PUSHKIN

LONDON : HUMPHREY MILFORD
OXFORD UNIVERSITY PRESS

PUSHKIN

Pushkin

BY

ERNEST J. SIMMONS

CAMBRIDGE · MASSACHUSETTS · 1937

HARVARD UNIVERSITY PRESS

PRINTED AT THE HARVARD UNIVERSITY PRESS
CAMBRIDGE, MASS., U. S. A.

37622

To follow the thoughts of a great man
is a most interesting science.
Pushkin

PREFACE

For the sake of easy reference all dates in this book are reckoned according to the Old Style, that is, according to the Julian calendar. To change a date to the New Style, add eleven days in the eighteenth century and twelve days in the nineteenth century.

Notes which provide necessary information concerning matters in the text are placed at the bottom of the page. All other notes, which are indicated by numerals, have been relegated to the back of the book. In nearly every case these numbered notes refer simply to Russian works which have been mentioned or quoted in the text. They exist for the benefit of those who wish to ascertain the Russian titles or to check translations from the Russian.

I am deeply indebted to Harvard University for grants from the Milton Fund and the Fund for Research in the Humanities. This generosity has enabled me to have direct access to highly important material on Pushkin which has been brought to light in Russia in recent years.

Two eminent Soviet Pushkinists, Professors M. A. Tsyavlovski and B. V. Tomashevski, have kindly aided my researches.

The profound scholarship in the Russian language and literature of Professor Samuel H. Cross, my friend and colleague, has been ever at my service. I am grateful for his assistance.

E. J. S.

Leverett House
Harvard University
January, 1937

CONTENTS

ILLUSTRATIONS

TRANSLITERATION

There is no universally accepted method of transliterating the letters of the Russian alphabet into English. The system used for Russian names and titles mentioned in this book is that employed by the Library of Congress, with a few changes which seem to make for simplicity in English orthography without essentially violating the phonetic value of the Russian letters. However, the spelling of a few proper names, which have become fixed in English by long usage, is retained.

а	a		с	s
б	b		т	t
в	v		у	u
г	g		ф	f
д	d		х	kh
е	e		ц	ts
ж	zh		ч	ch
з	z		ш	sh
и	i		щ	shch
і	i		ъ	(omitted)
й	i (omitted after й)		ы	y
к	k		ь	(omitted)
л	l		ѣ	e
м	m		э	e
н	n		ю	iu
о	o		я	ya
п	p		ѳ	f
р	r			

PUSHKIN

Introduction

Alexander Pushkin, Russia's greatest poet, is little known in Western Europe or America. Compared to those giants of the novel, Turgenev, Dostoevski, and Tolstoi, he is almost a nonentity outside his native land. The comparison of literary artists is hazardous, and the conclusions rarely have any validity in fact or in aesthetics. Yet one may venture to compare Pushkin by way of placing him among his better-known contemporaries. If we except Goethe, it is not an exaggeration to say that during the first forty years of the nineteenth century no poet of Western Europe surpassed Pushkin in sheer genius or in sustained quality of literary accomplishment. For over a hundred years he has been Russia's most beloved poet. His countrymen have continued to read him, as we read Shakespeare, sometimes more and sometimes less, depending upon the intellectual interests of a given generation. But no native poet has ever had such a large and unfailing number of enthusiastic readers. Turgenev and Dostoevski called themselves his pupils; Tolstoi learned his verses by heart and acclaimed his literary significance. The best pages of Russian criticism have been devoted to his poetry, and many profound judgments have been pronounced upon his life and works. Russians in general recognize a perennial charm in Pushkin's poems, a timelessness which evokes as much delight today as it did when he was a living literary hero. In view of these facts it may be illuminating to dwell briefly on the reasons for the relative lack of interest in Pushkin among peoples outside of Russia.

The difficulty of translation, of course, has been a large factor in preventing a correct estimate of Pushkin among non-Russian readers. To render adequately the bare contents of his poetry is simple enough. Although there is a distinct Russian flavor to the substance, in foreign dress it will seem equally worthy to the Englishman, Frenchman, or German. But invariably some quintessential quality, which for lack of a better word we may call "form," is lost in translation. The form is so significant that failure to reproduce it in a foreign version robs the original of its chief poetic virtue. By form is meant not merely meter, rhyme, and the mechanical ordering of lines, but also phrase-making and the extraordinarily subtle choice and arrangement of words, a talent which critics recognize as peculiarly Pushkin's own — as "Pushkin's language." Very often this language connotes or suggests much more than any literal rendering can possibly indicate. Form with Pushkin is inseparable from the content and contributes in a high degree to the perfection of a poem. It is never a kind of shell, but the very essence of poetic expression. He will prune and polish until he has achieved the ultimate degree of simplicity. But when a translator attempts to catch this simplicity, the results are often simple in the worst sense of the word. No doubt Pushkin could be translated adequately, but it would take another Pushkin to preserve all the harmonious effects of the original.

A second difficulty which foreigners meet in Pushkin's works is that they seem quite alien to the customary Western European and American conception of Russian culture. This is not entirely the fault of foreigners, for in some respects Pushkin appears to have little in common with the ideals and objectives of the Russian culture and literature which developed after his death. The country's great novelists have been largely responsible for the widespread notion of this culture which is shared by many foreigners today. We have been taught to expect a preaching tendency in Russian literature, a justification of moral good in the world and the unmasking of moral evil. In the works of Turgenev, Dostoevski, Tolstoi, and their followers we find a social-humanitarian teaching which makes for a weak, oppressive, but sincere democratization. This literature has also revealed to us an instinctive and conscious antipathy to accepted government and its inevitable attributes — force and judicial oppression. And there is often expressed an ideological enmity towards Western Europe and its whole political and social structure. Finally, we perceive a neglect of external form in the name of significant content, and a cult of simplicity and unpleasantness.

Now Pushkin's literary attitude is diametrically opposed to these forces in Russian culture. One must not search for a moral in his works; his muse is truly on the side of both good and evil. There is no tendentiousness, no social teaching, no moral pathos. Although a sincere patriot, he was never a Slavophile, for intellectually he felt as much at home in the culture of Europe as in that of his own country. He opposed evil, but he never preached a crusade against it. In him there is nothing of Christian humility, mysticism, or nihilism. The brotherhood of man would have appealed to Pushkin, if he had thought about it at all, as an excellent subject for a satiric poem. As for purpose in art — he summed it all up in one phrase: the purpose of poetry is poetry.

Such a Russian and such a poet may well confuse the foreigner's conception of Russian literature and culture. Pushkin had followers, but, like Shakespeare, he had no real continuators. He stands a solitary figure, and his poetry, like Chaucer's, is in a sense the glittering capstone of the past. However, this is not the whole story. To change the figure, the stream of Russian culture was not sharply divided by Pushkin; it simply flowed into a different channel. But even here the discerning critic can detect the precious life-stream of Pushkin. Despite political and economic change, national catastrophes, and social upheavals, he has left his mark on Russian culture, and few of the succeeding great writers have escaped his influence. His true position in Russian literature is that of a preserver of the past and a prophet of the future.

Any biographical study of Pushkin has its own meaning and value. He was great not only as a poet but as a man. And as a man it is difficult to find in the whole range of Russian literature anyone who was as vital, brilliant, and unfortunate as Pushkin. He felt life deeply, and he gave to it all his passion, all his genius. He approached it directly and fearlessly, yet he found it no unmixed blessing. Life beat him down, persecuted him, and rarely cheered him with moments of happiness. It is not necessary to idealize him. He knew both weakness and greatness, but his genius towered triumphantly above everything that was small and mean in his nature. He lived in a difficult time, difficult for him as for any man, during the reigns of Alexander I and Nicholas I. He belonged to a definite historical epoch, conditioned by well-defined cultural, social, economic, and political forces. And his life and poetry were so intimately involved in all these forces that to ignore them would result in a most distorted picture. A biographer must study Pushkin as a man, as a poet, and as an historical figure.

CHAPTER I

"Russian Scribblers Call Me an Aristocrat"

"So you have become an aristocrat," a poet-friend wrote to Pushkin in 1825. "This makes me laugh. Are you proud of your five-hundred-year-old nobility? I see in this a piddling imitation of Byron. For God's sake, be Pushkin! You are a clever enough fellow in your own right." [1]

Ryleev, the poet-friend, had touched Pushkin on a sensitive spot. Aristocrats do not boast of their pedigrees. The romance of genealogy is the darling foible of the middle classes. Pushkin felt obliged to explain himself — and, incidentally, to correct Ryleev.

"You are angry," he replied, "that I praise my six-hundred-year-old nobility. (N.B., my nobility is older.) Why do you not see that the spirit of our literature depends in part on the status of our writers? We cannot offer our works to a lord, for by our own birth we esteem ourselves his equal. . . ." [2]

The pride of birth went deeper than this shuffling explanation implies. Unlike Dr. Johnson, Pushkin never had to wait for favor in an outward room; nor was he ever repulsed from the door of a noble lord. If he wished for a patron, he had one in the Tsar of All the Russias. Pushkin insisted upon his aristocracy because the title of "poet" was held in contempt by the new nobility and uncultured bureaucracy. He knew his worth and had divined his immortality. Before the snobbism of crass officialdom he flaunted his six-hundred-year-old pedigree. "A lack of esteem for one's ancestors," he defended, "is the first sign of wildness and immorality." It was also comforting to think that his name was writ large in the annals of Russian history, and that he was a living force carrying on the ancient glory of his race.

Not a little of the tragedy of Pushkin's life, however, is implicit in this arrogance of ancestry. Like a falcon towering in his pride of place, he was capable of circling scornfully above condescending courtiers and venomous critics. But too often he met them on their own level. They sneered at his ancestry, dubbed him a mere "writer," and provoked all the fierce resentment of his nature.

A shaping Divinity somehow or other never provided Pushkin with those blessed tokens of aristocracy — small ears and white hands — which so fortified Byron's family conceit. But the line of his ancestry went back as far as Byron's, and was certainly more distinguished in that kind of historical fame which noble families cherish.

There is often little justification for the biographer's zeal in digging away at the roots of the family tree, but in Pushkin's case extenuation is not lacking. He was proud of his ancestors, though he never tried to conceal their various faults and crimes. They were links connecting him with his country's past, and in many ways they helped to foster in him a love for Russian history which he expressed in memoirs, scientific works, historical romances, dramatic productions, and many poems. This interest developed his knowledge of the historical process, which provided an effective counterbalance to his flair for political freethinking and revolutionary ideas. Finally, this six-hundred-year-old ancestry was strangely involved in his emotional and intellectual reactions to the society in which he lived.

II

> I am a descendant of old boyars.
> *My Genealogy*

The Pushkins were a numerous clan. They claimed descent — as did many other noble Russian families — from Radsha, a half-legendary, half-historical Prussian who entered the country in the second half of the thirteenth century to serve the sainted Great Prince Alexander Nevski. Like Ivan the Terrible, then, and perhaps with more right, the Pushkins could lay claim to Teutonic origin. Radsha was described in the chronicles as an "honorable man"; that is, explained Pushkin, "an illustrious or noble man." [3] At the beginning of the fifteenth century Grigori, a descendant of Radsha, was the first to bear the family name "Pushka." And from Konstantin, Grigori's youngest son, Pushkin descended in a straight line.

The Pushkins had a right to the hereditary title of "boyar," which originally belonged only to the highest officials of the state. Their name was included in the famous Pedigree Book of Ivan the Terrible among those of the most noble families of Russia. Members of the clan played important parts in the affairs of the realm, especially in the seventeenth century. They served on the council, as court officials, governors of provinces, and ambassadors, always close to the Muscovite Great Princes and to the tsars. Pushkin himself singled out for special praise Grigori Gavrilovich as "one of the most remarkable figures in the epoch of the Pretender." [4] For his part in the conspiracy Grigori was rewarded with a place close to the False Dmitri when the latter ascended the throne. Pushkin put Grigori's father, Gavrila, con amore, into his play, Boris Godunov. "I portrayed him," he proudly remarked, "exactly as I found him in history and in my family papers." [5] Nor did the poet fail to point out that no less than four Pushkins (actually five) signed the Act of Election which placed the first of the Romanovs on the throne, a service which Nicholas I hardly regarded as a family debt to his troublesome poet. Down through the reign of Peter the Great the Pushkins continued to play a significant role in governmental matters, and one of them the great tsar executed for his "significance" in the Streltsy conspiracy. In the eighteenth century, however, new stock, coming from obscure provincial gentry, pushed the descendants of the old boyars into the background. The Pushkins were among those families that lost their luster and importance.

But blots in the scutcheon were not rare on the male, as well as on the female, side of the family tree. Unhappy and sometimes tragic marriages dogged the fortunes of Pushkin's ancestors and gave the poet unpleasant food for thought on the eve of his own marriage. His great-grandfather, Alexander Petrovich Pushkin, murdered his young wife in a fit of jealousy or madness. And his grandfather, Lev Aleksandrovich, Pushkin described as a "passionate and cruel man." [6] He did not hesitate to repeat a story that his grandfather's first wife died in a domestic prison where she had been confined by her husband because he suspected her of a real or imaginary affair with the French tutor of their son. In good Russian feudal fashion the grandfather hanged this presumptuous pedagogue to the gates of his estate. Nor did his second wife fare much better. Though in agony, she did not dare, on one occasion, to refuse her husband's demand that she accompany him on a visit. On the road, said Pushkin, she gave birth to a child. It is interesting that years later (1840), after the poet's death, Pushkin's father took pains to deny these stories, and gave his own father a clean bill of health. [7]

By his second marriage Lev Aleksandrovich had two daughters and two sons. The elder of the sons was Vasili Lvovich, born in 1767. This uncle of Pushkin's became a well-known poet and the literary guide of his more famous nephew. He carried on the unhappy-marriage tradition of the Pushkins, for his wife, a great beauty, deserted him for another, curiously justifying herself by charging Vasili with unfaithfulness.

Sergei Lvovich, the second son and the poet's father, was born on May 23, 1770. Like his elder brother, he received a typical worldly, French education, and followed the fashion of many young members of noble families at that time by entering the army. He became an ensign in the Egerski regiment and retired with the rank of major in 1798. Two years before his retirement he married "a beautiful creole," Nadezhda Osipovna Hannibal, who was then living with her mother in Petersburg. Their second child was Alexander Sergeevich Pushkin.

III

> But I, a rake on pleasure bent,
> Ugly offspring of negro descent . . .
> *To Iurev*

With amusing abandon, critics allow their imaginations to run wild on the fetching question of the negro blood which Push-

kin inherited from his mother. Few traits of his life or poetry
have failed, at one time or another, to be subjected to the argument ethnological. A rare flamboyancy in imagery and an unfailing sense of poetic rhythm must reflect the Negro in him.
Or, his nature is passionate — again a positive indication of hot
African blood. If on occasions he grows insanely jealous, affects
garish clothes, or changes swiftly in mood from deep melancholy to childlike gaiety, then these traits, too, become the in-
dubitable stamp and seal of the blackamoor. Nor is there lacking that chauvinistic type of biographer who attributes all the
faults of Pushkin's nature to his negro strain and all the virtues
to his pure Russian ancestry. More pardonable, perhaps, but
none the less biased, are those American Negroes who claim
Pushkin for their own and see in his genius a glorious expression of his ultimate African origin.

Here we are obviously treading on dangerous ground. The
riddle of genius defies solution, and particularly the solution of
race. A passionate or jealous nature, fluctuating moods, and
a love for ostentatious clothes are traits that might appear
among any of the sons of Ham, Shem, or Japheth. Heredity is a
fascinating subject, but the unknown factors in any line of descent make the derivation of human characteristics a mere
guessing game. Browning's creole grandmother may explain a
certain mental gaudiness in the man, but he could, when the
spirit moved him, be as plain and severe as an Eskimo. Clearly
to understand cause and effect in Pushkin's nature on the basis
of heredity would require a thorough knowledge of much more
than the negro blood in his mixed ancestry. And the effort, no
doubt, would be as fruitless as trying to run down the source of
the maze of cracks in some ancient Byzantine mosaic. Indeed,
it would be profitable to dismiss here and now the whole mud-
dled question of negro blood. But Pushkin himself prevents
this. If he had written his own biography, he would have devoted considerable space to the subject. For unlike Browning or
Alexandre Dumas, Pushkin took his African ancestry very
seriously. On more than one occasion he referred poignantly to
his negro descent. He thought and dreamt about the black

founder of his family in Russia, traced his physical appearance
to him, and felt that this strain of African blood gave him a
unique position in society. In short, Pushkin's so-called negro
ancestry had a deep psychological influence on him, and for this
reason, at least, it is necessary to state the facts in the case.

It is not a matter of ethnological hairsplitting to say that
Pushkin's great-grandfather on his mother's side, Abram Petrovich Hannibal, was an Abyssinian and not a Negro. In derision
the Arabs applied the term "Abyssinian," which means
"mixed," to the inhabitants of Ethiopia, a fact which truly indicates their polyglot nature. History flung into this melting pot
Beja, Somalis, Arabs, Turks, Hebrews, Portuguese, Negroes,
and other peoples. The fairest description of the population of
Abyssinia is that it is largely of Hamitic and Semitic base, with
a negro admixture. That is, the Abyssinians belong funda-
mentally to the Caucasian division of races. How much or how
little of negro blood coursed through the veins of Abram Petrovich no one can pretend to say. All we know is that he passed on
to his descendants in Russia certain physical characteristics,
such as a dark skin, full, thick lips, and a somewhat broad but
not negroid nose. However, these characteristics did not make
Pushkin a Negro any more than the other possible strains in the
mixed blood of Abram Petrovich made the poet a Hebrew or an
Arab or a Somali.

The maternal great-grandfather of Pushkin was born in
northern Abyssinia in 1697 or 1698. His father was a sovereign
prince, but in the position of a vassal to the Turks, who from
the early sixteenth century had made frequent incursions into
the country. When he was eight years old Abram was sent to
Constantinople, with other youths of noble Abyssinian families,
as a hostage. There he lived in the sultan's seraglio for a year.

At that time Peter the Great was on the throne of Russia.
This extraordinary and quixotic monarch had a passion for all
manner of bizarre specimens of humanity, among which he included dwarfs and Negroes. He surrounded himself with
strange or monstrous creatures, much as the medieval rulers of
Europe kept at their courts simpletons and jesters. And the

great nobles of Russia imitated this practice. Even as late as Pushkin's childhood it was not uncommon for a powerful noble to include dwarfs and Negroes in his entourage.

The story goes that Peter wrote to his envoy at Constantinople to procure several bright negro boys. With some difficulty the envoy complied — it is said by bribing the sultan's vizier — and in 1706 Abram was taken from the seraglio and brought to Russia. In an old German biography of Abram, found among Pushkin's papers, we are told that he always insisted that he came to Russia of his own free will; and Pushkin himself scornfully denied the allegation of a literary enemy that his great-grandfather was bought by Peter the Great for a bottle of rum. Another and more gratuitous explanation has been offered for Abram's journey to Russia. The tsar's subjects bitterly opposed his educational reforms. Accordingly, Peter wished to prove to them, in the person of the little dark Abyssinian, that even members of another race would take kindly to his educational schemes and benefit therefrom. The course of schooling to which young Abram was subjected almost lends credence to this dubious explanation.

The tsar quickly made a favorite of the boy, and in 1707 he was christened at Vilna in the Orthodox Church, with Peter and the queen of Poland for godparents. He preferred to use his own given name instead of the tsar's, which he employed simply as a patronymic. Many years later Abram Petrovich added the family name "Hannibal," why and on what authority it has never been determined. It is said that Peter gave him the name because of its African associations; and in the German biography it was good-naturedly argued that Abram was descended directly from the great Carthaginian Hannibal.

In 1717 Peter sent his fosterling to Paris to be educated in engineering and the mathematical sciences. He took part in the War of the Spanish Succession, acquired a veneer of French culture, and returned to Russia in 1723. On his deathbed Peter made provision for him, and Abram was given an engineering post in the army and became teacher of mathematics to the heir apparent. In the course of the next few years, however, he was persecuted by the ruling favorite, Menshikov. On various pretexts he was sent further and further into Siberia to undertake petty engineering tasks, and on one occasion his arrest was ordered. Only under the Empress Anna Ivanovna did his star once again begin to rise.

In 1731 Abram married a Greek girl and soon began to contribute his share to the marital difficulties that accumulated on both sides of Pushkin's family. His wife hated him as a "Negro not of our kind," and seems to have been unfaithful to him. A "white baby" said to have been born to her gave rise to the motive of infidelity which Pushkin intended to use in the unfinished historical romance, *The Negro of Peter the Great*, which he wrote about his great-grandfather. Abram applied domestic correction in the form of stringing up his wife to a ring in the wall and beating her unmercifully. Then he had her confined to a civil hospital for five years, which gave the unhappy husband leisure enough to fall in love with another woman, Khristina Sheberkha, a Livonian. Abram lived with her for some time, and they finally married in 1736. His bigamous position was eventually terminated many years later in an ecclesiastical trial. The first wife was judged guilty and shut up in a convent, and after Abram had performed a slight act of penance, the second marriage was declared legal.

During the reign of Elizabeth the list of Abram Petrovich's engineering feats and of the ranks and rewards he received makes an imposing picture of activity and success. He became a highly important figure in government and army circles, and the empress, shortly before her death, conferred on him the title of general in chief and the order of St. Alexander Nevski. He lived well on into the reign of Catherine II, dying in 1781 surrounded with honors and wealth.

Abram Petrovich had no children by his first wife, but the second marriage was blessed with eleven, of whom nine survived, five sons and four daughters. One of the sons, Ivan Abramovich, achieved almost as much fame as his illustrious father, and Pushkin celebrated in verse his victory at Navarino in 1773, where he was admiral of the fleet. He was also noted as the builder of the fortress of Kherson, and rose to a position of influence and to the rank of major general.

The other sons did nothing of consequence, although two of them succeeded in adding material to the history of unhappy marriages among the Hannibals. One of these, Osip Abramovich, was Pushkin's grandfather. He was born in 1744 and served in the artillery, where he achieved the rank of major. In 1773 he married, curiously enough, Marya Alekseevna Pushkina, a collateral descendant of the medieval Radsha. Nadezhda Osipovna, the only surviving child of this marriage, was Pushkin's mother. The poet wrote: "The African character of my grandfather, and his flaming passions, united with a terrible levity, involved him in amazing mistakes." [8] Pushkin put it lightly. The jealousy of the wife and the inconstancy of the husband soon brought about a separation. Then Osip conveniently forgot about Marya Alekseevna and married a rich widow, representing himself as a recently bereaved husband. Their felicity, however, did not last long. His first wife soon discovered the "mistake," and an interminably long court case ensued in which poor Osip was torn between the demands of both women. Rusticated by command of Catherine II and forced to remit to Marya Alekseevna a fourth part of his estate, he died while his second wife was still trying to recover money she had signed over to him. Marya Alekseevna Hannibal brought up her daughter in the little village of Kobrino surrendered by her husband. Theirs was an isolated existence, often made unhappy by straitened circumstances. There is much reason to suppose that Marya Alekseevna petted and spoiled her only child. Kobrino was near Petersburg, and when Nadezhda reached marriageable age her mother frequently took her to the capital. Their hopes were eventually realized, for the girl soon met and married a young officer, Sergei Lvovich Pushkin. Nadezhda compensated him for her extremely meager dowry by an unusually attractive figure and a handsome swarthy face.

It is clear, then, that Pushkin on his father's side had a plain title to an old and honored nobility, whose members had at one time occupied positions high in the government and even close to the throne. From the Hannibals also he could justly claim descent from a noble strain, for the founder of the family in Russia was the son of an "Abyssinian prince." But it is equally clear that at the time of the poet's birth both branches of his family had lost their high official standing, along with much of their wealth. As in the case of many other ancient Russian families, the Pushkins over the centuries had gradually slipped into a respected but undistinguished class of middle nobility.

CHAPTER II

Childhood

O Moscow . . . for a Russian heart
How much is mingled in that sound!
Eugene Onegin

The young couple did not remain long in Petersburg. A year after their marriage (1797) Nadezhda gave birth to a daughter, Olga. In the following year her husband, with a grand gesture, retired from the army to live on his dwindling income. Perhaps the rigorous Prussian discipline which Paul I enforced among his troops bored the lackadaisical Sergei Lvovich. He was a poor officer, always forgetting his gloves or committing some breach of strict army etiquette. Besides, it was the fashion for young men to resign after a reasonable period of service. But life in Petersburg was expensive. Opportunely, grandmother Marya Alekseevna sold her village of Kobrino, and in 1799 the whole family packed off to Moscow.

At the end of the eighteenth century Moscow was like a huge village, dotted here and there with imposing estates of rich noblemen and the golden cupolas of many churches. Most of the houses were little more than miserable peasant huts. The busy center of the present city was then a vast swamp, and ducks and geese swam in stagnant pools of water by the roadside. It was a city of showy luxury and dire poverty, and this contrast in extremes was everywhere noticeable. Here one found a strange mixture of ancient and recent architecture, of European and Eastern manners and customs, of ignorance and culture, of sophistication and barbarism. On the street one encountered every variety of European mingling with Greeks, Turks, and Tatars in their native costumes. Moscow was a capital without a court and lived its own independent life, an existence quite different from that of Petersburg. Petersburg was a stage but in Moscow were the spectators, as one Russian author defined the difference. For the older city was thronged with superannuated generals and government officials, members of the highest nobility or of no nobility at all, and poor and wealthy landowners from the provinces seeking official favors, rich brides, or the varied pleasures of Mother Moscow.

In this half-Asiatic, half-European city the Pushkins arrived, much, one likes to think, as the Larins did in *Eugene Onegin* — their carts loaded to the spilling point with furniture, mattresses, pots and pans, jars of preserves, and bird cages. In those days people were obliged to travel with all the comforts of home. The couple took a house on German Street in what was at that time a rather fashionable section of the city. There Pushkin was born on May 26, 1799. It was Holy Thursday, and the church bells rang the whole day. He was christened Alexander, no doubt after his great-grandfather Alexander Petrovich, not a hopeful augury, to be sure, for this was the same Pushkin who had murdered his wife. Adoring posterity has placed a marble tablet on a house in German Street to mark the place of birth of the great poet. But exacting scholars are now agreed that the tablet is on the wrong house.

The future poet's father and mother were in some respects ideally mated, for they shared the same weaknesses and each was an effective counter-irritant to the other. There was a touch of the Micawber about Sergei Lvovich. He had a genius for getting into debt and an illusion of grandeur that was well supported by a hypocritical trust in God and a measure of self-pity altogether offensive. After he had resigned from his regiment, circumstances again forced him to enter government service, in which he rose to be the chief of the commissariat commission of the reserve army. But in 1817 he once again took up a life of complete leisure, for which his talents, as well as his inclinations, admirably suited him. He belonged, as one critic has said, to that class of people called "loafers."

Since the reign of Catherine II, Gallomania had been all the rage in Russia, and Sergei Lvovich followed the fashion. He was devoted to French culture in every form, and his command of the language was perfect. Molière, he was credited with knowing by heart, and he possessed a facile ability at composing French verses which he indulged frequently. In fact, nature had created Sergei Lvovich to shine in society. He possessed all the address and ornament of the *salon* lion, and it was in the *salon* that he spent most of his time. For him a public was as necessary as for an actor. No one punned or versified better than Sergei Lvovich, and his efforts in this direction went the rounds of the town. No one declaimed poetry better or wrote and staged better amateur plays. He busied himself with everything but work, was concerned with everybody else's affairs but his own and those of his family. Like most social successes he was a colossal lump of egotism. The cheerful appearance and kind nature he presented to the world would degenerate into irascibility or maudlin sentimentality the moment he was faced with the cold realities of life. He was always in debt, mismanaged his estate, and was continually swindled by his peasants. All the business of the household he left to his wife, who was as poorly fitted for the task as her husband. With such a nature it is easy to see why Sergei Lvovich was utterly incapable of understanding his talented son. The failure was unfortunate, and the consequences most unhappy for both.

Like her husband, whom she thoroughly dominated, Nadezhda Osipovna lived in society. She loved theaters, receptions, and balls, and her gay French conversation and vivacious manner made her a general favorite in the *salon*. People liked to think that the irritable, stubborn, and capricious nature of Nadezhda Osipovna, as well as her dark-skinned beauty, was a positive trait of her Abyssinian grandfather. But it would be difficult to draw upon heredity for her love of power, general impracticality, and the conspicuous neglect with which she treated her children. She was capable of sulking for days and months, and on one occasion it is recorded that she refused to talk to little Sasha (Alexander) for a whole year because of some petty grievance. The children, indeed, feared her much more than their father. She had a passion for moving, which the Pushkins did with monotonous regularity, and when she was unable to change quarters, she sublimated her desires by shifting the furniture around or by transforming the study into the parlor or the dining room into a bedroom.

The Pushkins' door was never closed to visitors, and the household was invariably in a state of chaos. Nadezhda Osipovna was as charming as her husband in the matter of entertainment, and just as irresponsible in the business of running a house. It followed almost as a matter of course that their children — a third child, Lev, was born in 1805 — would be neglected. The father had little time for them, and the mother was capricious in her affection. At one moment she was all kindness, and at the next she would fly into a rage over some slight act of childish disobedience. In these fits of anger she was capable of slapping her grown daughter's face at a public ball.

It soon became apparent to everybody that little Sasha was the ugly duckling in this family. As a small boy he was unattractive, fat, and awkward in his movements, and his dark, coarse features betrayed his Abyssinian blood. Large, lively blue eyes, however, suggested a forming spirit and intelligence. He was moody and timid, shy in the presence of grown-ups, and preferred his own devices to the company and the games of playmates. Whether or not he deserved it, he was soon regarded as a difficult problem by his unsympathetic parents. His mother wanted him to be sociable, and introduced him into the drawing room. But he ran off at the first opportunity. She took him out for a walk. He lagged behind and finally sat down in the middle of the street. Neighbors in the windows smiled at him. He got up and said petulantly, "Well, you don't have to grin!" [1] and ran home in anger. It seems that when he was still an infant Pushkin was taken to Petersburg, for he tells a family story of an encounter there with Paul I in the city gardens. The mad tsar scolded the nurse for not taking off the child's bonnet at his majesty's approach. And the tsar proceeded to remedy the matter by removing the bonnet himself.

Nadezhda Osipovna invented punishments to cure Sasha of his awkwardness and bad habits. Visitors would come and find him in a corner of the hall surrounded by chairs, condemned to sit there for some prank or other. His mother was particularly offended by his habit of rubbing the palms of his hands together and of everlastingly losing his handkerchiefs. To cure the first offense she tied his hands behind his back for a whole day and deprived him of food. For the second crime he was punished in a more ingenious fashion. She ordered a handkerchief sewed to his jacket, in the manner of a shoulder-knot, which was changed twice a week. Much to the boy's mortification, she compelled him to show himself to guests with the tell-tale handkerchief in place. His awkwardness at children's dances also irritated her. Comrades laughed at him, and, blushing angrily, he would retire to a chair, pout, and refuse to be drawn from his corner. Nadezhda Osipovna's patience with her ugly duckling soon wore out. Besides, like her husband, she had other more interesting things to do than bother with a moody, recalcitrant child. Her indifference turned to coldness, and when the maternal spirit moved her she lavished her affection on Olga and Lev, who were, and always remained, the favorites, especially the younger brother. Sasha became the unloved child of the household and was soon left to himself, a position which he seemed to prefer.

Fortunately, little Sasha's friendless state was not without its consolations. Vexed to tears by the nagging of his mother, he often ran out of the room and hid himself in the large clothes basket of Marya Alekseevna. From this safe retreat he would silently watch his good, kind grandmother go about her work. Marya Alekseevna lived with the Pushkins and was a steadying influence in the disordered ménage. She was wise with the wisdom of years, and the misfortunes of her own troubled existence had filled her with sympathy for the unhappy. She brought comfort and understanding to her neglected grandson. Although she often worried over his intractable nature and fluctuating moods, she did not attempt to punish him. In a sense, she was his first Russian teacher. French was the language of the household, but from his grandmother Sasha heard absorbing tales about his ancestors in strong, simple Russian. His literary friend at school, Delvig, went into raptures over the pure Russian style of the letters which Marya Alekseevna sent to her grandson.

Perhaps a greater comfort to Sasha in his childhood, and even later when he had grown to manhood, was his old nurse, Arina Rodionovna, whose name he glorified in poetry. She was a freed serf, devoted to the family, and the general nurse of all the Pushkin children. Arina occupied a special position in the household, ate at the same table with her master, and expressed her opinion with the fearlessness of a privileged domestic. She belonged to a familiar type of house serf whose earthy wisdom, severe virtues, and unfailing loyalty were a bulwark against a variety of disintegrating influences common among Russian noble families of the time. She performed the most menial tasks with a simple dignity. And in her sturdy nature she united goodness with querulousness and infinite patience with a pretended severity. She was the guiding genius of the children, but clumsy little Sasha was her favorite, perhaps for the obvious reason that he was nobody else's. Little wonder that he called her "mama," for he found in her a loving tenderness which his own mother failed to give.

Those evenings when his parents went off to a ball or *soirée* were memorable for Sasha. Then he was left alone with his beloved nurse and could expect a story-telling hour. Like many old peasant women, Arina's strong memory was stocked with fascinating tales drawn from the rich storehouse of Russian folklore. Years afterwards Pushkin recalled with pleasure those "golden moments," the transition from prose to poetry, from waking to sleeping, as he eagerly waited for these stories. The old woman entered the room in her nightcap and frayed dressing gown. She bent over the crib, her lively eyes peering down at him through large spectacles. After blessing her nursling, she began in a tense whisper to tell her tales of ghosts and witches, and of the romantic exploits of Bova Korolevich. Sasha's childish imagination grew more and more excited. He crouched fearfully under the bedclothes, scarcely daring to move, to breathe. At last he dropped off to sleep and had marvelous dreams of magicians and ogres, of strange lands and miraculous transformations of beautiful princesses into majestic white swans.[2]

Pushkin was always able to look back on these "secret nights" and wondrous dreams with undiminished delight. They were among the few happy recollections of his childhood. Arina Rodionovna awoke and fostered in him a love for the folklore of his native land which was to inspire some of his greatest poems. He never ceased to treasure her memory. Pushkin's father and mother are not once mentioned in his poetry, but to Arina Rodionovna he dedicated many lines, remembering her affectionately as his "ancient little dove," [3] "the kind friend of my wretched youth." [4] And as Tatyana's nurse in *Eugene Onegin* he immortalized her for posterity.

II

> . . . not one of my tutors could cope
> with such an insufferable boy.
> *A Russian Pelham*

About 1806, grandmother Marya Alekseevna bought the village of Zakharovo, a short distance from Moscow. Here the Pushkins spent their summers, for then, as now, all Moscovites who could afford it abandoned the city during the hot months. The estate consisted of a ramshackle old house surrounded by fir trees and peasant huts. But the peasants were a jolly lot, and sang country songs and danced. These visits were a joyful period for young Sasha. Indeed, a remarkable change, or perhaps development, in his nature took place at about this time. Like the male-Cinderella of folk tales, he suddenly came to life and revealed characteristics which were to stick by him. From a quiet, phlegmatic, and uninterested child he was transformed into a lively youngster, swift of movement, and filled with an impish propensity to play all manner of pranks. His apathetic parents were startled and then horrified by this abrupt change — a change all for the worse, they thought. They admonished and scolded, and finally tried a variety of severe corrections. But kindness or severity were now all to no purpose. The seed of rebellion had taken root in the child and was to grow with the years. They set him down as undutiful and incorrigible, and with these amenities they again left him in peace, content to place their parental aspirations in Lev and Olga. Sasha had already begun his fight for freedom. Personal freedom was one of the conditions of existence which Pushkin valued most in his lifetime. Yet he was condemned, to the very day of his death, to pursue it like a will-o'-the-wisp.

In the country surroundings of Zakharovo Sasha felt free. He loved the woods and the little pond near the house. As a boy, Coleridge, imagining himself one of the Seven Champions of Christendom, used to roam the fields, cutting down weeds and nettles with his stick. And like Coleridge, young Pushkin, driven in upon himself, lived in a fanciful world, the fairy world of Arina Rodionovna's tales. He, too, wandered the fields, beheading the flowers with his cane as he pictured himself a doughty *bogatyr*, a Russian knight. In one of his schoolboy poems he remembered these carefree days in the village of Zakharovo with evident delight.

In a youthful and fragmentary *Program for Memoirs* Pushkin jotted down: "First annoyances — governesses." Further on, under the caption, "My disagreeable recollections," he lists his tutors, and significantly adds, "An insupportable situation!" [5]

Throughout his life Pushkin remained interested in Russian education, and on more than one occasion he expressed himself in no uncertain terms on the subject. His own childhood experiences left a bad taste in his mouth and undoubtedly influenced his mature judgment. It was inconvenient for his parents, and also unfashionable, to bother much with little Sasha's schooling. They preferred, like many modern parents, to shift the burden. Sasha was turned over to the tender mercies of foreign tutors, and he wore out several before they gave him up.

It is hardly an exaggeration to say that the wave of migration consequent upon the French Revolution literally changed the whole conception of elementary education in Russia. Hundreds of Frenchmen, from titled gentlemen to forthright adventurers, poor soldiers, lackeys, cooks, and unhappy tradesmen, flocked into the country. France and French culture were held in high esteem. What could be better than to have these *émigrés* impart their culture to Russian youths? Soon every family that could afford it engaged one or several French tutors. It became a fashion indiscriminately indulged in. Abuses were many. Any foreigner inevitably possessed a prescriptive right to pedagogy. There is the story of the Finn who for years taught his own language for French. And in the satirical literature of the time the French tutor became the accepted butt of witty journalists and dramatists.

The Pushkins, of course, subscribed to the vogue, and little Sasha's first instructors were drawn from this *émigré* class. The earliest seems to have been a certain Count de Montfort, a capable man of some education, with a talent for painting and music. But he was soon followed by M. Rousselot, who fancied himself a second Racine and was for one reason or another cordially hated by young Pushkin. He gave way to M. Chédel, another *émigré*, about whose efforts we know nothing except that he spent most of his time in playing cards with the servants, for which offense he was finally dismissed. In an unfinished prose romance, *A Russian Pelham*, Pushkin has left an account of his hero's tutors which has an autobiographical savor. He writes: "Father, of course, loved but did not at all trouble himself about me and left me to the solicitude of Frenchmen who were continually being taken on and discharged. My first tutor turned out to be a drunkard; the second, not a stupid man and not without information, had such mad habits that once he almost murdered me because I spilled ink on his waistcoat; a third, living with us for a whole year, became insane. . . . However, it is true that there was not one of them whom, in two weeks after his introduction to the position, I did not turn into a family joke." [6] Whatever their abilities may have been, there is no doubt that Pushkin's instructors quickly found in their charge a young Tatar.

In general, little Sasha's education went slowly. He was clever and eager, but he studied badly and had periods of protracted laziness. He was taught Russian and arithmetic, and learned theology from a Russian priest. From his sister's governess, Miss Bailey, he acquired a smattering of English; and a German governess effectually prevented him from learning that language because she preferred to talk in Russian. The four rules of arithmetic vexed him to tears. He placed his whole trust in his memory and would repeat the examination answers well, after listening to his sister's recitation. But if by chance he was examined first, he quickly became inarticulate.

It is easy to believe that as a child Pushkin was anything but a model student, and his attitude during his later schooling was hardly an improvement. Yet one has more than a suspicion that his childhood tutors and governesses were largely to blame. Pushkin certainly thought so himself, for he never forgot the unfavorable impression they made on him. Many years later Nicholas I suggested that he write something on education in Russia. Pushkin was quick to seize the opportunity to work off the ancient grudge he bore the system to which he had been subjected as a child. The tsar was not pleased with his effort, feeling that he did not give an important enough place in his treatise to the moral responsibility involved in education. His early experiences are clearly reflected in the following statement: "In Russia domestic education is most inadequate and most immoral: the child, surrounded by servants, sees certain odious examples, becomes self-willed or servile, does not receive any knowledge about justice, the mutual relations of people, or sincere honor. His education is limited to the study of two or three foreign languages and the elementary basis of all science, taught by any hired teacher whatever." [7]

III

Unseen, my genius
Hovers over me.
The Town

There were compensations in this domestic education, however, that did much to shape and inform the bright young mind of Sasha. The Pushkins knew everybody in Moscow, and among their friends were most of the literary celebrities of the town. Sergei Lvovich had a well-known weakness for authors, and he possessed some of those qualities of the brilliant *salon* mistress which are so successful in attracting literary people. He amused without boring, flattered without offending, was humble in the matter of his own talent, and lavished the necessary hospitality on his guests. It is little wonder that cultured foreigners with high-sounding titles, or none at all, and many of the foremost Russian writers found it congenial to make his home a kind of literary center.

His own brother, Vasili Lvovich, was a general favorite of this group. He was a talented versifier, and a light, obscene poem, *The Dangerous Neighbor*, gained him considerable renown. Vasili was no doubt one of the magnets that helped to draw the Moscow littérateurs to the home of the Pushkins. A dandy and a gastronome, he had much in common with his brother and belonged to the same circle of intellectual *bons vivants*, in which the period abounded. Everybody liked him for his genial nature and attractive naïveté. But in his character was none of the moral shuffling of Sergei Lvovich.

The Pushkin children were always thrilled with the visits of jolly uncle Vasili, and he was a glittering focal point at the literary evenings. His lively tales of life abroad and his personal acquaintance with many famous French writers of the time enthralled his young nephew. These evenings were further hallowed by the frequent presence of great figures in Russian literature — I. I. Dmitriev, Karamzin, Zhukovski, and Batiushkov. Such a brilliant group would have done honor to the most distinguished literary *salon* of Europe at that time.

With these advantages the future poet was, so to speak, born into literature. He fell heir not merely to a literary tradition but to the living representatives of this tradition. Imagine the ten-year-old Byron sitting quietly of a night in a corner of one of those big, impoverished rooms of Newstead Abbey, listening to the absorbing conversation of Coleridge, Scott, and Wordsworth. Only some such conception can give an idea of the privilege which was often afforded young Sasha Pushkin. The

guests would arrive. Sergei Lvovich at the appropriate moment
led his literary friends into his well-stocked library. Sasha would
steal in and snuggle up in a corner of the divan. His father
noticed but did not mind. The boy knew well that absolute
silence was the one condition of his presence in the room. Wine
and cigars were served, and the conversation began. The youthful ears took in everything — clever puns, brilliant discussion,
readings of poems, literary gossip, and town chitchat. On such
occasions female guests, of course, avoided the study. For after
the wine had flowed freely it is safe to say that the conversation
contained much that was unsuited to women or to the young
listener. However, no one seemed to care. Sasha heard and
remembered everything, and his abnormally quick intelligence
matured swiftly under such tutelage. Literature was a part of
the domestic atmosphere of the Pushkin home, and he eagerly
breathed it in. He early learned to pronounce with childish awe
the word "poet." Soon Karamzin and Zhukovski were to read
his own youthful compositions, and then they recalled the dark,
curly-headed child with lively eyes who sat on the divan and
listened attentively. At first they were pleased, and praised,
and as the compositions continued they marveled and were
proud to play the part of literary foster fathers to this promising
young poet.

The stimulation which the boy received from the conversation of his father's literary friends was not the only compensation for a shoddy formal education. Like many of the cultured
nobles of the time, Sergei Lvovich had collected a rich library,
composed largely of eighteenth-century French philosophers,
translations of the classics, and writers of belles-lettres. Here
the young Sasha, who by the age of nine had developed a passion for reading, could browse to his heart's content. As usual,
his indifferent parents set no restrictions upon their son's reading. Under such conditions it was natural enough that he should
have indulged to the hilt a boy's customary hankering after
erotic books, and French eighteenth-century sensualist literature became his favorite reading material.

Fortunately, however, his instinct for knowledge was sure

and his taste broad. Young Pushkin spent sleepless nights in his father's library poring over Racine, Molière, Voltaire, La Fontaine, Parny, Gresset, Rousseau, and French translations of the *Iliad*, the *Odyssey*, the *Aeneid*, and of Juvenal, Tasso, Ossian, and Wieland. This seems rather heavy fare for a ten-year-old scholar. But Pushkin, like the young Browning devouring the splendid library of his father, found reading books of any kind an enjoyable pastime, and the knowledge gained therefrom necessary food for a growing imagination.

A constant companion of these reading sprees was his sister. Pushkin sincerely loved Olga Sergeevna, and throughout his life they were devoted to each other. Several years after this period, when he was away at school, he addressed a poem to her, his "precious friend," in which he pleasantly recalls their hours in the library.[8] Olga's literary taste, however, had little in common with his. Like his heroine Tatyana, and for that matter like most of the young girls of the time, Olga was an omnivorous reader of sentimental literature. Pushkin twits her in his verses on her love for the lachrymose romances of Mme. de Genlis and the elegiac poetry of Gray and Thomson, which had been translated into French and Russian.

In another early poem, *The Town*,[9] written in the same year as these verses to his sister (1814), the young poet casts a backward glance over the reading he had done in his childhood, and his comments indicate that he had read with more than ordinary youthful discrimination. He describes how with rapture he forgot the whole world in the company of "these ghosts" of the past, these "priests of Parnassus." Voltaire, "the hoary jester," he worshiped as the "first poet among poets," and his works he read again and again. The vogue for Voltaire, which had penetrated Russia during the reign of Catherine the Great, died hard. La Fontaine was a "carefree idler," but his poetry was "charming"; and with these he includes among his favorites a list of minor French poets of the eighteenth century. One can appreciate, if not believe, the proud exaggeration of his brother, that by the age of eleven Pushkin "knew all of French literature by heart!"[10]

Nor in this beadroll of prized childhood authors does Pushkin neglect to tell off the names of Russian writers. Derzhavin, Dmitriev, Ozerov, Karamzin, Fonvizin, and Knyazhnin are mentioned. But their meed of praise is small. The native authors who really called forth his enthusiasm — Bogdanovich, Batiushkov, Vasili Pushkin, Krylov, and Barkov — were more or less imitators of the light poetry of his French favorites. What he sought and admired most in literature at this time was a frivolous attitude towards the serious things of life, a playful scepticism, and a cynical eroticism. Such was the literary climate of his father's house; and such were the compositions of his Frenchified uncle Vasili. Even the serious works of his beloved Voltaire he could not abide; but his *La Pucelle*: that was a "glorious little book, golden and unforgettable." [11] Klopstock, the precocious boy tried to read but failed to understand, for which it is not difficult to forgive him. And "without wings" he was afraid to soar after Milton and Camoëns, nor would he attempt to imitate Vergil.

This catalogue — and more could be added — of Pushkin's childhood authors is astounding enough. But the intention is not to emphasize his precocity. He early fell into the habit of substituting for the normal experience of a boy the experience one learns from books. The fact was important. Such reading not only helped to compensate for his lack of early formal schooling, but the light, amorous, and cynical French literature unfortunately fed the first passionate emotions of youth, and also deeply influenced his initial attempts at poetry.

Tradition has it that these attempts began at the age of eight. Obviously, writing poetry came to him as naturally as leaves to the trees. Nor was there any lack of incentive. The Pushkin ménage was a nest of singing birds. On those rare occasions when guests failed to appear, Sergei Lvovich would gather the children around him and declaim French verses. The father fairly exuded poetry. It became contagious in the household. Even the servants, male and female, were infected. The most proficient was the valet, Nikita Timofeevich, who composed doggerel ballads on folk-tale subjects and on the lives of robber-heroes. Uncle Vasili provided distinguished models of his own fashioning, and the frequent literary *soirées* kept poetry in the air. The small Olga, and Lev when he was old enough, were also caught up in the fashion and later were to try their hands at versemaking.

Young Sasha acquired a command of literary French before he learned to write in his native tongue. At any rate, the first known examples of childhood verses by the greatest of Russian poets are in French. His earliest model, naturally enough, was his favorite Voltaire. And, with youthful presumption, nothing short of an epic attempt would satisfy the eight-year-old bard. This was *La Tolyade*, a grandiosely-planned parody in six cantos of Voltaire's *Henriade*. It was to tell the story of a war of dwarfs in the time of Dagobert, led by the hero Toly. He read the first four lines to his French tutor, M. Rousselot, who drove the poet to tears by laughing and ridiculing the performance. To make matters worse, the tutor complained to his mother that Sasha wasted time over such trifles, and was idle and lazy to boot. Nadezhda Osipovna punished her son. In a rage Sasha threw his manuscript in the stove and revenged himself on M. Rousselot by the various devices with which small boys make their teachers acutely unhappy. The memory of Pushkin's sister retained the opening quatrain of the destroyed *Tolyade*:

> Je chante le combat que Toly remporta,
> Où maint guerrier périt, où Paul se signala,
> Nicolas Mathurin, et la belle Nitouche
> Dont la main fut le prix d'une horrible escarmouche.

The muse, however, was not silenced by this initial frustration, and the next attempt was hardly less ambitious than *La Tolyade*. Sergei Lvovich had taught his children to admire Molière, and his own imitations, which he staged, earned him a local reputation as a dramatist. The father's efforts no doubt inspired the son. Sasha liked to compose comedies which he acted out for his sister. She was older, and Sasha looked up to her as a critic. It is recorded that one of these attempts, *L'Escamoteur*, Olga hissed off the boards, and the offended author promptly wrote an epigram:

> Dis-moi: pourquoi *L'Escamoteur*
> Fut-il sifflé par le parterre?
> Hélas! c'est que le pauvre auteur
> L'escamota de Molière.

It is possible that these childhood verses have gained something in correctness and smoothness from the clever Olga Sergeevna, who recalled them after Pushkin had died. She also remembered that he wrote imitations of the fables of La Fontaine. Sasha most certainly won the reputation of a child-poet, and there is an incident of an occasion on which the little girls of the neighborhood surrounded the blushing, curly-headed author and begged him to write something in their albums. The few extant French verses of this period, light and humorous, gain in authenticity from the fact that they are precisely in the tradition in which he wrote his later youthful poems.

Thus Sasha Pushkin grew up in his father's house to the age of twelve, reading quantities of books, scribbling light French verses, and living more and more in a world of his own creating. Suddenly the thought struck his carefree parents that it was time for the boy to be shipped off to school. Obviously he was making little progress in the accepted rudiments of an education under the pitiful guidance of his frequently-changed *émigré* tutors. To be sure, he was stuffing his head with a more worldly knowledge garnered from a wide and varied reading, but such self-teaching had no place in the conventional ideas of an education at that time. His parents were the kind to avoid responsibility in any form. After their first unsuccessful attempts to make him a good little boy like all the other good little boys, they had more or less dismissed him from their thoughts. He went his own way, guarding his independence with all the childish obstinacy of a stubborn nature. At this time, said one of his friends, he had the character of a child of twelve and the mind of a youth of twenty. The budding seeds of genius went unnoticed, for his mother and father never took the trouble to understand their son's difficult character, which was full of contradictions and passions. The good in him was not nurtured, and the evil was sharpened by unnatural childhood adversities.

The boarding schools at Moscow were mediocre; at Petersburg they were expensive. The Pushkins preferred the latter but could not afford them. They were considering a Jesuit school when a friend of the family, Alexander Turgenev, informed them that the emperor had just opened a lyceum at Tsarskoe Selo. The applicants were to be admitted by a competitive examination. The fact that there was no stipend involved unquestionably helped to settle the matter in the minds of the parents. They entered their son as a candidate. In the summer of 1811, accompanied by uncle Vasili, he set out for Petersburg to take the examinations. His kind grandmother gave him a little purse of a hundred rubles, which the jolly Vasili borrowed on the road and then forgot to repay. The boy left his mother and father without any regrets on either side. He was sorry to be parted from his sister, but in the chaotic Moscow home of the Pushkins Arina Rodionovna was perhaps the only one to weep sincere tears at the departure of her nursling.

CHAPTER III

An Emperor Establishes a Lyceum

> O drink, my friends, this first, the flowing
> cup!
> In honor of our union never fail!
> Bless our muse victorious; drink it up;
> To our Lyceum, God bless her, all hail!
> *The Nineteenth of October*

Pushkin seemed destined to annoy monarchs. While still in swaddling clothes he had provoked the anger of mad Paul I. In school a prank aroused the ire of his son, Alexander I. Later Pushkin offended that emperor in a more serious manner. And on various occasions Nicholas I found Pushkin a most vexatious subject. Since tsars provided him with an education and lent him money, perhaps they had some reason to think him ungrateful.

Pushkin, however, never ceased to be grateful for the opportunity to spend six years in the Lyceum of Tsarskoe Selo, and this experience exercised a great influence on his development as a man and a poet. A fine excess of idealism lay behind most of the constructive projects of Alexander I, and the idea of a lyceum was no exception. The institution was unlike any school then existing in Russia. Children of noble families scorned the gymnasium as "too common"; and the universities at Moscow and Petersburg did not command much respect. Yet the government wished to attract well-educated members of the best families into civil and military service. To train such government officials was the guiding factor in the establishment of the Lyceum of Tsarskoe Selo. Ironically enough, its most illustrious graduate was to be Russia's greatest poet.

La Harpe, the Swiss tutor of Alexander I, had no doubt encouraged some of the liberal educational ideals which his pupil wished to incorporate in the new school. And that other extraordinary liberal influence on the emperor, Count M. M. Sper-

anski, had a hand in fashioning the curriculum. It is pretty certain, also, that the newly-formed Napoleonic *lycées* and the
famous public schools of England served as models for Alexander. The program of studies was to eliminate sciences, such as
chemistry, astronomy, and higher mathematics, which were of
no use to future judges, ministers, and diplomats. The history
of philosophical opinion about the soul, and the teaching of abstract ideas in general, were ruled out as inconsequential in
forming the intellect of youth. Above all, there was to be no
narrowing, pompous pedantry. The curriculum called for
strictly liberal studies: languages, moral philosophy and logic,
simple mathematics, law, history, geography, literature, art,
rhetoric, drawing, writing, gymnastics, dancing, fencing, riding,
and swimming. Here was an educational paradise, perhaps better calculated to produce cultured men of the world than skilled
diplomats and learned judges. The enrollment was limited to
fifty, the age of entering students set at ten to fourteen, and the
course divided into two periods of three years each. At first
Alexander intended that his two young brothers, Nicholas, the
future tsar, and Mikhail, should be educated in the Lyceum.
He hoped that these royal youths, by coming in contact with
such studies and with a group of boys drawn from cultured
homes, would learn some of the liberal idealism that had inspired their emperor. Apparently this was carrying liberalism
and democracy too far. Their mother objected, and the young
princes were never allowed to sit at the benches of the Lyceum
of Tsarskoe Selo.

From the very outset this liberal training school for future
statesmen took a privileged position among the educational in-
stitutions of Russia. The Lyceum was designed to be something
more than a gymnasium, and to retain the best features of a
university without subscribing to the narrow scientific curricula
then much in vogue. To add dignity to the school it was placed
under the control of a director who was responsible to the emperor. And its teachers were to be among the best in Russia.
In certain cases they were even sent abroad to acquire a final
polish which would better fit them to instruct boys from whom

so much was expected. A concluding touch of imperial favor was the decision to locate the Lyceum in a great wing of the tsar's palace at Tsarskoe Selo, only a few miles from Petersburg. Here the prospective students would be close to the royal family, and they would have as their playground the beautiful and expansive gardens of the emperor. One can readily understand why the Pushkins were eager to avail themselves of this golden opportunity to further the education of their son. Besides, it was all free.

II

On a day in August 1811 an official in a large room of the Ministry of National Education at Petersburg solemnly read off a list of names. "Alexander Pushkin!" he intoned. A lively, curly-headed, quick-eyed youngster stepped forward, looking somewhat confused. Other boys in turn answered to their names, and soon they were all busily at work on the examinations which were to prove their fitness to enter the Lyceum of Tsarskoe Selo.

This account is taken from the *Memoirs* [1] of I. I. Pushchin, also a hopeful aspirant. Uncle Vasili, who knew young Pushchin's grandfather, paid a call. The two boys were introduced. Pushkin had found his "first friend," and their friendship was to remain a constant one, filled with devotion and touched with tragedy. Pushchin grew up to be a pure-souled, selfless man, one of the active figures in the unhappy Decembrist Revolt which came so close to engulfing his poet-friend.

The joyful news that they had passed the examinations and would soon be schoolmates strengthened the feeling of comradeship. Pushkin's success was hardly a favorable reflection on the schooling he had received in his father's house. The tests were not difficult, and one suspects that influence was as much a factor in securing admission to the Lyceum as ability. He was rated fourteenth in a list of thirty successful candidates. In the Russian language Pushkin received a grade of "very good"; in French, and in his particular bête noire, arithmetic, "good." In geography and history his examiners piously conceded that

Sovfoto

PUSHKIN AT THE AGE OF FIFTEEN

"he has information"; and against the German language was placed the laconic remark, "Not studied."

During the several weeks that preceded the opening of the Lyceum the two boys saw much of each other. They took walks in the Summer Garden and made friends with future students who were on the ground, especially with I. V. Malinovski, the son of the director. Pushchin, who was a good observer, has left his impressions of his companion at this time. "We all saw," he writes, "that Pushkin outstripped us, had read much about which we had not even heard, and that everything he read he remembered; but his worth consisted in the fact that he did not in the least show off or put on airs, as often happens with precocious youngsters at that age (each of us was twelve years old), who through some special circumstance find it possible to learn things sooner and more easily. Apart from his natural talent, the situation of Pushkin in his father's house and in the company of his uncle, in a circle of littérateurs, hastened his education but did not at all make him overbearing — an indication of fine material." [2]

The day on which the new students obtained their uniforms was a banner occasion. They were gorgeous outfits, freighted with all the color, braid, and shiny buttons thought necessary to distinguish the favored pupils of the emperor's new school. The uniform consisted of a blue, double-breasted frock coat with a specially designed red collar, tight-fitting white trousers, high, glossy jackboots, and a three-cornered hat. The start of school is rarely a welcome event for the average boy, but it is easy to understand the impatience of this group for the opening of an imperial Lyceum, and for the opportunity of parading about in such resplendent uniforms.

At last the great day arrived, October 19, 1811. Every effort was made to lend dignity and importance to the formal inauguration of the Lyceum. The emperor and his wife and mother were present, along with ministers, senators, members of the Holy Synod, and various other dignitaries. After prayer at the royal chapel they all went to the audience hall of the Lyceum, which was decorated for the occasion. The imperial charter was solemnly read. With thumping hearts the three erect rows of boys heard the concluding words: "We expect that the young people will obtain here an excellent knowledge in the sciences, a most honorable feeling of love for their native land, and a most pure morality to the honor of this institution, to the use of the fatherland, and to their own and to our satisfaction!" [3]

Then the director, pale as death in the presence of his tsar, made a few remarks in which he generously promised, in the name of the whole staff, "to apply every minute of our lives, all our power and abilities to tilling this new garden." But the high point of the ceremony was the fiery oration of the young and brilliant adjutant professor, A. P. Kunitsyn. He harangued the wide-eyed, wondering students on their duty to the fatherland and abjured them to make the most of their opportunity to grow and increase in knowledge. Carried away by the sound and fury of his words, he swung into a flowery peroration: "Surrounded by examples of virtue, will you not be inflamed with a love for it? Will you not prepare yourselves to serve the fatherland? . . . Sweet hope of parents! Are you not afraid to be the last in your generation? Do you wish to mingle with the crowd of ordinary people, cowering in obscurity, and every day sucked under the waves of oblivion? No! Do not let this thought corrupt your imaginations!" [4] The twelve-year-old scholars grew restless. The long speech reminded them of the sumptuous banquet ready to be served. But the emperor was well pleased with his official orator. The next day he sent him the Vladimir Cross.

The ceremonies finally came to an end. The students filed before the platform, and the emperor smiled kindly at each in turn in acknowledging their awkward bows. With happy faces the boys were at last led into the dining room. Members of the royal family remained to inspect the meal. While the tsar chatted with the minister of education, the empress condescendingly tasted the food.

"Fine soup?" she said to a member of the staff.

"Oui, monsieur!" stammered Kornilov, bewildered by the glittering array of royalty.

She smiled, passed on, and refrained from asking any more questions. The boys snickered. Kornilov had earned his nickname. For ever after he was "Monsieur" in the Lyceum.[5]

A few days later, at the tea hour, the director announced to the boys that the minister of education forbade them to leave the Lyceum, and that parents could visit them only on holidays. The decree was part of the new educational scheme. Later it was modified to some extent. The students heard this unexpected news with many misgivings. Six long years within the walls of the Lyceum! Silently they looked at one another, and then a few of the more daring protested against such high-handed procedure. Their agitation, however, was soon forgotten in the novelty of their new life. The prohibition merely served to draw them closer together, uniting them in their isolation into a compact student family.

III

The tender roots of the twelve-year-old Pushkin had taken little hold on the rocky and shallow soil under the paternal roof. To transplant them to the fertile ground of the Lyceum was an easy, almost effortless task. The ties denied him at home were quickly formed in school, and he cherished them all his life. Pushkin gained there a rich experience, and his Lyceum days stimulated a sentiment and a devotion which never faded from his memory and found expression in some of his sincerest poetry.

But the sprouting individualism and self-assertiveness of Pushkin's nature often made it as difficult for him to get along with his companions and teachers as with his parents. He was not naturally combative, but a certain youthful shyness betrayed him into extremes of behavior. At times he would seem standoffish, the result of timidity, no doubt, rather than of any youthful desire to pose. Then suddenly he would become all life and action, a leader in boyish adventures.

There were no age-old traditions of social fitness in this new school; no hazing or fagging or winning of spurs to test the spirit and temper of the newcomers. They had all entered on an equal footing, and they were all about the same age. As a little homogeneous band of thirty students making their own school traditions, each boy was strictly judged by his companions on his merits and on his adaptability to the Lyceum community. Pushkin was not very adaptable. He was inclined to be touchy and failed to arouse any general sympathy. Although not attempting to play a role, he had something of the eccentric about him and paid the usual price for strangeness in a conventional schoolboy society. Pushchin says of him that often his misplaced jokes and caustic remarks placed him in difficult situations, and then his awkward efforts to extricate himself did not serve to improve the strained relations with his companions. "I, as his neighbor," he writes, "when everyone was already asleep (listening at the wall on the other side of his room), frequently discussed with him in a low voice through the partition some nonsense or other in the course of the day; then I clearly saw that, because of his sensitiveness, he attached a particular importance to every prank, and this agitated him. Together we tried, as best we could, to smooth out the rough spots, but we did not always succeed. In him was a mixture of personal daring and shyness, and at times one or the other brought him to grief." [6] Even at this early age Pushkin was beginning to show that lack of tact which later, in more important social contacts, caused him no little misery.

But a few more discerning companions found another side to Pushkin's nature. Besides his marked abilities, they discovered an unusually strong sense of honor, and an affection, and a passionate loyalty. The first to take a place with Pushchin and Malinovski in his esteem was the young Baron Delvig. Pushchin was a general favorite with the students, for he had a warm personality and entered into all the activities of the school with enthusiasm. He was Pushkin's companion in various escapades; and in all the "terribly important" secrets of schoolboy existence they were confidants. Pushkin's feeling for Delvig was something different. In the Lyceum the lazy, phlegmatic Delvig led his own life, the best expression of which was his love for poetry. It was as the first and most sensitive appraiser of

Pushkin's poetic creations that Delvig recommended himself. Their feeling for each other, which deepened in their devotion to the muse, remained the most profound and touching of all Pushkin's literary friendships.

Pushkin was also admired by another Lyceum follower of the muse, V. Kiukhelbeker. "Kiukhlya," as he was familiarly called by his comrades, or "Tapeworm," because of his height and thinness, was the standing joke of the whole school. Pushkin himself was one of the most persistent of his tormentors. He was an inoffensive, kindly boy whose German accent, unfailing awkwardness, and passion for poetry provided irresistible subjects for cruel schoolboy humor. Pushkin could not resist ridiculing his bad poetry, but this did not prevent him from repaying in kind the sincere devotion of Kiukhelbeker. Years later they were to fight a duel because of one of Pushkin's sallies, and it was much in keeping with "Kiukhlya's" Lyceum reputation that the combat should have ended in a joke.

These friendships were lasting ones, and continued long after Pushkin had left the Lyceum. But as time went on he widened the circle of his schoolboy acquaintances. Despite the antagonistic side of his nature, he did not remain aloof. For he was always ready for a prank, and took an active part in school games and exercises. His comrades quickly gave him the nickname of "Frenchman," no doubt because of his excellent knowledge of that language.

IV

> Little by little we all learned
> Both something and somehow or other.
> *Eugene Onegin*

The daily program of the school during the first year was perhaps more exacting in theory than in practice. The boys, who had individual rooms, arose at six and went to prayers in the hall. From seven to nine, classes; then tea, and walking to ten; from ten to twelve, classes; from twelve to one, walking; dinner at one; from two to three, writing or drawing; from three to five, classes again; tea at five, and walking till six; then the recitation of lessons or auxiliary classes. At eight-thirty they assembled for supper. After this meal, recreation until ten; at ten, evening prayers and lights out. The six-o'clock hour on Wednesdays and Saturdays was varied by dancing and fencing. Linen was changed twice a week, and Saturday was bath day. On holidays four dishes instead of three were served at dinner. In general the food was excellent, but this did not always prevent the customary rebellion of students against favorite dishes of the cook. On such occasions the boys vented their spleen by hurling pastry at Zolotarev, the unfortunate steward with the Dundreary whiskers. After the English fashion, a half glass of port was served at dinner. But this soon gave way to native kvass and water.

The fine educational ideals of the emperor quickly disintegrated under the fire of practical application. The mild chaos that took hold of the institution was hastened by the early death of the first director, V. F. Malinovski. Until 1816 the Lyceum was run by the professors, each trying to foist his own pedagogical theories on the students. This "interregnum," as the boys called it, was a period of pleasant license and little work. No doubt the extremely excited state of the country also had something to do with the lax discipline. It must be remembered that the great events of 1812 took place during the first year of the Lyceum. Moscow was taken by Napoleon and burned. So great was the fear of an invasion of Petersburg that officials contemplated moving the school further north into the Archangel region. Teachers and students alike followed the news of the campaign with frenzied interest. The boys played war games, wept over Borodino, and rejoiced over the repulses of the French. Caught up in the national patriotic fervor, they daily cheered the long columns of troops that filed by the Lyceum walls; and Pushkin tells how he and his schoolmates envied those who "marched past them to their death." [7]

The professors hardly lived up to their advance reputations. Perhaps something was lost in trying to realize the worthy ideal of a measure of familiarity between student and teacher. If this familiarity did not exactly breed contempt for their preceptors, it did entice the boys to take an uncommon interest in the private lives of the teachers. They quickly learned that the erudite professor of Russian and Latin, N. F. Koshanski, had a weakness for strong drink, was a bit of a dandy, and favored the fair sex. F. M. Gauenshild, the German teacher, they disliked both for his sternness and the fact that he chewed licorice continually. Professor A. I. Galich, who replaced the sick Koshanski, was admired by all the students, and especially by Pushkin. They enjoyed his lectures and even more his relations with them outside the classroom. The level of his familiarity with the students may be judged by Pushkin's tribute to him as "a true friend of the cup" [8] and the companion of their nightly revels. The very excellent French instructor, De Boudry, chattered much about liberty and equality, for he was a brother of the famous Marat. But he was a favorite because of his jollity and cleverness, and the students pardoned the fact that he never took a bath on the score that it was a penance for the violent death of his brother. The only teacher who seems to have won the wholesome respect of the boys was the learned professor of moral philosophy, A. P. Kunitsyn. They complained that he turned them into machines, but for a time they listened attentively to his lectures, and the highly critical Pushkin admitted that "he formed us, he fed our flame." [9]

On the whole, the students were not overworked. Whoever wished to avoid classes could do so with some impunity. The prescribed punishments for laziness and bad behavior would have earned the scorn of the birch-wielding masters of English schools at that time. An offender was obliged to sit apart from his comrades, and for some particularly heinous offense he was placed on bread and water for no more than two days. Certain subjects were badly taught, and German literature was imparted through French lectures, perhaps because hardly any of the students knew the German alphabet.

The free life of the Lyceum left the boys much time to read. This favorite occupation outside the classroom played almost as large a part in their education as the more formal instruction. No doubt the chief fault of the school was the "general-culture" ideal of the curiously liberal, yet bureaucratic founder. In the

attempt to teach everything that would fit them for government service, they were taught nothing well. In place of the
intended purpose and aim, there were continual vagueness and
indecision. As one of the students complained, "the Lyceum
was not a gymnasium, not a university, not a preparatory
school, but a kind of vile mingling of all of these." [10]

It has become a commonplace in the biographies of great men
to indicate how ineffectual their early schooling was in laying a
sure foundation of knowledge. A talented boy may learn a great
deal from his instructors, but he often insists on learning only
what he pleases. In the Lyceum Pushkin benefited from his
educational opportunities in ways that his teachers never
suspected and that his biographers often ignore.

For one thing, Pushkin learned with an ease that discouraged
his comrades. They marveled at his phenomenal memory.
One of them tells how he could read a page of poetry once or
twice and then recite it without a mistake. Zhukovski, it is
said, used Pushkin's memory in correcting his own verses. For
he reworked any line which Pushkin forgot, accounting it as
unsuccessful. But the boy applied himself only to what he
liked. The broad, undisciplined reading done in his father's
library gave him an advantage over his schoolmates which they
were quick to recognize. His domestic education had also encouraged habits of independence and self-direction in study
which ran counter to the customary regimen of school work.
Pushkin may have been a lazy scholar, but one is inclined to
think that what his instructors often set down as laziness was
simply a talented youth's unwillingness to learn some things
which he instinctively felt were unnecessary to him.

The testimony of Pushkin's teachers represents a certain uni-
formity of opinion. Most of them were aware of his brilliance
and quick receptivity, but they condemned him for his negligence. A report by the supervisor sums up the general impression of the instructors: "He has a talent more brilliant than
well-grounded, a mind more passionate and clever than profound. His diligence in study is mediocre, for industry has not
yet become a virtue with him. In reading a quantity of French

books, without the selection proper for his age, he has stored his memory with many successful passages of famous authors; he is quite well read in Russian literature, and knows many fables and verses. His knowledge in general is superficial, although he is beginning to accustom himself to sound reflection. Pride, together with ambition, sometimes makes him self-conscious. A sensitive heart, a hot, passionate temper, giddiness, and especially a sharp disputatiousness are characteristic of him." [11] This is a rather searching evaluation of a fourteen-year-old boy, but the separate judgments of most of his teachers confirm it.

Koshanski suspected his talent and tried to encourage it, but he found Pushkin incorrigible. "Aroused by competition and a feeling of his own worth," wrote Koshanski, "he wishes to be compared with the first writers." [12] The stern Gauenshild bemoaned the fact that Pushkin had not occupied himself with German before entering the Lyceum and was not disposed to do so in his class; but he did admit that, if he wished to, "he would make the most rapid progress, being endowed with much penetration and memory." [13] Kunitsyn sang the same burden: "Pushkin is very intelligent, thinks, and is witty, but he is extremely unindustrious. He is capable only in those subjects which demand least application, and therefore his progress is not very great, especially with logic." [14] Naturally enough, De Boudry found Pushkin one of his best pupils in his specialty, French literature. And I. Kaidanov, the history teacher, felt that for the little effort he put in Pushkin "showed very fine progress, and this must be attributed only to his excellent talents." [15]

In a list of comparative ranks, made up by the teachers a year after they had been in the Lyceum, Pushkin was rated as poor in German, logic, ethics, and mathematics; good in Russian and in French literature. But in drawing, fencing, and calligraphy his instructors unconditionally praised him — perhaps not a bad prophecy for a future poet.

Despite this rather uncomplimentary testimony, Pushkin, on other evidence, was rarely idle in the Lyceum. When he was not up to some deviltry, the time he stole from classes or from his prescribed homework he spent in writing poetry or in feverish reading. With a sure instinct, most of what he did seemed designed to feed the flame of his genius.

v

Restrictions on individual conduct in the Lyceum were not very severe, and during the "interregnum" they lapsed more than ever. Members of the staff were considered legitimate victims for practical jokes, and students roamed at will about the emperor's gardens, stole his prize apples, and in general made themselves obnoxious to everybody. The machinery of surveillance was weak, for guards were easily bought off. Even contraband sweetmeats and liquors had their price, and with these luxuries as incentives forbidden parties were often arranged at night.

Pushkin, with the "face of a monkey," was a leader in these escapades, a "vrai démon pour l'espièglerie," [16] as he described himself in a poem of this time. Before supper one evening the "Frenchman," with his trusted confidant Pushchin and a few other more hesitant companions, smuggled into the room hot water, sugar, eggs, and rum. Then they proceeded to concoct a beverage which was called "egg flip." One of the less staunch of the conspirators was unequal to the drink. A supervisor detected him and reported the matter to the inspector. After supper the inspector questioned the slightly tipsy boy, and the ringleaders came forward and admitted their guilt. They were reprimanded and for two weeks were obliged to say their morning and evening prayers on their knees. Pushkin celebrated the prank in a poem.

A favorite diversion in the considerable leisure at the students' disposal was dramatic entertainment. The teachers themselves encouraged this, and several actually wrote plays, to the no small amusement of their charges. Sergei Chirikov, the drawing instructor, was not very proficient in his specialty, but he imagined himself a dramatist and read the students his long verse tragedies. He was known to them as "The Hero of the North," the title of one of his dramas. The fact that he bemoaned his childless marriage was common knowledge in the Lyceum. And when a son, named Sergei, eventually arrived, the students gleefully hailed the new member of the family with two lines from a well-known play:

> Sergei Sergeich, long belated!
> How we have waited, waited, waited! [17]

The boys themselves staged classical French and Russian dramas and occasionally the productions of another member of the staff who sought literary glory. This was a tutor, A. N. Ikonnikov, a talented man with an unfortunate passion for vodka. One of his plays, pleasantly entitled "A Rose Without Thorns," was put on by the boys with sad consequences for the author. The principal role was taken by the student Maslov. He did poorly in the first act, and in the next, without any warning to the spectators, the author himself appeared in the role, minus a costume and very drunk. While the mystified audience continued to guess whether or not Maslov and Ikonnikov were one and the same person, the new leading man soon managed to disorganize the whole cast by his tactics. For a time dramatics were forbidden, "in order that the students should not be diverted from their studies." [18] Nor did Ikonnikov remain much longer at the Lyceum. Pushkin, it appears, took little part in these spectacles, but the enthusiasm for drama among his comrades no doubt inspired his own attempts at playwriting in the school.

But Pushkin's love of pranks, his sharp tongue, and his passionate nature got him into difficulties with both his preceptors and comrades which he deeply regretted. His quick repartee was often amusing, as in the story of the emperor's visit to a classroom.

"Who is first here?" asked Alexander.

Pushkin promptly replied: "There is no first here, your imperial majesty; all are second." [19]

But Pushkin could offend as easily as he could amuse. Even his schoolfellow, Baron Korf, though never very kindly disposed to him, could say with some justice that, apart from his particular literary cronies, Pushkin was not especially liked by the students; and that his teachers, "afraid of his evil tongue and poisonous epigrams, peeped through their fingers at his epicurean life." [20]

In short, like any full-blooded youngster, the "Frenchman" made both friends and enemies at school. It would be idle to argue whether he made more of one or the other. The unfortunate traits of his character were simply nearest the surface. A Delvig or a Pushchin saw beneath the surface. "In order to love him," wrote Pushchin, "one must look on him with that complete benevolence which knows and sees all inequalities of character and other insufficiencies; for only then does one become reconciled and ends by loving them. . . ." [21] After all, it was only Pushchin who, in the quiet of a sleepless night, heard through the wall the penitent sobbing of "the young man in No. 14." [22]

CHAPTER IV

Literature and Love in the Lyceum

> At life's beginning I remember school;
> There we were children, many and untamed;
> A happy family with no thought or rule.
> *Imitation of Dante*

The general disorganization of the Lyceum during the "interregnum" came to an end when E. A. Engelhardt was appointed director in March 1816. He was a kindhearted man, adept at gaining the confidence of his students, and determined to remedy the growing reputation of the boys for bad behavior. Engelhardt's first principle was that his pupils should be pure in heart, but, unlike the stern Dr. Keate of Eton, he had no intention of flogging them until they were. For one thing, corporal punishment of any sort was forbidden, a prohibition that would have amazed the masters of similar schools in Western Europe. Engelhardt's method was one of kindness, persuasion, and good example. For him, social and moral influences were of the utmost importance in any system of education. He was convinced that the boys, shut up in their Lyceum for so long, had grown wild. They must be brought into contact with society and with normal home life. Accordingly he gained them the privilege of going outside the school walls, provided they kept within the bounds of Tsarskoe Selo. And, following his example, certain families in the town opened their doors to the students. In the summer vacation months Engelhardt took the boys on hiking trips in the neighborhood, and in winter he went skating and sleighing with them. Such treatment worked miracles, and most of the students formed a strong attachment for their new director. Engelhardt's chief fault was that he carried his paternalism too far, and where he failed to find a pure heart in a boy, judging by his own rather narrow standards, he was too quick to condemn him as altogether bad.

Pushkin soon ran afoul of the new director. One of the measures in Engelhardt's reform was to give the students, now several years older than when they had entered the Lyceum, an opportunity for wholesome feminine company. On certain evenings he invited the boys to his house, where they were entertained by his own daughters and their friends. At first Pushkin attended these *soirées* and joined in the various parlor games and songs. A young and pretty woman, who had recently lost her husband, was living with the Engelhardts. The seventeen-year-old Pushkin at once began to court her; he sent her an immodest but excellent verse epistle, *To a Young Widow*.[1] Perhaps the widow was offended by his rather mature protestation of love, or she may not have relished the poetical innuendo that her tears were for him instead of for her dead spouse. At any rate, she showed the poem to Engelhardt. What the director did in the matter is not known, but Pushkin suddenly ceased to appear at his house, and a coldness grew up between them which lasted for the rest of the Lyceum term. Pushchin, who worshiped Engelhardt, was much troubled by his comrade's attitude.

The estrangement was furthered by other unhappy events which throw light on Pushkin's character. It was the custom for the regimental band to play in the court quarters of the Guards before sunset. The noisy students were inevitable and bothersome spectators at these performances. A long, dark corridor, off which were the apartments of the empress' maids of honor, connected the Lyceum with that wing of the palace in which the Guards' room was situated. The boys used this passageway as a short cut. Then there was always the likely chance of meeting Natasha in the dark corridor and of making love to this pretty serving-girl of Princess Volkonskaya, one of the maids of honor. Natasha was well known to the students.

One afternoon the boys were going through the corridor in small groups. With his usual bad luck Pushkin went alone on this occasion. In the darkness he heard the swish of feminine skirts near him. He thought it was the sly Natasha and seized the girl in an effort to kiss her. At that unfortunate moment

one of the room doors flew open, and in the light he saw standing before him not the giggling serving-maid but her stern mistress, Princess Volkonskaya! Pushkin fled as though he had
just come to grips with the devil. When he reached his comrades he at once told Pushchin of the terrible mistake. And
with customary stubbornness he refused to accept his friend's
wise advice that he should throw himself on the mercy of Engelhardt. Pushkin thought that a letter of apology to the princess
herself would remedy the whole affair. But the princess had
already complained to her brother, who in turn brought the
matter to the emperor's attention.

The next day Alexander paid a visit to his director.

"What will it be next?" exclaimed the tsar. "Your students
not only steal my juicy apples through the fence and beat the
garden caretaker, but now they do not even permit my wife's
maid of honor to go about her business!"

By this time Engelhardt had learned of the incident, and in
his kind way he pleaded Pushkin's case and told how the offender wished to write a letter of apology to the princess. The
tsar seemed mollified but advised that the idea of a letter should
be dropped.

"I will take it upon myself to be Pushkin's advocate," said
the monarch. "But tell him this is to be the last time." Then,
smiling, Alexander whispered in his director's ear: "Between
ourselves, the old lady is no doubt enchanted with the young
man's mistake." [2]

This most recent of Pushkin's escapades naturally went the
rounds of the Lyceum, and it is said to have caused no little
scandal at the court. A French quatrain, which pretty clearly
bears the marks of Pushkin's claws, celebrates his revenge in
language most uncomplimentary to the Princess Volkonskaya:

> On peut très bien, mademoiselle,
> Vous prendre pour une maquerelle,
> Ou pour une vieille guenon:
> Mais pour une Grâce — oh, mon Dieu, non! [3]

Pushchin tried to use this instance of Engelhardt's kindness
to prove to his friend how well disposed the director was to him.

But Pushkin remained adamant. Engelhardt, in protecting him, said Pushkin, was merely protecting himself. Clearly his grievance against the director was deep-seated. Engelhardt worried over the matter. During a recreation period he approached Pushkin, who was sitting at his desk, and asked the reason for his hostility. The boy grew confused and protested that he had no reason, and that he did not dare to be angry with his master. "Then you do not love me," replied Engelhardt. He sat down beside Pushkin and in a voice filled with emotion explained to him the strangeness of his behavior. Pushkin listened attentively, frowned, and blushed. Finally, he burst into tears and threw himself on the director's neck.

"I am at fault," he sobbed, "in that up to this time I have not understood and have not been able to appreciate you."

The fatherly Engelhardt wept himself and departed, well pleased with the boy's penitential actions. Ten minutes later he suddenly returned to say something to Pushkin. The boy, noticeably embarrassed, hastened to conceal a sheaf of papers in his desk.

"Verses, no doubt?" the director jokingly remarked. "Show them to me, if it is not a secret."

Pushkin declined.

"One does not keep secrets from a friend," said Engelhardt sweetly, and he firmly opened the desk cover and took the papers. He saw a horrible caricature of himself, adorned with several vile epigrams, amounting almost to a libel. Quietly handing back the papers, he said icily: "Now I see why you do not wish to come to my home. However, I do not know why I have merited your dislike." [4]

II

Friends, young and choice,
In idle hours of pleasant leisure,
You loved to listen to my voice.
Eugene Onegin

Engelhardt and certain of the teachers encouraged literary efforts among the students, and the easy curriculum left plenty of leisure for such pursuits. The boys needed no prompting in this respect. A number of them, like Pushkin, had entered the Lyceum with their pens already exercised. The lush gardens of Tsarskoe Selo and the palace surroundings, filled with monuments and reminders of the country's great historical deeds, provided an inspiring atmosphere for youthful poets; and the stirring events of war that were thrilling the nation suggested no end of patriotic subjects. Literary societies were quickly formed. Communal storytelling games were cultivated, and a whole series of so-called "national songs" came into existence. These popular songs, known to all the students, were usually anonymous. Pushkin, however, played a leading part in composing them. They consisted of nonsense verse about school pranks; or they pilloried particular instructors and students. A whole volume of such poems on Kiukhelbeker alone was collected.

A more formal kind of literary production were the school journals. These began to appear soon after the Lyceum opened. They were ordinarily short-lived attempts, bearing such fetching titles as *For Entertainment and Profit*, the *Inexperienced Pen*, and the *Youthful Swimmers*. The best, and certainly the most characteristic, was the *Lyceum Sage*. With a flourish the youthful editors announce in the opening number that the paper is the repository "of all antiquities and curiosities of the Lyceum members. To this purpose we shall insert in the journal all judgments, new poems, in general everything that has occupied, and occupies the reading public (i.e., the Lyceum)." [5] This announcement was obviously inspired by the professional satirical journals of the time, which in turn had taken their departure from English works of the *Spectator* and *Tatler* variety. With a sense of aping, there appeared on the title page in longhand: "Printing permitted. Censor, Baron Delvig. Typography, K. Danzas"; and the Lyceum Sage humorously warns his readers "not to expect the issues to appear periodically, if at all." [6] There is much bad grammar and childish foolery in the numbers, together with some fine drawings and excellent poetry. On the whole, the *Lyceum Sage* is superior to the average school journal.

Pushkin, of course, was one of the leading spirits in these literary ventures, and he was ably seconded by Delvig, A. Illichevski, S. Komovski, and the insatiable poetaster, Kiukhelbeker, whom Pushkin jokingly advised to write German verse, since his Russian was so bad. For a time Illichevski, who had a clever wit and a facile pen, attempted to rival Pushkin, but he soon bowed to his vastly superior talent.

As a matter of fact, Pushkin was the poet laureate of the Lyceum. There was never any doubt about the matter. His talent was at once recognized by the boys and by his teachers. The school was not long open when Illichevski wrote to a friend: "Concerning my poetic occupation, I have made great progress, having as a comrade a certain young man who, living among the best of poets, has gone far in poetic knowledge and taste." [7] And in a later letter, this same seventeen-year-old poet, who has been busily engaged in composing an opera, gravely informs his friend: "Apropos of Pushkin, he is now writing a comedy in five acts, in verse, under the title of *The Philosopher*. . . . May God grant him patience and constancy, which rarely exist in young writers. . . . May God permit him to finish it — this first great work begun by him, a work with which he wishes to open his career on leaving the Lyceum. May God grant him success; the rays of his glory will be reflected on his companions." [8] God did not grant all these things; *The Philosopher* was never finished. But there was a bit of unconscious prophecy in Illichevski's concluding remark. The Lyceum and the students of this first course were to bask in the reflected glory of Pushkin.

"From the very beginning," recalled Pushchin, "he was our poet. How I see now that class of Koshanski's after dinner when, ending the lecture somewhat earlier than the fixed time, the professor said: 'Now, gentlemen, let us try our pens; write for me, if you please, some verses on a rose.' Our verses in general did not stick, but Pushkin in a twinkling read two quatrains which delighted all of us." [9] Another schoolmate describes how "our poet, withdrawing to the deserted hall of the Lyceum or to the shady walks of the garden, would stormily knit his brows, pout, and bite his pen from vexation as he wrestled mightily with the capricious, coquettish muse; but nevertheless we all saw and heard how his light verse flew forth like 'a puff from the mouth of Eolus.'" [10]

Although not very talkative with most of the students, with his literary coterie Pushkin would discuss poetry endlessly. He scribbled verses everywhere — in church, in the detention house, in the recreation hall, and especially in the mathematics class of Kartsov. Once the professor called him up to the board to do an algebra problem. For some time Pushkin stood on one foot, then on the other.

"How is it coming out? What equals X?" Kartsov finally bellowed.

"Zero!" he smilingly answered.

"Fine! In my class, Pushkin, everything ends in zero with you. Take your seat and write verses." [11]

Pushkin's literary superiority was not questioned, not even by the professors. If a school event had to be celebrated or a distinguished guest entertained, Pushkin was called upon to provide the official ode. When the emperor returned from abroad, the Ministry of National Education requested some verses. Pushkin modestly offered "to his majesty this weak production of an inexperienced poet." [12] In honor of the nuptials of the Prince of Orange and the Grand Duchess Anna Pavlovna, Pushkin also wrote a solicited ode, for which the empress rewarded him with a gold watch and chain.

In the eyes of his comrades Pushkin's literary glory was immeasurably enhanced by his contacts with great authors. He not only wrote letters to such celebrities as Karamzin, Zhukovski, Batiushkov, Vyazemski, and his uncle, but they answered him and discussed his literary plans. At first, in fact, uncle Vasili seemed a bit envious of his nephew's talent, and finally he grudgingly admitted that "Alexander's verses do not smell of Latin and are entirely free from the mark of the seminary." [13] But the boy showed little deference to Vasili. "And so, most amiable of all the uncle-poets of this world," Pushkin writes on sending him some verses, "may I hope that you will forgive this nine-months' pregnancy from the pen of the laziest of poet-nephews?" [14] Once his uncle, Karamzin, and Vyazemski visited the Lyceum, and the renowned Karamzin is reported to have said of the boy: "In him I see a great poet." [15] One may be sure that Pushkin let his literary schoolmates know that his uncle, in a letter following this visit, wrote: "We expect much from you." [16]

Pushkin's greatest triumph, however, was the occasion of Derzhavin's appearance at a Lyceum public examination in 1815. The students were thrilled with the prospect of seeing with their own eyes the patriarch of Russian letters, the illustrious poet of the reign of Catherine II. Pushkin never forgot the spectacle. The interest created would compare favorably with that which Pope might have aroused had he put in an appearance at Harrow when Byron was there. The old Derzhavin, who had not long to live, dozed through most of the examination. But when the subject of Russian literature was reached he came to life. His eyes shone and he was completely transformed. Finally Pushkin was called to deliver perhaps his best Lyceum poem, *Reminiscences in Tsarskoe Selo*.[17] He read with unusual animation. Tears filled the old man's eyes as he heard his own poetry glorified by this boy-poet. "It is not in my power," recalled Pushkin years later, "to describe the state of my soul when I came to the line where I mention the name of Derzhavin; my youthful voice rang out and my heart beat with transporting rapture. . . . I do not remember how I ended my reading; I do not remember where I ran. Derzhavin was in ecstasy: he called for me, wished to embrace me. . . . They looked but did not find me." [18]

"I am not dead!" [19] the ancient bard enthusiastically exclaimed at the conclusion of the performance; and later he remarked to a friend: "He is the one who will replace Derzhavin." [20]

Such triumphs might well have turned an older head than Pushkin's, and no doubt he became somewhat vain about his growing talent. These Lyceum successes early taught him to expect applause. Indeed, some of his schoolmates seem to have resented his attitude, if we may judge by a "national song" which was leveled at him:

> Our "Frenchman" is in haste
> To praise his own taste,
> While he grubs for obscenities.[21]

But Pushkin came by his youthful fame legitimately. For he devoted himself to the muse with zeal, and the record of his school achievement is considerable. In his Lyceum diary for 1815, Pushkin lists some of his literary and other activities: "Yesterday I wrote the third chapter of *Fatama*, or *Human Intelligence*. Read it to S. S., and in the evening with comrades I extinguished the candles and lamps in the hall. A fine occupation for a philosopher! In the morning I read *The Life of Voltaire*. I began a comedy — I do not know whether I shall end it. The day before yesterday I wished to begin an ironic poem, *Igor and Olga*, but I wrote an epigram. . . . In the summer I shall write *A Picture of Tsarskoe Selo*." [22]

In the Lyceum Pushkin wrote more than one hundred and thirty poems on an extraordinary variety of subjects. They range all the way from precise lyrics on the joys and sorrows of Venus and Bacchus to imitations of Ossian, formal odes, epigrams, and verse epistles. From a literary point of view, their form is perhaps more significant than their content, which was too often dictated by the cynical works of the eighteenth-century French poets which he read in his father's library and in school. In these youthful compositions he strove for, and in an unusual degree achieved, a purity of diction, clarity of expression, and pervasive beauty of style. Everything is kept on an even level, there are few purple patches, and adjectives are sparingly used. To be sure, there is little originality, and the marks of his models — Parny, Voltaire, Batiushkov, Zhukovski, V. L. Pushkin — are clearly discernible. It is poetry of the French classical school. But his youthful dependence could not always prevent him from expressing his own sincere emotions and thoughts.

A few of the Lyceum poets achieved a larger audience by getting their verses into print. In June 1814 Pushkin published his first poem in the most influential Russian magazine of the day, the *Messenger of Europe*.[23] This was *To a Poet-Friend*,[24] written when he was only fourteen, and signed by an anagram of his name. It is a fair performance in which the author humorously advises a friend (one would like to think it was the Lyceum metromaniac, Kiukhelbeker) to abandon the art of poetry. With unconscious irony Pushkin warns him that the life of a poet is "a series of griefs, and the thunder of glory a dream." [25]

Several other poems were published, and while still at school Pushkin received the signal honor of being elected to the Arzamas Society. This was composed of a half-serious, half-humorous group of writers, who organized themselves in 1815 to further the development of everything new in literature and to oppose a similar, though much more serious organization, the Beseda, headed by Admiral Shishkov. The Beseda championed an extremely nationalistic and conservative literary platform. Karamzin was recognized as the head of the Arzamas, and the organization included such authors as Zhukovski, Vasili Pushkin, A. Turgenev, Batiushkov, and Vyazemski. The members took nicknames (Pushkin's was "The Cricket"), and their gatherings were usually fun-fests in which they parodied the solemn and pedantic meetings of the Shishkovians, and poked fun at their literary enemies in witty satires.

However, this early and rather unique fame of the young Pushkin must not be rated at more than its face value. It is easy to forget that Russian literature at this particular time was a kind of mutual admiration society, and that such controversies as those between the Arzamas and the Shishkovians were tempests in a teapot. Authors published little, and many poets owed their fame primarily to manuscript verses. Literature had small dissemination, and the leading figures formed a more or less closed corporation, hardly known to the world at large. Although it meant a great deal to Pushkin to be accepted by such men as Karamzin and Zhukovski, the cream of Russian intellectuals, its significance hardly got beyond the limits of their own small circle. It meant that his schoolboy poetry had

achieved an elegance and finish according to the standards of
very brilliant and exacting writers. Pushkin himself, after 1820,
by his own enterprising talent, was to carry literature to a much
wider public and to make poetry more popular than it had ever
been in Russia. It is little wonder that his elders read and believed these remarkably prophetic verses of his friend Delvig,
published in 1815, two years before Pushkin finished his school
days:

> Pushkin! Not even the woods can hide him:
> The lyre betrays him with resounding song,
> And Apollo will ravish him from mortals
> To the immortals on divine Olympus.[26]

III

> I learned the pain of secret bliss.
> *Eugene Onegin*

Although many of Pushkin's Lyceum love poems were of the
synthetic variety, largely inspired by the erotic productions of
French writers, a few of them were based on personal emotional
experiences. Like his hero, Eugene Onegin, Pushkin began
very early to cultivate "the science of the tender passions." [27]
The notation "early love" in his *Program for Memoirs* [28] refers
to a time when he was only six or seven years old. A little girl
whom he saw at the dances his mother obliged him to attend,
had caught his childish fancy.

By the time he entered the Lyceum the addition of a few
years had deepened his perception and turned his mind to the
more serious aspects of love. He began to evince an unusual
responsiveness to feminine charm which did not escape the
attention of his schoolmates. "Pushkin was so susceptible to
women at this time," writes one of his comrades, "that when
only fifteen or sixteen, by merely touching the hand of his
dancing partner at a Lyceum ball, his glance grew passionate,
and he snorted and wheezed like a high-spirited horse in a drove
of colts." [29]

Students roamed the Lyceum gardens and the town, when
they were permitted, sniffing pretty servant girls, such as the
Natasha of Princess Volkonskaya. But there was another

Natasha, an attractive but poor actress in the domestic troupe
of V. V. Tolstoi. The boys were allowed to attend the performances at Tolstoi's house, and naturally they all fell in love with
Natasha. Pushkin dedicated two poems to her, in which he
describes how she appears in his dreams, how he is "languishing
with love" and "growing weaker every hour." [30] The expres-
sions are conventional and his feeling anything but profound.
However, he could hunt more ambitious game, as in the unfortunate case of the young widow at Engelhardt's; and it is
even reported that he thought himself in love with the charming
but middle-aged wife of Karamzin. Pushkin visited the family
when they stayed at Tsarskoe Selo, and took it upon himself to
send the wife a love note. She showed it to her husband, and
they both laughingly reprimanded the boy. The incident did
not prevent her from remaining one of his closest and best
friends.

None of these affairs of the heart occupied Pushkin for long.
But an entry in his Lyceum diary for November 1815 tells us of
his first serious love, and, poetically speaking, a very fruitful
one. "I was happy!" he writes. "No, yesterday I was not
happy; in the morning, standing by the window, I was tortured
by expectation, by an indescribable agitation; I looked out on
the snowy road — she was not to be seen! At last I lost hope;
suddenly I meet her unexpectedly on the stairway. Sweet
moment!

> He sang of love, but his voice was so sad.
> Alas! from love he learned only pain!

How nice she was! How the black dress clung to dear Bakunina!
But I have not seen her for eighteen hours — ach! What a
situation, what torture! But I was happy for five minutes." [31]

The object of this youthful passion was Ekaterina Bakunina,
the pretty sister of one of his schoolmates. She often visited
her brother and attended the Lyceum balls. The students were
in raptures over her, and Pushkin had serious rivals in Illichevski and Pushchin. But Ekaterina seems to have been par-
tial to the young poet, and no doubt they had secret meetings
in the quiet garden walks. She must have been flattered by the

fact that Pushkin's first poem to her, *To an Artist*,[32] had been set to music and was sung by the students.

However, if we may judge from the whole series of poems Pushkin wrote about her, Ekaterina did not return his affection with quite the abandon her lover wished. In the first group, written when his feelings were still in the uncertain stage, he merely indulges in sad thoughts about the hopelessness of his love. At "life's feast" he appears always as a "gloomy guest," [33] and he regrets that "the flower of my youth withers from suffering." [34] These verses carried him over the winter of 1815 to 1816. But in the second series, written in the summer of 1816, he is for a time more hopeful and the expression of his passion more daring. He dreams about Ekaterina, tells of his "voluptuous raptures," and of the purely imaginary "consolation of secret pleasures." [35] But in the autumn Ekaterina left for Petersburg. The lovers had a last rendezvous, and in a poem on the event the unhappy youth tells of his premonitions of an early death. He is prepared to bid farewell to this "sad world." [36]

Of course, Pushkin soon got over his sorrow in the active life and pleasures of the Lyceum. But the impression Ekaterina Bakunina made on his young heart long remained with him. Years later, in describing the love of the unfortunate Lenski for Olga in *Eugene Onegin*,[37] he had in mind his own affection for Ekaterina. And in a rejected stanza of this poem he returned, with all the force of an unforgettable memory, to this first serious love, poignantly recalling the "lively features of the charming maiden" and the emotions that "agitated my young blood." [38]

IV

Dear friend of our Lyceum life,
With thee I share these parting moments.
To Kiukhelbeker

Towards the end of the six-year course the students made the most of Engelhardt's desire to broaden their young lives through social contacts beyond the walls of the Lyceum. The new freedom often degenerated into license. Uniformed boys smoked openly in the gardens, roamed noisily about the town, ogled girls, and spent much time in the coffee shops. Some of them frequented the barracks of the loose-living Hussars stationed at Tsarskoe Selo. Here they indulged in drinking bouts and ribald nonsense with the officers until late hours of the night. Then they would straggle back to the locked gates of the Lyceum; a small tip quieted the porter, and the tutors had long since been asleep. Nor was it unknown for a student who had suffered defeat in a drinking contest with the Hussars to pass the whole night at the barracks.

Pushkin, impatient of restraint, abused Engelhardt's good intention more than any of the students. The stuffy bourgeois atmosphere of the game-playing families of Tsarskoe Selo, and even of Karamzin's household, where he was always welcome, bored him. He preferred making friends with the peasants and servants in the town, and the jolly Hussars he found much to his taste. The officers reciprocated by at once placing him on a comradely basis at their lively evening parties. One of the worst rakes in the regiment, Captain P. Kaverin, became his particular friend. The young Pushkin drank with the officers, addressed cynical poems to them, and in their company chased after the pretty actresses of Count Tolstoi. Under the allure of their gay life, he even dreamed of entering the regiment after he graduated. But father Pushkin quickly pricked this bubble. Yes, he might enter the infantry, but to maintain his son as a cavalry officer was much too expensive. The youth was obliged to give up the idea, but he continued his vicarious army life with the Hussars. These new acquaintances and diversions had a bad influence on his studies. Four months before graduation he received grades of zero in several subjects, even in his beloved Russian poetry.

For a youth of Pushkin's mature intelligence there was much more to be found in the company of these Hussars than valorous wassailing and smutty anecdotes. As a young cynic he could pretend to be a sworn enemy of "cold wisdom," [39] and to value a "fine dinner" more than "three whole dozens of philosophers." [40] In reality his active mind was eager for wisdom and philosophy, and certain of his soldier-friends had both. Like most of the aristocratic officers of the Guards regiments, the Hussars were a curious combination of intellectually ambitious men and forthright rakes. They had recently returned with the Russian army of occupation at Reims, where they had become infected with dangerous European liberalism. The revolutionary ideas which were to sweep so many of them into the disastrous dragnet of 1825 had already borne fruit. Pushkin and some of his schoolmates listened attentively to the Hussars' conversations about constitutional liberty, social evils in Russia, and the necessity of changing the system. Their impressionable minds were much influenced, and several of them, to their sorrow, were to attempt to realize this liberal heresy after they graduated from the Lyceum.

The one Hussar who most affected Pushkin in this respect was Colonel P. Chaadaev. Although only twenty-three in 1817, he was already a dispassionate observer, and before many years he was to be regarded as one of the most brilliant philosophical minds in Russia. Chaadaev was an idealist, devoted to the highest type of moral thinking. Pushkin had many long and earnest discussions with him which must have been a revelation to a youth who up to this time had lived, as he says, "not knowing either care or purpose or system." [41] Their talks awoke in him a consciousness of Russia's destiny and opened up new paths in life. They became fast friends, and Pushkin remembered Chaadaev in verse as the first to influence him in the direction of serious and independent thought.

These contacts with older men increased Pushkin's impatience with his schoolboy life. Before the course was fairly ended, he was pluming his wings for a flight into the great world. In a letter to Vyazemski he protests that isolation is an evil to all philosophers and poets. "To be sure, the time of our graduation approaches. But a year still remains. A whole year of pluses and minuses, of laws and taxes, of the lofty and the beautiful . . . a whole year still to doze before the teacher's desk — this is terrible!" [42]

In truth, the Lyceum had done about all it could for him.

Perhaps, like Onegin, he knew enough Latin to decipher an epigraph and place a *vale* at the end of a letter; and he had fortified his mind with a stock of historical anecdotes.[43] The school possessed most of the defects of the virtues which its imperial founder had hoped to plant in it. The Lyceum hardly prepared Pushkin for life, and for years he was to curse his "damnable education" [44] and the obligation he always felt of supplementing it. He saw through the pretenses both of the system and of many of the teachers. Probably no other school in Russia would have served him any better, for his may have been the usual case of the misfit genius brought into contact with educational conventions and intellectual mediocrity.

Among his schoolmates and instructors he had gained the reputation of a giddy, thoughtless, irritable, and cynical youth, who was fond of pranks and proud of his ability to turn out scurrilous epigrams. In the minds of many of his contemporaries this reputation clung to him for the rest of his life. Engelhardt's severe and final judgment on his pupil had, perhaps, more justification than many critics will allow. "The highest and final purpose of Pushkin," wrote the director, "was to shine, and in poetry alone; but there is hardly to be found in him a substantial foundation because he is afraid of every serious instruction, and his mind, having neither penetration nor depth, is an entirely superficial and French mind. This is the very best that may be said about Pushkin. His heart is cold and empty; there is neither love nor religion in him; perhaps no young heart was ever quite so empty as his. Tender and youthful feelings are debased in his imagination, profaned by all the erotic productions of French literature which, before entering the Lyceum, he knew almost by heart as a worthy acquisition of a primary education." [45]

These are harsh words. It is clear that Engelhardt had little love for Frenchmen, and less for Pushkin. The opinion of his schoolmate, Baron Korf, was as harsh as the director's. "Hottempered to the point of madness," wrote Korf, "always scatter-brained, always steeped in his poetical dreams, with his ungovernable African passions, spoiled from childhood by praise

Sovfoto

PUSHKIN AT THE LYCEUM PERIOD

and flattery, Pushkin never had anything amiable or attractive in his manner, either at the school bench or later in society." [46] But Korf was an envious and smug climber (he was proud of the fact that he had restraint enough to avoid the student excesses with the Hussars), and Engelhardt, though well-disposed, lacked penetration, and morally was a bit of a prig. Pushkin gave them plenty of provocation for their ill opinion, but they were inclined to see only the bad side of his nature.

For those who had eyes to see and hearts to understand, there was a lovable side to Pushkin. Arina Rodionovna and his grandmother had discovered it in the sorry period of childhood. And in the Lyceum days such close friends as Pushchin, Delvig, Malinovski, Kiukhelbeker, and Chaadaev valued him as much for the likable qualities of his character as for his unquestioned talent. Herein lies Pushkin's debt to his school. The Lyceum gave him an opportunity to form lasting friendships and to develop his genius. Here he found an encouraging literary atmosphere and friends who at once recognized his ability. Fame came to him easily in the Lyceum, as to one destined to it. There his imagination grew, and his responsiveness to various impressions of life quickened. At school Pushkin learned to sing of what he felt. Poetry was becoming the echo of his heart. And some notion of the divine mission of the poet was already beginning to dawn in his mind.

The strong feeling of comradeship among the members of this first Lyceum class, and the part Pushkin played in inspiring it, may have been somewhat exaggerated. However, his affections were anchored to the school and to his friends there as they never had become anchored to his home and his parents. For a time the old students met in Delvig's house in Petersburg, and every year a formal reunion was held. When it was possible, Pushkin always attended these gatherings. The most faithful members were largely his old literary companions, who speeded the hours of meeting with wine and verse. The sentiments of an alumnus for his alma mater grow mellow as the years pass. Pushkin was no exception. He forgot his unpleasant experiences, and the series of fine anniversary poems he wrote for these occasions is filled with devotion to the Lyceum and with tender recollections of his comrades and their doings. In the best of these poems, *The Nineteenth of October*, he could sincerely call upon his old schoolmates:

> Let each, as to his lips the cup he raises,
> The good remember, and forget the ill. [47]

And in those days they were more than proud of "their poet." Everybody was reading his verses; his old teacher, Koshanski, recited them to his classes. The students then at the Lyceum benches found glory for themselves in the glory of their great alumnus. For was it not Pushkin who had made their school famous?

But the road to this wider fame was still long and tortuous. The first step, however, was at hand. Graduation had at last arrived. At the public examinations which preceded the event Pushkin certainly won no fame, despite the fact that the questions and answers had been arranged beforehand by students and teachers. Only when a professor got the order of his questions mixed was there any chance of a candidate's doing badly. For Russian literature Pushkin read a cold didactic poem, *Disbelief*,[48] a theme which might have been suggested by Engelhardt as a penance for his erring student. The best Pushkin could do was to finish nineteenth on the list. For this performance he was given only a rank of the tenth class,* and a minor position in the Foreign Office.

The graduation exercises on June 9, 1817, were a kind of parody of the Lyceum's opening day, save that now the atmosphere was heavy with the sadness of farewell. The emperor graced the occasion with his presence and with fatherly tenderness addressed the graduates. Like Kunitsyn six years before, he told the boys of their holy obligations to their monarch and to the fatherland. And he concluded, having offered them the privilege of entering his service, with some well-meant advice on how to conduct themselves on the path of life. The prizes

---

* Peter the Great divided all public service into fourteen classes, corresponding to ranks in the army. The tenth rank was that of "collegiate secretary."

were then awarded, the Lyceum hymn sung, and after the students had filled their friends' albums with parting verses, they went their separate ways. At that moment Pushkin wept while saying farewell to the comrades with whom he had spent six years in the Lyceum of Tsarskoe Selo. But his sorrow soon vanished at the thought that at last he was free to enter the "great world."

CHAPTER V

In the Great World

J'aime et le monde et son fracas,
Je hais la solitude.
Mon Portrait

After graduating from the Lyceum Pushkin did not immediately plunge into the "great world." Instead he went directly
to his mother's estate at Mikhailovskoe, in the province of
Pskov, where the family now spent their summers. The simple
pleasures of village life, of which he had seen nothing for over
six years, amused him — the country baths, strawberry-picking,
and rustic dances. At Mikhailovskoe he met Peter Hannibal,
the last son of the famous Abram. The old man treated him to
some of his homemade vodka and was pleased with the youth's
drinking prowess. He also enjoyed the company of another
relative, good-natured Pavel Hannibal. But their friendship
and disparity in age did not prevent the quick-tempered Pushkin from challenging him to a duel — Pavel had stolen his
partner at one of the village dances. Ten minutes later the
quarrel was forgotten in wine, embraces, and impromptu verse.

Despite a genuine fondness for country life, Pushkin could
never endure it for long. "I love noise and the crowd," [1] he
wrote, and after little more than a month at Mikhailovskoe he
left for Petersburg. Except for two short intervals, he spent the
next three years there (1817–1820).

The comparatively young Russian capital was vastly different in appearance and population from ancient Moscow.
Petersburg was a European city, adorned with grandiose buildings and monuments designed by western architects and artists.
Its inhabitants reflected the excitement of new ideas and impressions brought from Western Europe. Half of the population was in uniform, for it was a city of nobles, army officers, and
officials. Something of the glitter and parade of Alexander I's

spectacular court was caught up by high society in general. Entertainment was done in the grand style, and the effect at state balls, the theater, the ballet, and in brilliant *salons* was one of extravagant ostentation.

But foreigners who visited Petersburg at this time often experienced a feeling of sadness and impending disaster beneath the city's external beauty and the gaiety of its high society. "Built on tears and corpses" by Peter the Great, the frightful history of its founding seemed to be indelibly stamped on the capital. Peter had intended his city to be a "window to Europe"; under Nicholas I, it soon became the "gendarme of Europe."

The restless Pushkins, who had by now moved from Moscow to Petersburg, lived in a modest seven-room apartment on the Fontanka, hard by the river. The neighborhood was poor, accommodating mostly artisans and tradesmen. Impoverished landowners, obliged to come to the city to fight lawsuits, and penniless widows with marriageable daughters also sought the cheap living-quarters in this district. Although the financial condition of the family was gradually growing worse, the Pushkins still attempted to live in style. An atmosphere of faded grandeur hung about the household. A dilapidated family carriage, harnessed to ill-fed horses, stood at the entrance, and ragged and drunken domestics cluttered the hallways. Some rooms were adorned with rich old furniture, others were entirely empty. There was an insufficiency of everything, from money to drinking glasses. When guests arrived, the servants were often sent scurrying to the neighbors for extra cooking utensils. Sergei Lvovich, untroubled by any gainful occupation, managed to keep his days occupied with the business of maintaining social contacts. He would start off in the morning in the rickety family carriage to pay his first visit, and often he did not finish his calls until well into the evening. Meanwhile, the household affairs were left to his indifferent wife. Nadezhda Osipovna ran things by fits and starts, in between her own social calls and the reception of visitors. Members of the household had grown accustomed to her tearing the sheets from anger, but it was not always easy to put up with her capricious nature. She could not abide beards. Hence the servants had to restrict themselves to side whiskers. Nor would she tolerate smoking. Up to her death Sergei Lvovich always had to smoke his pipe by stealth in his own house.

"My corner is narrow and simple," [2] Pushkin wrote to a companion. He occupied a tiny room on the floor above the family quarters, which enabled him to receive his friends with some degree of privacy. One of them describes this "corner": "We mounted the stairs; a servant opened the door and we entered Pushkin's room. By the door was a bed on which lay a young man in a striped Bokharan dressing gown, with a skull cap on his head. Beside the bed, on a table, were papers and books. In the room objects of the abode of a worldly youth were joined with the poetic disorder of a scholar." [3] Pushkin's servant was the devoted Nikita Kozlov, who literally never deserted his master from the cradle to the grave. He cared for Pushkin in his infancy, accompanied him into exile, and escorted his body to its last resting place.

The rift between Pushkin and his parents which had begun in his childhood was in no respects lessened by six years in the Lyceum. They paid him occasional visits at school, but the long separation was regretted by neither side. Now, living once again in the family homestead, Pushkin was bound to find plenty of cause for friction. The situation went deeper than clashing temperaments and mutual incompatibility. Although he never entirely lost a feeling of filial duty to his mother and father, they did nothing to stimulate in him any real affection. Later they took pride in his fame, but they were not inclined to understand or forgive his weaknesses, as they did repeatedly in the case of his younger brother. Nadezhda Osipovna's irritability increased as she grew older. And Sergei Lvovich, who spent most of his time trying to break into the circles of higher aristocracy, grew more niggardly as his financial circumstances became more straitened. Many of the quarrels between Pushkin and his parents, at this time and later, were over questions of money. Accustomed to indulge their own caprices, they were not inclined to cater to his. If they had anything left, they preferred to spend it on the two favorite children, Olga and Lev. Pushkin received only seven hundred paper rubles* from the Ministry of Foreign Affairs, and this sum was entirely inadequate for the kind of life he elected to lead in the gay Petersburg world. Sergei Lvovich, who thoroughly disapproved of his son's behavior, repeatedly refused requests for funds. Pushkin asked money to buy a fashionable pair of dancing pumps. Sergei Lvovich offered him instead his own old ballroom shoes, dating back to the time of Paul I. The son bitterly recalled how his father everlastingly nagged him over eighty kopeks which he paid a cabby for driving him home when he was feeling too ill to walk. No doubt the miserliness of his father gave rise to the story that Pushkin, while rowing on the river once with Sergei Lvovich, nonchalantly threw gold pieces into the water because he liked to see their glitter in the clear depths. The anecdote does not lose its point in the face of the extreme unlikelihood that Pushkin ever possessed any gold pieces at this time with which to give his father such a moral lesson in avarice. It was inevitable that Pushkin should once again feel himself alone in the family circle. His sister often sided with him in these quarrels, and Arina Rodionovna comforted him, but his unhappy family life was partly responsible for the compensating and furious existence he sought in the pleasures of the capital.

At the beginning of the Petersburg period Pushkin was eighteen years old. By now his form and features were fixed, and the essential traits of his nature, while still to develop and change somewhat, had achieved well-defined characteristics. He was short, not quite five feet six inches in height. But his small frame was muscular and well-developed. He was a tireless walker, passionately fond of swimming and horseback riding, and was considered one of the best pupils of a popular fencing teacher. His features, however, were anything but attractive — a shock of dark curly hair, a flat nose, thick lips, and a mulatto-like complexion. His smile revealed two perfect rows

* At that time a paper ruble was worth about thirty-five cents.

of unusually large, glistening teeth. And he affected extremely long fingernails, of which he was inordinately proud. But the face was remarkably expressive, animated by a pair of brilliant eyes that suggested a world of contemplation and poetic beauty. By both friends and enemies the unattractiveness of his "African" features was forgotten under the compelling power of these extraordinary eyes.

Vivacity was Pushkin's most pronounced personal trait. "Cricket" and "Spark," his nicknames at this time, are fairly descriptive of his unusual animation and swiftness of movement. In crowds he could be morose and silent, but in a small company of intimate friends he gave full vent to his natural liveliness of spirits. The famous actress, Kolosova, in whose family circle he was a welcome visitor, appreciated this quality in him. "At our home Sasha Pushkin made us laugh with his playfulness and childish pranks. He would not sit still for a minute in any one place; twisting, jumping about, shifting seats, he would overturn mother's sewing box, entangling himself in a ball of embroidery yarn; then he would scatter the playing cards arranged by mother. 'You think you are clever, you dragon fly!' my Evgeniya Ivanovna would cry. 'Stop; enough!' For a couple of minutes Sasha would be quiet, and then he would again begin to play his pranks. Finally mother would threaten to punish the restless Sasha. 'Snip his claws!' (So she called his enormously long fingernails.) 'Hold his hand,' she would say to me, taking her scissors, 'and I'll cut them!' I would seize his hand, but he would set up a howl over the whole house, and complaining that we were hurting him, he would begin a feigned sobbing and groaning until we were driven to tears laughing at him. In a word, he was a veritable child, but truly well-mannered." [4]

Throughout his short life Sasha Pushkin was regarded by many as a "veritable child" — the tsar's secret police would have preferred the epithet "enfant terrible" — but few, even among his close friends, would have agreed that he was "well-mannered." The mature, serious, and intellectual side of his character was too often obscured by his ebullient nature. However, this period was a time for sowing wild oats. He had the desire and plenty of leisure, for his position in the Foreign Office was purely nominal. The Cricket had the great new world of Petersburg to explore, and for a time he was to chirp gaily in it.

II

> While live we may, let us live!
> *To Kaverin*

The old caretaker extinguished the lamps on the bridge in the early hours of the morning. Most of Petersburg was still asleep. Only a few tradespeople stirred. A huckster's cart from the suburbs rolled noisily down the street, and a thick-limbed peasant woman with her milk pitcher hurried along. Thin columns of blue smoke rose from the chimneys of a few buildings. And the precise German baker in his paper cap opened the little window of his shop, ready for business.[5] A tired horse, driven by a drowsy *izvozchik*, halted before a stone house on the Fontanka. With some difficulty a young man, wearing a high hat and a Spanish cloak thrown back over one shoulder, got out of the carriage and disappeared in the gateway. This was the Cricket arriving home from an evening of revelry with his friends of the Green Lamp.

Through his father's contacts and the friendships he had formed in the Lyceum the doors of Petersburg society were open to Pushkin. He soon revolved in a circle of worldly and rich young men. The glittering officers of the Guards gave a certain tone to this youthful society. They provided a refinement and nobility altogether admirable. But debauchery and dangerous adventures, perhaps because of immemorial army tradition, were considered orders of merit among both the officers and their friends.

The Society of the Green Lamp — so called because of the large lamp in the room of Nikita Vsevolozhski's house where the members met — had enrolled Pushkin and some of the more prominent youths in his own circle of friends. Their meetings were described as "scandalous orgies" by contemporary outsiders and by subsequent commentators. One recalls the exaggerated gossip about the unholy mysteries of Abbot-Byron, his monk-companions, and the Paphian girls in the vaults of Newstead Abbey. Tales were told of wild debauches, drinking, card-playing, and indecent dramatic skits, such as "The Exile of Adam and Eve from Paradise" and "Sodom and Gomorrah." As a matter of fact, the Green Lamp was established largely for the purpose of reading original literary productions and for discussing subjects of contemporary interest. Nikita Vsevolozhski, one of the leaders, was a student of history and a translator of comedies; the gentle Delvig, Pushkin's poet-friend, was also a member; and Gnedich read parts of his version of Homer to the group. The morally stern Griboedov, greatest dramatist of the time, attended the meetings, as did the philosophically-minded Ya. Tolstoi. To be sure, the wine flowed freely, and there were merry feasts with female companions. Such gay young blades as Kaverin, Iurev, Yakubovich, V. Engelhardt, and Mansurov did their best to maintain the scandalous reputation of the Green Lamp. The lively Cricket was a favorite with these intellectual and pleasure-seeking bottle-companions. He was ready with witty conversation or an extemporary epigram; or he would read them a gracious poem. Nor did he falter in the pledges to Bacchus and Venus. "Everything goes as formerly," Pushkin writes to the absent Mansurov. "The champagne, thank God, is good, the actresses also — now they drink, now they . . . . — amen, amen, so it must be — the Green Lamp is snuffed, extinguished, it seems." [6]

The members of the Green Lamp were passionately fond of the theater. It is much to the credit of Alexander I that he encouraged one of the most brilliant periods of the Russian stage. The Imperial Theater was the center of elegant social life, and the Theatrical School, with its pretty novices, was a favorite hunting preserve of guardsmen and fashionable youths about town. Every dandy believed it his sworn duty to be at home backstage. Young men such as those of the Green Lamp were constantly devising schemes to circumvent the supervision of the stern duenna of the Theatrical School. The carriage bearing one of the pupils to a performance would break down under suspicious circumstances. A dashing officer would opportunely drive up, proffer his services, and the charming aspirant would fail to arrive at the theater that evening.

The devotion of these youths to the actresses did not improve their behavior in the course of the performance. Pushkin has left a picture of the typical dandy at the theater, and the description unquestionably is something of a self-portrait. "Just before the start of an opera, a tragedy, or a ballet the young man saunters up and down the first ten rows of seats, steps on everybody's feet, and converses with all his acquaintances and strangers. 'Where did you come from?' 'From Semenova's, from Sosnitskaya's, from Kolosova's, from Istomina's.' * 'How fortunate you are!' 'She is acting today. She is dancing. Let's clap her, let's call her out! She is so sweet! What eyes she has, what tiny feet! Such a talent!' The curtain goes up. The young man and his friends, moving from place to place, express their delight and applaud." [7]

The Cricket also stepped on feet and often made himself generally offensive to neighbors who really wished to enjoy the spectacle. One evening he entered the box of some friends in the Grand Theater, wearing a periwig (because of illness he had been obliged to shave his head). Suffering from the heat, he doffed the wig and used it as a fan during the most pathetic scene. The audience around him began to laugh. His friends remonstrated. But he slid off his chair to the floor, pulling the wig on like a hat. There he sat to the end of the performance, "making jokes at the expense of the play and the acting of the players." [8] On another occasion he applauded a scene by pounding on the bald head of a man seated in front of him. Or, for variation, he would assume the attitude of the bored fop, ignore the spectacle, yawn, stretch, stare at ladies in the other boxes, and ostentatiously display his long, golden-sheathed fingernails.

Despite this childish behavior, Pushkin soon grew deeply

* Well-known theatrical performers of the time.

interested in the theater and became a keen critic of the drama. His works contain many penetrating observations on actors, performances, and plays. Like all Petersburg society, he took sides in the fashionable theatrical war between the great actress Semenova and her rival Kolosova. The Cricket carried his partisanship to the extreme of vainly falling in love with the beautiful Semenova. He presented to her his *Notes on the Russian Theater*,[9] in which he glorifies her genius. But on Kolosova he wrote an insulting epigram, for which later he had the good grace to ask her pardon.

Organized demonstrations in the theater and rivalries for the affections of actresses sometimes ended seriously. Duels were in fashion. The young society man, officer or civilian, eagerly sought his baptism of fire. A duel was considered a gentlemanly perquisite as well as a badge of courage. Points of honor were never lacking; often there was hardly any provocation at all. The reputation of "duelist" was a mark of distinction among the gay youth of the capital. Yakubovich, a member of the Green Lamp, became a kind of epic figure in the eyes of his comrades because of his many duels. He was the "hero of my imagination," [10] wrote Pushkin. Of course, most of these battles of honor were bloodless affairs. But tragic exceptions did occur. Such was the notorious four-cornered duel fought by friends of Pushkin over the famous ballet dancer, Istomina. It ended fatally for one of the youths, and the others were seriously compromised.

The Cricket had more than his fair share of contests in the process of making his mark in the great world. "Pushkin has a duel almost every day," [11] lamented Karamzin's wife in a letter to Vyazemski. The Cricket had a touchy sense of honor, and he was also quick to give offense. We have already seen that he did not hesitate to call out his own relative, Pavel Hannibal. Even with good kind Kiukhelbeker, his Lyceum comrade, he fought a duel. The motive is uncertain and the details not fully supported. It seems that he offended Kiukhelbeker with one of his cruel epigrams. Pushkin was challenged. The duel took place in winter. The lanky "Kiukhlya," his eyes popping and his sparse Dundreary whiskers and beard bristling, shot first and missed. According to one account Pushkin dropped his pistol and wished to embrace his friend. "Shoot! Shoot!" [12] cried Kiukhelbeker hysterically. But Pushkin complained that the snow had got into his weapon. Another version insists that the Cricket simply refused to fire, saying: "It is entirely silly, my dear. Let us go and drink tea." [13] Still a third account insists that Pushkin shot in the air; and one contemporary even asserted that the pistols were loaded with cranberries. At any rate, the friends were quickly reconciled. Pushkin sincerely loved Kiukhelbeker, as future events were to prove.

According to an authentic incident recorded by the novelist Lazhechnikov, the young Pushkin appeared early one morning in the apartment of a certain bumptious Major Denisevich. He was accompanied by two officers of the Guards.

"What is your pleasure?" demanded the major, striking a martial pose.

"You should know that well enough," replied Pushkin in a soft voice. "You directed me to be at your place at eight o'clock. It is now a quarter to eight. We have time to select the weapons and decide on a location."

The major's face grew red.

"But I did not ask you here for that. I wished to tell you that for a young man such as you it is not right to shout in the theater, to prevent your neighbor from hearing the play. That is improper."

"You recited this lecture to me last night before many listeners," said the Cricket more forcefully. "I am not exactly a schoolboy, and I have come to discuss another matter with you. For this, few words are necessary. Here are my two seconds. This gentleman" — he indicated Lazhechnikov, who was in the major's apartment at the time — "will not refuse, I am sure, to be your witness. If it is agreeable to you . . ."

"I cannot fight with you. You are an unknown youth, and I am a staff officer . . ."

"I am a Russian nobleman, Pushkin!" the Cricket interrupted in a harsh and indignant voice. "My comrades will testify to this. You don't need to be ashamed of having such an affair with me!" [14]

The major retreated and called upon Lazhechnikov to play the part of mediator. And the upshot of the affair was that the major humbly begged Pushkin's pardon. The Cricket haughtily left the apartment, refusing to shake hands with his opponent.

In this young, hard-living Petersburg society Pushkin fully subscribed to the philosophy of his jingle:

> Love and wine
> We need together;
> Without them man
> Would yawn forever.[15]

With bottle-companions he visited disreputable pothouses. These escapades were of the nature of "slumming" expeditions, for the young dandies dressed in cheap clothes and professed to be interested in the morals of such places. But they were not above sampling the pleasures. On these occasions drinking prowess became almost a matter of self-preservation. Pushkin strove to excel, but his powers of consumption were not always equal to his ambitions. Sometimes the results were disastrous. His greatest feat in this respect, according to one account, was to wager that he could drink a bottle of rum and not lose consciousness. He stomached the liquor, but all sense of feeling seemed to vanish. The spectators, however, noticed that he continually moved the little finger of his left hand. When he regained his senses Pushkin stoutly protested that he had kept his finger moving as proof of the fact that he had not lost consciousness. The consensus of opinion declared him the winner of the bet. Kaverin has left in his diary an abbreviated account of one of these parties: "Shcherbinin, Olsufev, Pushkin dined with me in Petersburg — champagne placed on ice for twenty-four hours — by chance my ruling beauty (for the satisfaction of fleshly desires) went by — called her in — was insupportably warm — they asked Pushkin to perpetuate the memory of this evening for us in verses." [16] And Pushkin obliged, but the results were more indecent than poetic.

The Cricket, too, had his "ruling beauties." Although he

suffered from a consciousness of his unattractive features, the fact did not lessen a natural self-assurance in affairs of the heart. He possessed an enormous store of nervous energy and yearned after "youthful beauty with the shameless madness of desire," [17] as he exclaims in one of his poems of the time. His overtures were swift and usually successful. He had but to see a pleasing face, and he reacted at once. "More or less," he writes, "I have been in love with all the pretty women I have known." [18] He was talented in love no less than in poetry. Although most of these Petersburg affairs were of a transient nature, he was capable of almost every degree or kind of love. When he experienced a strong urge he was nearly out of his mind if satisfaction were denied him.

With companions of the Green Lamp Pushkin pursued the actresses and ballet dancers. Often he was seen standing outside the dormitory of the Theatrical School, hoping for a glimpse of his beloved of the moment at one of the windows. When the fair students of the theater failed him, he fell in love with a pretty ticket-seller. But like some of his comrades, he preferred the wider and easier field of amorous activities provided by the many girls of pleasure in Petersburg. Among the smart set, tradition approved the brothel with as much fervor as it did dueling. Pushkin appeared to be tireless in these adventures. Nothing stopped him — insufficient means, advice of good friends, or the danger of injuring his health. "The Cricket hops along the boulevard and into b . . . .," [19] writes A. I. Turgenev to Vyazemski, who at that time was in service at Warsaw. Pushkin himself told Zhukovski that he "does not sleep for whole nights on end, visits brothels all day, and sometimes plays at bank in the evening." [20] And again we find Turgenev keeping his friend in Warsaw posted: "Pushkin is very ill. He caught a cold while waiting at the door of a certain . . . . ., who would not let him in out of the rain, in order not to infect him with her own illness. What a struggle of nobleness, love, and debauchery!" [21]

It was inevitable, despite the Cricket's excellent constitution, that such dissipation should eventually take its toll. "Venus has nailed Pushkin to his bed," [22] the ever-watchful Turgenev finally announced to Vyazemski. And this unhappy sequel to his promiscuous amours was quickly celebrated in doggerel: "Condemned by fate for my old sins, I have suffered eight days now, with drugs in the stomach, with mercury, for being indiscriminate, and repentant at heart."[23] Pushkin's lowered vitality, however, laid him open to more serious illness. At the beginning of 1818 he was dangerously sick, and in 1819 an attack of typhoid fever proved almost fatal. A rest cure at Mikhailovskoe was prescribed. Once more village life bored him. The Cricket was soon back in Petersburg, pale, thin, and with shaven head, but again hopping along the boulevard or convulsing Zhukovski and his friends until two in the morning with the representation of a comic scene between a monkey and a dog.

In the light of such behavior it is difficult to dismiss Baron Korf's lurid and much-disputed characterization of Pushkin at this time. Korf was in an excellent position to know, for he lived in the same house with the Pushkins in Petersburg. His unsympathetic attitude of the Lyceum days was in no sense improved by this continued proximity in the capital. On one occasion, in fact, the former schoolmates had a serious quarrel. Pushkin's servant, a little tipsy, offended Korf, who gave him a beating. In a rage Pushkin immediately sent a challenge, which Korf promptly returned with a note: "I do not accept your challenge for such a trifle, not because you are Pushkin, but because I am not Kiukhelbeker."[24]

No doubt Korf's hostility considerably prejudiced his judgment in the altogether unfavorable picture he drew. "In society," he writes, "Pushkin gave himself up to debauchery of every kind, indulging day and night in an unbroken chain of bacchanalian orgies. One wonders how both his health and talent bore this mode of life, the natural accompaniment of which were frequent odious illnesses which often brought him to the brink of the grave. . . . Pushkin was not created either for society or social obligations, nor even, I think, for any higher love or sincere friendship. Two elements only dominated him — the satisfaction of fleshly desires and poetry, and in both he has gone far. . . . Always without a penny, everlastingly in debt, often even without a decent dress coat, with constant scandals, frequent duels, intimately acquainted with tavern keepers, bawdy houses, and Petersburg harlots, Pushkin represented a type of the filthiest debauchee." [25]

But it is easy to lose perspective and exaggerate the significance of Pushkin's life of dissipation at this time. For six years he had been shut up in the Lyceum, where his personal freedom had been restricted in many ways. Thoroughly uncongenial parents failed to provide him with the steadying influence of an attractive home life. When he was about the age of a college undergraduate, his passionate nature was brought into contact with the brilliant and youthful society of the capital, a social set that regarded dissipation as the hallmark of the fashionable gentleman. If he was immoderate, so were his young friends. In their own remarks members of the Green Lamp did not describe Pushkin as a monster of debauchery, but simply as "one of the crowd."

On the other hand, though Pushkin felt that he had a prescriptive right, by virtue of his nobility, to a place in the best Petersburg society, in reality his material conditions often forced him to cut a sorry figure among these rich young gallants. He gambled furiously — an unfortunate habit that was to stick by him — in hopeless attempts to obtain funds for the expensive pleasures of this set. Thus, even at an early age, he began to experience an insufficiency in the social world that hurt his pride. At times one strongly suspects that the ardor with which he led his convivial existence was simply an expression of fear that he would appear to be something less, socially, than his gay companions. Even the priggish and unsympathetic Korf admitted that Pushkin was inclined to exaggerate his own vices. "He would approach a society group and stagger," one of his friends observes. "'How are you, Alexander Sergeevich?' 'O, I just drank twelve glasses of punch!' But it was all nonsense, for everybody knew that he had not downed one glass." [26]

III

Of course, the dashing officers of the Guards and the polished youths of aristocratic families provided the colorful aspects of Petersburg society. But there were other more settled elements that made for a cultured and enlightened background. Pushkin was as welcome here as he was among the merry feasts of the members of the Green Lamp. With an infinite capacity for all manner of enjoyment, the Cricket would hop from his bacchanalian revels into the brilliant *salons* of the city's intellectuals.

One of the most popular of these *salons* was that of Princess E. I. Golitsyna. The victim of an unhappy marriage forced upon her by the Emperor Paul, she had separated from her husband, nicknamed "the fool," and lived a life of single blessedness in Petersburg. Her beauty, clever conversation, exemplary morals, and unusual personality attracted to her *salon* the most cultured people of the city. These gatherings lasted until three or four o'clock in the morning. A fear of dying at night, supposed to have been prophesied by a gypsy fortune teller, gained for Golitsyna the reputation of never retiring until daybreak. She was known in society as the "Princess Nocturne."

Not long out of the Lyceum, Pushkin was introduced into this *salon*, which was frequented by all of his more respectable literary friends. Although the Princess Nocturne was almost twenty years older than he, she at once fascinated him. "The poet Pushkin," wrote Karamzin in a letter, "fell mortally in love with Golitsyna at our house and now spends the evenings at her place. He lies because of love, gets angry from love, yet he does not write from love." [27] The princess had many worshipers, and whether or not Pushkin conceived a deep passion for her is hard to say. At any rate, her cold nature was sufficient protection against his customary ardor. Karamzin, however, was wrong. Pushkin's love did inspire two short poems to Golitsyna. But there is more respectful adoration than passion in them, the kind of token one would expect from an eighteen-year-old admirer of a handsome middle-aged woman who had gained a reputation in society for culture and impeccable virtue.

Another house frequently visited by Pushkin was that of the Olenins. A. N. Olenin, the president of the Academy of Arts and director of the State Public Library, was one of the best educated men of the time. In his beautiful home he gathered about him the most talented members of the artistic world, and here the young rake Pushkin played the part of brilliant conversationalist. Some ten years later he was to propose to Olenin's pretty daughter, Anna.

One evening in the spring of 1819, the Cricket was present at Olenin's among a company of artists and social luminaries in resplendent uniforms adorned with ribbons and glittering stars. Pushkin sat in a corner and listened to Krylov, the eminent fabulist, recite his fable of *The Donkey and the Peasant*.[28] Suddenly a young woman entered the room, escorted by one of Pushkin's friends, Alexander Poltoratski. There was an attractive languor in her beautiful eyes and smile. He quickly learned that she was his friend's cousin, Anna Kern. The company soon began to play charades. In the course of the game Anna Kern was obliged to portray Cleopatra. As she passed Pushkin, holding a basket full of flowers, he maliciously remarked, pointing to Poltoratski:

"And this gentleman, no doubt, will play the role of the asp?"

Anna remained silent. When the guests sat down to supper Pushkin, now captivated by the young lady opposite him, tried desperately to get her attention.

"Is it possible for one to be so beautiful?" he said in a stage whisper to Poltoratski. Then the two youths engaged in a joking conversation, intended for the ears of Anna Kern, about sinners and the possibility of their damnation.

"In any case," Pushkin concluded, "in hell there will be many pretty women, and one may play at charades there. Ask Mademoiselle Kern if she would rather be in hell?"

The young lady drily answered for herself that she had no desire to end up in hell.

"Well, how about that, Pushkin?" Poltoratski inquired with a laugh.

"I change my mind," he replied. "I do not want to be in hell, even though pretty women will be there." [29]

The time for departure arrived. Pushkin's eyes followed her as she entered the carriage, and her profile, outlined against the window, remained engraved on his memory. Some five years later he met Anna Kern again in entirely different surroundings. And the "fleeting vision" of that evening in the home of the Olenins returned to inspire one of his most beautiful lyrics. At this second meeting, as his "genius of pure loveliness," [30] Anna Kern responded to the poet's desires.

On the whole, young Pushkin's social connections with the best Petersburg families were well established. Wherever art and literature were honored he was a favorite guest. Besides Golitsyna and the Olenins, he frequented the homes of such well-known families as the Buturlins, the Vorontsovs, the Lavals, and the Trubetskois. He was also devoted to the dance, and few of the season's prominent balls were left unattended by him. There was to come a time when such entertainment palled, when he hated the very sight of the whirling figures and the affected gallantry of the ballroom. But then his young wife was the center of attraction, and her husband the jealous chronicler of every officer's ardent glance.

IV

My gift, like life, I squandered carelessly.
The Nineteenth of October

In the midst of dissipation and the pleasures of fashionable *salons* and balls, the poet laureate of the Lyceum did not forget his muse. It was not simply a desire for glory. Some inner compulsion obliged Pushkin to continue to pour out verse during this period of loose living. Something of his schoolboy literary fame had preceded him to the city, but naturally the sophisticated great world had nothing of the veneration of his Lyceum comrades. The youth's talent, however, was quickly recognized by Petersburg society, and especially among the younger set he soon became a literary idol.

Pushkin's graduation from the Lyceum did little to sever his literary connections. Delvig and Kiukhelbeker also moved to Petersburg, and Pushkin saw a great deal of them. Some of the new friends he made, even among the hard-living members of the Green Lamp, had positive talent or possessed literary aspirations. In the city he renewed his acquaintance with N. N. Raevski, whom he had met among the Tsarskoe Selo Hussars, and who was to become one of his best critics. P. A. Katenin, another of these young officers with literary inclinations, also became a real influence, although his criticism of Pushkin's poetry was not always sincere. Katenin was seven years older than Pushkin, had already acquired a reputation for erudition, and was an unusually fine poet and critic. Pushkin desired to meet him. He went to Katenin's quarters, handed him his walking stick, and said: "I have come to you as Diogenes to Antisthenes. Beat, but teach!" Katenin gallantly replied: "To teach a man of learning is but to spoil him." [31] These friends flattered the Cricket's verse, and applauded his witty epigrams and pointed criticisms.

More important than these young literary connections was the zealous guardianship of the older, established writers who had watched over Pushkin's muse in the Lyceum and now continued to encourage it during his dissolute life in Petersburg. Although the Arzamas Society disbanded in 1818, Pushkin continued to foregather with the members, such as Zhukovski, Karamzin, Batiushkov, A. I. Turgenev, Vyazemski, and Vasili Pushkin. Nor did he hesitate, in this brilliant company, to consider himself an equal among equals. They were afraid of his epigrams, coveted his verse epistles, and in general made of him the spoiled literary child of their circle. In 1818 he became a member of the rather select Free Society of Literary Amateurs.

During this time Pushkin grew closer to Karamzin, the oldest and most distinguished writer of the group. While he was convalescing from a long siege of sickness, his days in bed were brightened by reading the first volume of Karamzin's famous history. "Karamzin discovered ancient Russia as Columbus did America," [32] he wrote enthusiastically in his diary. But Karamzin's conservative views and his opposition to the young liberals of the time offended the freethinking Pushkin. To his face he boldly charged the ageing historian with preferring "serfdom to freedom." [33] And in a regrettable moment he aimed an unkind epigram at Karamzin. Karamzin overlooked the offense, however, and continued to befriend the rash poet in matters that were of the utmost consequence to his future.

With Vyazemski Pushkin maintained a lifelong friendship, and their extensive correspondence is one of the liveliest and keenest in Russian letters. Vyazemski was in the government service, but more for honor than need, for he was a wealthy noble. Pushkin envied his riches and resented his aristocratic and somewhat dilettantish attitude towards literature. However, Vyazemski with the "poisonous smile," as Pushkin described him, was one of his best critics and most faithful friends. Like Vyazemski, A. I. Turgenev, highly cultured and with excellent literary taste, was another of Pushkin's guardian angels. He knew everybody, and his influence in high places was always at the disposal of the young poet.

With Zhukovski, younger than Karamzin, Pushkin's friendship deepened into a lifelong attachment. The sad, idealistic Zhukovski, whose soul burned with a clear ecstasy, was now tutor to the Grand Duke Alexander and close to the empress. He had the Cricket's full confidence, shared in all his thoughts and feelings, and was faithfully consulted in most of the important decisions of his life. His relation to Pushkin was that of an older and responsible brother who never failed to come to his aid in time of need. Pushkin regarded Zhukovski as his teacher, and under his influence first began to value the charm of elevated poetry. At Zhukovski's famous literary Saturdays Pushkin was a frequent visitor, enlivening the gathering by his verses, witticisms, and inexhaustible merriment. Upon reading a splendid poem of his pupil's, addressed to himself, Zhukovski rapturously exclaimed: "A miraculous talent! What verses! He torments me, like a specter, with his gift!" [34]

The faith of these older men in his genius and ultimate accomplishment must have served as a profound inspiration. Perhaps with a conviction of their own inability to achieve truly
great poetry, they urged on their protégé. They regarded his
loafing, pleasure-seeking existence with dismay, and vainly
sought to restrain his madcap adventures. "Idleness, as the
terrible destroyer of everything fine and talented, rules over
Pushkin," [35] Turgenev reports to Vyazemski, and he sadly
itemizes the recent instances of his bad behavior. In turn
Batiushkov complains to Turgenev: "It would not be bad for the
Cricket to be shut up in Göttingen and fed for three years on
milk soup and logic. There will be nothing sensible from him if
he himself does not desire it; posterity will not differentiate him
from somebody with the same name if he forgets that for a poet
and a man there must be a posterity. . . . No matter how great
is the talent of the Cricket, he will squander it if . . . But then
his muse and our prayers will save him!" [36] Yet this same
Batiushkov, a great poet in his own right, after reading one of
the Cricket's perfect little crystal-clear poems, crumpled up the
paper and cried enviously: "O, how this rascal has learned to
write!" [37]

Pushkin had learned. In fact, despite his laziness and cease-
less carousing, by 1818 he had, through constant application,
almost reached the maturity of his style. Most of the products
were erotic elegies or polished epigrams which he poured out indiscriminately against friend or foe. With characteristic indifference he lost a whole volume of them, already prepared for
the press, to Vsevolozhski in a card game. But these licentious
lyrics and verse epistles attained the very acme of ease and
elegance. There was still some immaturity, and the fullness and
mellowness of his later poetry were lacking, but the Pushkin
form and diction, which set him apart from his contemporaries
and followers, were present in all their perfection.

The Cricket, however, was not content with mere anthology
pieces. His older literary friends were demanding something
"great," a work that would fully test his abilities. Perhaps they
also thought that such a major effort would wean him from his

youthful vices. But Pushkin insisted upon mixing pleasure and poetry. In the Lyceum he had begun a long poem on a folk-tale subject about Ruslan and Liudmila. This was to be his first bid for popular acclaim. Feverishly he worked at it in the mornings, after nights of debauchery. Fragments were read to visitors or at literary gatherings. Friends were jubilant. They prodded him on. Long periods of idleness would drive them to despair. Then sickness. Yet this was almost cause for rejoicing among the literary foster fathers. Venus might nail him to his bed, but periods of convalescence left him with nothing else to do but to compose. "Despite his disreputable form of life," writes Turgenev to Vyazemski, "he has ended the fourth canto of his poem. If there were only two or three more . . . . . ., then the matter would be in the hat. His first . . . . disease was the first nurse of his poem." [38] In shreds and patches the work went forward, written either in the bare little room on the Fontanka or at his mother's village of Mikhailovskoe during the long days of recovering from illness. Finally in March 1820 *Ruslan and Liudmila*,[39] a poem in six cantos of some three thousand lines, was finished. Towards the end he had become bored with it, but the composition had cost him infinite labor.

This poem is the story of the ravishing of the Princess Liudmila on her marriage night by the wizard Chernomor. Her bridegroom, Ruslan, and three rejected suitors set out to recover Liudmila, and after many fantastic adventures she is finally rescued by Ruslan. The delicate filigree work, malicious humor, and romantic novelties provide a charming poetic pageantry. But once again it was the perfection of Pushkin's verse that both astonished and delighted his contemporaries. The expectations of his literary friends were fully realized. *Ruslan and Liudmila* heralded the advent of Russia's greatest poet. The gay Cricket, however, was not destined to be on the ground to receive the public acclaim. Before the publication of the poem certain unfortunate events obliged him to leave Petersburg.

CHAPTER VI

Among the Conspirators

Hurrah! a wandering despot
Gallops into Russia!
Noël

An ominous cloud was gathering over this gay Petersburg society. Forces were at work which aimed at the very overthrow of the imperial Russian government. Pushkin became implicated, and the consequences profoundly affected his immediate future and shadowed the rest of his life.

The wave of patriotism that swept the country during the war of 1812 attracted many of the younger and better educated members of the nobility to the colors. These men were thrilled by the lofty liberal ideals of Alexander I, conqueror of Napoleon and "liberator of Europe." They applauded the charter he granted to enslaved Poland, and his speech before the Polish Diet in 1818, in which he promised constitutional government to Russia, filled them with hope for the future of their country. These young officers learned much from their experiences in the army. They saw and deplored the stark brutality of the life of the common Russian soldier. And they observed closely the existence of freedom-loving citizens abroad, which was such a violent contrast to the sorry lot of their own autocratically-ruled countrymen. In the case of the Hussars whom Pushkin had met at Tsarskoe Selo, something has already been said of the liberal ideas which these officers imbibed in their stay in France. They had suddenly grown politically- and socially-minded. Adam Smith, Bentham, and Benjamin Constant were eagerly studied. Political economy became almost a fashion. The movement spread to thinking young men in civil service. Constitutional government and the betterment or even liberation of the serfs were advocated as panaceas for Russia's ills. At the outset the reformers had some reason to expect that their emperor, much advertised as the great liberal of the age, would fulfil their aspirations for political and social improvements.

Then the reaction set in. After 1818 something very mysterious happened to Alexander I. No doubt the disintegration of his liberal idealism had begun several years earlier, but the reasons for the collapse have never been satisfactorily explained. Political and economic expediency played a part, yet strange emotional and psychological factors in the complex nature of the tsar unquestionably had much to do with the transformation. He fell under the influence of narrow-minded old men and pious women, extreme reactionaries and mystics. The hated tyrant and ignorant favorite, Arakcheev, practically ruled Russia.

This new situation drove the reformers to desperate measures. They had to be more discreet in expressing opinions. Secret societies were formed, much after the fashion of the contemporary Italian Carbonari. What was originally an open agitation for liberal reforms was now driven underground and spread over the whole of Russia as a forthright revolutionary movement. Many of these young officers and civilians were handicapped in their views and actions by a fluffy kind of idealism. On the whole, they were poor revolutionists. They lacked both the adversities, which would have tempered their misplaced enthusiasm, and the logic of experience, which would have corrected their impracticality. But among them were men of great sincerity and daring who possessed that capacity for sacrifice which makes for successful revolution. In any event, their efforts were soon to reach a climax in the disastrous December Revolt of 1825.

Many of Pushkin's friends in the young society of officers and wealthy youths which he frequented were involved in this widespread conspiracy. Too often their liberalism was the kind that is worked up over a bottle of wine, and their conspiratorial zeal had a large element of the tragicomic in it. But there was no essential paradox in the fact that they led, on one hand, a gay, carefree existence, and on the other were plotting the reformation of the government. Their youth, their training, and the social conventions of the time sufficiently account for their mixed allegiance.

The spirit of criticism toward things political and social which had been stirred in Pushkin by certain of his Lyceum comrades and the Hussars at Tsarskoe Selo was sharpened in the conspiratorial atmosphere of the capital. His friendship with Chaadaev continued in the city. Pushkin visited his quarters often, and their revealing conversations of the Lyceum days were renewed. Liberal discussions were not unusual even at the meetings of the Green Lamp. A few among this circle were also members of the secret political society, the Union of Welfare, and there is evidence that the Green Lamp was used as a medium for spreading radical ideas. In the letter to Mansurov, already quoted in part, Pushkin requests information from this comrade of the Lamp concerning the hated military settlements established by Arakcheev. "I love you and hate despotism," [1] he concludes, by way of justifying his request.

A few of the homes of intellectuals which Pushkin visited were hotbeds of dangerous political debates. This was particularly true of the Turgenevs. A. I. Turgenev, one of the most highly cultured men of the age, was a liberal, and his brothers, Sergei and Nikolai, the latter a member of the Union of Welfare, were both pronounced advocates of reform. In this family circle Pushkin heard frequent denunciations of conditions in Russia which must have whetted his own appetite for social betterment.

The Cricket was surrounded by conspirators. Many future Decembrists and members of secret societies were his intimate friends. Yet Pushkin himself never actually joined the conspiracy, and the fact has resulted in a good deal of unfavorable criticism of his political sympathies. His failure to enter a secret society has even been attributed to his superstitious fear of fatal consequences. He possessed perhaps more than the average man's belief in the supernatural. During this Petersburg period he had his fortune told by an old German woman. She immediately discovered in him a remarkable man and foretold several events in his life which later actually took place. Among other things, she predicted that he would meet death through a fair- or white-haired man (*Weisskopf*). This prophecy was curiously rationalized by Pushkin, if the account is true, and offered as one reason why he did not join a secret society. For all such organizations, he is said to have explained, were directed by a certain Adam Weisshaupt. And, he concluded: "*Weisskopf* and *Weisshaupt* are one and the same!" [2]

Whatever may have been Pushkin's political views later in life, it is not difficult to understand them during this youthful period. He enthusiastically exclaimed at the age of sixteen: "At heart I am a Roman; freedom boils in my breast. The spirit of a great people does not slumber in me." [3] And a few years later he could write to Chaadaev in a lofty strain:

> With wearied hope we have been waiting
> The moment of our sacred freedom.[4]

Despite the customary fervor of youth, however, he was in no sense a revolutionist. First of all Pushkin was a poet, and all his talents and interests were centered in his art. It was not that poetry and politics were incompatible. He could play the civic lyre with good effect. But such poems were the results of sudden inspiration and not of a rooted passion for social and political justice. There can be no question that at this time of his life he was a liberal and that he sincerely deprecated the abuses of an autocratic government. However, the plain truth of the matter is that Pushkin was not vitally interested in the new political movement that was taking form all around him. He was busy living life and thinking poetry.

It is more than likely that Pushkin would have joined the Union of Welfare had he been strongly urged. There was just enough of the flavor of danger, as well as of fashion, in the enterprise to have caught his ardent fancy. Indeed, there is reason to suppose that he narrowly missed becoming a member, and the failure was of great import, for he would unquestionably have suffered the fate of death or long exile which fell to the lot of nearly all the Decembrists.

His close school friends Pushchin and Kiukhelbeker joined the Union of Welfare shortly after leaving the Lyceum. Pushchin at once became an active worker in the conspiracy. Convinced that his whole purpose in life was immeasurably ennobled by the new role, he at first thought of sharing his happiness with Pushkin and of persuading him to join the secret society. He remembered that his friend had always agreed with him on questions of reform, and he believed that Pushkin could further the cause with his poetry. Fortunately, at that precise time Pushkin was at Mikhailovskoe, and before he returned to Petersburg the young conspirator had lost his first enthusiasm for imparting his secret. Meanwhile, Pushchin began to hear tales of the Cricket's dissipated life. He recalled Pushkin's close connections with the relatively conservative members of the Arzamas and of the government. The more he reflected on the matter the more he doubted the propriety of taking him into his confidence. He began to wonder why other members of the Union, also friends of Pushkin, had not asked him to join. They must distrust him, he thought. "The uncertainty of his flaming temper and his intimacy with unreliable people frightened me," [5] wrote Pushchin. Once in the theater he observed how Pushkin buzzed about important and reactionary government officials, who treated him in a condescending manner. In friendly fashion Pushchin rebuked him for such fawning behavior. Pushkin seemed disconcerted, but during the next intermission he did the same thing.

In the meantime Pushkin had noticed that a great change had come over his Lyceum comrade. Of course, he knew that secret political societies existed, and he suspected that Pushchin had joined one. On several occasions he probed him with questions, and again Pushchin was filled with the desire to enlist him in the Union. For a time he felt that the high purpose of the conspirators might transform Pushkin's wayward existence into one of noble activity. One evening they met at N. I. Turgenev's, where a session had been called to discuss the founding of a political journal. After the discussion the two friends had a quiet chat about their Lyceum days, and Pushkin expressed regret that an old schoolmate had failed to confide in him. Pushchin departed with his mind almost made up to ask him to join the society. But a couple of days later he met Pushkin's father on the street. The latter looked gloomy.

"How are you, Sergei Lvovich? How goes it with our Alexander?" asked Pushchin.

"Have you seen him?"

"Several days ago at Turgenev's."

"I have nothing better to do than to go about reëstablishing the reputation of my dear son. It is clear that you do not know his latest prank." [6] And Sergei Lvovich, with a self-pitying sigh, proceeded to relate the newest escapade of Alexander.

"I thought the matter over," said Pushchin, "and I confess that this meeting, quite by chance, made an impression on me. The idea of accepting Pushkin vanished from my mind." [7]

II

O tyrants of the world, beware!
And you, good men, take heart and dare —
Arise, O fallen slaves!
Ode to Freedom

Though Pushkin did not actually join the Union of Welfare, he contributed in no small way to the radical movement. The personal feelings and motives that guided his behavior are not always clear. His liberal convictions of this time provided an ever-present stimulation. No doubt certain acts may justly be attributed to a youthful spirit of bravado and to a desire to be in the conspiratorial "swim" along with many of his intimate friends. To some extent he may have been merely living up to the answer he is reputed to have made to the objections of his family over some prank or other: "Without an uproar no one has ever stood out among the crowd." [8]

Verse, of course, was the inevitable outlet for what liberal sympathies Pushkin possessed, and soon a series of political poems startled Petersburg. Epigrams dripping with sarcasm were leveled against reactionary government officials and prominent obscurantists. The Archimandrite Photius is excoriated as a "half fanatic, half rogue," whose chief spiritual instruments of persuasion are "the curse, the sword and cross, and the knout"; [9] the all-powerful Arakcheev is scorned as the friend and brother of the tsar, "without mind, without feeling, without honor"; [10] and even Alexander I is not spared the biting reminder that as a "brave captain he ran at Austerlitz and trembled in 1812." [11]

More sustained and serious political poems not only startled the city but decidedly horrified the conservative elements. In *The Village* [12] Pushkin laid bare the cruel and stupid existence of the peasantry. *Noël* [13] and *The Ode to Freedom* [14] amounted to deliberate warnings to all tyrants of the bloody fate in store for them. Even the most ardent reformer of these days must have been shocked by such lines as:

> Despotic miscreant,
> Thee and thy throne I hate! [15]

In verse Pushkin hailed himself as "the proud singer of freedom," [16] and this reputation quickly spread among his friends. Of course, such poems could not be printed, but they circulated in numerous manuscript versions. "Everywhere," says Pushchin, "people passed around, copied, and learned by heart *The Village, The Ode to Freedom, Hurrah, into Russia Gallops,** and other pieces in this spirit. There was not a living man who did not know his verses." [17] And another famous conspirator, Yakushkin, says of these poems that "there was scarcely a literate ensign in the army who did not know them by heart." [18] The whole liberal generation of Petersburg found in Pushkin's political verse a reflection of their own ideas and feelings. The fame of their author grew by leaps and bounds.

But the Cricket did not confine his revolutionary zeal to inflammatory poetry. No doubt his growing notoriety as the unofficial literary mouthpiece of the new movement helped to beguile him into rash public statements and acts. There was a boyish daring about his behavior which must have both irritated and frightened his conspirator-friends. Once, in the hear-

---

* The opening line of Pushkin's political poem, *Noël*.

ing of all present at the theater, he cried out: "Now is the most secure time, for the ice floats in the Neva!" [19] The obvious hint that the moment for revolt had arrived, since there was nothing to fear from the fortress in the Neva, was clear to all. A bear escaped from its keeper and ran loose in the tsar's garden at Tsarskoe Selo. The animal was killed, but people talked much about the dangerous possibility of a meeting between the bear and the emperor in one of the lonely walks of the garden. Had this happened, Pushkin declared to an audience, "only one kind creature would have been found there, and that a bear!" [20] A more blatant act, and one which came to the attention of the authorities, was that of the occasion when Pushkin freely displayed in the Imperial Theater the portrait of Louvel, the murderer of the Duc de Berry, which bore the inscription: "A Lesson to Kings." [21]

Pushkin's more mature friends grew deeply alarmed. A. I. Turgenev feared to send a copy of *The Ode to Freedom* to Vyazemski, explaining: "Walls may have eyes and even ears." [22] And Karamzin likewise apprised I. I. Dmitriev of the situation in a letter: "Over the poet Pushkin, at present, there is not simply a cloud, but a thunder-bearing cloud." [23] These wise friends knew whereof they spoke. The police already had the Cricket under surveillance.

III

In anger and without tears I forsook
The banquets' garlands and the tinsel of Athens.
To Glinka

One morning in March 1820 Pushkin set out for the home of his friend, F. N. Glinka, and met him just outside his quarters. Glinka noticed that the Cricket's usually cheerful smile was missing and that his face was a bit pale. "I was coming to you for advice," [24] said Pushkin, and hurriedly he related a strange occurrence. The previous day, when Pushkin was out, an unknown man had appeared and offered his old servant fifty rubles for permission to carry off the poet's writings. He promised to return them very shortly. But the faithful Nikita flatly refused.

After hearing this story Pushkin had burned all his papers. In the meantime he had been summoned to Count Miloradovich, the governor general of Petersburg. The friends discussed the matter at length, and finally Glinka advised him to go directly to Miloradovich and place himself at the disposal of the governor general. Pushkin went.

A few hours later Glinka, who knew Miloradovich well, visited him.

"Do you know what, my dear!" exclaimed the old count. "Pushkin has just been here. Indeed, I had been ordered to seize him and all his papers; but I reckoned it more delicate to invite him here and send for his papers. Well, he appeared, very quiet, with a bright face, and when I asked about his papers he answered: 'Count, all my verses have been burned! You will find nothing in my room. But, if it is agreeable to you, everything may be found here' — he pointed to his head. 'Order paper to be brought; I will write everything that has been composed by me — of course, with the exception of printed things — with a note that it is mine and has appeared under my name.' Paper was brought, and Pushkin sat down and wrote and wrote until he had filled a whole copybook. There it is" — pointing to a table by the window. "Now just fancy that! Tomorrow I shall carry it to the emperor. But do you know, Pushkin charmed me with his noble tone and the manner of his behavior." [25]

The young Pushkin was very much worried, and with reason. Rumors were flying: that the emperor had read *The Ode to Freedom* and was angered by the reference in it to the death of his father, Paul I; that his insulting epigram had reached the ears of the vengeful Arakcheev, who demanded punishment; that he was to be sent to Siberia or, even worse, to the Solovetski Monastery in the White Sea. Pushkin's worry turned into fear. The would-be radical appealed to influential friends. They had already begun to intercede. Chaadaev called upon Karamzin for help. Gnedich in tears begged Olenin to save Pushkin. Zhukovski, A. I. Turgenev, and Glinka all used their influence to avert the blow.

The situation was truly serious. It is reported that the emperor saw Pushkin's old lyceum director, Engelhardt.

"Pushkin must be sent to Siberia," said Alexander sternly. "He has deluged Russia with shocking verses. All the youths are learning them by heart." [26]

Engelhardt, with little reason to remember his former pupil kindly, pleaded his cause, explaining that the offense was one of youthful waywardness, and that Pushkin's talent would one day bring glory to Russia. Karamzin, after extracting a promise from the penitent poet that he would write nothing against the government for two years, promised to aid him. But the emperor had made up his mind. Pushkin's friends had softened the blow, but they could not entirely save him from punishment. Alexander decreed, apparently on the suggestion of Karamzin, that Pushkin be sent to the south of Russia for a short period. Here he was to serve under Lieutenant General Inzov, chief of the Board of Protection of Foreign Colonists in Southern Russia.

A. I. Turgenev hastened to inform Vyazemski at Warsaw. "The fate of Pushkin is decided," he writes. "Tomorrow he will set off with a courier to Inzov and will remain with him. He has become quieter and more modest, and in order not to compromise himself he even runs from me in public." [27]

No doubt fear and the narrow escape from exile to Siberia had chilled Pushkin's liberal zeal and chastened his conduct. It must not be forgotten that he was barely twenty-one years old when this blow fell. But there is reason to suppose that he was not entirely averse to leaving Petersburg for the south of Russia at this juncture. For one thing, the life of pleasure he had been living for three years had begun to pall, and his relations with political conspirators had left a bad taste in his mouth. Five years later, in a strange letter to Alexander I which was never sent, Pushkin retraces the events which led to his downfall and offers a curious justification for his behavior. He relates how the rumor had spread that he had been whipped by the police in a secret chancery because of certain satiric verses. Driven to despair by this humiliating story, he had contemplated both suicide and an attempt on the emperor's life. However, a friend had convinced him of the futility of either course. "I resolved, then," concludes Pushkin, "to fill my conversation and writings with so much indignation and bravado that the government would be obliged to treat me as a criminal. I aspired to Siberia or to the fortress as a rehabilitation of my honor!" [28]

The intention of this letter in 1825 was to secure his recall from exile, and Pushkin unquestionably drew upon his imagination in order to present to the emperor a satisfactory explanation of his acts. But it is true that the rumor of a whipping by the police had been spread by one of his acquaintances, Count F. I. Tolstoi, the "American." * For several years Pushkin bore him a grudge on this score which finally ended in a challenge. Yet evidence seems to indicate that much more than this rumor contributed to his dissatisfied state of mind in 1820. Pushkin thought of the army as an escape, and he actually appears to have contemplated suicide. It was almost inevitable that an "unfortunate love affair" should be predicated as the reason for his disillusionment. In fact, a considerable literature has grown up about Pushkin's "lost love" and the conviction that it explains his attitude at this time and for several years later. True, it is very likely that he suffered from an unrequited love. It is even more likely that he suffered from several of them. With a full awareness of the danger of reading biographical facts into a poet's works, it is still possible to say with assurance that several of Pushkin's poems after 1820 contain pointed references to a deeply-moving and unhappy emotional experience during the Petersburg period of his life. But the name of the lady and the circumstances in the case have remained a sealed book. It will be more illuminating to consider this question in detail later.

At any rate, Pushkin was not sorry to leave. Besides, he fully believed that it would be only for a short time. Like Eugene Onegin, he was afflicted with spleen. He was "wearied with the noise of balls and with turning morning into midnight." [29] The

---

* So nicknamed because of a trip he made to Alaska.

world-weariness of satiated youth was upon him. As early as March 1820 he wrote to Vyazemski: "Petersburg is stifling for a poet; I thirst for foreign regions. Perhaps the southern air will revive my spirit." [30]

On May 6, 1820, Pushkin set out for Ekaterinoslav. He was jauntily dressed in a red shirt with a girdle, and he wore a felt hat. Two Lyceum friends, Delvig and M. Yakovlev, accompanied him to the city limits. The government had softened its expulsion by a substantial appropriation of one thousand rubles for traveling expenses. Pushkin bore a sealed letter from the Ministry of Foreign Affairs to his future guardian, General Inzov. The contents of this letter are worth quoting in part, for they represent the government's official opinion of Pushkin at this time, although it is pretty certain that Karamzin, and perhaps Zhukovski, may have been responsible for some of the details.

"The young man designated in this letter," wrote Kapodistria, "places himself under your command and solicits for himself your benevolent protection. Permit me to report certain facts about him. Filled with bitterness during the course of his whole childhood, young Pushkin left his parental home without experiencing any regrets. His heart, destitute of any filial attachments, could feel only a passionate desire for independence. This student, even at an early age, evinced an unusual talent. His progress in the Lyceum was swift, his mind aroused astonishment, but his character, apparently, escaped the attention of his preceptors. He entered the world endowed with a flaming imagination, but weak in the complete absence of those inner feelings which take the place of principles when experience has not provided us with a correct education. There are no extremes into which this unfortunate young man has not fallen, just as there is no perfection which he might not have achieved by the excellence of his talents. . . . Certain poems, especially an ode on freedom, have brought Mr. Pushkin to the attention of the government. But along with the highest beauties of design and execution, this poem reveals dangerous principles issuing from that contemporary school, or perhaps it would be better to say, from that anarchical system which people maliciously call a system of the rights of man, of freedom, and of the independence of people. . . . Mr. Pushkin, it appears, will reform, if only we may believe his tears and promises. In any case, his patrons suppose that his penitence is sincere and that, removed for some time from Petersburg, provided with an occupation, and surrounded with good examples, one may make of him a fine servant of the government or, at least, a writer of the first rank. . . . His fate will depend on your good counsel." [31]

It would be interesting to know Pushkin's reactions on leaving Petersburg if he could have read these farewell amenities of the Russian government. Perhaps, in his unhappy frame of mind, they would have made little difference. He had promised to say good-by to Chaadaev. Sometime later he wrote an apologetic note, in which one can detect a suggestion of the emotional and spiritual weariness that filled him upon departure: "My dear, I visited you, but you were asleep. Of what use would it have been to awaken you for such a trifle?" [32]

The fact that his first great poem would see the light of day in a few weeks must have provided him with some consolation, albeit a cold one. And he had no doubt packed away in his baggage a portrait of Zhukovski, bearing the great writer's inscription: "To the victorious pupil from the conquered master, on this most solemn day on which he has finished his poem, *Ruslan and Liudmila,* 1820, March 26." [33]

CHAPTER VII

A Russian Childe Harold

> A seeker after new impressions,
> I fled from you, my native land.
> *The Sun Has Set*

Ekaterinoslav was over a thousand miles due south. The trip must have given the youthful exile plenty of leisure to repent his past indiscretions and to contemplate the uncertainty of his future. Officially, of course, Pushkin was not an exile. The Ministry of Foreign Affairs had simply transferred him, for the good of the service, so to speak. Nor did Pushkin regard his departure from Petersburg in the light of exile, for he fully expected to return in a few months. Only when the months lengthened into years and his appeals for a recall were denied, did he experience the bitter resentment of an outlawed person.

Pushkin arrived in the little town of Ekaterinoslav about the middle of May. He presented himself and Kapodistria's letter to General Inzov. Despite the chilling arraignment of the "recommendation," he was very well received. I. N. Inzov, a bachelor of over fifty, seemed designed by nature to tolerate a young scapegrace like Pushkin, and at the same time to inspire a certain amount of respect in him. Inzov had grown up in the army; he had learned to be severe with himself and extremely indulgent to others. A member of the Masons and the Bible Society, he possessed a softness of manner, kindness, and love for humanity that enabled Pushkin to accept any punishment from him without ever feeling offended. He was fairly well educated, read history omnivorously, and made a hobby of collecting manuscripts. Pushkin benefited much from his earthy wisdom, and in turn Inzov quickly learned to appreciate Pushkin's intellectual powers and poetic talent.

It is unlikely that the Cricket's Petersburg notoriety preceded him to Ekaterinoslav. Yet stories, of doubtful authen-

ticity, have been told of his visit to the city as though he were a
marked man even at this early age. Of course, the contraband
political poems may have reached Ekaterinoslav to give him a
certain fame. It is reported that several local celebrities, eager
to meet Pushkin, visited him in the hut where he was staying.
They found him with a piece of bread, spread with caviar, in his
mouth and a glass of red wine in his hand. "What is your pleasure?" he mumbled. The leader of the delegation humbly replied that they had come simply to see the poet. And the poet
promptly blurted out: "Well, now that you have seen him,
good-by!" [1] He is also reported to have shocked the guests at a
dinner given by the governor of the province. With malice pre-
pense, or perhaps because it was more comfortable in the hot
weather, he appeared before the ladies in transparent muslin
trousers, minus underwear. The shortsighted hostess, in the interests of morality, undertook a closer inspection which immediately caused her to hurry her young daughter out of the room.

In reality nothing very definite concerning Pushkin's visit to
Ekaterinoslav has come down to us. He remained in the town
not much more than ten days, and the only comment he himself
made on the stay is hardly rich in details. In a letter to his
brother he wrote briefly: "Upon arriving in Ekaterinoslav I
grew bored, went boating on the Dnieper, took to swimming,
and was seized with a fever, as usual with me. General Raevski,
who was going to the Caucasus with his son and two daughters,
found me in a delirium in a Jew's hut, without a physician and
with a mug of iced lemonade. His son (you know our close bond
and his invaluable service, never to be forgotten by me) proposed a trip to the Caucasian waters; a doctor who traveled
with them promised to cure me on the road." [2]

The appearance of the Raevski family at this juncture proved
to be of real consequence in Pushkin's life; and closely connected with this appearance are problems which biographers
have never satisfactorily solved. We already know that Pushkin had met Nikolai Nikolaevich Raevski, two years younger
than himself, among the officers at Tsarskoe Selo. They continued their friendship in Petersburg, but the nature of the "in-

valuable service" of young Raevski we have no means of knowing. Very likely it was connected with Pushkin's difficulties
with the government.

In the light of certain facts, it is hard to believe that the arrival of the Raevskis in Ekaterinoslav at this precise time and
the invitation to the Caucasus were matters of sheer chance.
On the seventh of May, the day after Pushkin left Petersburg,
Ekaterina, eldest daughter of the family, wrote from the capital
to her brother in Kiev. She explains that she is sending the letter by post, "because mother forgot to send it with Pushkin." [3]
To have gone to Kiev would have taken him much out of his
way. Hence such a request implies that Pushkin must have
known the family very well. Furthermore, among Pushkin's
friends there was a persistent rumor, just before he set out from
the capital, that he would go to the Crimea. This rumor may
easily be accounted for by the hypothesis that before he left
Petersburg the Raevskis, who had planned a trip to the Crimea,
had suggested to him the possibility of journeying with them.
In short, they knew that Pushkin was in Ekaterinoslav and
definitely planned to pass through, with the idea of picking him
up for a prearranged vacation trip. However, all this is mere
guesswork.

At any rate, when father and son arrived in the town, fairly
late at night, they lost no time in looking up Pushkin. They
found him in a vile hut, lying on a wooden bench, unshaved,
pale, and ill. Tears of joy came to his eyes when he saw them.
The army doctor of General Raevski, E. Rudykovski, was
quickly summoned. He diagnosed the ailment as a cold, accompanied by a high temperature. But Pushkin's illness did not
prevent him from setting out very soon with the Raevskis for
the mineral waters of the Caucasus. The kind Inzov offered no
objections, for General Raevski held himself responsible for the
suspected poet. Inzov's official explanation for the sudden departure of his charge is eloquent of the man's character: "Ill-
health in so young a person, and the disagreeable situation in
which he finds himself because of his youth, demanded on one
hand assistance, and on the other innocent distractions; there-

fore I let him go with General Raevski, who, on his way through Ekaterinoslav, willingly took him along. . . . I hope I shall not be blamed for this or be called overindulgent. In truth, he is a good lad, unfortunate only in that he ended his course of studies too soon; a learned shell remains forever a shell." [4] Old General Inzov well understood the temper of the exile.

II

> Before me there I now behold
> The proud Caucasian mountain tops.
> *Epilogue to Ruslan and Liudmila*

By the first of June Pushkin was well on his way to the Caucasian mineral springs. His host was an unusual man. In fact, the whole Raevski family, which consisted of two sons and four daughters, was much out of the ordinary. General Raevski, a well-known hero of the 1812 war, commanded the fourth corps of the Second Army, which was then stationed at Kiev. He was well educated, interested in literature, and brought his family up in the best traditions of native and foreign culture. Nikolai, the younger son, wrote poetry, loved music and art, and possessed a fine critical sense. Colonel Alexander, the other son, was a man of strange character and dominating personality. His relations with Pushkin will be discussed presently. The four daughters, ranging from thirteen-year-old Sofya to twenty-three-year-old Ekaterina, were all attractive, and for that time excellently educated. On his way through Ekaterinoslav General Raevski was accompanied by Nikolai and the two youngest girls, Sofya and Mariya. He expected to meet Alexander in the Caucasus, and to join his wife and two eldest daughters in the Crimea.

During the early stages of the journey Pushkin lay sick in the carriage. It was almost a week before he felt like himself, since his recovery was somewhat delayed by his unwillingness to follow the doctor's instructions. But by the time they reached Goryachiya Vody (now Pyatigorsk), in the very heart of the Caucasian mountains, he had fully regained his health and spirits, and he signified the fact by playing a prank. In the official register of the revenue commandant, he playfully described Raevski's army doctor as a "physician in ordinary" and himself as a "minor." Such a breach of legal propriety was not at all appreciated by the commandant or the doctor.

This region in the Caucasus, not long conquered by Russian arms, was still roamed by half-wild tribesmen. The lush, semi-tropical foliage of the foothills changes its variegated colors with magical swiftness. And over the impressive mountain chain towers the majestic, white, two-headed peak of Elbruz. The locality already existed as a kind of fabled paradise in Russian literature, but Pushkin was the first writer of consequence to celebrate its beauties from direct observation. Later the Caucasus inspired such authors as Bestuzhev, Lermontov, and Lev Tolstoi.

Pushkin had every opportunity to absorb new impressions, for once in the mountains the vacationists led a real outdoor life. Hikes, nights under the open southern heavens or in Kalmuck tents, the Tatar villages, and Circassian mountaineers were all a far cry from his recent Petersburg existence. "I love our Cossacks," he later wrote to his brother. "They are everlastingly on horseback, everlastingly ready to fight, and eternally cautious."[5] At times the party had to be provided with an escort of these same Cossacks as a protection against possible attacks by hostile mountaineers. "You will understand," he continues to his brother, "how this specter of danger pleased my fanciful imagination."[6] Pushkin thoroughly enjoyed traveling with the Raevskis. For the general it was a kind of triumphal march. Nearly every town and village provided a deputation to honor a hero of 1812. Naturally, the impressionable Pushkin was delighted to be in such company.

At Pyatigorsk Alexander Raevski joined them. The party remained in this region for almost two months, making the most of the opportunity to bathe in the healing waters of various mineral springs at Pyatigorsk, Zheleznovodsk, and Kislovodsk. On his own testimony Pushkin's health was much benefited by this treatment.

About the first of August the party set out on the return journey, heading for the Crimea by way of Kerch and Theodosia. In the little town of Kerch Pushkin sought out the so-called tomb of Mithridates. The ruins, however, failed to stir him. He plucked a flower as a token, and lost it the next day without any regret. From Theodosia the party went by boat over the Black Sea to Gurzuf on the Crimean coast. "All night I did not sleep," Pushkin later wrote to Delvig concerning this passage. "There was no moon, the stars shone; before me, in the mist, stretched the southern mountains. 'There is Chatyrdag,' the captain said to me. I did not distinguish it and, indeed, I was not curious. Before daybreak I was asleep." [7] Impervious to the scenery he may have been, but sad thoughts of home and the memory of far-distant friends troubled his soul. Eyewitnesses observed him pacing the deck in deep contemplation, muttering something to himself. One recalls the Byron of the first pilgrimage on the Malta packet, sitting in isolation on the deck and gloomily gazing out over the moonlit waves. There was no talented chronicler present to describe the Russian poet as "a mystery in a winding-sheet, crowned in a halo." [8] But the mystery of his fate profoundly stirred Pushkin on this occasion. That night he composed the beautiful and manly elegy, *The Sun Has Set.*[9]

III

> I grieve for her in exile.
> *The Bakhchisarai Fountain*

Next morning, when Pushkin awoke before Gurzuf, the captivating sight banished the memory of his doubts and sadness of the previous night. This little Tatar village is one of the most beautiful spots on the southern shore of the Crimea. A strip of sandy beach, gently washed by sunlit surf, merges into vineyards and woods. A ridge of mountains looms up in the background, and steep cliffs forming the bay drop precipitately into the water.

Here the Raevskis had obtained a large house overlooking the sea. The general's wife and his two eldest daughters, Ekaterina and Elena, were already on the ground. In these congenial surroundings Pushkin spent one of the happiest periods of his life.

He found among the Raevskis the understanding, affection, and domestic care which were so conspicuously lacking in his own family. The striking contrast both rejoiced and saddened him. In the letter to his brother, written shortly after this brief stay at Gurzuf, he gives vent to his pleasure, and at the same time plaintively suggests what a revelation this new kind of family existence was to him. "My friend," he writes, "I spent the happiest minutes of my life with the family of the honored Raevski. I did not see in him the hero, the glory of Russia's army. In him I loved a man with a clear mind, with a simple, beautiful soul; an indulgent, solicitous friend; always an agreeable, affectionate host. . . . All his daughters are charming; the eldest is an unusual woman. Judge for yourself whether or not I was happy; a free, secure life in the circle of a dear family, a life which I so love and which I have never enjoyed. The happy, southern sky; the delightful region; nature satisfying the imagination; mountains, gardens, the sea; my friend, my darling hope is to behold once again the southern shore and the Raevski family." [10]

So deeply did this experience engrave itself in his memory that four years later, in a letter to Delvig, he could recall it with all his original enthusiasm: "At Gurzuf I lived an idle existence, bathed in the sea, and stuffed myself with grapes; from the first moment I grew accustomed to the southern clime and enjoyed it with all the indifference and unconcern of a Neapolitan lazzarone. Awakening at night, I loved to listen to the noise of the sea — and I listened to it for hours at a time. Not two paces from the house was a young cypress tree; every morning I paid it a visit, and I grew devoted to it with a feeling akin to friendship." [11] About this same cypress a local Tatar legend exists. The natives tell how a nightingale flew to the tree and sang whenever Pushkin sat beneath its branches. Every summer the bird visited the tree. But after the poet's death the nightingale returned no more.

Pushkin spent three weeks at Gurzuf very much in the manner he describes in his letters. There were long walks in the mountains, swimming, reading, writing, and jolly conversations with the Raevskis. Among the daughters Pushkin found pleasant companionship. According to some biographers he found more than companionship, and for one reason or another evidence has been produced to prove that he was in love with the entire female half of the Raevski family, excepting the mother and the thirteen-year-old daughter, Sofya. One critic has jokingly suggested that even the Tatar serving-woman of the family was an object of his passion. It is impossible to dismiss this matter without further comment, for the question has become involved with the larger problem of Pushkin's "lost love" or "Northern love."

It has already been pointed out that Pushkin accepted his removal from Petersburg with a feeling of relief. For various reasons the capital had grown distasteful to him, and especially as the scene of an unrequited love. For some weeks after his departure Pushkin evinced an apathy and insensitivity to his surroundings which seemed to indicate the emotional deadness of a man trying to escape the memory of an unhappy and unfulfilled love. Furthermore, from 1819 to as late as 1828 we find veiled allusions in poems and letters to this mysterious experience. In support of the theory is the curious evidence of the unknown initials in the famous "Don Juan List." In 1829 he wrote in the album of Elizaveta Ushakova a long list of the Christian names of women he had loved. This "Don Juan List" was divided into "serious loves" and "light loves," and in the first part occur the initials N. N. With the exception of these initials, all the other names have been identified with reasonable certainty. Hence investigators have supposed that N. N. refers to Pushkin's "lost love." Some biographers, accepting the theory that he was actually in love with a Petersburg lady in 1819, have made determined efforts to identify her and connect her with N. N. But to date the evidence in each case has been unconvincing.

There is another school of biographers which insists that the "lost love" was one of the Raevski girls. This notion presupposes that Pushkin was not hopelessly in love with a Petersburg woman previous to his departure, or that, if he was, he quickly forgot it in his passion for one of the daughters of General Raevski. Here the principal difficulty has been to select the right daughter, for more or less evidence has been unearthed to plead the cause in turn of Mariya, Elena, and Ekaterina. However, the champions of Mariya appear to have made out for her the strongest case.

At the time when Pushkin first met her, Mariya Raevskaya was an attractive fifteen-year-old girl with a swarthy complexion, a little turned-up nose, flashing eyes, and a vivacious temperament. In the notable *Memoirs* that she wrote many years later, there is only one mention of Pushkin, and this scarcely indicates that she was aware of the profound love for her which has been ascribed to him. Recalling an incident of the Caucasian tour, she writes: "As a poet, Pushkin long accounted himself in love with all the pretty women and young girls whom he met. On this journey, not far from Taganrog, I remember how I was traveling in the carriage with Sofya, our English companion, and a Russian nurse. On catching sight of the sea a halt was ordered; we left the carriage and rushed down in a group to admire the sea. It was an open stretch of water, and, not suspecting that the poet was following us, I began to amuse myself by running after the waves, and when they rolled up I fled from them. I ended by getting my feet wet. Of course, I said nothing about this and returned to the carriage. Pushkin found this a very graceful picture, and, poetizing my childish prank, he wrote some charming verses." The verses she refers to, and which she quotes in part, occur in a stanza of *Eugene Onegin* where Pushkin, remembering the incident, exclaims:

> Then how I yearned with the sea waves
> To touch her dear feet with my lips.[12]

Pushkin had an admiration for women's feet which amounted almost to an obsession. His poetry contains many rhapsodic references to them, and the margins of his copybooks are adorned with drawings of women's feet. Perhaps it is unwise to read into the lines quoted above any deeper significance than that which Mariya Raevskaya suggests in the concluding sentence of her account: "In effect, he worshiped only his muse and poetized everything he saw." [13]

It is possible that references to his "lost love" in other poems may concern Mariya Raevskaya, but in each case the element of doubt has not been entirely resolved. And Mariya herself never gave the slightest indication that she was aware of anything other than a pleasant friendship with Pushkin. In a few years she married the Decembrist, Prince Sergei Volkonski. After the fatal revolt she bravely followed her exiled husband to Siberia, and Pushkin never saw her again. Whether his famous dedication to *Poltava* refers to Mariya and her unhappy fate will perhaps always remain a mystery.

If one were so disposed, almost as good a case could be made for the eldest daughter. In 1822 or 1823 Pushkin wrote a passionate love letter to an unknown woman whom one investigator has identified as Ekaterina Raevskaya.[14] Several references in his correspondence and poetry have also been connected with her name. But once again we have no positive proof that he was in love with this woman. Certainly Ekaterina never betrayed even the possibility of such a relationship.

From what evidence we possess it is extremely hazardous to say that Pushkin did more than flirt with the eligible Raevski girls at Gurzuf. Ekaterina soon married a friend of Pushkin, and later, when he visited the family at Kamenka, he gave no indication of any passion for the sisters. The important fact in this whole troubled question is not the identity of the woman but the profound emotional experience Pushkin underwent. His state of mind after he left Petersburg, and certain poignant passages of poetry testify to the burning reality of his "lost love." It is commonly supposed that Pushkin was extraordinarily frank and boastful in affairs of the heart. But text and verse do not indicate that he possessed any more than the average male's customary vanity in this respect. He distinguished between transient affairs, which might become common knowledge, and ideal love, which must be his secret alone. And his "lost love" seems to have been such an ideal. Because he was a poet, he gave expression to the hopelessness of his passion, but he jealously guarded from the world the woman's name. More than this, he appears to have kept her in ignorance of the deep love she inspired in him. There is some reason to believe that his "lost love" first told him the story which he later turned into his well-known poem, *The Bakhchisarai Fountain*.[15] He wrote to his brother in 1823 that he hesitated to print the poem because "many places in it refer to a certain woman with whom I have been very long and very stupidly in love." [16] And in still another letter, to Bestuzhev, Pushkin suggested the mysterious source of the poem in a couple of verses. The lines eventually found their way into print. In anger he wrote again to Bestuzhev, roundly rebuking him and declaring his fear that the journal containing the verses might fall into her hands. He concludes his censure: "I confess that I treasure a single thought of this woman more than the opinion of all the journals in the world and of all our public. My heads whirls!" [17] The growing library of investigations devoted to the vain search for the name of the woman testifies to the success with which Pushkin guarded the secret of his "lost love."

IV

> What is he, then? An imitation,
> A paltry phantom, or a sample
> Of Muscovite in Harold's mantle?
> *Eugene Onegin*

However apathetic he may have been after leaving Petersburg, Pushkin was stirred into activity by the congenial atmosphere of Gurzuf. The cultured Raevskis provided him with much intellectual stimulus. But in his low spirits the muse tempted him little. In the inspiring Caucasus the only thing that he wrote was the short and excellent epilogue to *Ruslan and Liudmila*. And in this piece he laments:

> The flame of poesy is dead,
> And I search in vain for impressions.[18]

Meanwhile, *Ruslan and Liudmila* had been published in Petersburg. But the praise accorded the work did not reach the dejected poet in his mountain exile. The young Raevskis, and especially Nikolai, were eager students of foreign literature, and English authors were among their favorites. At Gurzuf Pushkin read the poetry of Byron with them in the original. This fact was of great importance, for it marked the beginning of Pushkin's "Byronic Period," which, in a positive manner, colored the next two or three years of his life and literary output.

There is reason to suppose that Pushkin had become acquainted with Byron's works before his visit to Gurzuf. Byron's poetry had been noticed in Russia as early as 1815, and while Pushkin was still in Petersburg Byron had already begun to be loudly acclaimed and read by A. I. Turgenev, Vyazemski, and Zhukovski. It was almost inevitable that the enthusiasm of such close friends in this matter should be communicated to Pushkin. There is a tradition that even at this time he began to read Byron in the original. However, his knowledge of English then, and for some years to come, was sketchy. It was not until 1828 that he could handle the language with ease. Meanwhile, of course, he had access to French translations.

While in the Caucasus Colonel Alexander Raevski joined the group. This man, several years older than Pushkin, appears to have exercised a considerable influence over him. "He will be more than famous," [19] Pushkin wrote his brother. Alexander Raevski was the very embodiment of the Byronic spirit. A few years later Pushkin described him, with some poetic exaggeration, in the famous *Demon*, as his "evil genius," a man who laughed at life, scorned people, flouted love and freedom, and "poured cold poison into my soul." [20] And like an evil genius he continued to haunt Pushkin. Whether the cold cynicism and spirit of negation of Colonel Raevski were born of Byron or were real traits of his own nature, the English poet was most certainly his hero. And in their "sad meetings" he helped to infect Pushkin with the Byronic virus. Some critics are convinced that Alexander Raevski suggested the more Byronic characteristics of Eugene Onegin.

Of course, the circumstances of Pushkin's life at this time would naturally have predisposed him to a keen sympathy for Byron and his poetry. The accidents of fortune which banished both poets from their native lands may easily have suggested a similarity in their fates which would have appealed to the imagination of the twenty-one-year-old Pushkin. Like Eugene Onegin, he was for a time to play the role of the Muscovite in Childe Harold's mantle.

It was not long before the new role found expression in poetry. *The Sun Has Set*, the elegy written on board ship during the night when the Raevskis and Pushkin were on their way to Gurzuf, was actually printed with the subtitle, "Imitation of Byron." And the manuscript contained the epigraph "Good night, my native land!" incorrectly quoted from the song in the first canto of *Childe Harold*. There can be little doubt about Pushkin's immediate inspiration. The echoes of the Childe bidding farewell to his native land are heard once again. But Pushkin is a softer Childe, more realistic and humanly sentimental. He exhibits nothing of Byron's scorn on leaving England. Rather, his melancholy thoughts are filled with regret for the friends, the loves, and the youthful pleasures he has left behind.

Pushkin, however, soon wore his mantle of Childe Harold with more swagger. At Gurzuf he drafted a long poem which he had no doubt conceived while he was in the mountains. This was *The Prisoner of the Caucasus*,[21] the first of a series of verse narratives which were directly inspired by Byron's Eastern tales. They won for Pushkin a universal Russian popularity. There is unquestionably something of Chateaubriand's René in the Prisoner, but the poem as a whole bears the Byronic stamp. In the manner of Byron, Pushkin has imaginatively identified himself with his hero. The Prisoner has been captured by Circassians. Pushkin represents him as disgusted with the sophisticated life of cities and as suffering from an unrequited love. Here we have something of the author's own situation upon leaving Petersburg. A beautiful native girl falls in love with the Prisoner. Although he is obliged to reject her affection, she helps him to escape and then kills herself.

In truth, there is not much to the story. The significant fact is that Pushkin draws upon his own emotional and spiritual illness, somewhat aggravated by the Byronic poison, in the psychological development of his hero. The narrative method of the poem also shows the deep impress of Byron's method in the Eastern tales. But the real charm of *The Prisoner of the Caucasus* consists of the style and the splendid descriptions of mountain life and scenery, accomplishments which were Pushkin's own.

For the next two or three years Byron remained a determining factor in Pushkin's literary development, and it is not without significance that his life during this period has been described as "Byronic." The rather cold brilliance of his youthful verse vanished, and his poetry was suffused with a new life and feeling. Upon the appearance in print of his Southern poems, *The Prisoner of the Caucasus*, *The Robber-Brothers*, *The Bakhchisarai Fountain*, and *The Gypsies*,[22] with some unfairness critics enthusiastically hailed him as the "Russian Byron." Soon the country was deluged with "Prisoners," "Robber-Brothers," and "Gypsies." The whole Byronic movement in Russia must, indeed, be largely attributed to Pushkin, for the majority of imitators learned of Byron from Pushkin's own works.

v

Unhappily for Pushkin, the pleasant existence at Gurzuf terminated all too soon. General Raevski had to return to his post at Kiev, and Pushkin was under the necessity of rejoining Inzov. He set out with the general and his son, traveling on horseback along the southern shore and over the Crimean mountains to Bakhchisarai. The remarkable rock structure of Kikeneis left no trace in his memory. But in climbing the steep mountain passes he got some amusement out of the fact that they were obliged to grasp the tails of their Tatar ponies, which suggested to him some mysterious Oriental rite. After they had left the mountains behind, the first object that struck him was a northern birch. "My heart sank," he wrote. "I at once began to grieve for my beloved South!" [23] The memory of the happy days at Gurzuf was still fresh in his mind. Pushkin was much impressed by the famous Monastery of St. George and its remarkably long flight of steps running down to the sea. Close by were the fabled ruins of the Temple of Diana where Iphigenia was sacrificed. The temple interested him, and he wrote of it to Delvig: "Apparently, mythological traditions are happier for me than historical associations. Here at least I was visited by rhymes." [24]

Pushkin was ill when he arrived at Bakhchisarai. The city had been the center of the Crimean khans and with it were associated many Oriental legends. Although the palace of the khans with its storied "fountain of tears" was to be the setting of his most romantic and most Byronic poem, Pushkin was at this point in no humor to appreciate it. He described his visit later: "On entering the palace I saw a ruined fountain; water fell in drops from a rusty iron spout. I roamed about the palace, indignant at the carelessness with which it had been allowed to decay and at the half-European reconstruction of several of the rooms. Almost by force N. N. [Nikolai Nikolaevich Raevski] led me up the rickety staircase to the ruins of the harem and to the khan's graveyard.

> ... but not of that
> Was my heart then full.

I was racked with fever." [25]

It is not difficult to understand why these scenes, which were eventually recalled with such vividness and beauty in *The Bakhchisarai Fountain*, made little impression on Pushkin at this time. Sickness is a potent enough annihilator of interest in dead monuments and will enervate the healthiest poetic imagination. Yet Pushkin did wonder at his apathy in this case, and in the conclusion of the letter to Delvig four years after his visit to Bakhchisarai he asked: "Why is the desire in me so strong to visit once again the places I left with such indifference? Or is memory the most powerful faculty of our minds, and is everything that is subject to it likewise charmed by it?" [26]

The party continued to Simferopol, and there Pushkin took his leave of the Raevskis. In the meantime General Inzov had been transferred from Ekaterinoslav to Kishinev in Bessarabia,

and it was for this town that Pushkin now set out, going by way
of Odessa.

Pushkin said farewell to the Raevskis with many regrets. He
had spent some three months with them, and the stay at Gurzuf
always remained a delightful memory. He had been given an
opportunity to view the splendors of Caucasian scenery and the
exotic Oriental life and customs of the Crimea, all of which provided him with lasting material for his muse. In this healthy,
happy, and cultured circle the poison and disillusion of his dissipated existence in Petersburg were mitigated, if not forgotten. In the touching dedication of *The Prisoner of the Caucasus*
to Nikolai Raevski, Pushkin expresses his gratitude in deeply
sincere lines. When he had been ruined and saddened, when betrayed and hopeless love racked him, then, writes Pushkin:

> With thee I once again found quietude;
> Peace entered my heart, and we loved each other.[27]

In the unhappy days that soon followed it is little wonder that
Pushkin seized the first occasion to speed to the Raevski estate
in a despairing effort to recapture the comfort and solace he had
found in the bosom of this friendly family.

CHAPTER VIII

"*Accursed City of Kishinev*"

Pushkin arrived in Kishinev about September 20, 1820, and with the exception of a few intervals he lived there for more than two and a half years. The present capital of Bessarabia, with its Russified aristocracy of Greco-Rumanian descent, offers a striking contrast to the little town of Kishinev in Pushkin's time. Then it had all the ethnographical interest of an international bazaar, the prevailing flavor of which was Asiatic rather than European. It had only recently been annexed by Russia, and Russians constituted but a small part of the population, which was made up of an extraordinary mixture of Moldavians, Bulgarians, Albanians, Greeks, Turks, Jews, Russians, French, Germans, and Italians. Of course, the Moldavians (who had not yet discovered that they were Rumanians) were the most numerous. Many were suspiciously proud of their lineage, and even tillers of the soil called themselves "nobles." The older generation, in fezzes and waistcoats with large lace sleeves, spoke only their native language or Greek. But the young Moldavians modeled themselves after the French, and this Gallomania, not unlike that which existed among their Russian masters, was almost the only real point of social contact between conquered and conquerors. The town was situated on the muddy river Byk, and along the narrow crooked streets and dirty squares one met with a variety of dress — multi-colored caftans, Turkish pantaloons, fezzes, turbans, European frock coats, and military uniforms. There were nearly as many levels of society as there were racial types — peasants, cunning middle-class Moldavians, Greco-Moldavian aristocracy, Jewish merchants, and a small Russian administrative and army society. The unnatural gaiety and moral looseness of a frontier town existed among this conglomeration of adventurous men and exotic women. Theaters, balls, gambling, love intrigue, and hard drinking and gypsy singing in disreputable inns were the chief amusements. Pushkin liked to compare Kishinev with Sodom, but he complained that Kishinev had all the vices and none of the enlightenment or hospitality of the Biblical city.

Here General Inzov was lord and master, but the poet in his chancellery was probably the most incorrigible citizen of Kishinev. Shortly after Pushkin's arrival the good Inzov invited him to live in his own house, one of the finest in the city. It was perched on a hillock on the outskirts and commanded a splendid view of the valley, river, and mountains in the distance. The house was surrounded by vineyards and gardens, filled with singing birds, which Inzov loved. Pushkin was allotted two rooms on the ground floor, one of which was given over to his faithful servant, Nikita.

At first Pushkin spent little time in his sparsely furnished chamber. In the morning he busied himself with reading and writing, but at a fairly early hour he sallied forth into town to enjoy the company of acquaintances. Inzov wisely understood that his poet-charge had other uses for his pen than those of a chancellery clerk. Pushkin might have made a career for himself in the army; the passion of his Lyceum days for uniforms and military action never died. But civil service he heartily disliked. Inzov soothed his own conscience by giving him a few copying tasks. In reality, most of the small commissions he foisted upon Pushkin were designed as "punishments" for some instance of misconduct.

With the instinct of a reporter of life, Pushkin quickly made friends — and enemies — among the various levels of Kishinev society. He was as much at home with the native peasantry and aristocracy as he was with Russian army officers, and soon he became an inseparable part of both the city's formal and less respectable entertainments. But Pushkin had hardly got settled when he became involved in a characteristic scrape. With three of his new acquaintances among the Russian officers, F. F. Orlov, A. P. Alekseev, and I. P. Liprandi — the latter ultimately became a close friend — Pushkin repaired to a bil-

liard room for a game and bowl of punch. The liquor worked
fast, and Pushkin began to amuse himself by scrambling the
billiard balls of Orlov and Alekseev. They naturally objected.
Orlov called him a schoolboy, and Alekseev added that he ought
to be taught a lesson. Pushkin ended by challenging them both
and asking Liprandi to be his second. "I will show them that I
am not a schoolboy!" [1] he angrily told Liprandi on the way
home. The night air soon cooled his head. To fight a duel over
something as inglorious as a billiard game now seemed ridiculous. Liprandi suggested a reconciliation. No, it was too late.
His honor would suffer. Nevertheless, the next morning, over a
good meal, Liprandi did succeed in making peace, but only after
he had convinced Pushkin that his precious honor was un-
smirched. Honor was the polar star of his short life. He steered
his course by it unfailingly, and in the end it guided him to
destruction.

Thus early the Kishinev reputation of Pushkin got under
way. A small, rumor-mongering population did not have to
wait long for additional material, and even before he left Bessarabia Pushkin's deeds and sayings had grown to the proportions of a lengthy saga. To add flavor to the early notoriety,
very shortly after his arrival he turned a Moldavian song of betrayed love, which a beautiful native girl in the Green Inn sang
to him, into the popular stanzas of his famous *Black Shawl*.[2]
The lyric went singing through the town and soon was heard all
over Russia. V. P. Gorchakov, another army officer, has left
some interesting memoirs of Pushkin at this precise time. In a
Kishinev theater, he writes, "my attention was caught by a
young man of short stature but quite robust and powerful, with
swift and observing glance, unusually lively in his actions, often
laughing with an abundance of unnecessary hilarity, and then
suddenly becoming so meditative as to arouse interest. The
features of his face were irregular and plain. . . ." Gorchakov
was introduced to Pushkin and the next day he met him in a
group of friends. They were all talking about the *Black Shawl*.
Gorchakov asked him to recite it. "While repeating certain
strophes in fragmentary form," continues Gorchakov, "he sud-

denly seized a rapier and began to play with it; leaping about, he took up poses, as though challenging an opponent. At that moment Druganov entered. Hardly giving him time for greetings, Pushkin offered to fence with him. Druganov refused. Pushkin insisted, and like a naughty child he began to make passes at him with the rapier. Druganov avoided the rapier with his hand. But Pushkin did not desist, and Druganov began to get angry. To avoid a quarrel I again asked Pushkin to recite the Moldavian song. He willingly agreed, threw the rapier aside, and began to recite with great spirit." [3]

Despite the zest with which Pushkin threw himself into Kishinev society, he was unhappy in the town. It was not easy to forget the delightful weeks he had spent with the Raevskis. Moments of nostalgia for these friends and their ideal family existence disturbed his thoughts. Other factors contributed to a growing discontent which was at the root of the disordered life he led throughout his whole stay in Kishinev. He had scarcely been in the city two months when he availed himself of an opportunity to visit the Raevskis at Kamenka. Inzov was not loath to give him permission, for he seemed to understand thoroughly the restless and rebellious spirit of his young charge.

II

> Loving thee, Raevskis and Orlov,
> And Kamenka's fond memory,
> I wish to say two words to thee
> About myself and Kishinev.
> *To V. L. Davydov*

By the end of November Pushkin was at Kamenka in the province of Kiev, and on the fourth of December he wrote in a gay strain to N. I. Gnedich in Petersburg: "My time is spent between aristocratic dinners and demagogic discussions. Our society, now broken up, was not long ago a varied and jolly mixture of original minds, of people well known in our Russia and curious for the unacquainted observer. There are few women, much champagne, many clever words, lots of books, and a few verses. At the present moment you will easily believe that I am little concerned with the rumors of Petersburg." [4]

Kamenka, surrounded by orchards and extensive gardens, was the beautiful estate of the Davydovs. The mother of General Raevski had been married a second time to General L. D. Davydov, and the two sons of this union lived at Kamenka, the eldest with his wife, Aglaya, a pretty young woman of French birth. In the nearby city of Kiev, which Pushkin also visited on this "vacation," was the home of the Raevskis. Hence it was natural that the hospitable estate of Kamenka should have become the common meeting-ground of both families and their many mutual friends.

Life at Kamenka was as pleasant as Pushkin described it, much like the even, unbroken leisure on board an ocean liner. The central points of the day were meals and discussions, varied by reading, billiards, and occasional dances. Relatively speaking, there were "few women" present, but the attractive wife of Alexander Davydov was a legion in herself. Her husband, a retired officer and much liked by Pushkin, who compared him to Falstaff, was not especially intelligent. He possessed the sole distinction of an enormous appetite. With winning French manners Aglaya supported her boredom in "barbaric Russia" by sophisticated coquetry with the many males who visited the estate. Pushkin carried on a vigorous flirtation with her and then ungenerously dubbed her "fat Aristippus" [5] of a husband a "majestic cuckold," [6] a word which in a few years was to sear his own soul like a hot iron. In *To a Coquette* [7] he amusingly and not too discreetly celebrated this flirtation; and he capped the poem with an entirely ungracious epigram in which, after listing the superficial charms that had attracted Davydov's wife to certain lovers, he pointedly concludes:

> Now will you tell me, my Aglaya,
> How did thy husband ever win thee? [8]

Perhaps piqued by his failure with the mother, he also flirted with her twelve-year-old daughter, Adele. (This is not the only instance in which Pushkin transferred his affections from mother to daughter.) A visitor to Kamenka remonstrated with him for provoking the young girl almost to tears by his fierce grimaces across the dinner table. "I want to punish the coquette," he promptly replied. "At first she paid court to me, but now she pretends to be heartless and does not wish to look at me." [9] This curious lapse from good taste was hardly improved by his poem to Adele, in which he urges the child "to seize the hour of rapture" and "to give her youthful years to love." [10] Such strange conduct annoyed even his close friends and seriously damaged his reputation in their eyes. Of course, Pushkin also saw something of the Raevski girls at Kamenka. As in his travels with the family, nothing now occurred which would indicate that any one of the sisters was his "lost love." There is even a story that Mariya and Ekaterina treated him with some disdain during this visit.

The "original minds" and "demagogic discussions" that Pushkin wrote about no doubt provided the chief attraction for him at the estate of the Davydovs. The southwest of Russia was then an important military concentration sector. The growing revolutionary movement, which involved so many army officers, radiated out from Petersburg over the whole region. Such focal points as Tulchin, the staff headquarters of the Second Army, and Kiev were used as propaganda centers, feeding particularly the south of Russia.

Hospitable Kamenka soon became a stopping-off place for many of the prominent conspirators. V. L. Davydov himself was enmeshed in the movement. Agents on missions to the south, and interested officers from Tulchin and Kiev visited the estate. Warm political discussions were held, and quiet proselyting for secret political societies took place. Among the guests were the well-known conspirators, I. D. Yakushkin, Okhotnikov, and the two generals, M. F. Orlov and Prince S. Volkonski, who were soon to marry Ekaterina and Mariya Raevskaya. All these men suffered for their part in the December Revolt of 1825. Perhaps the most brilliant of the company was Orlov, "the only man whom I have seen," remarked Pushkin, "who is happy by virtue of his vanity." [11] He was the brother of the Orlov with whom Pushkin had already come so close to fighting a duel, and later in Kishinev Pushkin saw a good deal of the general and his bride.

Pushkin was once again thrust into the midst of political conspiracy. A tradition exists that Prince Volkonski was actually commissioned at Kamenka to enlist Pushkin in a secret society. He finally refused the task because he felt that Pushkin's service to literature was infinitely more important than anything he could do in the cause of political reform. However, there were other more realistic reasons for blackballing him. His position was not unlike that of his last year in Petersburg. He was aware of the scheming all around him, eager to take a part, but frustrated by the unwillingness of the conspirators to admit him into their circle. Like his schoolboy comrade, Pushchin, they distrusted his youthful frankness and passionate nature. The unfortunate first impression of irresponsibility which he so often made on people destroyed any incentive for confiding in him. One evening at Kamenka, to allay the suspicions of Pushkin and General Raevski, who was likewise kept in the dark, certain members of the secret Union of Welfare set up a smoke screen. They brought the conversation around to the question: Was the existence of a secret political society necessary and possible in Russia? The discussion grew heated, and Yakushkin, after emphatically arguing on the negative, dismissed the whole subject as a joke. Pushkin was much moved by this sudden turn in the conversation. He had previously expressed his belief that a secret society already existed and had declared himself as willing to join one in the interests of political and social reform. After his joking dismissal of the subject, Yakushkin describes the conclusion of the incident in his *Memoirs*. "Pushkin arose, red in the face, and said with tears in his eyes: 'I have never been so unhappy as now; I had already seen my life in the future as ennobled with a lofty purpose, yet all this was only a vile joke!'" "At that moment he was thoroughly splendid," [12] remarks Yakushkin. Although he may have been carried away by his feelings, there is no reason to doubt Pushkin's sincerity on this occasion. Before long, circumstances obliged him to recognize the wisdom of concealing his liberalism, but that liberal sentiment burned within him is an unquestionable fact. Indeed, his mind was occupied with some of the very reforms which the Decembrists were trying to bring about. In the fragmentary notes on Russian history [13] which he wrote on his return to Kishinev, he declares himself for emancipation of the serfs and against the excessive privileges of the aristocracy. He has also left us the plan for an article on feudalism,[14] which in intention, at any rate, indicates a serious and scholarly approach to the subject. A few months after this incident at Kamenka, Pushkin wrote *The Dagger*,[15] in which he glorifies assassination as a desirable fate for tyrants. The poem, which gained wide oral dissemination, was scarcely less offensive to the government than his *Ode to Freedom*.

Political disputes and the other distractions on the estate did not divorce Pushkin entirely from his pen. On occasion he shut himself up in the billiard room and, oblivious to the knocks of servants and calls to meals, wrote for many hours at a stretch. To this period belong several fine lyrics, and it was at Kamenka that he finished *The Prisoner of the Caucasus*, penning the last line, according to tradition, while sprawled out on the billiard table.

But Pushkin had unduly protracted his visit among the Raevskis and Davydovs. After he had been away from Kishinev for about a month he had felt it necessary to have A. L. Davydov write to Inzov to explain that he had not returned because he was recovering from a severe cold. Perhaps he had been really ill, or perhaps his conscience had been bothering him. The indulgent Inzov replied to Davydov, naïvely telling of his fears that Pushkin had lost his way while traveling over the steppes in the wintry weather. "But, receiving your letter of the 15th," he concludes, "I was reassured, and I hope that your excellency will not permit him to return until he recovers his full strength." [16] He had taken more than two months to "recover" his full strength, for it was the first of March before he finally returned to Kishinev.

Pushkin made one more short visit to Kamenka and Kiev in November 1822. Thereafter his connections with the Raevski family as a whole were broken off. But in his future travels he was to meet several members, and he maintained a correspondence with the youngest son. His stay at Kamenka served to increase his deep devotion to this family, a touching testimony of which was his plea to Nicholas I, several years later, for aid for the Raevski children and their mother after the death of the father.

III

> Kishinevian Pushkin struck a certain noble in the mug and fought a colonel with pistols, but without any bloodshed.
> *Letter of A. I. Turgenev, 1822*

On his return to Kishinev Pushkin let loose all the devils of his nature on this Bessarabian "Sodom." It was more than mere youth or a proud insistence upon his individuality that inspired such behavior. A certain purposefulness appeared to dictate his actions, and the terrific energy he threw into dissipation seemed born of despair. Enemies, and some friends, set it all down as a pose.

In the morning, lying naked in bed, Pushkin traced patterns on the walls of his room by shooting wax bullets with a pistol. At meals he delighted in confounding the pious Inzov by asking sacrilegious questions. Leaving the house early, he sometimes failed to return at night. In all social events he was an inevitable participator, and these failing, he engineered his own entertainment. Wherever there was a gathering, there was Pushkin. When he appeared in the public gardens the natives turned out to see him, dressed as a Turk, a Serb, a Jew, a Greek, or a Moldavian, always swinging a heavy iron cane which he carried in order to strengthen his trigger-hand. Perhaps extreme poverty had something to do with these masquerades, for he could hardly afford to dress in the best Russian style. For a time the government had forgotten his meager "salary" of seven hundred rubles. He asked his father for money; Sergei Lvovich offered clothes instead, which his son scorned. Inzov was finally obliged to declare his poverty to the government, and the usual allowance was renewed. Then the gaming table often claimed this pittance. The gambling habit, acquired in the Lyceum and nourished in Petersburg, became a passion in

Kishinev. Pushkin, like Dostoevski, always seemed to lose, but the hope of a "killing" soon brought him back to the green table. He had a reputation for bad luck and unintelligence at cards.

There was no end to his childish pranks and witticisms. A local beauty asked him to write some verses in her album. He willingly obliged, extolled her charms, and then wrote at the end of the poem, "April 1." At a party he observed that a young lady, whose feet hurt, had secretly removed and hidden her shoes under the divan. Pushkin filched them, and the embarrassed woman had to walk to the door in her stocking feet before he relented. He taught Inzov's parrot a Moldavian oath. When a native priest talked to the bird the parrot repeated its profanity with a loud guffaw. In church, behind Inzov's back, he made faces at the girls and thumbed his nose. And at a divine service, prompted by a happy motif on the organ, he invited a young lady next to him to dance a mazurka. She fled, thinking him mad. In general, irreverence was characteristic of his attitude during this period. For making a joking remark about the Bible in the presence of the rector of the local seminary he was threatened with a summons from the Holy Synod. Pushkin loved dancing, music, and gypsy songs. Walking hatless about the town — he had pawned his hat for wine — he did not hesitate to take part in a dance with native street performers.

Pushkin had a contempt for Moldavians and Greeks, and they soon learned to fear him. For the most part they regarded him as a young madcap who possessed special privileges beyond their understanding. From experience they soon became aware of his irritable temperament and took care to flatter rather than provoke him. The wives of these local nobles, only recently released from semi-Oriental seclusion, made a hero of Pushkin, surrounding him with a mysterious demonic glamour. They were proud of being courted by "Pushka," as they called him, a son of a Russian nobleman. With some of the natives he became very friendly. Of little Khudobashev, a long-nosed Armenian, he made an idol, searching him out in every company and playfully throwing him down on a divan and sitting on him (an expression of friendship not unusual with Pushkin).

But he was easily offended, both by natives and his own countrymen, and they in turn thought him a born trouble-maker. Often his pride and ambition knew no limits; whatever the company was doing, he wanted to be first. In a discussion about books a Greek expressed surprise that Pushkin did not know a certain work. Indignant, he at once challenged the sur-prised Greek to a duel. He shoved a pear in the face of another unfortunate native; and in a dispute over a card game he took off his shoe and struck a Moldavian in the face. For this Inzov sent him packing to Izmail for a brief spell. At dinner he im-pertinently doubted the drinking prowess of an old guest at Inzov's. The venerable drinker sarcastically called him a "milk-fed boy"; Pushkin retaliated by dubbing him a "wine-fed man." The guest wished to challenge, but Inzov made peace between then.

A quarrel with an important Moldavian merchant by the name of Balsh became the talk of the town. Pushkin courted his young wife, who spoke excellent French, and ended by flirt-ing with her thirteen-year-old daughter. The mother grew vexed, either because of the attention he paid her daughter or because he ceased to give her any. In a caustic exchange Push-kin joked about the courage of Moldavians, and Mme. Balsh in turn sneered at his own courage. Piqued, Pushkin went directly to the card table where her husband was playing and challenged him to a duel. Naturally mystified, Balsh sought an explanation from his wife, who told him that Pushkin had been offensive. Turning to Pushkin he asked: "Why do you demand satisfac-tion from me when you have allowed yourself to offend my wife?" [17] This was said in such a loud and angry voice that Pushkin lost his temper. He seized a candlestick and bran-dished it over Balsh's head, but a friend caught his arm. To prevent a duel Balsh was persuaded next day to apologize. "They have asked me to beg your pardon," he began. "What sort of a pardon do you want?" [18] Without saying a word Pushkin slapped his face and left the room.

The duel, however, did not take place. Inzov put Pushkin under arrest for two weeks, confining him to his room. This was the good general's customary military form of punishment for Pushkin's misconduct. As an extra precaution he sometimes deprived him of his boots. Then the patient old man would worry and inquire after his health and send him the latest issue of a Petersburg journal. These confinements were intended to avoid disagreeable consequences rather than to punish him. Indeed, there was no end to Inzov's kindness. He provided him with lodgings, food, money, and even clothes, and in return Pushkin helped to enliven the old bachelor's isolation by his clever, jolly conversation. They had a sincere affection for each other. "General Inzov," he wrote, "is a good and honored man, a Russian at heart. . . . He puts his trust in nobility of feeling because he himself has noble feelings." [19] Ingratitude was not one of Pushkin's vices, and he never failed to speak of Inzov with a kind of filial devotion.

Pushkin did not always escape the consequences of his bold behavior in Kishinev. Nor did he want to escape them. If anything, he courted danger during this period. He delighted in hearing about brave deeds, and like several poets of his temperament — Byron, for example — he would rather perform heroic acts than write about them. This is one reason why some of his friends felt that he was created for an army career. The light-hearted attitude toward the danger of duels which seemed to characterize him in Petersburg had now changed to the attitude of the fatalist. Life "staked on a card," as it were, was part of his new pose. Pushkin valued courage as one of the highest of virtues, something that was a necessary part of his great pride and of his Russian nobility. And it must be said that in the face of danger, when a man reveals himself fully, Pushkin possessed every fine quality of bravery. Before the barrier his passionate nature grew cold as ice. At that fatal moment, as one of his Kishinev comrades remarked, "it seemed that he was smiling satirically while looking into the muzzle, as though he were thinking up an evil epigram on the marksman or on a miss." [20]

To be sure, there was relatively little danger in offending

timid Moldavians, but Pushkin did not hestitate to treat his countrymen, who were often as nice about a point of honor as he, to the same brand of daring. His sharp language frequently ran counter to the army etiquette of officer-friends, and his quick temper was continually plunging him into difficulties.

Once at a card game he lost steadily to Zubov, an officer of the general staff. Pushkin implied that Zubov cheated. A challenge resulted. The duel took place in a field outside the city limits. According to the testimony of many, Pushkin appeared with some cherries in his hand and calmly ate then while his opponent took aim. Zubov shot and missed. "Are you satisfied?" asked Pushkin before he fired. Instead of demanding that he shoot, Zubov ran to embrace his cool enemy. "This is entirely superfluous," [21] remarked Pushkin, and refusing to take his shot, he left the field. The news of his behavior at this duel quickly spread through the town and added to his growing reputation. Inzov, however, could not overlook the affair. "The Kishinev air has a bad effect on me," Pushkin waggishly told one of his friends. "On the advice of my old doctor" — so Pushkin called General Inzov — "it is necessary for me to spend some time further south." [22]

Shortly after his return he got into another scrape, and this time with a much more formidable opponent. At a dance in the casino one evening a young officer of the Egerski regiment requested the orchestra leader to play a quadrille. Pushkin had previously asked for a mazurka. The leader, who knew him well, ordered the mazurka. The commander of the regiment, Colonel S. N. Starov, renowned in the army for his bravery, suggested to the young officer that he demand an apology. The timid youth argued that he was not acquainted with Pushkin, and the colonel at once took upon himself the obligation. A challenge quickly followed.

The duel was fought next morning in a blizzard. The opponents could hardly see each other. They each shot twice and missed, the distance having been shortened for the second try. Because of the intense cold it was difficult to load the pistols, and although both wished to continue, the seconds insisted that the duel be called off until more favorable conditions were available. On his way back to town Pushkin visited a friend, and not finding him at home he scribbled the following impromptu:

> I live;
> Starov
> Is well;
> The duel is not ended.[23]

Fortunately, before another meeting could take place, common friends managed to compose their differences. At the usual meal of reconciliation Pushkin said to Starov:

"I always respected you, Colonel, and therefore I accepted your challenge."

"And you did well, Alexander Sergeevich," replied Starov. "To tell the truth, you stand up under bullets as well as you write." [24]

The vanity of art and the vanity of courage were glorified in one stroke. Such a tribute from a brave man and a hero of the war of 1812 threw Pushkin into ecstasies. He embraced the colonel and never ceased to hold him in great esteem.

A new and vaster outlet for heroics was at hand. The dogs of war were about to be unleashed. At the beginning of 1821 Bessarabia was aflame with the spirit of the Greek revolt. All the classic catchwords were in the air — the "freedom of ancient Greece"; "Christians against Turks"; "the salvation of the cradle of civilization." Rumors flew. The tsar would declare for the rebels. His dream of ending the European power of the Turks was about to be realized. Had he not concentrated an army in Bessarabia for this purpose? The population of Kishinev was swollen by Greek refugees from Turkish atrocities. Patriotic Greeks were roaming the streets of Kishinev and Odessa, buying up every conceivable weapon. The Ypsilanti brothers appeared in Kishinev; and finally in March 1821, under the leadership of Alexander Ypsilanti, the standard of revolt was unfurled. The Greek rebels moved on the Turkish frontier.

Pushkin, like Byron two years later, was caught up in the excitement of the movement. The noble cause of Greek independence stirred his imagination. If Russia went in he would have his chance to strut in a uniform and engage in warlike deeds. He had written to S. I. Turgenev in Petersburg about the possibility of his being recalled. "But," he added, "if there is any hope of war, for Christ's sake, leave me in Bessarabia!" [25] The rumor even got around among his friends in the capital that he had run off to join the rebels. In his Kishinev diary he jotted down: "I am firmly convinced that Greece will triumph and that 25,000,000 Turks will surrender the flowering land of Hellas to the lawful heirs of Homer and Themistocles." [26] And like many of the sympathizers, he subscribed to the journal of the revolutionists. The muse provided him with a vicarious outlet for his mounting enthusiasm. In *War*, with an unintentional touch of the mock-heroic, he imagines the resounding din of clashing armies:

> Blood I behold; I see the feast of vengeance;
> The fatal bullets whistle about my head! [27]

And in *Arise, O Greece, Arise!* amid a star-cluster of classical names and allusions, he calls upon this "country of heroes and of gods" [28] to break the chains of slaves.

Meanwhile, the cause of the rebels went badly. For a time the infidel Turk had the situation well in hand. The cautious Alexander I submitted to the dictates of international diplomacy, and the Russian armies confined their efforts to protecting their own frontier. The revolutionists under Ypsilanti were defeated, and he himself lost caste among his followers. The mercenary motives of some of the Greek leaders were becoming more and more evident. Often the soldier-patriots took on the aspect of bands of brigands. The fundamental common sense of Pushkin began to assert itself, and his enthusiasm eventually turned into indifference. He observed the absence of sincere patriotism among the Greeks, and in the end he was not above ridiculing the whole movement. Concerning the bungling tactics of the rebels, he wrote to A. I. Turgenev: "In our Bessarabia there is no lack of impressions. Here there is such a mess that it is worse than an oaten kissel." [29] Three years later, completely disillusioned, he could deliver himself of the following to Vyazemski: "Greece has polluted me. . . . The Jesuits have stuffed us about Themistocles and Pericles, and we imagine that these filthy peoples, made up of brigands and shopkeepers, are their legitimate descendants and the inheritors of their school glory. You say that I have changed my opinion. If you should visit us in Odessa and gaze upon these compatriots of Miltiades, then you would agree with me." [30] The glory of combat and doughty deeds appealed to Pushkin, but he had no desire to die of a fever in the malarial flats of Missolonghi. He was wiser than Byron.

IV

> For long was pleasure strange to me;
> The very name gives new delight,
> But secret sadness of despite
> I fear; all that's sweet, false may be.
> *To a Greek Girl*

Exotic women of a variety of nationalities created an atmosphere of love-intrigue well calculated to appeal to Pushkin's cynical disposition at this time. In the course of his sojourn in Bessarabia he had many affairs, no doubt many more than we know about. But they were nearly all transient loves or flirtations with Greeks, Moldavians, Jewesses, and gypsies, characterized more by an ethnological curiosity than by any sincere passion. Gorchakov tells how Pushkin would come to him with a confession of some new conquest. "What a beauty! I cannot live without her!" he would exclaim. "But on the morrow," Gorchakov adds, "another took the place of this beauty." [31] Once he saw a pretty face at a window, and he spurred his horse up on the sidewalk to pay his addresses. The girl fainted, and her parents protested to Inzov. The punishment for this prank was two days' confinement without his shoes. In fact, his persistent and often unique courting of Moldavian women resulted in complaints to Inzov by irate parents or husbands. He had little respect for the husbands of these native wives, and he jokingly dismissed them as:

> Their husbands with horns,
> Both shaved and bearded. [32]

It was Inzov's custom to invite the aggrieved parties to state their case in Pushkin's presence. And the typical punishment that invariably followed gave young Moldavian daredevils plenty of occasion to run by the door and shout: "Look at master Pushka sitting without his shoes!" [33]

There was little moral satisfaction to be had from such nondescript amours. However, a few of the women he courted belonged to some of the best families of Kishinev; several even achieved the distinction of being remembered in the "Don Juan List." He was much attracted to Pulkheriya, the daughter of a rich Kishinev merchant, E. K. Varfolomei, at whose hospitable house Pushkin was a frequent visitor. But Pulkheriya was a cold beauty who had most of the eligible youths of the town quite mystified, and Pushkin was no more successful than they. Mariya, the handsome wife of his friend Aikhfeldt, a town official and zealous collector of old coins, received considerable attention from him and a poem to boot. The young daughter of another official, Mariya Shreiber, he courted unsuccessfully; and Kishinev's first beauty, Mariola Rali, was a powerful but inaccessible attraction. Pushkin also pursued the temperamental singer, Anika Sandulaki, as well as Elena Solovkina, the wife of the commander of a regiment.

A more serious attraction, and one that had an unhappy termination, was his love for a gypsy girl, Liudmila Inglezi. She was unusually beautiful, and after having been left a poverty-stricken widow by her first husband, who had taken her from a gypsy band, she entered into a loveless marriage with the rich Inglezi. Pushkin arrived in Kishinev shortly after the ceremony, was introduced into the household, and at once fell in love with Liudmila. She returned his passion, and they spent many blissful hours wandering about the fields outside the town. One day he burst into the room of a friend, demanding an asylum for himself and Liudmila, for he had suddenly discovered that her husband was trailing them. Inglezi had actually learned about the affair and challenged Pushkin to a duel. But the watchful Inzov promptly put his charge under arrest for ten days and advised the husband to leave Kishinev. Inglezi and his wife went abroad, and shortly after their return at the end of a year Liudmila died of consumption. Pushkin long remembered Liudmila, and it is said that he first heard from her the haunting song of Zemfira which he incorporated in his fine poem, *The Gypsies*:

> Old husband, dread husband,
> Rend me, burn me:
> Firm am I; I fear
> Neither knife nor fire.
>   I hate thee,
>   I scorn thee;
> I love another;
> Loving, I shall die! [34]

In 1823, shortly before he left the town, Pushkin wrote to Vyazemski: "If you go to Odessa in the summer, will you not take in Kishinev on the way? I shall introduce you . . . to a Greek girl kissed by Byron." [35] This new object of Pushkin's passion bore the fetching name of Calypso Polychroni, and she appears to have aroused much comment among his friends. Calypso, a refugee from the Turks, had escaped from Constantinople to Kishinev in 1821, and she apparently enjoyed Pushkin's society for two years. She was slender, small in stature, and her jet-black hair, large eyes, and heavily rouged lips lent an air of voluptuousness to a face which was otherwise made unattractive by a long, hawklike nose. Calypso had some talent for singing Turkish love songs, which greatly pleased Pushkin. His feeling for her was not very deep or lasting. She seems to have lacked discrimination in the matter of morals, and perhaps Pushkin was originally attracted because Byron had been before him, just as Bulwer-Lytton is said to have derived a special satisfaction from an affair with a woman whom Byron had previously loved. Calypso's acquaintance with Byron rests solely on her own assertion. It is unlikely, however, that Byron ever knew her, although Pushkin preferred to think so. He wrote a poem to Calypso, and after paying tribute to her genius for fanning "the flame of the imagination of poets," he wonders if she had not inspired the character of Leila in *The Giaour*:

> O thou wast born for soft retreat,
> For passion's ecstasy divine!
> Then say: when in his dreams sublime
> The bard of Leila would reveal
> His own immutable ideal,
> Was it not thee he etched in steel? [36]

There is a curious story that Calypso eventually entered a Moldavian monastery in 1824, disguised as a man, a fact which was revealed to the unsuspecting monks only upon her death several years later. However, Pushkin's friend, N. S. Alekseev, wrote from Kishinev in 1826, informing him, among other things, that Calypso was still in the town but had fallen into consumption.[37]

On the whole, these Kishinev loves and flirtations, though of some consequence in the history of his emotional development, left no deep trace in Pushkin's life or poetry. He was simply passing time, nothing more. They helped to compensate for the boredom of what he was beginning to understand as a real exile. The good Inzov punished him for his indiscreet amours by taking his boots away, as if he had been playing the pranks of a naughty boy. And the punishment was a just measure of the boyishness of many of his Kishinev love affairs.

CHAPTER IX

A Russian Ovid Among the Goths

> Ovid, I live beside those quiet
> shores
> To which thou once didst come,
> and where, bereft
> In exile of thy gods, thine ashes
> left.
>
> *To Ovid*

The "Sodom" of Bessarabia exhausted the senses. Pushkin's inquiring mind found little to tax its resources in Kishinev. A diet of the flesh never sustained him for long, and though the number of his follies might weary the arithmetic of memory, he accumulated them simply from lack of something better to do. Pushkin was not a rake by temperament. He dissipated partly because it was the fashion among his set, and partly to escape the spiritual and material oppression of adverse circumstances. He greatly missed the stimulation of his intellectual and literary friends in Petersburg, but among the more cultured army officers of Kishinev he found some compensation.

Pushkin frequently visited the home of General M. F. Orlov, whom he had met at Kamenka. In 1821 Orlov was sent to a command in Kishinev, where he settled with his new bride, Ekaterina Raevskaya. He was a highly-cultured officer, interested in literature, and a former member of the Arzamas. At his house gathered the best elements of the Russian army society of the town, such as P. S. Pushchin, Okhotnikov, Liprandi, V. P. Gorchakov, Druganov, A. P. Alekseev, A. P. Poltoratski, V. Kek, and A. F. Beltman. Pushkin was well acquainted with all these men, and in their company conversation was concerned with subjects far removed from the petty gossip of the native *salons*, such as theories of universal peace, a particular hobby of Pushkin's at that time. In these discussions he often showed himself over-eager and disputatious; his sharp tongue sometimes irritated, but his ideas, despite his youth, commanded respect. He also liked to visit at the home of the vice-governor, M. E. Krupyanski, where he found much stimulating conversation.

There were other smaller and more intimate circles which Pushkin frequented. He was a welcome guest at the home of his good friend, N. S. Alekseev, an official in the chancellery, with whom he lived after an earthquake had damaged Inzov's house; he saw much of Colonel Liprandi, who was one of his closest Kishinev acquaintances, and of Major V. F. Raevski (no relation to the Raevski family). Among these friends, particularly at Raevski's, the conversation often dealt with the dangerous subject of political and social reforms. The swiftly-spreading revolutionary movement had penetrated this southern province of Bessarabia. As usual, it found readiest acceptance among the numerous military stationed in and around Kishinev. A branch of the Union of Welfare, the Southern Union, had been formed, and not a few of the Kishinev officers were already members. Although apparent liberals, neither N. S. Alekseev nor Liprandi joined the conspiracy, and Liprandi was later credited with being a government spy. Major Raevski, however, the "first of the Decembrists," was a man of great force of character and of considerable intellectual powers. A vigorous reformist and a member of the Southern Union, he and Pushkin had many warm arguments. In a fragmentary account left by Raevski,[1] he relates a controversy over Pushkin's verses, in which the poet by no means had the better of the argument. A zealous adherent of constitutional government, Raevski felt that Pushkin neglected themes of a social and political nature in his poetry. In his special subjects of history and geography Raevski stirred Pushkin's curiosity to the extent that he applied himself to reading up on the matters discussed. Unfortunately, this salutary influence came to an abrupt end. In 1822 Major Raevski was arrested on the charge of belonging to a secret society. After the Decembrist Revolt of 1825 he was exiled to Siberia, where he died.

There seemed to be a positive fatefulness in Pushkin's connections with many of the active conspirators in the revolutionary movement. Unlike the proverbial moth, he flew close to the flame often enough but was never consumed in the fire. In Kishinev he met P. I. Pestel, one of the leaders of the Decembrists and perhaps the most vigorous intellect of them all. On April 9, 1821, he made an entry in his diary: "This morning I spent with Pestel, an intelligent man in every sense of the word. 'At heart I am a materialist,' he says, 'but my reason is opposed to it.' We discussed with him metaphysical, political, and moral subjects, etc. His is one of the most original minds that I know." [2] Some five years later Pestel was hanged for his part in the Decembrist Revolt.

As on previous occasions, the surface aspects of Pushkin's character were his best protection against being admitted into the Southern Union. Accounts of several of the conspirators on the ground leave no doubt concerning the reasons for their objections to him. One of them relates that members of the Union were forbidden to become intimate with Pushkin because of his debauched life and the fear that he would denounce them to the government. Another writes: "I did not become acquainted with him, but I met him three times in society. As a man, I did not like him. Something of a bully, he is conceited and has a desire to ridicule and to sting others. Even then many unacquainted with him said that sooner or later he would meet death in a duel." [3]

In Pushkin's Kishinev period such a prophecy would not have taxed the powers of any seer. Yet many of these conspirators, continually breathing the sanctified aroma of their holy cause, would not accept Pushkin as a revolutionist because he could never live by revolution alone. In short, there was nothing of the political idealist in him. He was a rational liberal. Yet in the south, as in Petersburg, he reaped the whirlwind, for he alienated as easily as he pleased.

Besides the intellectual discussions of the Orlov *salon* and talks with revolutionary friends, the monotony of pleasures in Kishinev was interrupted for Pushkin by several trips. His own restlessness and Inzov's desire to save him from the consequences of some scrape or other were the pretexts. He twice visited Kamenka and Odessa, and in December 1821 he traveled to the south of Bessarabia with Liprandi. This latter trip contained much of interest. At Akkerman they dined with the commander of the fortress, and Pushkin paid court to his daughters. A friend of Liprandi's irritated Pushkin by taking him for his uncle, the poet. He grew angry, not so much because he thought unkindly of Vasili Pushkin as a poet, but because anyone could think him that old. And in the mountains of Leovo he was vastly amused when his Cossack host served him partridge soup and roast chicken, when the Russian custom was just the reverse.

Historical and classical associations abounded in the steppes of southern Bessarabia, and gypsies roamed over the region. Pushkin was interested in the gypsy language, as he was in Rumanian, and made some slight efforts to acquire a knowledge of both. Curious tales exist of adventures and love affairs with gypsies. Most of them seem designed to read autobiographical facts into Pushkin's poem, *The Gypsies*. As in the case of Byron, attempts have been made, often farfetched, to identify Pushkin and incidents of his life with his imaginary heroes and their adventures. There are fairly good reasons to believe, however, that on this trip with Liprandi Pushkin actually joined a band of gypsies and roamed about with them for several days. And this experience, no doubt, bore fruit in his poem.

II

> My wayward genius in my exiled habitation
> Has learned both quiet work and thirst for contemplation.
>
> *To Chaadaev*

Poetry saved him in his black hour of despair. Pushkin had nothing of Byron's insincere contempt for the muse. His art was not a plaything or a refuge or an avocation; it was life itself. And when he finally ceased to be interested in poetry, when the complexities, the pain, and the tragedy of life eventually strangled his muse, he no longer cared to go on living. The lofty mission of the poet had dawned upon him in the Lyceum; in his exile it began to assume the proportions of a faith.

Despite the distractions of Kishinev and the fevered restlessness of his state of mind, Pushkin exhibited considerable intellectual and poetic activity during this period. He provoked discussions of unfamiliar subjects in order to obtain information, borrowed books from cultured friends, and plunged into reading, particularly in historical and ethnographical fields. The customs, languages, and folk literature of the conglomerate peoples of Bessarabia deeply interested him.

On his return from Kamenka in March 1821 he wrote to Delvig, telling him that *The Prisoner of the Caucasus* was finished. "You will not be entirely satisfied with it, and you will be right. Yet let me tell you that I have more poems fermenting in my head, but now I write nothing. I am digesting recollections, and I soon hope to compose some new things." [4] He had in mind recollections of his Petersburg life, of the Caucasus and the Crimea. And now Bessarabia was filling his mind with new images and new themes.

The business of accumulating a Byronic reputation by his escapades could not interfere with poetic enterprise. Only absolute despair and disillusion silenced his muse. The mornings that Pushkin spent at home were devoted to reading and writing. He arose at dawn, and in his nightshirt or stark naked, sitting cross-legged on the bed in his little room, he wrote. No one must disturb him. Breakfast went by, sometimes lunch. A knock at the door and he flew into a rage, often driving a servant out of the room with clenched fist. He tore his manuscript to bits and flung them in the face of Inzov's housekeeper for intruding, and then begged the frightened woman's pardon. Pushkin complained to the general and asked not to be bothered when busy, even if he had to miss meals. The servants soon learned to look in the window to see if he was occupied before they dared to cross the threshold.

On fine mornings Pushkin liked to walk in the garden and out into the fields with his copybook and pencil, halting occasionally to sit on a stone and write. He was unlike many authors in that no special time or locale was a necessary condition for the easy flow of his inspiration. Night and day, in his study or walking or riding, images, themes, rhymes, and whole lines flashed through his mind. He always read, and talked, literally with a pencil in hand. Invariably he had scraps of paper about him, and in the middle of a conversation he would pull out a piece from his pocket and write down something. On the trip to Izmail, Liprandi tells how he returned at midnight and found Pushkin on the divan with his legs drawn up under him, surrounded by bits of paper. He gathered them up and placed them under his pillow. After finishing off some wine the friends went to bed. In the morning when Liprandi opened his eyes he saw Pushkin sitting in exactly the same position on the divan, entirely unclothed, and the scraps of paper all around him. Using his pen as a baton, he beat time as he read verses to himself.

The dominating influence in the poetry of the Kishinev period was Byron. In the Caucasus Pushkin had already been attracted by the Byronic protest against society and by the strong personality of Childe Harold in exile. The hero of *The Prisoner of the Caucasus* had reflected the melancholy of isolation and the Byronic disdain of people and worldly culture. With Pushkin this melancholy, as with Byron, now turned into a kind of scorn. Like Eugene Onegin, Pushkin would have said of himself at this time: "That man who has lived and thought cannot, in his soul, keep from scorning people." [5]

In the summer of 1822 Pushkin began *The Bakhchisarai Fountain*, a poem even more Byronic than *The Prisoner of the Caucasus*. The Crimean Khan Girei falls in love with a beautiful Polish captive, Mariya, who languishes for her freedom. She dies mysteriously, and the khan suspects his former favorite, Zarema, who is thrown into the sea at his order by the noiseless guards of the harem. Girei then seeks forgetfulness in wars, and on his return to Bakhchisarai he erects a fountain in memory of Mariya.

The "Fountain of Tears" had left Pushkin unmoved when he first saw it in the palace of the Crimean khans. But the memory of it in Kishinev, now enhanced by his further reading of Byron, suggested the poem. The lyrical element predominates, the harem setting is in the best Byronic tradition, and Zarema has a good bit of Byron's Gulnare in her personality. The poem, however, is sentimental, and later Pushkin himself became one of its severest critics. "*The Bakhchisarai Fountain*, between ourselves, is trash, but the epigraph is charming," [6] he wrote to Vyazemski. Yet nowhere does the sheer musical quality of his early verse appear more triumphantly. It is a tour de force of metrical harmony.

Before he embarked on *The Bakhchisarai Fountain* Pushkin had already begun *The Robber-Brothers*, another romantic poem and one which he never completed. This tale, as Pushkin tells us, was inspired by a real occurrence that took place while he was in Ekaterinoslav — two robbers escaped their guards by swimming the Dnieper in chains. Dissatisfied with the second half of the work, he subsequently burned it. Apropos of the publication of the fragment, Pushkin wrote to Bestuzhev: "If the native echoes — tavern-keepers, the knout, and prison — do not frighten the tender ears of the *Polar Star's* * female readers, then print it." [7] The great critic Belinski disliked *The Robber-Brothers*, but Pushkin felt that for style he had written nothing better up to that time. Tender ears might well have been frightened by the lurid descriptions and the undertone of protest against society's attitude towards its outlaws. The Byronic stamp on the poem is plain, and echoes of *The Prisoner of Chillon* may be clearly heard.

Apart from these longer works, there was much else in this period to indicate that Pushkin's devotion to the muse more than kept pace with his devotion to Kishinev revels. His ode on the death of Napoleon in 1821 is perhaps the finest poetic tribute ever paid the great conqueror. In his Lyceum days he had written *Napoleon at Elba* [8] (1815), in which he had not failed to express his patriotic joy over Russia's defeat of the French and their leader. Now his attitude has changed — Napoleon has become a hero in his eyes. It must be remembered that he was

* A well-known magazine, edited by Bestuzhev and Ryleev, in which a number of Pushkin's works appeared.

Byron's hero, and soon he was also to become the hero of
Eugene Onegin. This majestic poem is inspired by a noble
feeling for the fallen emperor and contains a poetic justification of his fame:

> Then let him be obscured by shame,
> That coward who on this dire day
> Upbraids with his insensate blame
> His uncrowned shade.[9]

Napoleon was one of the first poems of Pushkin that Lev Tolstoi
as a boy learned by heart, and it always remained a favorite
with him.

The historical reading Pushkin had zealously pursued in
Petersburg continued unabated in Kishinev. He borrowed
books from Inzov, Orlov, Liprandi; and young Nikolai Raevski
sent them to him from Kiev. Pushkin had a profound interest
in Russia's past, and eventually he undertook historical works
of his own. The immediate fruits of this reading, however, were
two poems on subjects drawn from Russian history, *Vadim* [10]
and *The Song of Oleg the Wise*.[11] The latter is a simple para-
phrase, based directly on an account in Karamzin's history, and
before long it was chanted by every Russian schoolboy. It is
perhaps significant for this time that *Vadim*, which remained
unfinished, glorified the ninth-century rebel who tried to drive
Rurik out of Novgorod. Such a revolutionary theme appealed
to the Decembrists, and the poem was highly thought of by some
of the conspirators.

In Bessarabia the tradition of Ovid, who had been banished
to Tomi near the mouth of the Danube, still lingered, and it was
natural that Pushkin should have found in the exiled poet a
theme congenial to his muse. In a letter to P. V. Nashchokin,
reputedly by Pushkin, he could write lightly of the ancient
tradition: "I am living in the land in which Naso wandered. It
ought not to have been so boring for him as story says. All the
pretty women here have husbands; besides the husbands, there
are gallants, and in addition there is still someone or other to
keep one from being bored." [12] Yet was not the fate of the

Roman poet similar to his own? Pushkin modestly pointed the comparison:

> Like thee I bowed to an unfriendly fate,
> But not in glory have I reached thy state.[13]

On his trip to Akkerman with Liprandi he sought out the supposed grave of Ovid. There is an anecdote that he spent a whole night in an old tower opposite the town of Ovidiople, steeped in meditation over the misfortunes of the unhappy Roman. Pushkin's letters and poems of this time and later contain frequent references to him. Though he shed no tears for his own banishment, he sympathized with the lament of Ovid, far from his native land. With Ovid's shade, he wrote, "I often wander beneath the moon." [14] And he said of his verses, *To Ovid* (1821), no doubt somewhat prompted by his partiality for the subject: "*Ruslan*, *The Prisoner*, and *Noël* are trash compared with them!" [15] Pushkin returned to this favorite theme in *The Gypsies*. In one of the most beautiful passages of the poem he has the old gypsy tell a story of a tradition that still existed among his people of an exiled bard:

> He had the holy gift of song,
> A voice like murmuring streams,
> And all our people loved him.[16]

To this period also belongs a considerable body of lyric poetry in which a melancholy Byronic note is often heard. But on the whole these short poems fully reflect the variability of Pushkin's nature. With a lavish hand he poured forth songs in honor of wine and love, and warm elegies breathing the essential goodness of his soul. Laughter and tears, joy and grief, belief and disbelief mingle in kaleidoscopic fashion. To be sure, there were satire and downright viciousness in some of the impromptus and in many of the epigrams. Kishinev life and people inspired sharp jibes and scorn from Pushkin's pen. The epigram was his dagger. He spared neither the enemies of truth nor his own personal foes, and his stroke was deft and sure. But he was always ready to give satisfaction for his blows.

The Voltairean cynicism and literary influence of the Lyceum and Petersburg days, no doubt aided and abetted by the deeper cynicism of his Kishinev existence, resulted in two unique poems — *Tsar Nikita* [17] and the *Gavriliada*. The first, about Nikita and his forty daughters, is out-and-out pornography, and the second, if not altogether pornographic, is impure and thoroughly blasphemous. The *Gavriliada* tells in a highly irreverent fashion the story of the Annunciation, in which Mary is represented as being "seduced" by Satan, the angel Gabriel, and the Lord. Of course, the poem was never published in his lifetime, nor did Pushkin admit his authorship. But it circulated in many manuscript copies all over Russia and quickly won the reputation of a forbidden classic, eagerly sought after and secretly read. Pushkin is even better than Voltaire or Parny at this sort of thing, for without ever being militantly irreligious, he turns his irreverent and often obscene lines with a delicacy and elegance which excite admiration if not approval. Mary is delightfully characterized, and her fetching naïveté reaches a high point when, after the carnal visit of the Lord in the form of a pigeon, she exclaims:

> "What goings on!
> One, two, and three! Now tell me, is that bad?
> My, but I'll say that I've enjoyed a revel:
> On one and the same day I've really had
> The Deity, Archangel, and the Devil!" [18]

It would be charitable to dismiss this impious poem as a mere metrical exercise of a youth who took delight in his own cleverness. Some have seen in it a deliberate satire against hypocrisy in religion, others a reflection of the cynical disbelief into which Pushkin plunged during his existence in Kishinev. At any rate, he never ceased to regret the *Gavriliada*, would not permit it to be mentioned in his presence, and begged, borrowed, and stole the copies of his friends in order to burn them. Pushkin was not actually irreligious, and as he grew older his faith deepened. There were periods of doubt and a time when he flirted with atheism. Although a materialist at heart, like Pestel, his reason opposed such an attitude in religion. Some years later the *Gavriliada* turned up like a bad penny and caused him serious difficulties with the government.

This reversion to the joking, cynical, and blasphemous in-

МANUSCRIPT PAGE FROM THE KISHINEV PERIOD

decency of the erotic French poetry of his school days was a passing phase. Byron had captivated Pushkin, and the authentic stamp thoroughly pervaded his life and poetry during the Kishinev period. The psychological reasons for the ease and completeness with which Pushkin accepted this influence have already been suggested, and they will presently be elaborated; the Byronic influence on his poetic development followed as a matter of course. But it must be remembered that Pushkin was a truly cosmopolitan poet. The literatures of Western Europe were his natural birthright, as they were, indeed, of many cultured Russians. He borrowed where he pleased, but like any great author he thoroughly assimilated what he borrowed, and the final results were not mere imitations but original productions. All Europe was at the feet of Byron at this time, and in a sense Pushkin was simply following a fashion. Byron broadened his literary horizon and encouraged to a remarkable degree his budding romanticism. However, there was more of the classical than the romantic poet in Pushkin, and soon he was to regard with a coldly critical eye both Byron and his own Byronic works. But that time had not yet come. At night on the ninth of May, 1823, in Kishinev, Pushkin began his great masterpiece, *Eugene Onegin*. For some eight years he labored to complete this work. At its inception Byron was very much in his mind, but long before he reached the end *Eugene Onegin* had become Pushkin's own poem, filled with the indelible quality of his genius and convincingly Russian in characterization, expression, and thought.

III

> I sit behind bars in a noisome prison,
> An eaglet nourished in captivity.
> *The Captive*

It would be natural to regard Pushkin's dissipated Kishinev career as a continuation in kind of the life he had led in Petersburg. But this explanation is too simple. The excesses in the capital amounted to sowing wild oats. He was manifesting a released undergraduate's desire to taste all the forbidden fruits at once and without discrimination. The feeling that he must make up for the relatively secluded life of the Lyceum merely intensified the business of accumulating worldly experiences.

Pushkin was no angel. For the multitude of life's sorrows he sought perhaps more than his share of the compensations that pleasure brings. His enormous vitality required an outlet, and it would be idle to neglect the obvious fact that he often dissipated, like any full-blooded man, because he liked it. The usual paradox of duality has been the traditional explanation — or apology — for the swift transitions from good to bad behavior. But a certain amount of dualism is implicit in all human nature, and it explains nothing except that sometimes a man is good, sometimes bad, by one moral standard or another. Pushkin, however, was particularly given to these rapid transformations. In the middle of an entertainment, full of infectious laughter and gaiety, he suddenly grew somber and melancholy; or the goodness and generosity of his heart quickly changed to spite and bitterness. In Sodom-Kishinev this variability was especially prevalent, and the kind of existence he deliberately pursued was fostered, if not entirely enforced, by certain material circumstances.

For the first four months after leaving Petersburg Pushkin's pleasant associations with the Raevskis and the trip through the Caucasus and the Crimea had helped to restore his peace of mind. The desire to leave the capital behind him had also been real. But once having parted from the Raevskis, and left to his own devices in semi-Asiatic Kishinev, he began to experience a longing to return to civilization and his intellectual friends in Petersburg. A year passed and then another, and still the expected recall did not materialize. What he had thought was a temporary banishment of a few months now took on the appearance of an exile to which he could see no end. Had the government forgotten him? The local police did not forget him. On the occasion of his first visit to Kamenka the Kishinev police reported erroneously that he had gone to Moscow without permission. They also reported him for denouncing in coffee houses both high army officers and the government itself. Inzov soon received a letter from Count Kapodistria, Pushkin's immediate

chief in the foreign service, requesting an explanation. The kind
general was careful not to overdo it in giving his charge a clean
bill of health: "Aroused by that spirit which dominates all
dwellers on Parnassus to a jealous imitation of certain writers,
he sometimes reveals poetic thoughts in conversation with me.
But I am convinced that the passing of time will bring him to
reason in this matter and oblige him to confess the unsoundness
of conclusions inculcated by reading works inimical to the accepted principles of the present age." [19] This diplomatic rhetoric seems to have satisfied Kapodistria. But in a few months
the government again inquired about Pushkin, asking whether
he was not a member of a masonic lodge in Kishinev, and re-
minding Inzov that he was expected to keep the poet under the
strictest surveillance. Pushkin had joined the Masons, and
Inzov himself was a member. Masonic lodges were suspected of
anti-government agitation, and shortly after this incident the
emperor prohibited them altogether. Inzov replied with caution, defending both himself and his charge: "Mr. Pushkin,
living with me, conducts himself well. I occupy him with correspondence in French and with translations from Russian into
French, for, by virtue of his slight experience in affairs, I cannot
entrust him with other papers. Concerning his connection with
a masonic lodge, there could not be such an organization here,
even though there were a desire for one." [20]

Then the government grew silent. Kapodistria, who had
some interest in Pushkin and might have helped him, left the
service and Russia. Alexander I was lost in diplomatic exchanges and could hardly be expected to remember a mere collegiate secretary languishing in far-off Bessarabia. Pushkin
grew bitter. He complained to Zhukovski, imploring his aid in
obtaining a recall. Silence here also. Zhukovski had gone
abroad. In 1823 Pushkin boldly wrote to Count Nesselrode,
head of the ministry of Foreign Affairs, asking for permission
to go to Petersburg on family business. The request was referred to the emperor, who promptly rejected it. To make
matters worse, several of his close Kishinev friends had already
departed. There were few left who could appreciate his real

worth. Pushkin felt deserted, forgotten, ostracized. He was now convinced that his exile was real and permanent.

Loneliness and burning resentment are poignantly indicated in his letters. It is at Kishinev that Pushkin's extensive correspondence really begins. His collected letters compose one of the most extraordinary correspondences in Russian or any other literature. Frankness, gaiety, wit, penetrating observations on life and people, and brilliant literary criticism are revealed in these letters, which are written in a sparkling, unaffected prose. For sheer absorbing interest they compare very favorably with Byron's. But Pushkin's letters illuminate his character more faithfully, for he was natural in them, rarely posing or concealing himself.

The north was his home. In the south he could never entirely free himself from the feeling that he was a guest, a tourist. Separated from his Petersburg friends, he now valued them more than ever. In Kishinev he began to live on recollections for the first time. His letters stormed at friends in the capital for forgetting him. "I continue to write to Delvig and Gnedich," he remarks ironically to the publisher Grech, "but they do not breathe a word. What should this signify? If it is a simple forgetfulness, then I do not complain; to be forgotten is the natural fate of every absentee." [21] But when Gnedich did write he replies gratefully: "Thanks for the remembrances, the friendship, the praise, the censure, for the length of this letter — all indicate the interest your lively soul takes in everything that concerns me." [22] Upon receiving a note from Ya. Tolstoi, a comrade of the Green Lamp, his answer is touching, full of the loneliness of the exile: "My heartfelt thanks; you alone of all my comrades, the fleeting friends of my fleeting youth, remembered me. Apropos or not apropos, it is now two years and six months since I have had any news from them; not a single line or a word from anyone." [23]

At other moments he curses his fate, Bessarabia, and everything connected with it. "Pity me," he writes to Gnedich, "I live among the Getae and Sarmatians; no one understands me, there is no enlightened Aristarchus with me." [24] And to Vyazemski: "I flounder in filthy Moldavia, and the devil knows when I shall scramble out again." [25] Above all, he begs information, hungry for news of everything that concerns the success of his literary productions and the doings of his Petersburg friends. What of *Ruslan and Liudmila*, of the members of the Green Lamp and their merry feasts, of Delvig, Baratynski, Katenin, the theater, the actresses? — these and many other questions are constantly flung at his correspondents.

During this time Pushkin depended particularly upon his brother for news. Lev was known to his Petersburg friends and served as a kind of distributing center for literary and other information about his famous brother. Pushkin rarely wrote to his parents from Kishinev. Nothing had occurred since his departure from the capital to remedy the coldness between them. For his sister, however, he added warm little notes in his letters to Lev, inquiring after her health and playfully urging her to get married. The sixteen-year-old Lev had already been expelled from school and was thinking about an army career. He was a talented youth, wrote poetry, and had a memory as colossal as his brother's. Lev was a "living edition" of Pushkin's works and spouted them on the slightest provocation, or none at all, unfortunately favoring the more erotic and blasphemous verses. A genial personality won him many friends, but essentially he was giddy, shiftless, and irresponsible, continually spoiled by his parents. While in Kishinev Pushkin wrote to him frequently, demanding news, entrusting him with small literary commissions, and giving him careful advice about his behavior and his entering the army. There was a sincere affection between them, and Pushkin's concern even obliged him to beg certain of his Petersburg comrades to watch out for Lev and aid him in difficulties. Lev was never very circumspect with the confidences Pushkin imparted, often placing his brother in an awkward position by his babbling. He was to blame for much of the gossip about Pushkin's dissipated Kishinev life which was already current in Petersburg. Ultimately Lev's behavior and the many obligations he thrust upon his brother chilled their relations.

Under the circumstances, then, it is hardly correct to say that Pushkin's manner of living in Kishinev was merely a continuation of his Petersburg existence. He dissipated to escape from his unhappy thoughts. At times he grew frightened at his excesses, experienced periods of remorse, and promised himself to reform. In asking pardon for an offense he had given to his good friend, P. A. Pletnev, Pushkin writes: "You would really forgive me for my thoughtless lines if you only knew how often I am subject to the so-called spleen. In these moments I am vexed with the whole world, and no poetry can stir my heart." [26]

Although the attraction Byron had for him did not exactly inspire Pushkin's mode of life in Kishinev, it unquestionably gave it substance and form. Byron's name is mentioned frequently in his letters at this time, and friends noted Pushkin's worship. A. I. Turgenev wrote to Vyazemski: "Pushkin absolutely wishes to have not only the talent of Byron but even his stormy quality, and he distresses his father by his venomous apostasy." [27]

It was easy for Pushkin to slip into the Byronic pose, for there was much in the real and legendary Byron that strongly appealed to him. The Byronic protest against society, a hatred for every kind of oppression, a strong sense of individuality, a desire to excel, and a towering pride came naturally to Pushkin. And his insistence upon these attributes was often the cause of his duels and scrapes in Kishinev and elsewhere. In the famous letter of advice to his brother (1822), one recognizes the world-weary cynicism of a twenty-three-year-old Don Juan. Pushkin writes to Lev: "You will have dealings with men whom as yet you do not know. Begin always by thinking the worst imaginable; you will not go far wrong in this. Do not judge them by your heart, which I believe noble and good, and which above all is still young; scorn them as politely as possible. . . .

"Be cold toward everyone; familiarity is always injurious; but particularly beware of becoming intimate with your superiors, whatever their advances may be. They will very quickly leave you behind and humble you when you least expect it. . . .

"Never accept favors. A favor often turns into treachery. Have nothing to do with protection, for it enslaves and degrades.

"I should like to caution you against the seductions of friendship, but I have not the courage to harden a soul at an age when illusions are sweetest. What I have to say to you concerning women will be perfectly useless. I shall observe merely that the less one loves a woman the more certain he is of possessing her. But this pleasure is worthy of an old monkey of the eighteenth century." [28]

There is more of this, but enough has been quoted to indicate Pushkin's dark misanthropy. One searches in vain for the genial and correct tone of a Polonius. Lev, at sixteen, was treated to advice which may have been the fruit of disillusioning experiences, but which was none the less soured by a cynicism quite unnatural to Pushkin. But pessimism came hard to him. Pushkin laughed too loud and enjoyed living too much to make his Byronic pose anything other than a pose which could be shuffled off at the proper time just as easily as it had been assumed. He was altogether too powerful a genius to be a mere imitator or follower of anyone. With changed circumstances and the addition of a couple of years to his swiftly maturing mind, he doffed Childe Harold's mantle.

By 1823 close friends in Petersburg had grown thoroughly alarmed over Pushkin's behavior in Kishinev and his deep despondency. They set to work to effect a transfer. In May Turgenev wrote to Vyazemski: "Count Vorontsov has been made governor general of New Russia and Bessarabia. I do not know yet whether the Arabian devil* will go to him." [29] Vyazemski answered: "Have you spoken to Vorontsov about Pushkin? Without fail he ought to take him. Get busy, kind people! All the more so in that Pushkin really desires to steady himself, but boredom and vexation are bad counselors." [30] At the end of

* A double pun, much liked by Vyazemski and A. I. Turgenev, on Pushkin's so-called negro ancestry. The Russian *bes*, "devil," and *arabski*, "Arabian" (in sound quite like the Russian *arap*, "Negro"), together form *bes-arabski*, which might mean either "Arabian devil" or "Bessarabian."

May Pushkin visited Odessa, and this stay of a month appears to have intensified his desire to leave Kishinev for good. Turgenev in Petersburg was pleading his cause eloquently. He pointed out to Nesselrode the necessity of safeguarding the morals of the poet and of giving his talent the leisure and strength to develop. And to Vorontsov he made a personal appeal to save Pushkin from the kind of life he was leading. In the end Turgenev's friendly offices won out. Pushkin left Kishinev at the beginning of July 1823 for Odessa to enter the service of the new governor general, Count M. S. Vorontsov. He was sorry to part with Inzov, and the feelings of the old general, who had grown very much attached to him, were hurt by this apparent display of ingratitude. Before long Pushkin himself regretted the change.

Despite his iterated dislike for the "accursed city of Kishinev," it cannot be said that Pushkin's experiences there had been altogether unfruitful. Quite true, the moral fabric of his nature had been stretched to the breaking point. His contemptuous treatment of the natives, offensive pride, loose love adventures, and ugly scrapes lowered him in his own eyes. At times he felt like a pariah. Drawn figures of devils and their orgies persistently appear in his copybook and seem to indicate a state of mind verging on the pathological. But though Pushkin may have lost something in Kishinev, he found more than he lost. His dissolute experiences were a purging fire. It is noteworthy that toward the end of his stay friends observed that he was growing wiser and more reasonable. In the company of his few close intellectual friends in the town, his Byronism vanished like a cloud. Then he was all simplicity, kindness, and jollity. The Caucasus and the Crimea had nourished his feeling for external nature; Kishinev brought him into contact with a new world of social relations and revealed to him the workings of human nature. All this was fresh material for his pen. Kishinev was a furnace in which his fine quality was tempered rather than consumed. Some three years after he left the town, he wrote with sincere delight to his Kishinev friend, N. S. Alekseev: "I cannot explain my feeling to you on receiving your letter. Your neat and finical hand, the Kishinev sounds, the shore of the Byk, the Jewess, Solovkina, Calypso — my dear, you have brought me back to Bessarabia!" [31] This feeling of pleasure may have been the enchantment that distance and time lend. He had forgotten his bitterness and boredom. And it is noticeable that as the years passed he spoke of Kishinev with real affection and remembered with pleasure the experiences he had had there.

CHAPTER X

Odessa

Then I resided in dust-blown Odessa,
There where the heavens are always
serene.
The Journey of Onegin

At the end of August 1823 Pushkin wrote his brother: "I left my Moldavia and appeared in Europe — a restaurant and an Italian opera recalled the past and, by God, revived my spirits!"[1] Compared to semi-Asiatic Kishinev, Odessa seemed very European. The theater, opera, government and educational buildings, fine private houses, a good hotel, and botanical gardens contributed to a sophisticated city atmosphere. Situated on the Black Sea, it was a bustling port at this time, and in summer many tourists thronged the city to take advantage of the excellent bathing. The population was cosmopolitan but vastly different from that of Kishinev. Here dwelt mostly Russians and peoples of Western Europe — French, Greeks, Italians, and Poles. There was a large commercial class, but many important officials grouped themselves about Vorontsov, the governor general of the region, for Odessa was the administrative center of all Southern Russia. Members of fine old Russian and Polish aristocratic families visited the city, and in its streets, cafés, and public buildings was a slight suggestion of the noise and gaiety of Petersburg which Pushkin missed. Odessa enjoyed a reputation for culture, and despite a provincial staidness, the intelligentsia had some reason to be proud of their only newspaper, the *Journal d'Odessa*, and of their Italian opera, concerts, and *salons*. In his famous description of the city (*The Journey of Onegin*) Pushkin damns Odessa as "dusty" and "dirty,"[2] which it emphatically was. But he loved the cloud-

less southern skies, the quiet breathless nights, and the sound
of the sea:

> Odessa softly slumbers.
> No breath of air stirs there; the muted night
> Is warm, the moon with slow steps rises bright.
> A curtain, soft, diaphanous, enfolds
> The heavens. All is still. But from the shore
> Is heard the Black Sea waves' resounding roar.[3]

As though determined to reform his Kishinev manner of existence, Pushkin at first lived quietly in Odessa. After a short stay
at the Hôtel du Nord, he moved to private quarters in a house
on one of the main streets, where from the window of his room he
had a splendid view of the sea. In this European city his variegated Kishinev costumes gave way to conventional trousers and
a black frock coat and hat. He saw few people. In the morning
he read, wrote, shot at a target, and took walks about the city.
There were several good eating places, but he preferred the French
restaurant of César Authone, where he spent much of his leisure.
For a time the theater and the opera were his chief amusements.

During these first few months in Odessa Pushkin plunged into
literary matters. Such enterprise was not simply a reaction to
his Kishinev frivolity. A mature awareness of his importance to
Russian letters was dawning upon him, and he was also beginning to realize the commercial possibilities of poetry. Living in
style in Odessa was more expensive than in Kishinev. There
was no generous Inzov to fall back on; he had to pay for his
board and room. The need for money now became the burden
of his letters, and he was to chant it with despairing monotony
for the rest of his life. "Make it clear to my father," he writes
in exasperation to brother Lev, "that without money I cannot
live. To exist by my pen is impossible for me with the present
censorship; I was not trained for the carpenter's trade; I cannot
pass for a teacher. . . . I am deceived in everything — but from
whom may I hope for something if not from my kin, from my
parents? On Vorontsov's bread I will not live; I do not wish to
— and that is final. Need may bring me to extremes. I am sick
of seeing the indifference of my father to my situation — although his letters are very amiable." [4]

Only two of these letters from Sergei Lvovich have come down to us, and they are amiable enough. Pushkin's father could be tender, but his tenderness vanished in money matters. He had considerable landed property, and his eldest son had a right to expect some assistance. Despite his external show of kindness, Sergei Lvovich was often false in his dealings with Pushkin. To be sure, his income was constantly dwindling, for he was a poor manager, but the older he grew the more miserly he became, always inclined to quarrel over a few trifling kopeks. There is a fairly authentic story that when young Lev once broke a wine glass at dinner, his father growled about the accident during the rest of the meal. "Must you complain so long about a wine glass that cost twenty kopeks?" asked Lev. "I beg your pardon, sir," the father replied with feeling, "not twenty, but thirty-five kopeks!" [5]

With few prospects of obtaining money from home, and unable to live in the style he desired on his small salary, Pushkin now began to explore the financial value of poetry. The censor, that arch-annihilator of Russian literature, was not, as yet, an insurmountable obstacle. Pushkin simply exaggerated this difficulty for the benefit of his father. With his school Latin in mind, he would end his letters: *Vale, sed delenda est censura!*[6] And he raged to Vyazemski that the censor Birukov was "a cowardly fool."[7] But the censors, though stupidly severe and captious, would invariably certify his poems without completely emasculating them.

For all its success, Pushkin had received little or nothing from *Ruslan and Liudmila*. Necessity and added experience had set him to bargaining in the case of his next long poem, *The Prisoner of the Caucasus*. While in Kishinev he wrote of this work to the editor, N. I. Grech: "Do you want to buy from me a piece of a poem? About 800 verses long. The lines are broad — four feet — divided into two cantos. I'll give them cheap, in order that the goods may not lie long." [8] His hopes were not entirely disappointed. When the poem appeared in 1822 he received five hundred rubles and one copy. This was the first real money Pushkin made on poetry.

He began to feel his worth as a literary investment, and the fact stimulated his efforts and sharpened his business sense. The last months of 1823 and the first half of the next year found him hard at work, and his letters over this period, particularly to Vyazemski and his brother, are filled with literary dealings. *Ruslan and Liudmila* had long since been sold out, and speculators were demanding as high as twenty-five rubles for a copy. A second edition was called for, and on the heels of this came an offer of two thousand rubles for a new edition of *The Prisoner of the Caucasus*. Gnedich, who had been managing his printing, was now thrown over. Pushkin felt that this poet and publisher had cheated him. With foresight he asked Vyazemski to handle the publication of his recently finished *Bakhchisarai Fountain*, and to write an introduction. The move was wise. Vyazemski managed the affair so well that Pushkin received three thousand rubles, about five rubles per line. And when the poem appeared in 1824, with Vyazemski's brilliant introduction, it was eagerly bought up.

Pushkin found himself in a position entirely unique for any Russian poet up to that time. Literature, and particularly poetry, was still pretty much thought of as a gentlemanly pursuit, to be indulged in with talent and in one's leisure, but not with too much seriousness. Certainly the growing practice of many writers in Western Europe of regarding poetry as a salable commodity had not yet found widespread acceptance in Russia, and to obtain as much as five rubles per line simply astonished Pushkin's contemporaries. Later he was to receive as high as ten rubles a line, a rate that would compare favorably with the best Byron ever earned. In a sense Pushkin made poetry a profession in Russia. At least, he was the first to prove its real commercial possibilities.

It must not be imagined that Pushkin turned his literary activities into cash without a severe twinge of conscience. He was a noble, devoted to the conventions of his class, and it was difficult for him to dismiss the feeling that to write poetry for money was a violation of the ethics of his nobility of six hundred years. Necessity forced him to compromise with his convictions, and he found a way out, equivocal though it may seem, that satisfied at once both his needs and his pride. In answer to the question, "Why do you sing?" he wrote to his brother from Odessa: "I sing as the baker bakes, as the tailor sews, as Kozlov* writes, as the physician heals — for money, money, money. In my nakedness such is my cynicism!" [9] But in a letter to Vyazemski, after receiving the news of the financial success of *The Bakhchisarai Fountain*, he defends his position more cogently: "Since I do not belong to the authors of the 18th century, I write for myself and print for money, but not at all for the smile of the fair sex." [10] This was his real justification, which he never grew weary of repeating to his friends. He wrote for himself and printed for money, and he sincerely believed in the aphorism. He sold the fruits of his work but not the work itself, and in this sense he always felt his lyre to be free. In truth, he composed a large amount of poetry which he knew, for one reason or another, had no chance of publication; and much that he wrote never was published in his lifetime. Even his masterpiece, *Eugene Onegin*, he began with the belief that it would never be printed. In the last few years of his life, when his own livelihood and that of his family depended upon his writing, he never prostituted his art for gain. Pushkin refused to cater to popular literary tastes, and he wrote as his inspiration dictated, on what subjects he pleased, and in the manner he pleased. This integrity of art in a commercial world Pushkin reaffirms in the person of the bookseller in the noble poem written at this time (1824), *The Conversation of a Bookseller with a Poet*:

> Permit me simply this to tell:
> Although your manuscripts you sell,
> You must not sell your inspiration.[11]

Back home his poems were creating a sensation. Members of the older generation of writers and critics viewed them with distrust, but the younger critics hailed Pushkin as a new and great force in Russian literature. Bestuzhev in his article, "A

* V. I. Kozlov (1792–1825), a writer of little talent.

View on Old and New Literature in Russia" (1823),[12] lavished the highest praise on the young Pushkin. And Vyazemski in the introduction to *The Bakhchisarai Fountain* had placed him in the very forefront of Russian poets. All were reading and talking about his latest verse tales. As though convinced of his own leadership, Pushkin now began to lay about him in criticism with a daring but sure pen. In letters to Vyazemski, Bestuzhev, Delvig, and Ryleev he expresses a desire to begin a new criticism of Russian literature with a revaluation of the old writers. To some extent, in these letters, he appears as the logical predecessor of the famous critic Belinski, whose precise service lay in his revision of the Russian Parnassus. Pushkin saw correctly that Russia had come to a parting of the ways in literature; that it was time to shuffle off the sterile influence of French neo-classicism and strike out along the new paths indicated by the fresh romanticism of England and Germany. But he had his own conception of romanticism, which was quite different from that of contemporary critics. Pushkin saw in romanticism simply a negation of the old school and its rules, and a medium that permitted complete freedom of creation and the full expression of the individual. His own works were to pass through the romantic stage and beyond into the broad region of artistic realism. On the whole, he was much ahead of his time in criticism. His remarks on the older writers were trenchant and just, and his own works were blazing the way to Russia's golden age of poetry.

Feverishly he labored away in Odessa on *Eugene Onegin*. In November 1823 he wrote to Vyazemski: "As for my occupation, I am now writing, not a novel, but a novel in verse — a devilish difference! It is in the nature of *Don Juan*. The first canto or chapter is finished; I will get it to you. I write it with a rapture that I have not experienced for a long time." [13] With sure taste Pushkin's admiration had switched from Byron's Eastern tales to the more realistic and satiric *Beppo* and *Don Juan*. In this first chapter the young Eugene has much of Don Juan in him, with a dash of Childe Harold. But the brilliant picture of Petersburg fashionable life throws the hero into the shade for the time being. As yet Pushkin was hardly aware of the vast canvas he was going to cover, and the world-weary, cynical Eugene had only just emerged from the creative shell. As a character he developed over the next eight years of Pushkin's preoccupation with him into something quite other than a Don Juan. Pushkin objected, at this time, to Nikolai Raevski's calling the poem "romantic," a criticism that indicates the growing realistic tendency in his literary development. "It [*Eugene Onegin*] is my best production," he writes his brother. "Do not believe N. Raevski, who abuses it — he expected romanticism from me; he found satire and cynicism and did not understand them very well."[14]

At the end of 1823 or the beginning of 1824 Pushkin interrupted his work on *Eugene Onegin* to write *The Gypsies*, the most mature and significant of his Southern verse tales. Though he may have finished it while in Odessa, he continued to polish it and hesitated a long time before publishing. The poem did not actually appear in complete form until 1827. Its story is simple. Aleko, a wandering-Cain type, becomes disgusted with civilization and joins a gypsy band. He falls in love with Zemfira, and they live together in the tent of her old father. All goes well in this nomadic life until Zemfira, a free child of nature, wearies of Aleko and has an affair with a young gypsy. The old father tries to console Aleko by telling of his own unhappy experience. His wife had deserted him for another, but he accepted his fate, for he felt her justified. He asks Aleko:

> Who may say to a young girl's heart:
> Love only one, you must not change? [15]

But Aleko refuses to be comforted. One night he trails Zemfira to a rendezvous with her lover and kills them both. In the presence of all the gypsies the heartbroken father addresses Aleko in a passage that has become famous among all readers of Pushkin:

> Leave us, thou proud and haughty man!
> For we are wild, we have no laws,
> We punish not nor kill from hate;
> For blood and groans there is no cause;
> We will not share a slayer's fate.

Thou wast not born for a wild life,
Thou for thyself desirest freedom;
Thy voice with fright will make us start:
Thou art harsh and bold — let us be,
For we are shy and kind of heart.
Farewell! and may peace be with thee.[16]

As the gypsy band trails off down the valley, Aleko, grief-
stricken, is left sitting alone by the grave of Zemfira and her
lover.

There have been attempts by famous critics to read a deep
philosophy into this poem and to point out a special purpose in
its contents. Generally speaking, Pushkin fought shy of thesis-
writing. Perhaps the best answer to the critics is the classical
one Pushkin himself made to Zhukovski: "You ask what is the
purpose of *The Gypsies*? What should it be? The purpose of
poetry is poetry."[17] If Pushkin was preaching anything in
The Gypsies, it was the simple lesson contained in the single line:
"Thou for thyself desirest freedom."[18] Aleko had deserted civilization because his liberty was crushed and he hoped to find
liberty among these nomads of the steppes. But he ended by
denying them the very freedom that he cherished. The tragedy
taught him the eternal rightness of the community of man as
opposed to man the proud individualist. A man who wishes
freedom for himself alone is only a rebellious slave of his own
nature. In the last line of the poem Pushkin leaves Aleko with
a very pessimistic consolation for his grief:

Against fate there is no defense.[19]

The Gypsies is remarkable for the considerable advance in
both form and treatment over the other romantic poems written
during Pushkin's exile to the south. Here, as in *Eugene Onegin*,
the truth of art and the truth of life successfully merge. The
easy mellifluence of *The Prisoner of the Caucasus* and *The Bakhchisarai Fountain* is now sacrificed for a more masculine,
dramatic, and almost metallic style. Although the descriptive
passages and Zemfira's song have all the wonderful harmony of
the early verse, the dialogue is swift, pithy, and most artistically shorn of superfluous words. Belinski dates the beginning

of Russian realism from the splendid descriptions of the gypsy camp. There is also an intellectual quality quite lacking in the simple narratives of the early works. Aleko is Byronic, but with a difference. The individual will of Aleko is defeated by the will of the community. Such a resolution of his problem is entirely unorthodox for a Byronic hero. Clearly, Pushkin was moving away from Byron. And Aleko, in certain respects, was simply a forerunner of a still greater character — Eugene Onegin.

Byron died while Pushkin lived in Odessa. He carefully noted the date on the cover of his copybook, and a year later he "ordered an evening mass for the peace of his soul."[20] He also paid Byron a modest tribute in his poem, *To the Sea*,[21] but he persistently refused Vyazemski's demand that he commemorate Byron's death by composing a fifth canto to *Childe Harold*. He wrote to Vyazemski on the occasion of this request: "You are sad about Byron, but I am quite happy in his death as a glorious termination of his poetry. Byron's genius faded from his youth. . . . His poetry obviously changed. He had always created in the wrong manner. There was no gradation; he suddenly ripened and matured, sang and then grew silent, and his first melodies never returned to him."[22] Critically Pushkin had traveled far since his first enthusiasm for Byron at Gurzuf. Now he studied Italian, read Dante and Ariosto, Shakespeare and Goethe. The period of his romantic Southern poems was nearly ended.

II

Always a social animal, Pushkin soon began to take a prominent place in the gay life of the city. His lively nature and love of sheer enjoyment made him popular in certain circles. The theater found in him a faithful patron. Although the Odessa stage was a far cry from the brilliance of the Petersburg theater, Pushkin easily slipped into his former habits of the capital. He visited the boxes to exchange greetings with pretty wives of merchants; he became a familiar figure backstage, courting the young actresses; and after the theater he amused friends with his witticisms in favorite coffee houses. Young Poles visiting the city particularly liked to listen to his conversation. With their patriotic hatred of Russia they regarded the exiled poet as an enemy of the government and hence a natural ally in their own cause. But Pushkin never liked the Polish language, nor was he sympathetic to Poland's struggle for freedom. The rich merchants of Odessa thought him merry company, but he was much beyond his depth in this gambling society. Their stakes were too high; thousands of rubles changed hands in the course of an evening.

A few government officials, native families, and visitors to Odessa became his fast friends. In the family circle of the merchant Sikar, in whose house he lived, Pushkin felt entirely at home and saw much of them. Some understanding and sympathetic members of Vorontsov's chancellery, such as A. I. Kaznacheev, A. I. Levshin, and V. I. Tumanski, befriended him. He especially liked Tumanski, a rather sentimental romantic poet, and he continued to correspond with him after he left Odessa. "He is a fine fellow, but as a poet I do not like him,"[23] Pushkin wrote to Bestuzhev. Kaznacheev, an older man and the director of Vorontsov's chancellery, was very kindly disposed, and did his best to save Pushkin from the pitfalls of the service, which he soon fell into.

As with the funny little long-nosed Armenian, Khudobashev, in Kishinev, Pushkin now made a particular favorite of the strange Ali of Odessa. The gossip of the city had it that Ali was an enormously wealthy Egyptian pirate. Pushkin humorously dubbed him "a corsair in retirement."[24] His appearance and behavior encouraged the rumors of piratical adventures. Ali was tall, had fine regular features and a swarthy complexion, and dressed in an outlandish Turkish costume with pistols sticking in his girdle. He spoke excellent Italian, smiled mysteriously when the townspeople quizzed him about his sea expeditions, and occupied most of his leisure in gambling. His originality and inscrutable pose attracted Pushkin, and Ali returned the friendship. Liprandi, in a visit to Pushkin's quarters in Odessa, found him sitting on the tall Ali's knee. Pushkin was tickling his companion, and they both appeared to be enjoying themselves hugely. He interrupted the procedure long enough to say to Liprandi: "He has a place near my heart. Who knows, perhaps my ancestors were closely related to his forebears."[25] He then resumed his tickling.

Liprandi made several visits while Pushkin was in Odessa, and on these occasions the two got together to gossip about Kishinev and their common friends. In January 1824 they took a short trip to Tiraspol and Bendery to interview a man, reputed to be a hundred and thirty-six years old, who had taken part in the campaign of Peter the Great against Charles XII. The object was to discover the grave of Mazepa — Pushkin always had a deep interest in historical matters and monuments. But the antique warrior disappointed them with the vagueness of his recollections. At Tiraspol, where his Kishinev friend, Major V. F. Raevski, was confined, Pushkin had an opportunity to visit him in prison. He refused. The reason is curious, but indicates his cool common sense. Pushkin feared that information concerning such a visit to a convicted political conspirator would at once be forwarded to the army base at Tulchin and thence to the authorities at Petersburg. And he was probably correct. He still hoped to be recalled from exile and did not want deliberately to irritate the government any further.

There appeared in Odessa at this time F. F. Vigel, future vice-governor of Bessarabia. He was an old member of the Arzamas, well acquainted with many of Pushkin's Petersburg friends, and in his famous *Memoirs* he has left interesting material concerning the poet's life in the south of Russia. Vigel's impressions of Pushkin in August 1823 are worth translating in part. He writes: "In the room next to me lived Pushkin, the exiled poet. . . . In Odessa, where he had just settled, he had not yet succeeded in finding any jolly company; in Bessarabia the sounds of his lyre were heard in silence, as though in a noisy wilderness. There was no one with sufficient interest to hear them. Meeting with a man who could understand his language must have been agreeable. . . . My simple good will pleased him, and every day our conversations and walks became more frequent. How can one fail to believe in the power of magnetism when one observes the action of a particular individual on

another? The conversation of Pushkin, like electricity coming
in contact with the black meditations of my overburdened head,
suddenly produced in it a thousand thoughts, live, happy,
youthful, and made our disparate ages seem the same. . . .
Often, in the midst of some idle, amusing conversation, there
flew from his soul or his heart a bright new thought which
astonished me and showed all the breadth of his intelligence.
Frequently, with laughter bordering on disdain, he spoke to me
of the pranks of comrades in his Petersburg life, or with touching esteem he told of the teachers who had been stern with him
in the Lyceum. Little by little I discovered the whole buried
treasure of his sound reasoning and his noble ideas, over which
was thrown a soiled cloak of cynicism."[26]

It was given to few people to understand Pushkin in this
fashion, or perhaps it would be more correct to say that he rarely
chose to reveal himself as he apparently did to Vigel. But Vigel
was an extremely human person, not always reliable in statements of fact, but capable of judging genius with a thumb of
gold. Unfortunately, this understanding friend did not remain
long in Odessa. Vigel left for Kishinev, and Pushkin wrote him
a humorously consoling letter in verse and prose. "You are
bored in that den where I was bored for three years," he remarks; and after inquiring about his various Kishinev friends,
male and female, he concludes with the gratuitous information:
"I am drinking like Lot of Sodom, and I regret only that I have
not even one daughter for myself."[27] In the middle of March
1824 Pushkin paid Vigel a visit in Kishinev, remaining for about
two weeks.

Once thoroughly acquainted, Pushkin became a familiar
figure in Odessa society; and on the streets, with his broad-
brimmed black hat and frock coat, everybody knew him. As
though more sure of himself, he eventually began to vary this
costume with a fez and a Caucasian overcoat. But always he
carried that huge iron cane, swinging it ponderously, or shoul-
dering it like a musket. Gossip about his Kishinev fame had
reached Odessa, and his enormously successful poems made him
a marked man. There is a story that on one of his walks he

stopped to inspect a field piece belonging to a battery stationed on the outskirts of the city. An officer, growing suspicious, asked his name. When told, he ordered the gun fired in the great poet's honor. A crowd of soldiers gathered, and the officer announced that they were favored by a visit from the distinguished Pushkin. He was borne in triumph to their tents, where they made much of him. No doubt these officers were well acquainted with his prohibited political verses.

Once he strolled into the Odessa lyceum and found a student in the empty study hall. The boy had received special permission to go there to read Cicero. In reality he was secretly poring over a copy of *Ruslan and Liudmila*. Hearing someone approach, he hastily hid the forbidden book.

"What are you reading?" asked Pushkin.

"The speeches of Cicero."

"What is your name?"

"Sumarokov."

"A glorious name,"* said Pushkin. "Surely you write verses?"

"No," replied the student.

"Do you read Pushkin?"

"We are forbidden to read his works."

"Have you seen him?" asked Pushkin.

The student replied that he had not, for he rarely had an opportunity to leave the school. But he added that he would like to, for all his comrades were talking about him.

"I am Pushkin," [28] said the poet with a smile, and bidding the dumbfounded boy farewell, he left the building. The students, however, soon came to know his familiar figure, and when he passed by their classroom on a stroll they ran to the windows shouting: "Here's Pushkin! Pushkin!"[29]

About Count Vorontsov and his attractive wife was grouped the best society of Odessa, and it was precisely in this circle that Pushkin felt most ill at ease. Indeed, he had not been long in the city before he experienced a distinct hostility on the part of his chief and his more aristocratic adjutants, officials, and

* A reference to A. P. Sumarokov (1717–1774), a well-known poet and playwright, often called "the father of Russian drama."

friends. Vorontsov was the sort of person who would especially
resent a man of Pushkin's temperament. A member of a distinguished family, and the son of Catherine the Great's well-
known ambassador to England, Vorontsov had spent most of
his youth in that country. His father had been a pronounced
Anglophile, and the son followed suit. Anglomania had made
its way into Russia at the end of the eighteenth century as a
kind of reaction to the all-pervading Gallomania. But both
fashions were objectionable to those Russians who insisted on
preserving their own national integrity. Vorontsov dressed like
an Englishman, assumed English mannerisms, and favored the
English in everything. He was an enlightened official and could
be kind to his friends, but he was closemouthed, cold, faultless
in his address, and excessively proud of his lineage. The polite
smile of condescension to his subordinates irritated, and his
gracious politeness with his peers had the flavor of insincerity.
Vorontsov's career in the army had been brilliant, and now as
the governor general of New Russia he was bent on creating
a distinguished place for himself as an administrator. "Order"
was the keyword in his chancellery as well as in his private life.
In fact, he was a good bit of a pedant on the subject. All this,
naturally enough, was inimical to Pushkin's nature.

At first Vorontsov had not looked with disfavor on the idea
of having a poet in his suite. Perhaps he had some notion that
out of gratitude Pushkin would honor him in his verses. In
interceding for him, A. I. Turgenev had impressed Vorontsov
with the necessity of aiding the youthful poet and of giving his
genius an opportunity to flourish. The idea of playing the part
of a Maecenas was congenial to the lordly nature of the governor general. He invited Pushkin to his evening gatherings, but
the part he was expected to play there was that of a favored
employee of the count. The host was polite to him, even affable
at first, but Pushkin was not allowed to forget the chasm of
rank that separated them. It was a new experience for him to
be regarded in society as a mere clerk. The tone of this *salon*
was English. The conversation was conservative; liberal subjects were eschewed, and literary discussion, if any, was more

or less confined to the dead immortals. Pushkin sensed a degree of contempt in the aristocratic Vorontsov for his own family. What was worse, the toadying officials in the count's service and the highborn friends who visited his house began to reflect Vorontsov's attitude toward Pushkin. They could not understand his title of "poet"; to them he was just an idler. Pushkin began to wonder if he had not jumped from the frying pan into the fire in this move from Kishinev to Odessa. The vast difference between the kind and understanding Inzov with his "pure Russian heart" and the haughty Anglophile Vorontsov pained him. A marked coldness soon grew up between him and his chief. He continued to visit Vorontsov's house, but the real attraction was not the society there but the count's wife.

III

Preserve my talisman:
It has a secret power!
The Talisman

Several months after his arrival in the city Pushkin wrote two Kishinev women of easy morals (their identity is unknown), begging them to come to Odessa for a frolic. He pictures himself as a hermit and says that he has grown "chaste and virtuous." [30] All kinds of inducements are offered, among them the promise to imitate a monkey and to draw a certain lady in the thirty-eight postures of Aretino. Whether or not these gay Kishinev friends ever came we do not know. But that Pushkin was "chaste and virtuous" in Odessa is hard to believe. He may have been chaste, but it was no fault of his. Pushkin's love affairs in this city were intense and deeply significant, emotionally and poetically.

On one of his earlier trips from Kishinev to Odessa Pushkin had become friendly with a wealthy Serbian wheat merchant, Ivan Riznich. He was well educated, a patron of the theater and opera, and occupied a prominent place in the social life of the city. In 1822 Riznich had gone to Vienna to marry, and he returned to Odessa in the spring of 1823 with his young wife, shortly before Pushkin settled in the city. Amaliya Riznich was unique in both appearance and behavior. Her husband let

it be known that she was an Italian, but town gossip added to
this a mixture of German and Jewish blood. All were in agreement, however, on the question of her beauty, for she was tall,
well-formed, with luminous, ardent eyes, a long, transparently
white neck, and raven-black hair to her knees. She dressed un-
conventionally, usually affecting masculine attire. She was
seductive, and knew it, a flagrant coquette, and loved to dance
and play cards. The lofty social circle of the Vorontsovs balked
at Amazonian Amaliya, but she lost nothing by this. Her house
was continually filled with young and old worshipers, not a few
of them coming from the count's own serviceable toadies. In
the gay life at Riznich's the husband began to play a secondary
role.

Pushkin was at once attracted, and haunted the house. Before Amaliya had been in Odessa long he was passionately in
love with her. He even overlooked what was her one physical
defect in his eyes — large feet. (Pushkin, it will be remembered,
greatly admired pretty little feminine feet.) There were plenty
of rivals, the two most formidable being the Polish Prince Yab-
lonovski, a descendant of the Jagellons, and the old but rich
landowner, Sobanski. Pushkin was madly jealous and never
quite trusted Amaliya. His brother tells a story, which has been
repeated almost as often as the account of Byron's swimming
the Hellespont, that once in a jealous rage over Amaliya, Pushkin
ran five versts under the burning hot sun. But the reason for
the jealousy and just what relief he obtained from this extraordinary feat we do not know. His devotion was patent to everybody, even to the husband, who resented Pushkin's playing
about his wife, as he said, like a kitten. And the husband soon
had enough of it. All through the winter of 1823–1824 Pushkin
pursued Amaliya. In May 1824 Riznich sent his wife to Italy
for her health. The rumor was that Sobanski followed and lived
abroad with her. But he soon deserted her, and she died of
consumption, a disease that appears to have taken a heavy toll
of Pushkin's loves.

How intimate were Pushkin's relations with Amaliya Riznich
it is hard to say. Naturally, her husband denied that there were

intimacies, but if the poems Pushkin wrote about her have any
authenticity, his love was returned. This little corpus of some
six or seven "Riznich" poems constitutes a vexed problem in
Pushkin's biography. The agglomerators and separators have
struggled with the matter, but their additions and subtractions
have done little to clarify either the question of what poems
may be safely attributed to Amaliya or of the underlying significance of her love in Pushkin's life. One theory holds that his
passion was turbulent and real but in the end unsuccessful, and
terminated when she left Odessa; the other maintains that his
love was consummated and that it was an enduring passion
throughout his life. On the basis of this latter notion three
beautiful elegies,[31] written in 1830, shortly before his marriage,
are offered as evidence that the memory of Amaliya was still
fresh and green in Pushkin's mind, even at this highly important moment in his career. The simple fact remains that there
is no positive proof for the ascription of any of these poems to
Amaliya Riznich. Most critics are agreed, however, that a
passionate elegy, written in 1823, was inspired by this love affair.
But the only biographical facts one can safely extract from the
poem are simply that at times Amaliya was kind to him, that
her kisses were "flaming," and that she succeeded very well in
torturing him with jealousy:

> My dear friend, I pray, do not torture me:
> Dost thou not know how fiercely I love thee?
> Dost thou not know how grievously I suffer? [32]

When in 1825 he heard the news of her death abroad, Pushkin
wrote a poem which seems to indicate that not even the ashes
of his passion smoldered any longer. He writes:

> From lips indifferent I heard the news of death,
> And I indifferently listened.

He begins to wonder now about this woman whom he had loved
with "such madness and suffering." "Where are the torments?
Where is love?" he asks. But love has vanished, and he sadly
concludes:

> For the sweet memory of days irrevocable
> I can find neither tears nor grief.[33]

Before Amaliya Riznich had left Odessa Pushkin had also fallen in love with the wife of his chief, Countess Elizaveta Vorontsova. The names of both these women appear on the "Don Juan List," and, knowing Pushkin's nature, it is not difficult to understand how he could be in love with both at the same time. The countess was a vastly different woman, and his love for her was something other than his stormy passion for Amaliya.

Elizaveta Vorontsova, of Polish birth, was almost as highly connected and cultured as her husband. When Pushkin met her she was thirty and had been married four years. With typical Polish lightness of manner she flirted freely, wished to be liked by all, and in the social circle of the Vorontsovs she set the tone. "About her," remarks Vigel, who knew the countess well, "there was nothing which we call beautiful; but the swift, tender glance of her small eyes transfixed one; the smile of her mouth, the like of which I have never seen, appeared to invite kisses." [34] Other contemporary accounts testify to her unusual charm, and that she had many admirers is certain.

The exact nature of the relationship between Pushkin and Elizaveta has remained a mystery. With customary secrecy in the case of women for whom he had a deep and lasting love, he nowhere directly mentions her name in this connection. The truth of the attachment rests upon the authority of a few contemporaries who were in a position to know, and on certain poems and material circumstances which seem to be consequences of his love. His manuscript pages at this time were covered with many drawings of a feminine head which is supposed to resemble the features of Countess Vorontsova. We can be fairly certain that she presented him with a seal ring bearing a Hebrew inscription. Pushkin regarded the ring as a talisman, always wore it, and liked to think that in a supernatural way it preserved his poetic talent. His sister tells that at Mikhailovskoe, after he left Odessa, Pushkin received letters bearing the same seal as that on the ring. On these occasions he locked himself up in his room to read the letters, which presumably were written by the countess. The ring inspired a famous lyric, *The*

Talisman, which has been set to music. Whether or not the woman mentioned in the poem, who "caressed" him and gave him the talisman because of "her love," [35] refers to Elizaveta Vorontsova is anybody's guess. The countess, at all events, never ceased to remember Pushkin with affection. When she was an old woman, long after he was dead, she read his works every day. Perhaps this was a touching proof of the lasting bond between them; perhaps she read the poems simply because they recalled the pleasant memories of her youth. It is interesting to note that Elizaveta Vorontsova has the distinction of being the first of a long line of favorites selected by critics as the original of the lovely Tatyana in *Eugene Onegin*.

However deep his love for Elizaveta may have been, its course was not untroubled by a serious rival. Alexander Raevski, Pushkin's "demon," turned up in Odessa at this time. The strange influence he had exercised on Pushkin in the Caucasus was resumed. Rank cynicism and a worldly contempt for all that was fine and virtuous still poisoned Raevski's nature; even in his sleep, it is said, a sardonic expression remained on his face. His apparent purpose in coming to Odessa was to be near the Countess Vorontsova, whom he had known previously. His devotion to her may have been the only real thing left in his life. It is unlikely that she returned his affection, but Pushkin certainly knew of the relationship. A story is told that once, when he was dining at the Vorontsovs, the countess asked what was playing at the theater. "*La sposa fidele, contessa,*" Pushkin answered with a wry smile. "*Quelle impertinence!*"[36] she replied indignantly.

In this curious triangle Alexander Raevski made Pushkin his dupe. Taking advantage of his friendship, he encouraged Pushkin's love for Elizaveta, feeling secure in his own position. Then, too, adds Vigel, no doubt embroidering a bit, "The sighs, the sweet torments, and the rapture of Pushkin, of which he [Raevski] was the sole witness, provided him with continual amusement." [37] But Raevski's real purpose was to screen his position and turn the jealousy of the husband upon Pushkin. In this the "demon" was successful. Count Vorontsov was not averse to philandering himself, but like most married men he had no intention of sharing this privilege with his wife. The light finally dawned on Pushkin. In *Guile*, a bitter poem which pretty certainly refers to Alexander Raevski, he condemns him for finding amusement in his grief and humiliation; and for his treachery Pushkin declares him "unworthy of his friendship." [38]

Once again the clouds were gathering over Pushkin's head. The self-esteem of Count Vorontsov had already been injured by Pushkin's attitude and actions. Now it was an added insult to discover that this clerk of his chancellery courted his wife. That a person of Pushkin's social status should dare to pursue the countess made the offense all the more intolerable in the husband's eyes.

IV

The reasons for Pushkin's enforced departure from Odessa are not entirely clear. There is an unknown factor in the chain of circumstances which may or may not center in his love for Count Vorontsov's wife. In many respects, however, his own indiscreet conduct was largely to blame for the fate that overtook him. The transfer from Kishinev to Odessa had revived his spirits, and for the first six or seven months he took a new interest in life and work. But the novelty soon wore off, and he once again grew restless. Even the large sums he began to receive for his poetry were not sufficient to cover his manner of living in Odessa. The fact worried him. He took to gambling again. Once he set out for a town some distance from Odessa to attend a ball. A certain lady was an added attraction. But upon arriving in the town he got into a card game, played until morning, missed the ball and the lady, and lost all his money. There were times, indeed, when he lacked the few necessary kopeks to pay a cabby. Jealousy and unfulfillment in his love for two married women also helped to destroy his peace of mind. His relations with Vorontsov and the indifferent, sometimes contemptuous, attitude of Odessa aristocracy positively enraged him. This discontent fed once more his passionate desire for freedom. In despair, he asked himself if his exile would ever end. He wrote to his brother in January 1824, wondering whether they would meet again. "You know that twice I have asked Ivan Ivanovich,* through his minister, about a furlough, and twice his most gracious refusal has been the result. One thing remains: to write to him direct . . . or otherwise quietly to take my hat and cane and go to look over Constantinople; Holy Russia is becoming unendurable. *Ube bene ibi patria.*"[39] This threat to leave Russia was one of many in Pushkin's lifetime. But it was not easy to escape from his prison, and perhaps this was fortunate, for outside of Russia he would never have been happy for long.

The increasingly hostile attitude of Vorontsov soon began to manifest itself. As early as March 6, 1824, he wrote to his friend at Tulchin, General P. D. Kiselev: "With Pushkin I have spoken only four words in fifteen days; he is afraid of me, since he knows very well that on the first bad report I will send him away from here, and then nobody else wishes to be responsible for him; I am fully convinced that he conducts himself much better and in his conversation is much more restrained than formerly when he was with the kind General Inzov, who entertained himself in discussions with him, attempting to correct his ways by logical reasoning, and then allowed him to live alone in Odessa while he himself remained in Kishinev.† On the whole, from what I learn about him through Gurev [governor of Odessa], Kaznacheev, and the police, he is now very prudent and discreet; if he were otherwise, I would ship him off, and personally I should be delighted, for I do not like his manner and I am not such an admirer of his talent — it is impossible to be a real poet without study, and he studies nothing."[40]

It is clear that Vorontsov had little respect for Pushkin's poetic ability and that he would be happy to see him out of Odessa. But to remove him was not so easy as Vorontsov's cocksure attitude would suggest, and if Pushkin himself had not expedited matters, the count might have failed. In the

* The Emperor Alexander I.

† Here Vorontsov is registering his disapproval of the permission Inzov gave Pushkin to visit Odessa before he actually settled there.

course of the next few weeks Vorontsov's desire to see Pushkin go became a fixed determination. What happened to close his mind on the subject we do not know. It may well be that gossip about Pushkin and his wife convinced him. In the meantime Pushkin had not been idle. Insulting epigrams on Vorontsov were convulsing the town. The haughty governor general of New Russia and viceroy of Bessarabia would have required no other reason than the following quatrain to convince him that his clerk must leave the district at once, before more damage was done:

> Half-hero and half-ignoramus,
> Let's add half-villain to this toll!
> However, there is still the hope
> That he will finally be whole.[41]

Vorontsov's mind was made up. Some three weeks after his letter to Kiselev, he wrote to Count Nesselrode, head of the Ministry of Foreign Affairs. The letter is a masterpiece of diplomatic shuffling. Vorontsov knew that Pushkin had influential friends in the capital, and perhaps he wanted to protect himself. The theme of the letter is his sincere desire to do Pushkin a service, but at the same time he insinuates to the government that it has to deal with a truly dangerous subject. "I cannot complain of anything about Pushkin," writes Vorontsov. "On the contrary, it seems that he has grown much more reserved and moderate than formerly, but the proper interest of this young man, not devoid of talent, and whose failings come more from the mind than the heart, obliges me to request his removal from Odessa. The chief failing of Pushkin is his ambition. He has spent a season here sea-bathing, and already he has a quantity of flatterers praising his productions; this turns his head and supports the illusion that he is a famous author at a time when he is only a weak imitator of a writer whose usefulness may be said to be very slight — Lord Byron. ... If Pushkin lives in another district, he will find more stimulation for work and will avoid his present dangerous society. I repeat, count, that I request this only for his sake; I hope my request will not result in any injury to him, and I am fully convinced, if you will only agree with me, that it ought to give him more means to cultivate his growing talent, while separating him at the same time from that which is so harmful to him, from flattery and from contact with erroneous and dangerous ideas." [42]

I have translated this and the previous letter of Vorontsov at some length for the light they throw on his character and for their information about Pushkin. They will also serve as a background for future events. Under the circumstances Vorontsov's avowal of good intentions in asking for Pushkin's removal does not hold water; and that he was interested in furthering Pushkin's literary career is ridiculous. Vorontsov was known to be relentless in his enmities. As a conservative, with the best interests of his career at heart, he may well have been trying to serve his government. But considering his high position, these letters display smallness of nature, even envy, and his personal grudge against Pushkin sticks out all over. In an unquoted part of the letter, he insists that Pushkin should not be returned to Kishinev, and later he emphatically repeats this request. If Vorontsov's purpose was simply to get Pushkin out of Odessa, one might suppose that any other locale would have been agreeable to the dissatisfied count. But there is just a suggestion in this demand that he did not want Pushkin living close enough to be able to continue the pursuit of his wife. At all events, Vorontsov's next moves hardly support his professedly disinterested desire to encourage Pushkin's poetic education.

The expected answer from Nesselrode did not come. Vorontsov began to show impatience. While waiting he wrote on April 8 to his friend M. N. Longinov, who was in the service of the empress, complaining about Pushkin and mentioning how glad he would be to get him out of Odessa. Three weeks later he again wrote to Longinov, remarking that he had not yet heard from Nesselrode about Pushkin's removal. Vorontsov's impatience grew. In an official state report to Nesselrode on May 2, he did not fail to slip in a reminder: "Apropos, I repeat my request — deliver me from Pushkin. He may be an excellent fellow and a fine poet, but I do not want to have him

any longer, either in Odessa or Kishinev." [43] And as though he
hoped that Longinov might use some influence in the matter, he
once more wrote on May 4, telling him about Pushkin's insulting epigram and his disreputable behavior.

Throughout all this period Pushkin had no precise knowledge
of the gathering storm. Unknowingly, however, he committed
an error which eventually tripped him up. In the first half of
March he wrote a letter to Moscow (the recipient is not definitely known, but presumably it was Vyazemski) in which he
said: "While reading Shakespeare and the Bible the Holy
Spirit is sometimes in my heart, but I prefer Goethe and Shakespeare. You want to know what I am doing: I am writing various strophes of a romantic poem, and I am taking lessons in
pure atheism. There is here an Englishman, a deaf philosopher,
the only wise atheist whom I have ever met. He has written a
1000 pages in order to prove *qu'il ne peut exister d'être intelligent Créateur et régulateur* — destroying, by the way, the feeble
arguments for the immortality of the soul. The system is not so
comforting as is usually imagined, but, unfortunately, it is
more plausible than any other." [44]

The teacher of "pure atheism" appears to have been a certain Dr. Hutchinson, a familiar figure in Odessa when Pushkin
was there, and according to one account the physician to the
Vorontsov family, which is very likely, in view of the count's
love for Englishmen. Whatever may have been his religious be-
liefs in Odessa, or lack of them, five years later he had become a
zealous minister of the Church of England in London. For this
time, one of violent religious obscurantism in Russia, his teach-
ings were indiscreet, and Pushkin's letter about them even more
indiscreet. With his customary bad luck in such matters, the
contents of the letter entered the stream of Moscow gossip and
eventually found their way to the city police.

Pushkin's Moscow and Petersburg friends were aware of the
new danger and tried to help. Rumors were flying. His prohibited verse floated to the surface again. General I. N. Sko-
belev wrote to the commander in chief of the First Army that
the author of certain poems, which were Pushkin's, ought to

have a "few tufts of his hide"[45] taken off. But the first hint of danger was conveyed to Pushkin in a secret dispatch from Vyazemski, sometime about the beginning of April. No doubt his warning was issued with the "atheism letter" specifically in mind. "Do me a favor," Vyazemski writes, "and be careful with your tongue and pen. Do not play with your future. Your present place of exile is better than any other." After warning him not to place any trust in Vorontsov, he concludes: "You have played enough of your page's jokes on the government; you have provoked it enough, so have done with it!"[46] Vyazemski knew whereof he spoke, but Pushkin had no intention of placing any trust in Vorontsov. And the count's next move resulted in open warfare.

On May 22, still not having heard from Nesselrode, Vorontsov sent Pushkin an official communication in which he ordered him to accompany an expedition to Kherson and the surrounding neighborhood for the purpose of aiding in the campaign against a plague of locusts. He also required him to write a report of the activities. Pushkin was deeply offended, and with some justification. In the letter which Count Kapodistria sent to Inzov in 1820, recommending Pushkin, he had specified no duties. He simply indicated that Pushkin was on a "furlough" and placed him under the guardianship of the general. Pushkin was aware of this, and although he was still enrolled in the department of Foreign Affairs, Inzov had been careful to treat him as a "special case," never regarding him as a regular civil servant. Pushkin assumed that his position under Vorontsov was the same as that under Inzov. He expected no official duties. The notion has been advanced that Vorontsov, by this commission, actually wished to give Pushkin a chance to distinguish himself and to win the favor of the government. On the face of things such an explanation deserves little respect. The quoted correspondence of Vorontsov hardly supports the idea that he wished to strengthen Pushkin's position in the eyes of the government. He simply wanted him out of his sight, and since Nesselrode moved so slowly, exterminating locusts was a good temporary way out of the difficulty. The count's feeling

on the matter is clearly revealed in a conversation with Vigel.
When the latter brought up the subject of Pushkin's commission
to go to Kherson, Vorontsov "grew pale," Vigel writes, "and
his lips trembled, and he said to me: 'Dear Philip Philippovich,
if you desire that we continue our former friendly relations,
never mention this scoundrel to me!' And in half a minute he
added: 'Nor his worthy friend Raevski!'" [47] It is a fair assumption that the main cause of this venom was the love of both
these men for his wife. And Raevski, like Pushkin, did not
escape the count's jealous wrath. Vorontsov eventually saw to
it that Pushkin's "demon" also left Odessa.

v

> Farewell! O ocean free and brave!
> For the last time before my eyes
> Will roll thy deep and dark blue
> wave.
>   *To the Sea*

Pushkin did not hesitate to declare his feelings. On the same
day that he received the commission, he wrote to A. I. Kaznacheev, Vorontsov's first in command and an official kindly disposed to Pushkin: "For seven years I have been idle in the service, and have not written a single document or had relations
with a single superior. These seven years, as you know, have
been entirely wasted for me. There were no complaints on my
side with the position. I stood in my own path, for I chose another objective. For God's sake, do not think that I regard
poetry with the childish vanity of a rhymester or as the relaxation of a sentimental man: it is simply my trade, an honorable
branch of industry, providing me with subsistence and domestic
independence. I believe that Count Vorontsov does not wish to
deprive me either of one or the other. They will tell me that I,
receiving 700 rubles, am obligated to serve. You know that
only in Moscow or Petersburg may one conduct the business of
writing books, for only there are to be found journalists, censors,
and booksellers; every minute I have to reject the most advantageous propositions for the simple reason that I find myself

2000 versts from the capitals. It pleases the government to recompense me for my losses to some extent, for I receive these 700 rubles, not as the salary of an official, but as the allowance of an exiled slave. I am ready to renounce this if I can be made master of my own time and affairs. I enter into these details, for I value the opinion of Count Vorontsov, likewise your own, as the opinion of any honorable man. I repeat here what is already known to Count Vorontsov: if I desired to serve, then I would not select any other chief in the place of his excellency; but feeling my own complete incapacity, I have already declined all advantages of the service and every hope of future success in it. I know very well that this letter, as they say, will finish me. If the count orders me to resign, I am ready; but I feel that by exchanging my independence I lose much, yet I do not hope to gain anything. Still one more word: you may not know, perhaps, that I have an aneurysm. For eight years I have been plagued to death with it. I can present the evidence through any satisfactory doctor. Surely it is possible to leave me in peace for the remainder of a life which truly will not last long." [48]

This letter is a curious combination of pride, vanity, exaggeration, pathos, and comedy. Pent-up resentment over his long exile flares forth, and both his pride in his art and his desire for independence make themselves evident. But Pushkin is careful to put his best foot forward. Though furious over the prosaic commission, he no doubt remembered Vyazemski's advice about Vorontsov, and accordingly he does not permit himself too many liberties with his chief. And there is a seriocomic aspect about the aneurysm. In his battles with the government, he was to pull this illness out of his bag of tricks on various future occasions.

What reply Pushkin received from Kaznacheev we do not know. At least, there was no relenting on the side of the count. Alexander Raevski advised him to submit, and it seems that he had an understanding with Vorontsov. Pushkin went off to the Kherson district to fight the locusts, whose ravages, from all accounts, were most severe. If Vorontsov had any notion that the task would keep Pushkin away from Odessa for a long period, he was mistaken. He was back by the end of May, having remained away about a week. The required report was handed in, but perhaps a much shorter impromptu one, which has been attributed to Pushkin, more correctly reflects his disgust with the whole expedition:

> The locust
> Flew and flew —
>   And sat down.
> It sat and sat,
>   Ate all around;
> Again it flew.[49]

Upon his return the accumulated vexations of the past few months drove Pushkin to the exploding point. He engaged in polemics with Vorontsov and expressed his determination to resign. Kaznacheev, as a friendly service, tried to dissuade him. Pushkin replied in a frank letter which leaves no doubts concerning his real opinion of Vorontsov. "You speak to me," he writes, "of protection and friendship, two things which are incompatible, to my way of thinking. I cannot and do not wish to pretend to a friendship for Count Vorontsov, still less to his protection; nothing that I know of degrades more than protection, and I esteem that man too much to wish to lower myself before him. On this score I have democratic prejudices which are worth more than the prejudices of the aristocracy. I aspire only to independence (pardon me the word in favor of the fact), and by strength of courage and perseverance, I will end by enjoying it. I have already conquered my repugnance to writing and to selling my verses in order to live; the greatest step has been taken; if I still write only under the influence of capricious inspiration, the verses once written, I regard them merely as merchandise at so much a piece. I do not understand the consternation of my friends (I do not know too well who are my friends). I am bored with depending upon the good or bad digestion of this or that superior. I am weary of being treated in my own country with less respect than the first English blackguard who comes to air among us his platitudes and his gibberish. No doubt Count Vorontsov, who is a man of worth, will represent me in a bad light to the public: victory is very flattering, and I will let him enjoy it to his own satisfaction, since I care as little for public opinion as I care for the admiration of our journals." [50]

These are strong sentiments for a youth of twenty-five about a man in Vorontsov's high position. Pushkin was no doubt pleased with his palpable hit at the count's Anglomania, which had always annoyed him. And he followed up this letter by sending in his resignation, which was in Vorontsov's hands by the eighth of June. The count quickly forwarded it to Nesselrode with an explanatory letter.

With a feeling that he had closed the door behind him, Pushkin's Kishinev devil-may-care attitude, compounded of despair and a longing for liberty, took possession of him again. "Now I write nothing," he remarks laconically to his brother in a letter of the thirteenth of June; "there is trouble of another kind. Disagreeableness of every sort; it is boring and dusty here." [51] At times he disappeared, spending days on ships in the harbor, drinking and reveling. "Farewell," he ends a letter to Vyazemski. "I am writing you in bed, half-drunk." [52] A rumor even reached Petersburg that he had shot himself. There also exists good evidence to the effect that Pushkin planned an escape abroad. But nothing came of it. The wife of his close friend, Vyazemski, was visiting Odessa at this time, and Pushkin saw a good deal of her — it was even said that he was a bit in love with her. She kept a weather eye out for him, and her reports home to her husband eloquently suggest Pushkin's distracted state of mind. "(13th June) I can say nothing good about the nephew of Vasili Lvovich [Pushkin's uncle]. His brains are quite disorderly; no one can prevail upon him. . . . I have never met so much levity and such a tendency to malignant talk. (23rd June) What a head and what chaos in that poor head! Often he embarrasses me, but more often he invokes laughter. (11th July) I showed your letter to Pushkin, who always laughs like a madman. I begin to like his friendly way. I believe that he is good, but his mind has been embittered by misfortunes." [53]

There is much more in these comments of Vyazemski's wife about Pushkin's love for Elizaveta Vorontsova and his bitterness towards her husband. That the count's actions still rankled in his mind is emphatically clear from a letter to A. I. Turgenev on the fourteenth of July: "You have already learned, I think, about my request for retirement; with impatience I await the resolution of my fate. Is it not strange that I got along with Inzov and could not agree with Vorontsov? The fact is this, that he suddenly began to treat me with disrespect. . . . Vorontsov is a vandal, a court cad, and a petty egoist. He saw in me a collegiate secretary, but, I confess, I have a different opinion of myself." [54]

Pushkin, however, got more than he bargained for in his resignation, and perhaps Vorontsov was a little sorry for the kind of triumph he won. Nesselrode's long-awaited dispatch arrived. In addition to what Vorontsov had reported, the government had learned of the "atheism letter." The emperor, it is said, had read Pushkin's *Prisoner of the Caucasus* with pleasure and had remarked that he ought to become reconciled with the author. But Alexander I was now far gone in religious mysticism. Atheism was as reprehensible in his eyes as treason to the state. It made no difference that Pushkin was not an atheist. His jocose and idle note was enough to condemn him in this reactionary period. "As a consequence of this," Nesselrode sums up, "his majesty has commanded me, as a legal punishment, to strike his name off the list of civil servants in the Ministry of Foreign Affairs for bad behavior; however, his majesty does not agree to leaving him entirely without surveillance, on the ground that, making use of his independent position, he will, without doubt, spread more and more those harmful ideas which he holds, and he will compel the authorities to employ the most severe measures against him. In order to avoid, if possible, such consequences, the emperor thinks that he cannot be kept under control in retirement, and hence he finds it necessary to send him to the estate of his parents in the Pskov government, under the surveillance of the local authorities. Your excellency will not delay in reporting this decision to Pushkin, which he must act on punctually, proceeding to Pskov without delay, once having been provided with traveling money." 55

Pushkin had lost again. In the eyes of the government he was still a criminal, even more so than when he left Petersburg. To political he had added religious offense. Certainly his material position was worse. In his southern exile he had had a fairly wide territory to wander over. Now he would be confined to a village. The prospects were dark. Anyway, Mikhailov-skoe, the Pskov estate of his parents, was nearer the capital, closer to the civilization he loved. But this was cold comfort.

On the thirtieth of July, 1824, having collected some three hundred and eighty-nine rubles for traveling expenses, he left Odessa for the long trip north. His financial situation was unusually bad. It is said that friends helped him out; then he had, for him, a phenomenal stroke of luck in winning nine hundred rubles at a card game. Perhaps another circumstance ought to be reckoned as luck. Shortly after he departed Prince S. Volkonski, with his young bride, Mariya Raevskaya, settled in Odessa. Their home became the headquarters of revolutionists who soon rose up in open revolt against the government. Had he remained, it is difficult to imagine that Pushkin would have escaped the severe punishment of these southern rebels, so many of whom he knew.

As Pushkin's hired carriage took him beyond the limits of Odessa he could hardly have been in a happy frame of mind. More than four years ago he had left Petersburg, a mere youth; he was now returning north at the age of twenty-five, a relatively mature man. In this southern exile he had seen much, thought much, and experienced and felt a good deal more. It had been a period of scepticism, of tortuous doubt in himself and in everything. But this residence in the south had been a fruitful school of life for him. He had met many highly-cultured and interesting people who had enriched his mind with their own knowledge. His extensive travels, vivid experiences, and innumerable impressions had provided him with a vast store of creative material. He had written a great deal during these four years, published much, and he was carrying away in his luggage the draft of *The Gypsies* and three marvelous chapters of *Eugene Onegin*. It can truthfully be said that Pushkin in these four years in the south had come of age, as a man and as Russia's greatest poet.

But the future did not look promising. Instead of leaving the south, as he had hoped, a "free" man, he was traveling to a village where his freedom would be even more restricted. Then, too, perhaps the thought of leaving behind him in Odessa the passionate love that had agitated his soul for the last year, and his southern sky, and the bright sea which he took such delight in, saddened him. When he left, neither Amaliya Riznich nor Elizaveta Vorontsova was there to say farewell. But it must have been some comfort to place distance between himself and Count Vorontsov. In December he wrote from Mikhailovskoe to a friend in Odessa: "Here there is no sea, no blue southern heavens, no Italian opera, nor you, my friend. But then neither are there any locusts or Milord Vorontsov." [56]

CHAPTER XI

The Exile of Mikhailovskoe

Tears, pain,
Betrayal, slander — everything has
crashed upon
My weary head. . . . What am I?
Where am I? I am
A traveler, struck down by lightning
in the desert,
And all grows dark before me.
The Desire for Glory

The road north was long, over a thousand miles, and infinitely boring, for the authorities had very carefully planned the "atheist's" itinerary, with strict injunctions to abide by it. He must go directly to the village of Mikhailovskoe by way of Nikolaev, Elizavetgrad, Kremenchug, Chernigov, and Vitebsk. Of course, Pushkin understood their precautions — this roundabout route was intended to prevent him from stopping over at Kiev and Kamenka, dangerous localities for a political and anti-religious suspect to visit.

Chastened and discouraged, Pushkin stuck to his orders, or nearly so. We have fugitive glimpses of him on the road. He turned up at the estate of a friend, the erotic poet, A. G. Rodzyanko, in the Khorolski district. Like a man from another world, Pushkin bewildered the country yokels with his costume — wide, varicolored Turkish trousers, a Moldavian cloak, and a fez with a long tassel. His thick curly hair fell to his shoulders, and he twirled his iron cane like a drum major. The faithful valet, Nikita, dressed as a Tatar, trailed after him. At Chernigov he met a student who had been to school with his brother and was now on the way to Kiev. Pushkin asked him to take a letter to General Raevski, in which he no doubt apprised his old friend of the new misfortune that had befallen him. Several weeks later at Mikhailovskoe he received an answer from young

Nikolai Raevski, in which he tried to comfort the exile and begged him to be more prudent.

At Mogilev the townspeople thought him mad because of his bizarre costume. But he was recognized here by the nephew of Engelhardt, the director of the Lyceum of Tsarskoe Selo. At once the news got around that Pushkin was in town. Everybody had heard of him, for everybody was reading *The Bakhchisarai Fountain*. Immediately Engelhardt's nephew and his delighted army friends took him in tow. Champagne flowed. Pushkin drank lustily, grew excited, jumped on the table and declaimed one of his Petersburg drinking poems:

> How I love the evening feast,
> When mirth is in the chair,
> And my idol, liberty,
> Is the table's ruler fair;
> Where till morn the good word "drink"
> Will drown out the wailing song,
> While the line of bottles lessens,
> And the line of guests grows long.[1]

The tipsy and enraptured officers were all for giving their honored guest a champagne bath. But Pushkin had had enough. "Friends, I sincerely thank you; really, it would be excellent, for I have no objections to being rinsed in champagne, but I am in a hurry. I must go." [2] At four in the morning the revelers escorted him to the carriage, drank a final toast, and sent him on his way.

Pushkin arrived at Mikhailovskoe on the eighth of August. Seven years before, he had visited this estate of his mother's and drunk homemade vodka with the black Peter Hannibal, the last son of the famous Abram. The Hannibals had been settled in the region since the middle of the eighteenth century. Fresh from the Lyceum, young Pushkin had enjoyed the village on that first visit. But he had soon grown weary of it and hastened to Petersburg to learn about life. Since then he had learned a great deal about life, but not enough to keep himself out of the clutches of the government. Now he could not run off to the capital; Mikhailovskoe was his prison.

The village of Mikhailovskoe, in the province of Pskov and

the Opochetski district, was situated in a country of much natural beauty. The region was hilly and covered with a thick forest, broken here and there by wide rolling meadows. By the side of the village ran a stream which further on formed a lake of considerable size. The surroundings were charming, among the most attractive in Great Russia. The word "estate" requires qualifications. Though the possessions of Nadezhda Osipovna were extensive in area and contained close to two hundred peasants, male and female, Mikhailovskoe had deteriorated through poor management. The manor house was a sprawling one-story wooden building, badly furnished, and extremely uncomfortable in winter.

When Pushkin arrived he was met by his surprised mother and father, and his brother and sister, who were there for the summer months. Their greetings were pleasant. After all, they had not seen this son for four years, and they were fully conscious of the fact that in the meantime he had become a great writer. His parents looked much older, and little was left of their former social brilliance. However, they did not grow old gracefully, for with a loss of social position nothing remained but empty pride and invincible egoism. Eternally capricious and faultfinding, they wearied the servants and even their favorite children with constant nagging over trifles. The mother had long been a master at working up scenes; and now Sergei Lvovich ably seconded his wife in creating trouble within the family circle.

Pushkin's literary glory fell away from him like a discarded cloak the moment his parents learned of his new exile and the reasons for it. They were terrified by the hostile attitude of the government toward their son and were convinced that his new offense would reflect upon them and very likely involve them in serious trouble with the authorities. Sergei Lvovich complained that his son did not love him, and Pushkin believed that his father was entirely indifferent to him. Thus, at the very outset of his new exile, Pushkin found himself in the position of a criminal in his own family, an atheist whose contagious influence in the domestic circle was dreaded by his parents.

The situation rapidly grew worse. Nesselrode, as indicated in his communication to Vorontsov, had never intended that Pushkin should roam about Mikhailovskoe unwatched. The authorities in the region had all been informed of the exile in their midst, and arrangements were quickly made to keep him under surveillance. This responsibility principally concerned the local head of the nobility, A. N. Peshchurov. To facilitate the business Peshchurov proposed to Sergei Lvovich the task of spying on his son, and the father, with uncommonly bad taste, accepted. When this fact became known to Pushkin the house was scarcely large enough for both of them. The son tried to keep out of his father's sight, roaming about the fields or riding horseback all day, or else staying in bed. He was miserable, and in his misery his thoughts fondly wandered back to Odessa, to its clear sky and bright sea. A letter from Vyazemski's wife, who was still in the city, "calms the madness of boredom which consumes my stupid existence." And he added in his reply to her: "I believe that a beautiful sky would make me weep from rage." [3] The wounds of his love in the southern city were still open. A letter from Alexander Raevski, in which the "demon" passes on to him the regards and sympathy of Countess Vorontsova, could only have added to his agitated feelings. Pushkin's few letters during these first three months at Mikhailovskoe eloquently testify to his wretchedness.

The hostile attitude and spying of his father eventually became unbearable. Sergei Lvovich accused him of teaching atheism to brother Lev. Scene followed scene until father and son came to an open rupture. In desperation Pushkin wrote to B. A. von Aderkas, the civil governor of Pskov, requesting the authorities to remove him from Mikhailovskoe and place him in a fortress-prison. Fortunately, this letter never reached its destination. At the same time (October 31, 1824) Pushkin hurried off a letter to Zhukovski, telling him of the last bitter quarrel with Sergei Lvovich and imploring his aid. "My father," he writes, "terrified by my exile, continually declares that he expects the same fate; Peshchurov, commanded to keep me under observation, had the shamelessness to propose to my father that he open my correspondence; in short, that he be my spy." Pushkin then goes on to tell of his unsuccessful attempts at an explanation, and continues: "Father called my brother and ordered him to have nothing to do *avec ce monstre, ce fils dénaturé*. (Zhukovski, think of my position and judge for yourself.) My head boiled. I went to father and found him with mother, and I unburdened myself of everything that I have had in my heart for the past three months. I ended with this, that I was speaking to him for the last time. My father, availing himself of the absence of witnesses, ran through the whole house, declaring that I *struck him, wanted to strike him, raised my hand, could beat him* — I do not justify myself before you. But what does he desire from me with this criminal accusation? The mines of Siberia and deprivation of honor? Save me either by the fortress or by the Solovetski Monastery. . . . Make haste: my father's accusation is known to the whole house. No one believes it, but all repeat it. The neighbors know. I do not wish to explain matters to them — if it reaches the government, judge for yourself what will happen. It will be horrible for me to go to law to prove my father a slanderer, but for me there is no law. I am *hors la loi*." [4]

One recalls the mad rages between Byron and his mother. The letter is obviously that of a frightened person, and it illustrates at once the farcical melodrama and the real pathos that were so often a part of domestic existence in this household. Pushkin was excitable and very impulsive, and his actions on this occasion may be partly attributed to these factors. So fiery was his temperament that even under the excitement of harmless entertainment he would run out of the room to throw cold water on his head in order to get himself under control. It appears that he did not actually strike his father. Yet it is little wonder that at the moment he was frightened. Such an offense was severely punishable in the Russia of those days. Had the report come to the attention of the authorities, Pushkin's position, especially in view of the charges already lodged against him, would have been most precarious.

In Petersburg the mild-mannered Zhukovski was deeply concerned. Even Pushkin's neighbor, Praskovya Osipova, took it upon herself to write to Zhukovski and beg his assistance in the affair. Zhukovski, so different in every way from the young man he felt duty-bound to protect, both out of friendship and because of his genius, soon ascertained that there was no immediate danger. His reply to the unhappy Pushkin is most characteristic. He refuses to judge between father and son, maintaining that both are no doubt in the wrong, and he concludes: "For everything that has happened to you and for what you bring upon yourself, I have only one answer: Poetry. You have not talent but genius. You are rich, for you have the inalienable remedy of rising above this unmerited unhappiness and of turning it to good service; you more than anyone must have moral worth. You were born to be a great poet; be worthy of it. In this phrase is all your moral, all your possible happiness, and all your reward." [5] Such advice was not a mere comfortless anodyne. Zhukovski knew his subject, knew the vanity of art and the power that poetry had over the soul of Pushkin. And what little sustained happiness Pushkin enjoyed at Mikhailovskoe came largely through his poetry.

Fortunately, shortly after this last incident with his father, the impossible situation cleared up. By the nineteenth of November, for the best interests of all concerned, the family returned to Petersburg, and Sergei Lvovich sent in a formal resignation of his duties as spy. It was a long time before this break with his father was healed. Whatever offense Pushkin gave him, the responsibility for the ugly rumor that his son had struck him rests with Sergei Lvovich. In the reply to Zhukovski's letter Pushkin describes the kind of ranting that gave rise to the rumor: "Father said afterwards: 'What a fool! In what does he justify himself! Indeed, if he had dared to beat me, I would have ordered him to be bound! . . . How did he dare, while speaking with his father, to gesticulate indecorously with his hands? Yes, he struck his father with words!' A pun and that only. If you please, here even poetry is of no avail." [6] Yet it was hard for the old man to forget the affair, and his everlasting protestations to friends seem to condemn rather than justify him. Zhukovski and A. I. Turgenev tried to explain it all away by telling Sergei Lvovich that his son's bad behavior was merely the result of his imitating Byron, who detested even his own wife. In a letter to his brother-in-law * in 1826, he alludes to this explanation: "Alexander Sergeevich has chosen me for his victim; but these reasons are not consoling to a father, if I can still designate myself thus." [7]

Pushkin was now alone at Mikhailovskoe except for the company of his good old nurse, Arina Rodionovna. The calm after three months of family wrangling was a welcome relief. Yet he could never forget the deep pain and humiliation of the treatment he had received. Some ten years later, when visiting Mikhailovskoe, the bitter memory returned, and he wrote: "I saw a betrayer in a chance comrade . . . everyone seemed to me a betrayer or an enemy . . . I grew bitter . . . tempests raged in my heart, and hate and dreams of pale places." [8]

II

> Life is fine for an anchorite!
> At Trigorskoe till night,
> Then Mikhailovskoe till dawn.
> *To A. N. Vulf*

Pushkin drew directly on his experiences at Mikhailovskoe in describing the country existence of Eugene Onegin. Like his hero, he lived pretty much the life of a recluse, getting up at seven in the summer mornings, swimming in the stream, then having coffee, and scanning the journals. There were long walks and rides in the country, dreaming in the leafy shade; but Pushkin did not content himself, like Eugene, with merely kissing some passing black-eyed peasant girl. In winter the days and long nights were spent indoors in reading and in playing billiards with a blunt cue. To these occupations we must add writing poetry, for which his hero had some slight contempt. Unlike the self-sufficient Eugene, however, Pushkin in his isola-

---

* We owe the preservation of this, and other excerpts from Sergei Lvovich's letters concerning the quarrel with his son, to the police. They were very much interested in the quarrel, and recent searches have brought to light their transcriptions of passages concerning the incident in the father's letters.

tion was unable "to forget both the city and his friends, and the boredom of his idle ways." [9]

Of course, many small landowners lived about the countryside of Mikhailovskoe. Pushkin could have cultivated their society if he had chosen. They tried to be neighborly with him, but the description of Eugene running out the back door and galloping off when he heard his neighbors at the front was perhaps poetry drawn from Pushkin's own experience. With the peasants he was more hospitable. He liked to stroll among their huts, talk and joke with them, and listen to their songs. The peasants accepted him on his own terms, but they were quick to notice that he never bothered about the practical affairs of the estate. At the fair held at the Svyatogorski Monastery, near his village, Pushkin scandalized the local gentry by his appearance and actions. In a straw hat and peasant shirt, his hair unkempt, and with a growth of beard, he joined in the singing of the beggars on the monastery steps. The authorities regarded such behavior as highly suspicious.

Of his neighbors at Trigorskoe Pushkin made an exception, and their jolly company and endless solicitude sustained him in many a dark hour of his country exile. Trigorskoe was the beautiful estate of Praskovya Aleksandrovna Osipova, a distant relative of the Pushkins. It was situated only two miles from Mikhailovskoe, surrounded by extensive, well-kept gardens, and the exile visited it so often that he jokingly called it his home. During one of his expansive moments he even contemplated buying a plot of land nearby and settling on it. Praskovya Osipova was a women of forty-three, twice widowed, and the mistress of a large family of children and nieces and nephews. Although never a beauty and now rather plump, she was not unattractive and possessed a good deal of soft feminine charm. With a love for poetry and reading, she quickly became a devotee of Pushkin's genius and a watchful guardian over his material welfare. In her own home Praskovya Osipova was a real despot, firm with her children; and in all questions of economy and family matters she could be most resolute. It is said that when Pushkin stayed overnight at Trigorskoe she pre-

ferred that he sleep in the bathhouse (rather commodious struc-
tures on large estates), for she disliked to have a strange man
sleeping in the house. Her relations with Pushkin, however,
were a bit baffling. He always showed the highest respect for
Praskovya Osipova, and long after his departure from Mikhailovskoe he continued to write her friendly letters. But at
times she revealed a sense of possession and jealousy that indicated a feeling for Pushkin much stronger than simple friendship. All his words were listened to and his wishes carried out as
something sacred. He seemed to have an unlimited influence
over her. Yet whatever may have been her own notion of the
part she played, Praskovya Osipova takes a place in Pushkin's
life beside his nurse, his grandmother, Princess Vyazemskaya,
and other older women. They provided the affection and domestic care which he so dismally failed to obtain from his own
family.

There were girls without end at Trigorskoe. By her first husband, Vulf, Praskovya Osipova had two daughters, Anna and
Evpraksiya; by her second husband, a stepdaughter, Alexandra
Ivanovna. Then there were a niece, Netty, and some younger
children; and other nieces and relatives of various degrees were
constantly turning up at Trigorskoe. In this wholly female
society there was only one male, Aleksei Vulf, the son of Praskovya Osipova.

During the early months of scenes and recriminations Pushkin
had visited Trigorskoe largely to escape the endless quarreling
at Mikhailovskoe. For at first he was inclined to be a bit scornful of these neighbors. In the letter to Vyazemski's wife in October, he remarked: "My only resource is to go often to an old
neighbor [Praskovya Osipova]. I listen to her patriarchal conversations; her daughters, bad enough according to all reports,
play for me the Rossini which I have just copied out." [10] And as
late as December he wrote his sister that her "Trigorskoe friends
are insufferable fools, except the mother. I am rarely with
them." [11]

This attitude soon changed after his family departed from
Mikhailovskoe. Pushkin's yearning for human companionship

helped to reveal the solid virtues and genuine hospitality of the Trigorskoe circle. Perhaps Aleksei Vulf, the one male member, had something to do with it, for Pushkin and he became friends at once. He was a youth of twenty and a student at the University of Dorpat. Pushkin first met him during his summer vacation at Trigorskoe, and in September he wrote to him in verse at Dorpat, asking him to come back for a holiday and to be sure to bring a full case of bottles with him. Young Vulf had a veneration for Pushkin and looked up to him as a preceptor in all worldly and intellectual matters. But it seems that he felt himself most indebted to his master for teaching him the "science of love." For Vulf love was a science to which he devoted perhaps a disproportionate amount of his time. At Trigorskoe his sisters called Pushkin a Mephistopheles and their brother a Faust. And Vulf set out to master what he called Pushkin's "Mephistophelian method." The technique was ridiculously simplified. At first the conquering male occupies a woman's imagination with voluptuous pictures. Then the prospective victim, after having tasted this vicarious fruit, loses interest in everything else except that on which she feeds her mind. Thus mesmerized, she finally gives herself up to experiencing the reality of her dreams. Vulf, in many of his statements, has laid himself open to suspicion, but if he learned this "Mephistophelian method" from Pushkin, then his preceptor was simply teasing him. There is no doubt that Pushkin was something of an accomplished Don Juan. Vulf says of him that no one knew women as well as Pushkin. And his brother Lev observed: "Pushkin liked women; he was unusually attractive to them, and they inspired more than one passion in his life. When he flirted with a woman, or when he was really interested in one, his conversation became unusually alluring." [12] But there was nothing of the cold, designing rake about Pushkin, the picture of him that Vulf draws. Vulf himself was a Lovelace for whom the methodology of seduction, and not the fact itself, was the principal enjoyment. His singular diary, an important document in understanding the morals of the time, reveals him as a calculating and cynical rake. Pushkin had little appreciation for

his mind and called him a Philistine. Although Vulf unquestionably learned a good deal about women from Pushkin, he had
nothing of his master's impulsiveness and sincerely passionate
nature. It is ironical that the pupil soon practiced his lessons on
a woman his teacher loved.

There was certainly plenty of laboratory material for the
"science of the tender passions" in the Trigorskoe houseful of
girls. Romance hid in every corner. All these young ladies
coquetted with Pushkin. Some fell seriously in love with him.
And he, as was his custom, fell a little in love with all of them.
Anna Vulf, a plain and sentimental girl of twenty-five, had up
to this time found romance only in French novels. At her age,
and unmarried, Anna would have been considered virtually an
old maid. Toward the end of his stay in Mikhailovskoe, she
fell deeply in love with Pushkin, and in this one instance his
conduct seems to have been reprehensible. As though from lack
of something better to do, he returned her affection for the moment. An apologist might say that he pitied her, for Anna's was
a lost cause — she died an old maid. The affair ran its course
through 1826. To her pleading letters, the letters of a girl who
has given herself and is afraid of being cast aside, he replied
jokingly, flippantly, and eventually she grew resigned to her
fate. It would have been cold satisfaction for her to know that
he placed her name on the second part of his "Don Juan List"
— that is, among the "light loves."

To Anna's young sister, Evpraksiya, a girl of only fifteen,
Pushkin was much attracted, and it is difficult to say how far he
carried his flirtation. She was the life of the household, and male
visitors prized her ability at mixing punch. Pushkin immortalized her as Zizi in *Eugene Onegin*. The neighbors, as in the case
of Eugene when he first arrived in the country, began talking
about a match for Pushkin, and Zizi was the favorite choice.
But Pushkin had no thoughts of marriage during his exile.
Evpraksiya's pert, buoyant disposition, such a complete contrast to her sister's, was like a tonic to him. In a letter to Lev he
tells how he measured his waist with Zizi's girdle and found
their sizes the same. "As a consequence," he concludes, "we

have one of two things: either I have the waist of a 15-year-old girl, or she has the waist of a 25-year-old man. Evpraksiya pouts and is very sweet." [13] Aleksei Vulf seems to be responsible for the notion that Anna and Evpraksiya were models for the sisters Tatyana and Olga in *Eugene Onegin*. There are some superficial resemblances, but the comparison has no more authenticity than a half-dozen others. Pushkin felt his affection for Zizi deep enough to place her among his "serious loves" in the "Don Juan List."

Pushkin flirted with the other eligible girls of Trigorskoe, with the stepdaughter, Alexandra Ivanovna, and especially with the attractive niece, Netty. Fifteen years later his father, in his dotage, fell in love with this same Alexandra Ivanovna. Pushkin helped the younger children with their French lessons and wrote poems in the albums of the older girls. But this household of Trigorskoe misses was a hotbed of small intrigues, jealousies, and conflicting desires, and the exile was often exasperated by female pettiness. As in the provincial ménage of the Larins on a holiday in *Eugene Onegin*, one could hear excited conversations and girlish laughter resounding from morning to night throughout the long, one-story manor house of Trigorskoe. The change from his debauched life in semi-Asiatic Kishinev to the harmless pleasures of this typical provincial family must have struck him forcefully. But he was more the spectator, or let us say the umpire, of these Trigorskoe games than an active participator. When he grew weary from his literary labors at Mikhailovskoe, habit turned his steps in the direction of Trigorskoe. He found there the relaxation that he needed, the restful change that demanded nothing from him and always left him free to return to his poetry.

III

> The bard's disgraced home,
> O Pushchin mine, thou wast the first to visit.
>
> *The Nineteenth of October*

On a bitter cold day in January 1825 Pushkin was awakened early in the morning by the sound of bells. A sleigh drove into the yard. He ran to the door in his nightshirt, and in a moment he was in the arms of Pushchin, his Lyceum comrade. They stood off, looked at one another, kissed, and were silent. Pushkin forgot the cold and the fact that he was almost naked; his friend was unmindful of his snow-covered fur coat. Old Arina Rodionovna stood by. She understood, and tears appeared in her bespectacled eyes.

They quickly came to their senses and went indoors. A stream of questions followed. Neither waited for answers. Pushkin's warm and expressive nature was deeply touched. This was the first contact in five years with his old school life. A visit by one of his closest friends at this time in his loneliness, in the depth of winter, and at God-forsaken Mikhailovskoe, meant much, very much, to him. The initial confusion of greetings and impulsive questions finally subsided. Coffee was brought, and the two comrades settled down to more or less chronological accounts of what had happened to them since last they met.

Pushchin had left the army and taken a humble position in the courts, where he thought his services would be helpful to poor victims of the law. He had heard of Pushkin's exile to Mikhailovskoe and grew alarmed over the various rumors about his latest offenses against the government. An opportune vacation coming along, Pushchin decided to visit his friend. In Petersburg he informed A. I. Turgenev of his intentions. "What, you wish to go to him?" asked Turgenev in surprise. "Do you not know that he is under the double surveillance of the police and the church?" [14] For Pushchin, however, this was no hindrance. (Turgenev, no doubt aware that Pushchin was involved in the political conspiracy, may have been worried over the consequences of his visiting the exile.) Vasili Lvovich, on learning of the projected trip, begged Pushchin, with tears in his eyes, to embrace his unfortunate nephew for him. Pushchin had a married sister at Pskov, whom he first visited. He left there on the night of January 10, picked up three bottles of champagne on the way, and set out in a sleigh to cover the seventy-odd miles to Mikhailovskoe.

Pushchin took stock of the exile's disorderly room, strewn

with papers, books, and stubs of quill pens. It was not large or elaborately furnished. In general, Pushkin was simple in his tastes. He preferred to work in a bare room and disliked rich furniture, statues, and pictures which distracted his attention when he wrote. Opposite was a corridor, off which were the old nurse's quarters. For the winter the rest of the barnlike house was shut off as an economy measure. In fact, fuel was used sparingly, and Pushchin found the dwelling extremely cold. In the interests of his friend he even complained to Arina Rodionovna.

To Pushchin the exile seemed little changed. He had grown side whiskers and appeared to have become more serious. But once the reminiscences began to flow, Pushkin's eager, vivid conversation reminded his friend of old times. He appeared unwilling to talk about the reasons for his exile, laconically charging it up to the jealousy of Vorontsov and to certain epigrams and irreligious remarks. Abruptly he asked what they thought of him in Petersburg and Moscow, and he related, as authentic, an improbable story. The emperor, he said, had been terribly frightened upon finding his name on a list of visitors to the capital, and he had regained his composure only when told that it was Lev Pushkin and not the poet. His friend frankly answered that Pushkin's belief in his political significance was a vain dream and that hardly anyone thought of him in this connection. What the reading public expected from him, said Pushchin, was great poetry; and he added that his close friends loved him and hoped for a speedy termination of his exile. Pushkin was not offended by this deflation of his self-conceived political importance.

Pushchin observed that his host, as of old, was still very suspicious about his possible connections with a secret society. When the visitor mentioned that he was not alone in his new efforts to better the legal corruption in the country, Pushkin jumped from his chair and cried: "Surely all this concerns Major Raevski, who for five years has been held in the Tiraspol fortress, and they can still get nothing out of him!" Then, more quietly, he continued: "However, I do not oblige you, dear

Pushchin, to talk. Perhaps you are right in not trusting me. Truly, because of my many stupidities, I am not worth such confidence." [15] Pushkin understood the answer in his friend's silent embrace. Perhaps he wanted to believe that his latest clash with the government had increased his importance in the eyes of political conspirators. But his natural common sense must have told him that Pushchin was right — his path to glory was by way of poetry and not political reform. Deep in his own mind he never had any doubt about it. It was well for him to face the fact now, for the time would soon arrive when he would have to declare his allegiance one way or the other.

After this chat the two friends took a walk. They visited the quarters of Arina Rodionovna, where the peasant seamstresses were gathered under the watchful eye of the old woman. Pushchin noticed one young girl who, by virtue of her figure and appearance, stood out among the rest. He at once suspected that she occupied a special position, but he did not wish to question his host for fear of offending him. As he looked at the poet, however, Pushkin smiled significantly, having guessed the thought that was running through his head. There was no need of words, Pushchin decided, as he winked at the master of Mikhailovskoe.

Dinner time arrived. The first bottle of champagne was uncorked, and toasts were offered to Russia, the Lyceum, their absent friends, and to *her*. (Was *she* the pretty peasant seamstress, or the ideal woman of their dreams?) Soon the second bottle was opened, and the old nurse and a few of the favored domestics joined, in a modest way, in the simple festivities of these two warm friends. Pushchin presented his host with a manuscript copy of Griboedov's famous satirical comedy, *Woe from Wit*, which had not yet been printed. After the meal Pushkin began to read the play aloud, offering some penetrating comments on the work. In the course of the reading someone was heard approaching the house. Pushkin looked out the window and hurriedly hid the manuscript. A monk from the neighboring monastery entered and was invited to some tea and rum. When the monk began to quiz him, Pushchin realized that his

PUSHKIN AT MIKHAILOVSKOE

visit had already been reported, and that the monk had been sent to investigate. (It must be remembered that Pushkin was also under religious surveillance, and this task fell to the lot of the holy brethren in the Svyatogorski Monastery.) Eventually the monk got his fill of tea and rum, if not of information, and excused himself. After his departure Pushchin expressed indignation at such petty spying, but his host laughingly dismissed the matter as something that he had become accustomed to.

Pushkin continued his reading of the comedy and also read some fragments of *Boris Godunov*. The time passed swiftly. It was already midnight. The guest had to leave. A small repast was served and the last bottle of champagne opened. Pushchin lingered. There was much more conversation, until they suddenly realized that it was three in the morning. The sleigh was ready, the driver impatient. The friends embraced, expressing the hope that they would soon meet in Moscow. It was a vain hope. Pushchin recalls the parting in his *Memoirs*: "We clinked glasses once more, but I drank sorrowfully, as if I felt that this was the last time we would drink together, and that I was drinking to an eternal farewell! In silence I threw my overcoat over my shoulders and ran out to the sleigh. Pushkin called something after me; I heard nothing and looked back at him. He was standing at the entrance, a candle in his hand. The horses started downhill. I heard: 'Farewell, friend!' The gate creaked behind me." [16]

Pushchin's premonition was correct — they never met again. His pure-souled reformatory zeal came to an end with the Decembrist Revolt. He was condemned to Siberia. Almost exactly three years after that cold January day when they had drunk champagne at Mikhailovskoe and recalled their Lyceum frolics, Pushchin arrived in far-off Chita to begin his exile. At the palisade the brave wife of one of the prisoners slipped him a piece of paper. He unfolded it and read:

O, my first friend, my precious friend!
I blessed my fate that happy day,
When in my isolated yard,
With sad snow buried deep and hard,

The little bell announced thy sleigh.
I pray to holy Providence
That to thy soul my voice in praise
Will come and bring thee living cheer.
That it will light thy prison drear
With beams of our Lyceum days.[17]

"The voice of Pushkin consolingly called to me!" his friend exclaimed joyfully. "Full of profound, revivifying gratitude, I could not embrace him as he embraced me when I first visited him in his exile." [18]

IV

In his visits to Trigorskoe during the fall of 1824 Pushkin learned an interesting bit of news. At that time Anna Vulf, the unhappy adorer of Pushkin, was corresponding with her cousin in Lubny, Anna Petrovna Kern. Of course, Anna Vulf told Pushkin of her cousin, and the name brought back vividly to his memory that night at the Olenins, five years before, when the languorous eyes and quiet smile of beautiful Anna Kern had made such a deep impression on him. No doubt he also learned her history to the smallest detail from her cousin. The Trigorskoe misses had little else to talk about. Anna Kern was then twenty-four years old. As a child, at the Tver estate of the Vulfs, she had seen much of her aunt Praskovya and her cousin Anna. Then the two Annas had read sentimental French and English romances together, skipping the risqué passages that they did not understand. In girlish fashion they gushed over these lengthy stories; Anna Vulf lost herself in sentimental dreams; her more attractive cousin seems to have acquired from the romances a taste for gallant love adventures.

As she grew up Anna Kern had many admirers, but at the age of seventeen her exacting father unceremoniously married her off to General Ermolai Fedorovich Kern, a man over fifty. To catch a general was the hope of every provincial damsel, and Anna was much envied by her friends. Yet she hated this unromantic match, about which she had had little say, loathed her husband, and would rather be in hell, she said, if she were certain not to meet him there. General Kern was a good soldier but a stern, unimaginative, and not very intelligent husband. Seven years of this married life, during which she bore her husband one child, had made her a most unhappy woman, though she had had her triumphs and many tributes to her beauty. During an army inspection at Poltava, Alexander I showed her marked attention, and, connoisseur of women that he was, he invited her to visit him in Petersburg. The young bride respectfully declined, naïvely explaining that her husband had to remain at Lubny. And then she countered: "Come to Lubny instead! It is so beautiful at Lubny!" Alexander laughingly replied: "I will come; absolutely, I will come." [19]   The emperor was even credited with comparing Anna Kern to Queen Louisa of Prussia.

Anna yearned to be separated from the general, but he kept a tight rein on his wife, and most of her efforts were directed toward thinking up excuses for visiting relatives and friends in order to get away from her husband. This was the purpose behind her visit to her parents in Lubny in 1824. Not far from her family's estate lived the erotic poet, A. G. Rodzyanko, whom Pushkin had visited on his way to Mikhailovskoe. (The two authors had become acquainted in Petersburg, and had had a slight quarrel, but time had mended this.) Anna saw much of Rodzyanko, and there is reason to believe that he was in love with her.

Pushkin took a lively interest in the correspondence between the two women and told Anna Vulf of his meeting with her cousin. Naturally, this was reported in a letter: "You made a vivid impression on Pushkin when you met him at the Olenins; he always says: 'She was so brilliant.'" [20]   Rodzyanko soon acquainted Anna Kern with Pushkin's poetry, and she eagerly read *The Prisoner of the Caucasus* and *The Bakhchisarai Fountain*. Naturally enough, both correspondents asked and answered many questions about Pushkin in their letters. From the information he obtained from Anna Vulf, and from current gossip, Pushkin did not form a very high opinion of Anna Kern at this time. Apparently the scandalous talk of her unhappy married life had reached his ears. When he learned in December that she was friendly with Rodzyanko, he wrote the poet a letter in which he refers disrespectfully to Anna Kern: "Explain to me, my dear, who is this A. P. K., who has written many tendernesses about me to her cousin? They say that she is a charming thing. . . . In any case, knowing your amorousness and *unusual talents* in all respects, I suppose your business is done or half done. I congratulate you, my dear; write an elegy or even an epigram on this." [21]

Pushkin wrote again in February, but Rodzyanko did not reply until May, and the answer was a joint effort by him and Anna Kern. Rodzyanko jokingly asserts that she will not have "legal children" by her husband and yet refuses to accept him as a substitute, which he blames on her "youth and inexperience." [22] Pushkin answered with a verse epistle to Rodzyanko in which he quite indecently celebrates his love and urges him to have the children. Later Pushkin presented the poem to Anna in person. Throughout this correspondence he exhibits the cynical attitude of a man who is winking at the affair of a friend with a woman of easy morals. To him she seemed the giddy wife of a laughable old general. However that may be, Anna Kern in Lubny had been reading his poetry and his letters and those of her cousin. Her mind was full of Pushkin, and she eagerly desired to see him. The opportunity soon presented itself.

In the middle of June 1825 Anna's aunt invited her to Trigorskoe. The superstitious Pushkin did not know of her coming, but he had a premonition. In her *Reminiscences* Anna tells of their meeting, and with keen feminine insight she makes several shrewd observations about Pushkin: "We were sitting at dinner and laughing. . . . Suddenly Pushkin entered with a great thick cane in his hand. Afterwards he frequently appeared at dinner time, but he did not sit down at the table; he ate alone, much earlier, and very little. He always arrived with huge watchdogs, wolf hounds. My aunt, next to whom I sat, introduced me; he bowed very low but did not say a word: shyness was apparent in his actions. I also found nothing to say to him, and we did not very quickly become acquainted and converse. Indeed, it was difficult to make friends with him; he was very awkward in his address: now he was boisterously jolly, then sad, then shy, then saucy, then endlessly obliging, then tiresomely boring; in fact, it was impossible to guess what mood he would be in at any minute. . . . In general, one must say that he was not able to conceal his feelings; he always expressed them sincerely and was indescribably splendid when anything agreeable moved him. . . . When he resolved to be pleasant, then nothing could compare with the brilliance, cleverness, and attractiveness of his conversation. . . . With this purpose he once appeared at Trigorskoe with his big black book, on the margins of which were drawn feet and heads, and said that he had brought it for me. We gathered about him and he read us his *Gypsies*. We were the first to hear this remarkable poem, and I shall never forget the rapture that gripped my soul. I was in ecstasies, as much from the flow of the verses of this marvelous work as from his reading, in which there was so much musicalness that I melted from happiness." [23]

The account is interesting, although perhaps somewhat overdone in the matter of Pushkin's reading. Yet we know that Anna Kern loved poetry and could inspire it, and in her reminiscences she is essentially truthful. And we know that Pushkin could read his verse with extraordinary effectiveness. The remark on his initial shyness in her presence is curious. Certainly he had shown no such shyness in his letters to Rodzyanko about her. Anna may have been a bit naïve in these matters. Pushkin was not shy with women, and by this time he had had much experience with them. Aware of her relations with the rakish Rodzyanko, he perhaps sensed the fact that any immediate impropriety would offend her as an indication that she did not value her reputation. It is clear from what followed, however, that this meeting with the beautiful Anna Kern had powerfully affected him. Pushkin, like Browning, was a creature of the single moment. Not the fruit of experience, but experience itself was the end. At this period of his life love had to burst into flame at once or not at all.

In the course of the next few weeks they saw each other almost every day. His initial awkwardness, real or feigned,

quickly vanished. She was delighted with his genuine tenderness and the cascade of witticisms he treated her to. The initial
idealized impression he had formed at the Olenins now returned
to displace the frivolous regard for her that gossip and Rodzyanko's letters had taught him. No doubt Anna's own cautious
and reserved behavior had much to do with his changed attitude.

One beautiful moonlit evening Praskovya Osipova suggested
that they all take a drive to Mikhailovskoe. Pushkin sat in one
carriage with the two Annas; Aleksei Vulf and his mother were
in the other. Anna Kern remembered how genial and entertain-
ing he was on the drive. And when they reached Mikhailovskoe
her aunt hinted to Pushkin that he show Anna the garden. "He
quickly took my arm," Anna recalled, "and hurried off impatiently, like a schoolboy who had suddenly received permission for a stroll. The details of our conversation I do not remember; he recalled our first meeting at the Olenins, and spoke
charmingly, rapturously about it, and at the end of our conversation he said: 'You have such a virginal manner; have you not
over you something like a cross?'" [24]

This budding romance was abruptly interrupted. Praskovya
Osipova decided next day that she, her niece, and other members of the family would set off for Riga. The reason for this
sudden decision is puzzling. She may have been angry with
Anna for taking Pushkin's attention away from her own marriageable daughters. Annenkov, the first biographer of Pushkin, says that Praskovya Osipova carried off her niece in order
to avoid a catastrophe. But it may well be that the aunt was
jealous and wanted to remove a young and seductive rival, and
that her moral considerations were merely a pretext. Pushkin
himself and the two Annas were convinced of this.

The morning after their walk in the garden, July 19, was the
date of departure. Pushkin appeared at Trigorskoe to bid Anna
farewell. As she was about to leave, he presented her with a
copy of the second chapter of *Eugene Onegin*. When she tried to
conceal it in her basket he looked fixedly at her and then
snatched the gift away. She pleaded, and he returned it. In the

cut pages of this little book Anna Kern found the manuscript containing the beautiful stanzas dedicated to her, which later were set to music by Glinka and others. The poem is one of the most perfect of Pushkin's lyrics, one in which form and content are so exquisitely joined that no translation can adequately produce the effect of the original. At least the sentiment, if not the exquisite harmony, is duplicated in the present rendering:

> Oh, I remember our brief meeting;
> Thou didst appear, all tenderness,
> Like some fair vision past me fleeting,
> Some genius of pure loveliness.
>
> By pain of hopeless grief surrounded,
> Amid the fears of noisy care
> Thy tender voice to me long sounded,
> And I recalled thy features fair.
>
> Years passed. The rebel blast, still stronger,
> Scattered my former dreams to air;
> I heard thy tender voice no longer,
> Remembered not thy features fair.
>
> Far off in exile's desolation
> Slowly my days dragged on in strife,
> Without God, without inspiration,
> Without tears, without love or life.
>
> Then something in my heart came beating;
> I saw thee now, all tenderness,
> Like some fair vision past me fleeting,
> Some genius of pure loveliness.
>
> My heart now beats in exaltation;
> There steals into it from above
> Both Deity and inspiration,
> And life, and tears, and holy love.[25]

Once more, though he was not yet quite aware of it, Pushkin was passionately in love. He desperately wanted to get in touch with his "genius of pure loveliness," but at first he hesitated to write, and he could not leave Mikhailovskoe. Two days after the separation he rushed a letter to Anna Vulf at Riga, knowing full well that she would show it to her cousin. At the conclusion of a stream of unkind advice to poor, adoring Anna Vulf — in which he tells her to wear her skirts short, for she has pretty feet, and to beware of ruffles, since her figure is plump — Pushkin suddenly gives way to his feelings about Anna Kern. "I walk every night in my garden," he writes, "and say to myself: She was here; the stone over which she stumbled lies on my table beside her cherry sprig. I write many verses — all this, if you wish, very much resembles love, but I swear to you that it is nothing of the kind. If I were in love, on Sunday [the day of Anna Kern's departure] I should have had convulsions of rage and jealousy, and I should not have been merely piqued. However, the idea that I mean nothing to her, that, having awakened and occupied her imagination, I have only amused her curiosity, that the memory of me will not for a moment return to distract her in the midst of her triumphs or make her days of sadness more somber, that her beautiful eyes will gaze upon some coxcomb of Riga with the same heart-rending and voluptuous expression — no, that idea is unbearable; tell her that I will die from this — no, do not say that; this delicious creature will mock me for that! But tell her that if her heart has not for me a secret tenderness, a melancholy and mysterious inclination, then I scorn her, do you hear? Yes, I scorn her, despite all the astonishment such a new sentiment must create in her. . . . Damnable visit, damnable departure!" [26]

This is quite a different language from that which Pushkin used in his letters to Rodzyanko. Not yet sure of himself, he resorts to a playful exaggeration. But an undercurrent of strong feeling is there. His personal contact with Anna Kern in the ideal setting of Trigorskoe, and her unquestioned charm had acted strongly on Pushkin. It is clear also that she had returned his affection, but with that moderation demanded by a romance in its early stages. At this precise time she was trying to obtain a separation from her husband, and perhaps the tale of a beautiful young wife in misfortune had helped to capture the poet's heart as well as his imagination.

Four days after this letter to Anna Vulf (July 25), Pushkin, out of patience with an indirect correspondence, made bold to write directly to Anna Kern. The fact marks the beginning of a series of unusual love letters. They are particularly precious, for Pushkin wrote to many women he loved but his letters have been lost. In these letters to Anna Kern we get an opportunity to learn how Pushkin wrote to a woman whose heart he wished to conquer.

"I know that a correspondence leads to nothing," Pushkin tells her in this first letter, "but I could not resist the desire to have a word from your pretty hand. Your visit to Trigorskoe has left a deeper and more painful impression on me than that of our meeting at the Olenins. In the isolation of my sad village I have nothing better to do than to try to keep from thinking about you. If you have even a drop of pity in your soul, then you ought to bestow it on me — but frivolity is always cruel, and all you ladies, while turning everybody's head, are delighted to know that a soul is suffering in your honor and glory. Farewell, divinity; I am enraged, and I am at your feet. A thousand tendernesses to Ermolai Fedorovich [General Kern], and my compliments to Mr. Vulf." Then he adds a postscript, advising her to read the letter in secret and conceal it in her bosom. If she feels that she will be compromised in writing to him, he suggests that she use another name. And he concludes: "On rereading these lines, I am ashamed of their sentimental tone." [27]

In the ironical "thousand tendernesses" to her husband and the "compliments to Mr. Vulf" one can detect a jealous pang. In fact, the Trigorskoe Lovelace, Aleksei Vulf, had already begun to practice his teacher's precepts on his fair cousin, and, from all accounts, with some success. Anna at once answered this letter and eagerly waited for a second. Unfortunately, none of her letters is extant, but we can judge of the encouragement she gave him from her reminiscences. Before he received her answer, he sent a second letter. He made the mistake, however, of enclosing it in the same package with a letter to Praskovya Osipova. The angry aunt, still determined to put an end to the romance, refused to give the letter to her niece, and hence we have no means of knowing its contents. Pushkin was annoyed and worried over the behavior of Praskovya Osipova, and he did his best to allay her suspicions and to remedy the ill-

feeling between aunt and niece. With this purpose in view, no
doubt, he wrote to the aunt after the incident of the purloined
letter: "You wish to know what I think of Mme. Kern? She is
complaisant; she understands everything; she is easily afflicted
and consoles herself as easily. She is timid in manners and bold
in actions; but she is very attractive." [28]

Pushkin's heart was in Riga. Immediately after receiving
Anna's first letter he replied, on the fourteenth of August: "I
reread your letter both long and large, and I say: Dear! charming! divine! And then: Ach, villainous! Pardon, my beauty, my
sweet, but it is so. There is no doubt that you are divine, but
sometimes you have no common sense." After playfully scold-
ing Anna for her desire to know something of the seal he uses,
Pushkin continues in a cynical vein: "You tell me that I do not
know your character. Of what import is your character to me?
I do not deride it at all. Ought pretty women to have a character? The essentials are eyes, teeth, hands, feet (I would add
the heart, but your cousin [Anna Vulf] has overused this word).
You say that it is easy to know you; do you wish to say to love
you? I am of this mind and am myself proof of it. I have behaved like a child of fourteen with you — it is unworthy of me,
but since I shall see you no more, I shall regain little by little
the ascendency which I have lost, and I will use it in order to
scold you. If ever we meet again, permit me . . . No, I do not
wish your promises; and then a letter is so cold; a prayer by
post has neither force nor emotion, and a refusal neither grace
nor voluptuousness. Then to our meeting — but let us speak of
other things. How is the gout of monsieur your husband? I
hope that he had a good attack of it the day after your arrival.
In fact, if you knew what an aversion mingled with respect I
feel for this man! Divinity, in the name of God, arrange it so
that he should play cards and have the gout at the same time!
This is my only hope!" After instructing her on the ways and
means of obtaining an excuse to visit Trigorskoe again, Pushkin revealed his jealousy once more in his remarks about Aleksei
Vulf: "What are you doing with your cousin? Answer me
frankly. Send him at once to his university; I do not know why,

but I do not like these students any more than I do M. Kern. He is a very worthy man, this M. Kern, a wise and prudent man, etc.; he has only one fault — it is that he is your husband. How can one be your husband? I cannot conceive this any more than I can conceive paradise." [29]

Letters and answers now continued with as much speed as the relatively slow post would permit over the two hundred and seventy miles between Mikhailovskoe and Riga. The main theme was the usual one of separated lovers. Pushkin's passion in the letters grows in intensity, and his persistent prayer is for Anna to find some excuse to return to Trigorskoe. She was a passive woman, and he despaired of arousing her to action. There can be no doubt that she earnestly wished to come, but there were obstacles — her jealous husband, her angry aunt, her reputation, and her lack of freedom. Anna's beautiful form continually haunted him. "Farewell," he writes at the end of one letter. "It is now night and your image appears to me, all sad and voluptuous; I see your glance, your mouth half-opened. Farewell! I believe myself at your feet, I press them, I feel your knees — I would give all my blood for one minute of reality. Farewell, and believe me in my madness; it is ridiculous but true." [30] In another he goes further. "If monsieur your husband bores you too much, leave him; but do you know how? Leave the whole family, take the post to Ostrov, and you will arrive — where? At Trigorskoe? Not at all! But at Mikhailovskoe. This is the fine project which has plagued my imagination for the last quarter of an hour. Yet imagine what would be my happiness! You will say: 'But the explosion, the scandal?' What the devil! Upon leaving a husband the scandal is complete, the rest is of no consequence. . . . If you come, I will be gay on Monday, exalted on Tuesday, tender on Wednesday, carefree on Thursday, and Friday, Saturday, and Sunday I will be everything that will please you, and the whole week at your feet." [31] At the same time he wrote to Praskovya Osipova in an effort to reconcile her with Anna. But the aunt, who was now also aware of her son's interest in Anna, had already left Riga for home in disgust. Shortly afterwards (September 22) Pushkin, in another letter to Anna, begs her to make peace with her aunt and to cease writing to Aleksei Vulf. Then he once again urges her to come, if only to neighboring Pskov, and advises her to use the sickness of her cousin Netty as a pretext for the visit. "Do not speak to me of admiration," he concludes. "This is not the sentiment. Speak to me of love, for which I have a thirst. But especially, do not speak to me of verses." [32] After this letter, on the testimony of Anna herself, Praskovya Osipova prevailed upon Pushkin to cease writing, or else he would make the relations between husband and wife worse than they were.

Finally, in early October, Anna managed to visit Trigorskoe again, but this time with her husband. The brave general had come to make peace between his wife and Praskovya Osipova, and in this he seems to have been successful. Apparently it was the only possible excuse for a visit that could be trumped up. According to Anna, Pushkin did not get along with the general; but he wrote later to Aleksei Vulf: "Her husband is a very dear man — we were introduced and became friendly." [33] However, Pushkin was no doubt leading his young rival off on a false scent. Despite the presence of General Kern, Pushkin saw his wife alone several times, and in her reminiscences Anna declares that "as formerly he was again tender to me, even more so, but afraid of all the eyes turned on him and me." [34]

The Kerns soon left Trigorskoe, and on the eighth of December Pushkin wrote Anna a last letter — with the exception of a brief impersonal note — in which his feeling for her does not appear to have diminished much. He thanks her for an edition of Byron she had sent him, asserts that he sees in her Byron's ideal heroine, and concludes: "It is you, then, it is always you that fate sends to delight my solitude! You are an angel of consolation, but I am only an ingrate, since I still complain. You are going to Petersburg; my exile weighs on me more than ever. Perhaps the change* which has just taken place will bring me closer to you, but I do not dare to hope for this. Put no faith in hope; it is a pretty woman who treats us as she treats old

* A reference to the death of Alexander I.

husbands. How is yours, my sweet genius? Do you know that in his image I conceive the enemies of Byron, among whom is his wife." And in the postscript he adds: "I take up my pen again to tell you that I am at your knees, that I love you always, that sometimes I detest you, as the day before yesterday when I said horrid things about you, that I kiss your beautiful hands, and I kiss them again in the hope of something better, that I can do no more, that you are divine, etc." [35]

This letter was the last of the series, but he had not seen the last of Anna Kern. Shortly after her second departure from Trigorskoe, she went to Petersburg, virtually separated from her husband. In the next few years she became closely associated with Pushkin's family and literary friends in ways that indicate her personal charm and attractive spirit. Pushkin's love for Anna soon grew cold, but for some six months he had loved passionately, with all his soul. Her own nature could not match the flame of his, and there seems no good reason to believe that she submitted to him on either of these two visits to Trigorskoe. Her very passivity unquestionably added fuel to the fire that burned within him. The letters she inspired, with their turbulent, mad transitions from endless tenderness to reproaches, to jealousy, almost to hate, eloquently reflect his overwrought feelings. To be sure, this was no pure love, and the beautiful lyric he dedicated to her must be interpreted as an idealized sublimation of his passion. Certainly Pushkin's future relations with Anna Kern are a little disillusioning when considered in the light of that period when she was his "genius of pure loveliness."

CHAPTER XII

"I Choke Him with a Tragedy"

> While wandering beside my lake,
> Wild ducks in noisy flocks take fright:
> Hearing my plaint in tuneful verse,
> They flee the shore in soaring flight.
>   *Eugene Onegin*

The statement has been made that all Russian poetry is a dream of self-oblivion. With some reservations this generalization is surprisingly true when applied to Russian poetry written before Pushkin's time. Not only did the poet forget himself, but the reality of his native land evaded him. A slavish devotion to foreign literatures merely served to remove the poet further from Russian reality. Pushkin inherited the tendency. His early works, the Southern verse tales for example, contain few essentially Russian features, and the Byronic flavor that pervades them only emphasizes their non-Russian aspects. Apart from his educational background and initial literary influences, Pushkin's wandering life over a part of the empire that had little connection with Russian reality no doubt had a direct bearing on the kind of poetry he wrote. His enforced sojourn in the village of Mikhailovskoe brought him back to the reality of his own country, to its history, peasants, and provincial life. Despite his vexations and despair, he underwent there a kind of moral regeneration, and he took a revived interest in the national Russian existence which was soon reflected in his poetry.

Not a little of this new interest was inspired by closer contact, through correspondence and in person, with the Lyceum friends of his youth. In January 1825 Pushchin had come; at the end of April, after much urging and impatient expectation on Pushkin's part, Delvig also visited Mikhailovskoe for a few days. It was a gala occasion for both. If anything, Delvig was dearer to him than Pushchin. Their devotion to each other, beginning with their boyish love for poetry at the Lyceum, was a rare example of mutual understanding and sympathy. A

remarkable poet in his own right, Delvig was indolent in literature, a refined pagan in his life, a simple and noble man with a
deep but quiet sense of humor. With frankness Pushkin pointed
the difference in their youthful attitudes toward poetry:

> But I already loved the crowd's applause:
> You for the muses sang and for your soul.[1]

He valued Delvig's taste and advice in literary and personal
matters to the utmost. On this visit they spent the days in endless talk about literature, varied occasionally by a game of billiards. After a late dinner they would walk over to Trigorskoe.
Praskovya Osipova's daughters and nieces made a great deal of
Delvig, but he listened phlegmatically to their admiration, and
preferred to lie on the divan and read poetry. This lack of interest in the young ladies may have been due to the fact that
Delvig was already engaged. Pushkin resented the news when
he first heard it. "May the devil take your marriage, your
marriage may the devil take!" [2] he wrote. But he eventually
grew much attached to Delvig's wife. In one of the anniversary
poems written for his Lyceum comrades Pushkin remembered
the visit of his friend:

> You came, inspired son of indolence,
> O Delvig mine: in me your happy voice
> Awoke a heartfelt warmth, long since grown cold . . .[3]

Another Lyceum friend, Prince A. M. Gorchakov, to whom
Pushkin had never been very close, visited in the neighborhood
of Mikhailovskoe in September. "We met," Pushkin wrote to
Vyazemski, "and parted quite coldly, at least on my side. He
is terribly lofty." [4] For lack of something better to do Pushkin
read his poetry, which was not much appreciated by his old
schoolfellow. Gorchakov, an aristocrat and successful careerist
in the foreign service, was inclined to look down on Pushkin.

A much more memorable visit was that of the poet, N. M.
Yazykov, who was the friend of Aleksei Vulf at the University
of Dorpat. Pushkin had become acquainted with his early
verse, and Delvig praised his talent. Through young Vulf,
Pushkin began making friendly overtures to Yazykov. In his
letters to Vulf at Dorpat he rarely failed to inquire after Yazy-

kov and to urge him to visit Trigorskoe during vacations.
There was an unusual generosity, rare enough among authors,
in Pushkin's relations with his fellow-writers. Mean envy never
cankered his criticisms, which were invariably just. His own
indebtedness to older writers he overstated, and he was always
ready with encouragement and advice to beginners. Yazykov
at Dorpat was not very responsive to Pushkin's friendly overtures, nor can it be said that he had a high opinion of him as a
poet. Several vacation periods passed without his acceptance
of the invitations urged upon him. But finally, in June 1826,
he came to Trigorskoe with Aleksei Vulf for a stay of several
weeks. At once Yazykov was charmed with Praskovya Osipova and her numerous family, and his opinion of Pushkin, by
whom he was now much impressed, radically changed. There
was revelry and literary conversation, and Yazykov remembered the visit as one of the happiest occasions of his life. He
dedicated to it several fine poems, in which he spoke of himself
as Pushkin's "listener" and "apprentice" [5] in poetry.

The visits of such friends cheered the country exile and gave
him a sense of contact with Russian reality which he had missed
in the south. And the peasants of Mikhailovskoe helped to
bring him closer to the soil of his native land. He was interested
in their customs and speech, and particularly in the vast popular lore which is the heritage of the Russian peasant. However,
he was not above playing the traditional part of the serf-owning
landlord. In May 1826 he wrote to Vyazemski: "This letter
will be presented to you by a very dear and good girl whom one
of your friends has imprudently fattened up. I am counting on
your philanthropy and friendship. Give her a refuge in Moscow and as much money as is necessary — and then direct her
to Boldino (my patrimony, where chickens, cocks, and bears
wander about). I ask you to take care, with fatherly tenderness, of the baby, if it should be a boy. I do not want to send
him into an educational institution — is it not possible to place
him in some village or other, even in Ostafevo [Vyazemski's
estate]? My dear, I am conscience-stricken, as God is my judge
— but now this is not a matter of conscience." [6] Vyazemski

succeeded in taking care of the pregnant peasant girl to Pushkin's satisfaction. As directed, she was sent to Boldino, the
Nizhni Novgorod estate of Pushkin's father.

There has been a good deal of speculation concerning the
identity of this girl, whom Pushkin called his "Eda," after the
name of the unfortunate heroine who had been seduced by the
hussar in Baratynski's well-known poem. It is very likely that
she was the same girl whom Pushchin noticed on his visit as outstanding among the seamstresses of Arina Rodionovna because of her appearance and figure. One of the most brilliant
students of Pushkin, P. E. Shchegolev,[7] believes that he has
positively identified her as Olga Mikhailovna, the daughter of
M. Kalashnikov, peasant steward of the Mikhailovskoe estate.
He even goes so far as to say that the name "Olga" on the
"Don Juan List" refers to her, and that Pushkin's romance
was the most satisfactory and helpful emotional experience of
his village exile. If emotional relaxation were necessary for the
unusual period of poetic composition at Mikhailovskoe, certainly Pushkin's turbulent and unfulfilled passion for Anna
Kern could hardly have contributed anything to it. It may
well be that his happy love for a simple peasant girl brought
him the peace and contentment he needed. In this instance,
however, speculation is idle. We know entirely too little about
the facts in the case. Pushkin enjoyed himself with his peasant
girl — and perhaps with more than one — as so many Russian
landowners did. But he seems to have had a real concern for the
child of "Eda," a unique corollary to such affairs in those days.
Somewhere in the Nizhni Novgorod district there probably
exists to this day a peasant line springing from Russia's greatest
poet.

II

> The fruits of my imaginings,
> My efforts in sweet-sounding verse,
> I read to her, my childhood friend,
> To her alone — my ancient nurse.
> *Eugene Onegin*

We have observed that contact with literary friends and with
the village life around him helped to bring Pushkin back to an

awareness of his native land and its importance as material for poetry. There was one other factor in this process — his old nurse. This peasant woman of seventy was all that remained to him, now that his kind grandmother had died, of the few precious memories of his childhood. Arina Rodionovna was the moving spirit of Mikhailovskoe. All the affairs of the estate revolved about her. She assumed responsibility for everything, but her chief care was the welfare of her nursling. A natural tendency to idealize this old woman has only served to obscure the essential traits of her character. She no doubt had the usual faults of advanced age and was certainly too much given to vodka. But her loyalty and devotion to her young master were beyond question. Their relations were touching, as deep as those of a devoted mother and son. In 1826, shortly after he had left Mikhailovskoe, and two years before her death, Arina dictated a letter to Pushkin that reveals something of the intimate bond that existed between them. "My beloved friend, Alexander Sergeevich," she wrote, "I received the letter and money which you sent me. For all your kindnesses I thank you with all my heart. You are constantly in my heart and mind, and only when I sleep will I forget you and your kindnesses to me. . . . Come to us at Mikhailovskoe, my angel — I will get all the horses ready for the road. . . . I will expect you and pray to God that He will permit us to meet. . . . Farewell, my little father, Alexander Sergeevich. For your health I have prepared a wafer and said prayers — live well, little friend — let us love one another. I am in good health, thank God — I kiss your hands and remain your much-loving nurse, Arina Rodion-ovna." [8] Not only Pushkin's own affectionate tributes in prose and poetry, but the praise of his observing literary friends, such as Yazykov and Delvig, testify to the strong and endearing personality of Arina Rodionovna. Remembering his visit to Mikhailovskoe, Yazykov dedicated a poem to Arina in which he recalls her "hallowed hospitality" and her wise talk; and upon her death he wrote a sincere tribute to her memory. [9]

In the long winter evenings Arina was Pushkin's sole companion. He enjoyed talking with her, and often he read her his

ARINA RODIONOVNA'S HUT AT MIKHAILOVSKOE

own productions. When the rhymes stuck and he wearied of
work, then he called upon his old nurse to amuse him with folk
tales from her endless store. A little vodka quickened her slow
speech, and she told her tales far into the night. "Do you know
my occupation?" he wrote to brother Lev in October 1824.
"Before dinner I write my reminiscences; I eat late. After dinner I ride; in the evening I listen to folk tales — and I make up
for the insufficiencies of my damnable education. How charming are these folk tales! Each one is a poem!" [10] And two
months later he repeated to a friend: "In the evening I listen to
the folk tales of my nurse, the original of Tatyana's nurse; you,
it appears, have seen her once; she is my only real friend, and
with her alone I am not bored." [11] In *Winter Evening* [12] he
pleasantly recalls these storytelling hours with Arina Rodionovna.

Pushkin was deeply appreciative of the peculiar charms of
folk literature. At Mikhailovskoe he wrote down, in outline, a
number of the tales that he heard from his old nurse, and later
several of them served as sources for excellent poems. He
learned from her the idiom of the people and that curious artlessness which distinguishes folk from sophisticated literature.
One of these popular tales, *The Bridegroom*, he turned into verse
at this time. Though not entirely successful, it marks the beginning of a practical interest in folk literature which remained
with Pushkin for the rest of his life and inspired some of his
most characteristic productions.

During the two years spent at Mikhailovskoe Pushkin had
plenty of leisure — perhaps more than he wished — to devote
to literature and study. And on the whole, it cannot be said
that he wasted his time. Country life, nature, and contacts
with his old nurse, peasants, and literary friends — all contrived to provide him with inspiration. He continued his
studies of Italian and English, and embarked on extensive
reading programs to remedy his "damnable education." He
completely subscribed to the conviction that mental discipline
was a prime requisite for a poet, and valued learning, never
ceasing in his efforts to acquire knowledge. One of the chief

attractions at Trigorskoe was a large library; and the demand
for books was a most persistent one in his letters. The works
he read and those mentioned in his correspondence at this time
make up an extraordinary list of classical and important minor
productions drawn from antiquity and from Western European
and Russian literature. He now began to build up a library of
his own which would have reflected credit on a profound scholar
in the humanities. Some thirty-five large boxes were required to
move this library when he left the village. And he read these
books with care; many of them contain his marginal annota-
tions.

Pushkin's correspondence at Mikhailovskoe grew tremendously. In fact, no two other years of his life are so rich in this
respect. Very many of these letters were to literary friends —
Bestuzhev, Ryleev, Vyazemski, Delvig, Pletnev, Zhukovski,
Baratynski, Nikolai Raevski, and Katenin. And often their
chief subject is literature, not only his own productions but
those of his contemporaries. The sense of artistic maturity
that had begun to dawn upon him in Odessa now became a
settled conviction. "I feel that my soul is quite developed; I
can create," [13] he wrote with assurance to Nikolai Raevski in
1825. His early productions he began to shoulder aside, after
surveying them in the light of new critical criteria. He was not
only aware of the influences on his own works, but he knew the
extent to which he was influencing contemporary poetry. His
critical sense was intuitive and profound, like that of Coleridge
or Keats, and he possessed a wide background of literary knowledge to support his judgments. He began to turn his creative
eye inward in an effort to examine his own method of composition. "Poetry," he declared, "is ordinarily the exclusive
passion of the few who are born to be poets; it embraces and en-
gulfs all the observations, all the powers, all the impressions of
their lives." [14] Though limited by the aesthetic jargon and ideas
of his time, Pushkin was inclined to throw over the traditional
eighteenth-century notions of poetry, particularly in the matter of inspiration and the part it theoretically played in composition. "To seek inspiration," he wrote toward the end of

his life, "always seemed to me a ridiculous and absurd whimsy: do not hunt for inspiration; it must find the poet itself." [15]   But he had been thinking about the significance of inspiration much earlier.   In an unusual passage (1826–1827) he objected to the views on inspiration of his old school friend Kiukhelbeker, whom he valued as a critic.   "The critic," Pushkin maintained, "confuses inspiration with exaltation.   Inspiration is the disposition of the soul to a lively acceptance of impressions, hence to a swift consideration of ideas, so that it contributes to an explanation of the same.   Inspiration is as necessary in poetry as in geometry. . . .   Exaltation excludes tranquillity, a vital condition of the beautiful.   Exaltation, having arranged the parts in relation to the whole, does not presuppose the forces of the mind.   Exaltation is not continuous, unbroken; hence it has not the power to produce truly great perfection (without which there is no lyric poetry). . . .   Exaltation is an intense state of the imagination itself; inspiration may exist without exaltation, but exaltation does not exist without inspiration." [16]   The explanation is essentially rational — the divine role of inspiration among the romantics is minimized.   At the age of twenty-six Pushkin had arrived at the mature conclusion that the intellect plays the larger part in so-called poetic inspiration.

This consciousness of his leading position in literature is clearly reflected in Pushkin's literary enterprises throughout the two years of the Mikhailovskoe period.   Of course, money was a driving force.   He was now virtually dependent upon poetry for his whole income.   Though his life in the country was relatively simple, there were demands to be met, necessities to buy.   At times his needs were acute.   "By Christ and by God, I ask you to get *Onegin* away from the censor at once," he wrote to Lev. "Let glory go . . . . its . . . . . . — I need money.   Do not haggle over the verses — let them cut, tear, lacerate the whole 54 strophes, but money, for God's sake, money!" [17]   He was even forced to try to collect the hundred rubles which uncle Vasili had borrowed fourteen years ago when he was taking him up to Petersburg for his Lyceum entrance examinations.   Yet when money from *Onegin* began to come in, we find him instructing

his brother to use some of the proceeds to help the victims of
the terrible Petersburg flood, cautioning him, however, not to
breathe a word of his philanthropy to anyone. Though by necessity he grew more and more exacting in money matters,
Pushkin was really generous, spent freely, and could never refuse
a friend a loan.

While at Mikhailovskoe Pushkin at first entrusted the business of publishing his poetry to his brother. But he soon discovered that Lev was too irresponsible for this task. On the
whole, he handled the business badly and was not above dip-
ping into the profits. Pushkin quarreled with him and finally
turned his publishing affairs over to Delvig and Pletnev. The
latter assumed the larger share of the burden. Pushkin had
known Pletnev, who was a young professor in the University of
Petersburg, since his Lyceum days, and had complete faith in
his taste and general honesty. On his own side, Pletnev was devoted to Pushkin, and the publication of the poet's works could
hardly have fallen into better hands.

Of course, it was not only money that drove Pushkin on to
composition. He had to write poetry. If he had any doubts
about the service he was performing, his friends, such as Zhukovski, would have destroyed them. They impressed upon him
the fact that he was a genius and the country's adornment; and
Pushkin himself was aware of the revolution he was effecting in
Russian letters. Previous to his time, writers in Russia had not
regarded themselves as artists; they were moralists. Certainly,
eighteenth-century writers would have been puzzled by Pushkin's notion that the object of poetry is poetry. He was deeply
conscious of his position as an artist, and in Mikhailovskoe his
renewed contact with Russian life filled him with the desire to
treat that life artistically.

While in Kishinev, Pushkin had been anxious to publish a
volume of his short poems and lyrics, and he bethought himself
of the manuscript he had lost at cards to his bosom friend of the
Green Lamp, Vsevolozhski. At that time his efforts to buy
back the manuscript had failed. He continued these efforts
when he was living in Odessa, but it was not until he got to

Mikhailovskoe that he succeeded in obtaining the manuscript. These youthful verses were now rigorously overhauled, and he also added a number of short poems.

At Mikhailovskoe Pushkin's lyrical production was not extensive; he was definitely leaving this genre behind, though he never abandoned it entirely. However, he wrote some of his most remarkable lyrics during these two years. A few of them have biographical significance, but on the whole he was growing more objective, more concerned with transmuting emotional commonplaces through perfect form and expression. The lyric grows by its own inner laws; the poet cares little for subtleties of thought or psychological analysis. His aim is to discover the precise form for the relatively simple idea which he wishes to express. There is a quality in these short poems which recalls the lyrics of Herrick, with their compact union of form and expression. And it is as impossible to catch their rare quality in translation as it would be in the case of Herrick's. Among the best of the short poems written at Mikhailovskoe are three already mentioned — the one addressed to Anna Kern, the poem on the death of Amaliya Riznich, and *Winter Evening*. To these must be added *The Prophet*,[18] which goes as far in the direction of mysticism as anything Pushkin ever wrote. Critics have strained at the sense in an effort to read the author's religious views into the verses. But this famous poem is simply an extraordinarily brilliant representation of a Biblical theme, and nothing more. It proves only that Pushkin was reading his Bible at Mikhailovskoe, and that he had put far behind him the religious cynicism of the *Gavriliada*. A more personal lyric, and the longest and one of the finest, is *The Nineteenth of October*, composed in 1825 for the anniversary of the Lyceum. A wonderfully sustained mellowness and nobility run through it. Nowhere else has Pushkin conveyed with such sincere feeling a sense of the close bond of friendship which united him to his schoolfellows. In January 1826, supervised by Pletnev, who was assisted by Delvig and Zhukovski, his first volume of short poems appeared, bearing the simple title, *Poems of Alexander Pushkin*.[19]

III

> I am able to value Poetry, and I
> know that you were born to be a
> great poet and ought to be the
> honor and jewel of Russia.
>
> *Zhukovski in a letter to*
> *Pushkin, 1826*

Pushkin's main creative activities during the Mikhailovskoe period, however, were directed towards long poems. He put the finishing touches on *The Gypsies*, which upon its appearance in 1827 received more unqualified approval from both critics and public than any of his works up to that time or later. Meanwhile, he worked hard on *Eugene Onegin*, completing the third through the sixth chapters during the two years of his country exile. The story had expanded since the Kishinev conception, and the characters had developed into finished personalities. *Eugene Onegin* is a psychological novel in verse; in design and execution it is more like Chaucer's *Troilus and Criseyde* than *Don Juan*, which pretty certainly inspired it.

The plot is as simple as that of *Troilus and Criseyde*. Eugene is a typical young dandy of the period. With a superficial Frenchified education, he plunges into the dissipations of fashionable Petersburg society, leading a life similar to Pushkin's during his first sojourn in the capital. Although he enjoys considerable success, Eugene soon tires of balls, theaters, and love affairs. He grows melancholy and cynical, despises his existence, and assumes a kind of Childe Harold pose of frustration (though this is less of a pose than a genuine *taedium vitae*, not rare among young men of the time). His father dies, leaving him nothing but debts. At the same time he hears of the illness of his uncle, and the poem opens with his cynical reflections as he drives with all speed to the bedside of the sick man. He arrives too late, but he finds himself the sole inheritor of his uncle's estate.

The second chapter opens with Eugene's decision to settle down in the country. He feels that life there will agree very well with the melancholy disposition of his soul. His existence in the country, as already observed, is not unlike that of Pushkin at

Mikhailovskoe. He scorns his neighbors, who set him down as a madman and a freethinker. At this point a young poet, Vladimir Lenski, returns to his estate in the district, fresh from his studies at Göttingen. He is an idealist, full of German romanticism, and writes sentimental lyrics on Platonic love. As the only two educated people in the neighborhood, Eugene and Lenski become friends. Though their views on most things are poles apart, Eugene grows to like Lenski for his naïve enthusiasm, and condescendingly listens to his poetry, which is all that is necessary for Lenski. Lenski is engaged to a childhood sweetheart, Olga Larina, a young, giddy, carefree girl. The Larins are a typical provincial family, such as Pushkin met at Trigorskoe. Tatyana, however, is in striking contrast to her younger sister, Olga. She is a sensitive girl who has been nourished on the romantic nonsense of sentimental novels and the superstitions of her old nurse. But her simple, dreamy nature betrays a frankness, loyalty, and depth of feeling which make her the most superior character in the whole poem.

At the beginning of the third chapter Lenski persuades Eugene to visit the Larins and see his bride-to-be. On the way home Eugene unfeelingly comments on Olga and tells Lenski that if he were a poet he would have chosen the elder sister. Meanwhile, Tatyana has fallen in love with Eugene, and the neighbors begin to gossip about a match. He appeals to her as a romantic ideal, and after a sleepless night she writes him a letter filled with all the tenderness and longing of a girl in love for the first time. She frankly confesses her passion and throws herself upon Eugene's mercy. Two days pass without an answer, and she is desperate with impatience and shame. Then suddenly Lenski and Eugene appear again at the Larins. Tatyana runs out to the garden, and Eugene follows and meets her in one of the paths. At this point Pushkin characteristically ends the chapter, saying that he is tired and must rest.

The next chapter opens with Eugene's worldly thoughts above love. With annoying superiority he delivers a sermon-like answer to Tatyana's letter. He tells her that he admires her greatly, and that if he ever had a mind to marry, he would certainly select her. But he has no intention of marrying, and he pictures to her how unhappy married life with him would be. Smugly he has recourse to that last refuge of the pursued male:

> I love you with a brother's love,
> And, it may be, more tenderly.[20]

Then he departs, after telling Tatyana how fortunate she is that he has not taken advantage of her lack of experience in such matters. This cold rejection does not destroy her passion. If anything, her love grows stronger. She is convinced that he is the only man she will ever love, and she languishes and grows pale and thin.

A famous description of winter introduces the fifth chapter. Time has passed. After some persuasion, and by assuring him that it will be a small affair, Lenski induces Eugene to go to Tatyana's name-day party. The night before, Tatyana has a horrible dream (one of the most brilliant of the many brilliant passages in the poem) in which Eugene, under fantastic circumstances, takes possession of her and kills Lenski in a quarrel. On the name-day Eugene arrives late for dinner, and at once becomes out of sorts at finding a large gathering present, composed mostly of vulgar provincial landowners. He is further irritated by the effect his presence produces on Tatyana. She almost faints, and only by a great effort recovers herself. Eugene cannot abide any feminine show of emotion in public. Out of sheer spite he decides to punish Lenski for misrepresenting the number and character of the guests. When the dancing begins he purposely avoids Tatyana, asks Olga for most of the dances, and openly flirts with her. The giddy Olga enjoys herself hugely, and Lenski's rage mounts. Finally, when she refuses her betrothed the last dance because she has promised it to his friend, Lenski dashes out of the house, determined to challenge Eugene to a duel.

The very next morning, at the beginning of the sixth chapter, Lenski sends his challenge by an experienced duelist. Eugene, "without superfluous words, said that he was *always ready.*" [21] For a moment his conscience troubles him. He really likes

Lenski, but since an old and practiced duelist had been drawn in as his friend's second, he fears the ridicule that might fall upon him should he withdraw. The fight is scheduled for the next day. Meanwhile, Lenski forgets his resolve to punish the faithless Olga by not visiting her before the duel. He goes to the Larins, and his premeditated sternness is completely melted by Olga's ingenuous and gay affection. He says nothing of the imminent duel and returns home to bed in the airy mood of the reconciled lover. Unable to sleep, he opens his Schiller. But he cannot read, and finally ends by writing a pretty poem, filled with sentimental foreboding of the morrow. The next morning Eugene arrives late for the duel. He is very casual about the whole affair, and with studied rudeness brings his French valet along for a second. The opponents approach the barrier. Eugene shoots first, and Lenski is killed outright. The whole account of the duel, with the beautiful final lyric stanzas which end the sixth chapter, poignantly suggests the last duel Pushkin himself fought.

Pushkin did not get beyond this point while at Mikhailovskoe, but at the expense of chronology, something will be gained by finishing the summary of the poem now. In the seventh chapter, after the tragic outcome of the duel, Eugene departs on his travels, unable to bear the bloodstained shade of Lenski which haunts him in the country. After a surprisingly brief "decent" interval, Olga forgets her betrothed and marries an army officer. Tatyana remains alone, her mind still filled with Eugene. She loves the consolation of nature, and on one of her rambles she comes to Eugene's house. The attendant lets her in, and she surveys her hero's study. She returns the next day, and after some tearful memories sits down to read his books. This perusal of Eugene's favorite works throws new light on his puzzling character, and Tatyana begins to have a different opinion of him. Her mother finally takes her to Moscow to get a husband. At first Tatyana's country manners make her feel shy and appear ridiculous to the sophisticated city dandies. But the more discerning recognize her real qualities, and at last she is married off to a distinguished prince.

What Pushkin had intended for the next chapter, the story of
Onegin's travels, he relegated to an appendix. The eighth chapter begins with Eugene's return to Petersburg. At a ball he
meets an old friend, no other than the prince whom Tatyana
has married. The husband presents him to his wife. Eugene is
amazed at the transformation of Tatyana. She is no longer the
timid, provincial girl, but a beautiful, majestic, and cold queen
of Petersburg society. The next day he is invited to a party at
her house. Alone with her for a moment, he acts like a bashful
schoolboy. He can find nothing to say, and her complete indifference leaves him bewildered. It is now his turn to fall in love,
and his behavior is more extreme than that of the country girl
who once loved him. He dogs her steps everywhere, writes her
passionate notes, but always he is met with coldness and silence.
Tatyana has nothing but scorn for him. In despair, he shuts
himself up for a whole winter. And in the spring, determined on
a reckoning, he drives straight to Tatyana's house, enters, and,
finding no one to announce him, goes directly to her room,
where he discovers her in tears over his unanswered letters.
Eugene throws himself at her feet. After some confusion,
Tatyana bids him rise and says: "I once listened to your lesson;
today it is my turn." [22] She begins by rehearsing the love she
had for him in her country home and his rejection of it. And
she asks him why he loves her now. Is it her new position in
society? Or is it mere snobbishness? She wonders if he is
merely trying to bring about her fall, which would be noticed by
everybody and gain for him a flattering reputation in society.
Then she frankly admits that she is unhappy and would give
everything she possesses to return to those old days when happiness was so possible and so within her grasp. And she concludes her "lesson":

> I love you (why dissimulate?)
> But I was given to another;
> And I'll be true to him forever.[23]

She leaves the room. Completely crushed, Eugene remains
alone. At this moment he hears the clink of spurs on the stairs,

and the husband enters. Pushkin tantalizingly breaks off his narrative:

> And at this moment, bad for him,
> My reader, we now take our leave,
> For long . . . perhaps forever.[24]

With gentle humor mingled with regret, he ends his great work with the well-known lines:

> Blessed is he who left life's feast
> Early, not draining to the dregs
> The last full bottle of its wine,
> Who did not read the story through
> And suddenly could part with it,
> As I now part with my Onegin.[25]

In February 1825 the first chapter of *Eugene Onegin* was published. Because of the great length of time it took to write it, Pushkin preferred to print the chapters separately; besides, this method brought him in more money. The praise of the public and critics was not unmixed with censure. The public may well have been irritated by the tone of *The Conversation of a Bookseller with a Poet*, which was included in this printing of the first chapter of *Eugene Onegin*. In these verses Pushkin declared the poet's scorn for the public, a feeling he was to repeat often in the future. The poet stands apart from the people; he is an unfettered spirit, free in his life and work. The reviewers maintained that *Eugene Onegin* was an imitation of Byron. Even his friend Ryleev took him to task for this. "You may be our Byron," he wrote, "but, for God's sake, for Christ's sake, for your beloved Mahomet's sake, do not imitate him!" [26] Bestuzhev likewise, while admiring the poem, saw in it an imitation of *Don Juan*. Pushkin was vexed with these critics. He would not have denied that the poem was inspired by *Don Juan*; that he had learned from Byron (and also from Sterne) something of the narrative method which allowed him to write a loosely constructed tale of modern life in a mixed style, and which enabled him to mingle comedy and tragedy, to play with the plot by introducing sentimental or humorous digressions. The method is that of *Don Juan* and *Tristram Shandy*. Yet

Pushkin would have asserted that *Eugene Onegin* was the most original of his works. And in this he would have been correct. It is very likely that the criticism of Ryleev and Bestuzhev, who were deep in the conspiracy to reform Russia, was somewhat inspired by the feeling that Pushkin should have selected a subject more germane to the political and social struggle of the times. The tendentiousness which was ultimately to dominate Russian literature had already set in.

It was to take the critics some time before they realized that Pushkin's great poem was the most Russian thing he ever wrote. The resemblances to *Don Juan* are superficial, the differences tremendous. The work grew under the author's pen during the eight years it took him to compose it; the plan changed, and the poem reflects Pushkin's own changing spiritual, emotional, and artistic development. Despite this, *Eugene Onegin* is a well-rounded whole, with a definite beginning, middle, and end. The style also changes, but here too a certain consistency obtains. The light, sparkling manner of the opening chapter sobers in the later sections, but whenever Pushkin desires, even at the conclusion of the poem, he can reproduce the pure lyric flights of the first chapter. Above all, the faultless perfection of the intricately rhymed fourteen-line stanzas is sustained throughout the whole work of over five thousand lines with extraordinary artistry. The total effect of the style is that of light, easy spontaneity which never lapses from the beginning to the end.

A vast literature has grown up about *Eugene Onegin*, but this is not the place to consider in detail the various matters of verse technique, characterization, and poetic merits. It is sufficient to say that in *Eugene Onegin* Pushkin created a work of the utmost significance to the future of Russian literature. Succeeding authors from Lermontov to Chekhov have been indebted to the story and characters of *Eugene Onegin*. In the five thousand lines of this poem Pushkin has brought to life a definite period of Russian national existence with all the authenticity and brilliance of the historical picture of *War and Peace* to which Tolstoi devoted hundreds of pages. There is much lyricism, some conscious romanticism, and a good deal of sheer subjectivity in treatment. But the real direction Pushkin pursues is that of objective realism, the direction that had begun to manifest itself in the Odessa period. He had quite thoroughly broken with his early subject matter and method. Byron was behind him. He was now interested in Russian life and its treatment in realistic verse.

This desire to deal with Russian life in an objective manner lay behind the creation of the work that most absorbed Pushkin during his exile at Mikhailovskoe — *Boris Godunov*. In fact, he preferred to think this play his greatest production. He had begun to read Shakespeare in Odessa; at Mikhailovskoe Shakespeare was perhaps his favorite foreign author. Soon he informed Nikolai Raevski of his delight. "Probability of situation," he wrote, "and truth of dialogue, here is the veritable rule of tragedy. I have not read Calderon or Vega, but what a man is this Shakespeare!" [27] With all his enthusiasm he read discriminately. *The Rape of Lucrece* struck him as a very weak poem, and he wondered what would have happened if the harassed lady had slapped Tarquin's face at the appropriate moment. "Perhaps," Pushkin remarked, "that would have cooled his venturesome nature, and in shame he would have felt constrained to be on his way." [28] The idea occurred to him to parody Shakespeare's poem, and in two mornings he wrote the highly amusing *Count Nulin*.[29] The Russian Tarquin, Count Nulin, is a nobleman fresh from Paris. His carriage breaks down outside the house of a provincial squire. The count is led astray by his hostess's coquetry, and at night he sallies forth to her bedroom to make a real conquest. But he gets a resounding slap in the face for his pains and beats a humiliating retreat. The poem is a little gem of gaiety and realistic characterization.

Shakespeare's chronicle plays inspired Pushkin with the idea of writing a similar production on a theme drawn from Russian history. At this time the Russian stage, though remarkable for its acting and lavish production, had little in the way of truly fine native repertoire. Playwrights were still dully imitating French neoclassic drama, with its unities and Alexandrine couplets. At the opening of the romantic period Shakespeare was eagerly accepted by Russian critics, but as yet no one had appeared to write successful plays in his manner. This was the task Pushkin set for himself. He was convinced that the laws suited to the theater were the popular laws of Shakespearean drama, and not the courtly etiquette of the tragedies of Racine.

Pushkin was deliberate in this effort to impart a new direction to Russian drama. He felt that the attempt was to be of importance to his country's literature, and he set about planning the work with the greatest of care. The material of his play he obtained largely from Karamzin's *History*. The action covers the period from 1598 to 1605, and concerns the reign of Boris Godunov and the usurpation of the False Dmitri. Shakespeare's chronicle plays were his avowed models. He began by throwing over the sacred unities. "They have tried to base the laws [of drama] on probability," he wrote, "but it is precisely in this respect that the very nature of drama is forgotten; without mentioning times, places, etc., what the devil is there of probability in an auditorium cut in two, one part of which is occupied by 2000 persons who appear not to be seen by those on the stage!" [30] He thus explains his purpose to Raevski: "After the example of Shakespeare, I have limited myself to developing an epoch and historical personages without seeking theatrical effects, romantic pathos, etc. . . . The style is a mixture. It is trivial and low where I have been obliged to present common and rustic people." [31]

Pushkin had so completely assimilated the spirit of his model that the result was genuinely Shakespearean, not a mere imitation. He worked furiously on his tragedy. Even *Eugene Onegin* was put aside. His letters at this time are full of reports on his progress. Finally, at the end of October 1825, he announced with delight to Vyazemski: "My tragedy is ended. I read it over aloud, alone, and I clapped my hands and shouted: Hey there, Pushkin, hey, you son of a bitch!" [32]

Later, when he read *Boris Godunov* to Moscow friends, they hailed it as epoch-making. The blank verse and the complete objectivity were novel. Yet the play did not start a new movement in Russian drama, as Pushkin hoped, nor can it be said to justify the high place he gave it among his works. In sheer dramatic writing he was to surpass it. The central tragic situation is infected by Karamzin's sentimental treatment of the subject, and on the whole the verse is static. At times the scenes and characters do not come to life, and there is little of the sustained dramatic power of Shakespeare. But as a pioneer work it deserves high praise. There are some brilliant scenes and splendid passages of rhetorical poetry. Compared to any drama that had preceded it in Russia, *Boris Godunov* is an extremely fine performance, and its place in Pushkin's development is of prime significance. He completely effaces himself from the play, and this objectivity, so strongly developed during his exile at Mikhailovskoe, eventually became a chief characteristic of his later poetry.

CHAPTER XIII

The Tsar Commands

Sometimes my life was like
an epigram, but in general it
was an elegy...
*Pushkin in a letter to
Zhukovski, 1825*

Freedom of movement and freedom of expression were vital
conditions of existence for Pushkin. He never possessed either
in an unqualified degree. As a child he had resented the domi-
nation of parents; as a schoolboy he had fretted over the restrictions of the Lyceum; as a mature man he wore himself out
in a struggle to escape the shackles of both government and
society. Despite his literary industry at Mikhailovskoe and the
comfort afforded by his Trigorskoe neighbors or the visits of
dear friends, Pushkin was not at all happy. He could never
forget the fact that he was literally a prisoner in a kind of detention camp. Upon his arrival in the village he had been
obliged to promise von Aderkas, governor of Pskov, that he
would behave himself and not write anything objectionable to
the authorities. He could dismiss with apparent levity Pushchin's indignation over the petty spying, but in reality he hated
this surveillance. The authorities went so far as to interfere
with his correspondence, and sometimes his own letters and
those of friends did not reach their destination. Then, too,
though he enjoyed country life, he could not be content with it
for long. The city, with its pleasures, excitement, and friends,
was his natural habitat. During his exile at Mikhailovskoe
Pushkin's fondest hope was to escape from his village prison.
He was even ready, if possible, to escape from Russia.

While his letters from Mikhailovskoe are generally lively and
good-humored, time and again dissatisfaction with his situation
flares forth. Good friends in Moscow and Petersburg tried to
console him, but their epistolary encouragement did little to

alleviate his ennui. Everywhere, he complained, was mortal boredom. His resentment against the government grew intense. "Yesterday I received a ridiculously funny letter from Vyazemski," he wrote to Zhukovski. "How can he preserve his jollity in Russia?" [1] Had the Petersburg officials entirely forgotten him again? "Six Pushkins signed the Act of Election," he told Delvig. "From ignorance only two affixed their signatures. But I, their literate descendant, what am I, where am I?" [2]

The possibility of escape, as we have seen, had occurred to Pushkin while he was in Odessa. Now he began to entertain the idea in all seriousness. At first he had recourse to his aneurysm in a frank attempt to obtain legal permission to go abroad for a cure. There can be no doubt that Pushkin really suffered from varicose veins, but he patently exaggerated his complaint for purposes of his own. The initial step in his plan was to let friends and family know that he was badly in need of treatment, which, of course, he could not obtain at Mikhailovskoe. Friends and the family soon began to talk. Zhukovski heard and grew worried. He was close to the imperial family, tutor to the tsar's son, and hence his influence counted for something. Pushkin soon received an anxious letter from him. "My dear friend," wrote Zhukovski in May 1825, "I ask you to answer this letter as soon as possible, but answer it humanly and not insanely. I have heard from your brother and mother that you are ill. Is it true? Is it true that in your legs you have something like aneurysm, and that for ten years you have amused yourself with this guest without saying a word to anyone? I do not understand the reason for such a secret love for aneurysm, and I cannot share it with you." [3] Zhukovski then admits that treatment cannot be found in Pushkin's neighborhood, and that he will take steps to get him permission to go to Riga. He demands an immediate answer.

The ruse was working. Though not exactly abroad, Riga might serve as a jumping-off place. Zhukovski was not aware of the fact that his young friend had used this same aneurysm in Odessa as a reason for resigning from the government service.

Pushkin did not delay his reply. "Here is your human answer: I have had aneurysm for ten years, and with God's help I may be able to carry on for three more years. Consequently, the matter is not urgent, but Mikhailovskoe is suffocating me. If the tsar gives me permission to go abroad (in Europe), that would be a blessing for which I should be eternally grateful to him and my friends." 4 Pushkin incautiously suggests here his ulterior purpose: the illness can wait, but he must get out of Mikhailovskoe. And he was prompt in pressing the advantage of Zhukovski's interest, for with this letter to him he sent one to the emperor. The latter epistle is phrased most tactfully. Only absolute necessity has obliged him to break the respectful silence he has observed since his disgrace. Then he drags out the ten-year-old aneurysm and concludes: "Sire, I have formerly been reproached for having profited from the generosity of your nature, but today I swear it is to that only that I have recourse. I beg your majesty to permit me to retire to some place in Europe where I may not be deprived of all assistance." 5 He now sat back hopefully to await results.

His well-laid plans, however, soon received a check. Pushkin's mother experienced one of her rare moments of maternal solicitude for her famous son. Besides, the occasion presented an excellent opportunity for the dramatics which she fancied no less than her histrionic husband. It is certain that Zhukovski and Karamzin, who had no knowledge of Pushkin's real purpose, encouraged her. Nadezhda Osipovna took it upon herself to write a heart-rending letter to Alexander I, imploring the tsar to have pity on her son, whose life was threatened by ten years of aneurysm. The mother's plea brought a quick response. Pushkin was given permission to obtain treatment. But alas! not abroad, or at Riga, but in neighboring Pskov! The emperor, or his advisers, did not trust the prisoner of Mikhailovskoe beyond the jurisdiction of Russia. In a secret dispatch the Pskov officials were even commanded, if Pushkin should come there for treatment, to keep a close watch on his behavior and conversation. Pushkin was furious. He dispatched a stinging letter to Zhukovski: "The unexpected favor

of his majesty touched me unspeakably, all the more so in that
the local governor has already offered to obtain quarters for me
in Pskov, but I shall strictly adhere to the command of my first
superior. I inquired about the Pskov doctors; they informed me
that there is a certain Vsevolozhski there, a very clever veteri-
nary and famous in the learned world for his book on the curing
of horses. Despite all this, while still being sensible of the
fatherly leniency of his majesty, I have resolved to remain at
Mikhailovskoe." [6]

Pushkin accepted the unfortunate interference of his mother
in good faith, and was inclined to ascribe the miscarriage of his
scheme to the loose talk of Petersburg friends. He complained
bitterly to his sister of his ridiculous situation in a letter which
he angrily concluded: "I am told that the public is indignant;
I am, also, but because of the carelessness and frivolity of
those who mix in my affairs. Oh, my God, deliver me from my
friends!" [7]

Of course, Pushkin had no desire to go to Pskov. He knew
perfectly well that there he would be under the suspicious eyes
of the authorities, even more so than at Mikhailovskoe. But
he was not yet ready to admit defeat. A more ambitious plan
occurred to him in which the prime object of escape from Russia
was very thinly disguised again by the excuse of illness. In
this new scheme he enlisted the aid of Aleksei Vulf, who had
been so eager to assist that he had even offered to get his friend
to Dorpat in the guise of his servant, a suggestion that Pushkin
had rejected for fear of compromising the young student.
Praskovya Osipova was also involved in the new attempt. At
Dorpat lived a certain Dr. I. F. Moier, a distinguished surgeon
and a patron of art. Pushkin conceived the idea of making him
a pretext for a visit to Dorpat. The plan was to get Moier to
offer his services officially, in order to allay suspicion. Once in
Dorpat, a customary frontier point for travelers abroad, Pushkin hoped that the doctor would provide him with a professional
excuse for journeying further into Western Europe; and this
failing, he would simply take French leave.

The preparations were extensive and contained all the elements of a mystery story with a tragicomic ending. Young Vulf's task was to get Dr. Moier to persuade his good friend, Marquis F. O. Pauluchchi, governor general of the region and the official ultimately responsible for Pushkin, to permit the poet to come to Dorpat for an operation. To baffle spies who might interfere with their correspondence on this matter, a secret writing was devised in which the word "carriage," standing for Pushkin himself, was the key. The results of Vulf's dealings were to be conveyed to Pushkin in terms of the "carriage," which his accomplice had taken to Dorpat and would hold there or send back according as Moier accepted or rejected the proposal. Meanwhile, arrangements were under way to make Pushkin's old friend Chaadaev, who was abroad at this time, financial agent and the recipient of the poet's mail should he escape.

Lev Pushkin was in on the secret, but as usual he did a lot of unwise babbling in Petersburg. Pushkin had to warn him to be more discreet, for again he feared that gossip among his friends would ruin the plan. A rumor actually spread through the city that Pushkin was trying to borrow fifteen thousand rubles in order to escape to America. Yet Pushkin himself was indiscreet in his own letters. He wrote to Lev: "The devil take me, but I do not like the Petersburg talk about my escape. Why should I run away? It is so fine here!" [8] Then he incautiously asks pointed questions about Chaadaev and where he is staying in Europe. And in another letter to Lev he requests a quantity of books and "wine, wine, rum (12 bottles), mustard, Fleur d'Orange, a traveling bag, Limburger cheese (and a book on horseback-riding — I want to depart behind stallions: a free imitation of Alfieri and Byron)." [9] Such requests, which might easily have come to the attention of the authorities, are hardly those one would expect of a man suffering from aneurysm.

In truth, it seems that everybody in Petersburg knew of Pushkin's intentions, with the exception of Zhukovski. Or it may be that this wise friend knew and thought it best to interfere with the poet's dangerous scheme. It happened that Dr. Moier was related by marriage to Zhukovski. Learning of

Pushkin's desire for Moier's services, Zhukovski at once wrote to the doctor, asking him as a special favor to go to Pskov and operate on Pushkin for aneurysm. Moier readily agreed. But if he made the trip to Pskov, he would discover that the "dangerously ill" Pushkin required a mere prescription rather than a difficult operation. The exposal of his whole plan of escape was imminent. In despair he hurried off a letter to Moier: "I beg you, for God's sake, do not come, and do not worry about me. The operation for aneurysm is of too little consequence to take an eminent man from his affairs and abode." [10] And he followed up this weak refusal with a sad letter to Vulf, telling him in effect to forget about the "carriage." This sudden loss of interest in an operation was not so easy to explain to Zhukovski. Two letters were necessary. Pushkin finally did go to Pskov to inquire about local treatment in an effort to dispel the worries of Zhukovski and to justify his own actions. The upshot of the whole business was Pushkin's lame report to Zhukovski that he had been told an operation for aneurysm was a dangerous matter and hence he had decided against it. "It is all the same," he mournfully concluded, "to die from boredom or from aneurysm; but the first is more infallible than the other." [11]

In September 1825 Pushkin wrote to Vyazemski, revealing his real design and his chagrin over its failure: "For five years I have treasured my aneurysm as the last pretext for deliverance, *ultimo ratio libertatis* — and suddenly my last hope has been destroyed by this damnable permission to go and have myself cured in exile! My soul, my head really whirls. They are careful about my life; I am thankful — but what a devil of a life! It would be infinitely better to die from lack of treatment in Mikhailovskoe. At least, my grave would be a living reproach, and you could write over it a pleasant and useful epitaph." [12]

While all this scheming had been going on at Mikhailovskoe, Pushkin was writing passionate love letters to Anna Kern at Riga and working hard on *Eugene Onegin* and *Boris Godunov*. The hope of escape sustained him in this varied activity. However, when his last attempt at freedom seemed utterly frus-

trated, his feverish energy waned and he lost interest in work.
There was nothing left but to accept his fate and make the
most of his country exile. The future seemed black indeed.
Suddenly a great event occurred. About two months after his
pessimistic letter to Vyazemski, Alexander I died. While this
monarch reigned Pushkin had pretty much come to the conclusion that his unhappy lot would never be mitigated. A new
sovereign on the throne gave him new hope.

II

> . . . not in the position
> of a prisoner . . .
> *Order of the Chief of Staff to*
> *the Governor of Pskov*

As the cold weather of 1825 drew near Pushkin became restless. Another winter in lonely Mikhailovskoe was not pleasant
to contemplate. "What is there for me to do in Russia?" [13]
he ironically demanded of Pletnev in a letter of December.
Rumors of revolutionary preparations in Moscow and Petersburg aggravated his uneasiness. Recent investigations indicate
that at this time (early in December 1825) he received a letter
from his friend Pushchin, calling him to Petersburg, where the
conspirator himself had gone on orders from his secret society.[14]
It is certain, at any rate, that Pushkin decided to risk a trip to
the capital, either to fulfil his friend's request or because he
wished to set his own mind at ease about these alarming rumors
he had heard. A curious poetic story, for which Pushkin himself is a source, is told concerning this projected trip. He actually set out for Petersburg, but he had not gone far when a hare
crossed his path, and a little further on a second hare (another
account says that he saw three hares); and finally he met a
priest on the road. Such a run of bad omens was too much for
the superstitious Pushkin. He returned to Mikhailovskoe to
await further news from the city. In order to escape suspicion,
he had planned to arrive in the capital at night (actually the
night of the thirteenth of December) and to go directly to the
quarters of his friend Ryleev. If this intention had been fulfilled, he would have arrived that evening in the midst of a

final and memorable meeting of the Council of the Decembrists at Ryleev's home. He would have heard an inspired speech by Ryleev and the frenzied determination of the conspirators to strike on the morrow for a provisional government and the emancipation of the serfs. The next day these revolutionists and their adherents gathered on huge Senate Square. They were there to take advantage of the extraordinary confusion that followed the death of Alexander I. Constantine had refused the throne in favor of his brother Nicholas, who had been secretly designated as heir by the late tsar. The nation was completely bewildered by reports and counter-reports concerning which of the two brothers would be the next emperor. This state of affairs lasted for twenty-five days. Though woefully unprepared for such an emergency, the conspirators used the interregnum to foment open rebellion. Nicholas, aware that a plot was under way, selected the fourteenth of December to proclaim himself tsar; and this act was to be the signal for the revolutionists to strike. Old Count Miloradovich, governor of the city and the same man who had so cavalierly examined young Pushkin on his seditious poetry in 1819, tried to dissuade the rebels from their purpose on Senate Square. A conspirator stepped up behind the count and shot him dead. The efforts of the youthful Nicholas were also unavailing. Cavalry charges failed to disperse the mob. Finally, as a last resort, a few rounds of grapeshot were fired, and the conspirators broke and ran. Nicholas I was undisputed master of his country, and the first revolution of the Russian nobility and intelligentsia had ended in a dismal failure. If he had actually gone to Petersburg, Pushkin no doubt would have been among the rebels on Senate Square. Fate — or superstition — once again intervened to save Russia's great poet. Could he have foreseen his future, Pushkin might well have preferred to have taken a stand with his comrades on the fourteenth of December.

A new monarch had given Pushkin some hope of release from his exile, but the catastrophe of the Decembrist Revolt on the eve of Nicholas' reign filled him with apprehension for his own safety. His political verse came to his mind, and his proud

title of "poet of freedom." He recalled the liberal groups in
Petersburg, Kamenka, and Kishinev; and he remembered his
own impulsive desires to join the movement. Many of the conspirators he knew well, among them some of the most prominent. Almost up to the very outbreak of the revolt he had been
corresponding with Ryleev, Pushchin, Bestuzhev, and Kiukhelbeker, men who were now dangerous criminals in the eyes of
the government. The authorities, he learned, considered culpable even those who knew of the conspiracy and failed to report
it. For a time his friends ceased to correspond with him. Indeed, he had plenty of reason to feel alarmed. The memoirs he
had been writing at Mikhailovskoe he burned, for fear of im-
plicating himself and his friends.

Pushkin's first step in this critical situation was to write to
the faithful Zhukovski, explaining fully what he believed to be
his position. "No doubt the government is satisfied," he maintained, "that I did not belong to the conspiracy and that I had
no political connections with the disturbers of the 14th of December. . . . Still I cannot consider myself safe from the
gendarmes, and it may easily happen that I shall be charged
with political conversations with this or that one of the accused.
Among them were many of my friends." Then he goes on to
say that he is willing to make his peace with the new government; but he boldly asserts that his future behavior "will depend on circumstances and the government's treatment of me."
Hoping that Zhukovski will present his case to the new tsar,
Pushkin enumerates his contacts with conspirators, as though
he wished to convince the authorities, by a "full confession,"
that he had no active part in the affair. But he whitewashed
his record as completely as he dared, even going so far as to
point out that Alexander I had exiled him merely as a punishment for religious disbelief. This touch must have amused
Zhukovski. And at the end of his letter, after expressing the
hope that he would be allowed to return, Pushkin could not
resist the temptation to vent his spleen against the late tsar:
"They say that you have written verses on the death of Alexander — a rich subject! But in the course of ten years of his reign

your lyre was silent. This is the best reproach to him. No one more than you has a right to say: The voice of the lyre is the voice of the people. Consequently, I was not entirely at fault in hissing him down to the very grave." [15]

But as January and February wore on and news of arrest after arrest reached him, Pushkin's fears grew. "I am a peaceful man," he wrote to Delvig. "But I am worried, and may God grant that it be to no purpose." [16] He heard the news of the arrest of Pushchin, Kiukhelbeker, and the Raevski sons, and anxiously he inquired about their fate and hoped that the tsar would accord them mercy. Had he known what was going on in Petersburg, he would have expected his own arrest any minute. The Commission of Inquiry set up by Nicholas was busy examining scores and scores of conspirators. Very few of the noble families of Russia escaped suspicion. The leading questions of the Commission were: Where had the prisoner first learned his freethinking ideas; what persons, societies, books, or manuscripts had thus influenced him? A number of the conspirators, among them one of the leaders, M. P. Bestuzhev-Riumin, testified that Pushkin's manuscript poems, such as *The Ode to Freedom* and *The Village*, had helped to introduce them to revolutionary ideas. The Commission, composed mostly of generals indifferent to literature, was very much interested in this testimony and vainly tried to connect Pushkin with a secret society. It is little wonder that Pushkin's influential friends in Petersburg were deeply concerned for the poet.

Not hearing from Zhukovski, Pushkin wrote him again on the seventh of March. Pletnev had advised this step, for he had learned that Zhukovski was already at work in Pushkin's interest and required a straightforward expression of his attitude toward the government. Pushkin wrote just this, explaining the reasons for his disgrace in 1824: "His majesty [Alexander I] excluded me from the service and ordered me to be exiled to the country for a letter written three years ago in which an opinion on atheism was found, a thoughtless opinion, worthy, of course, of the disapprobation of anyone." [17] And he adds that he hopes for a pardon from the new tsar. Zhukovski finally wrote on the twelfth of April, and his information was disquieting. "You have not been involved in anything — that is true. But in the papers of each of the active figures your verses have been discovered. This is a bad way to make friends with the government." [18] His strict advice to Pushkin was to remain at Mikhailovskoe for the time being and write poetry. Other friends gave him similar counsel.

Pushkin assiduously followed this advice, but as the time passed without any news from Petersburg he began to fret again. To him nothing was more insipid than patience and resignation. "You, who are not bound, how can you remain in Russia?" he angrily wrote to Vyazemski at the end of May. "If the tsar gives me my freedom, I shall not stay a month." And in a postscript he digs up the old fable of his aneurysm once more, as though this might spur his friends to greater efforts on his behalf. "A young drunken doctor in Pskov told me that without an operation I shall not reach thirty. It is no joke to die in the Opochetski district," [19] he concludes lugubriously. At about the same time (not later than May 27) he wrote to Nicholas I through the medium of the governor general of the region. Again he rehearsed the history of his exile and begged the tsar's permission to go to Moscow, Petersburg, or abroad for treatment of his illness. To this letter he adds formal testimony concerning his relations with the conspirators which has some justification in fact; but only the law of self-preservation can wholly excuse him. He swore: "I, the signatory below, will not pledge myself henceforth to any secret society nor belong to any under whatever name it may exist, and I testify to this — that I never belonged to any such secret society, and do not belong and never knew about any." [20] At the same time he made a formal request to the Pskov authorities for his recall from exile and submitted to an official medical examination as proof of his illness. This request and testimony were forwarded to the capital.

On the twenty-fourth of July Pushkin heard of the execution of the five Decembrists — Ryleev, Pestel, Kakhovski, Bestuzhev-Riumin, and Muravev-Apostol. The event horrified him.

He was acquainted with every one of these men, and Ryleev he knew well, along with many of the hundred and twenty conspirators who had been exiled to hard labor. At the same time he learned of the death of Amaliya Riznich. On a manuscript page of his copybook, under the poem dedicated to the memory of this passionately loved woman of Odessa, he placed her initials and those of the executed conspirators. And he drew a rampart on which was a gallows with the suspended bodies of five figures. Beside this sketch are the laconic words: "And I, like a fool, might have been on. . . ." [21] (The word "fool" he intended as a bitter reproach against his country.) Despite his own fight for freedom, Pushkin did not and never could forget these executed men and their comrades in far-off Siberia.

Meanwhile, the tsar and the Commission of Inquiry were deliberating on Pushkin's case. The coronation was at hand. The Decembrists had been punished, and Nicholas hoped that the forthcoming festivities would help to dispel the gloom and terror that had settled over the whole country. He recognized in Pushkin a dangerous man, but he had plans of his own for him. Reports on the poet were solicited from Pskov officials. Governor General Pauluchchi wrote favorably of the exile's behavior, but he suggested that he be refused permission to go abroad. Finally a secret agent, A. K. Boshnyak, was sent to the Pskov region in the guise of a botanist to gather information about Pushkin. His report is amusing, but it favored the exile. One gathers from it the sort of information that was considered significant in condemning or exculpating suspicious persons. From various dwellers in and around Mikhailovskoe the secret agent learned: "That at the fair of the Svyatogorski-Uspenski Monastery Pushkin was in a shirt with a pink ribbon for a belt, in a broad-brimmed straw hat, and with an iron rod in his hand; that he is modest and discreet, does not talk about the government, and in general there are no rumors circulating among the people about him . . . that Pushkin is friendly with the peasants, and sometimes shakes hands when greeting them; that sometimes he rides on horseback and, on reaching his destination, tells his man to let the horse alone,

saying that every animal has a right to its freedom. . . . To
my question: 'Does Pushkin arouse the peasants?' the abbot
Iona answered: 'He does not mix into anything and lives like
a bonny lass.'" [22] There is much more testimony of a similar
nature in this report, but at any rate the authorities seemed to
be convinced that Pushkin had not been organizing a peasant
revolt of his own in the region of Pskov.

On the third of September Pushkin spent the day at
Trigorskoe and returned to Mikhailovskoe at eleven o'clock
that night. At this late hour a messenger from von Aderkas
suddenly arrived with a request that Pushkin set out for
Pskov at once. The governor had received an order from
the tsar by special courier, and the messenger handed him a
copy of it. One can imagine the poet's feelings as he read the
precise directions of his majesty's command: "Mr. Pushkin
may travel in his own equipage at freedom, not in the position
of a prisoner, and under the escort of the courier only; upon his
arrival in Moscow he must present himself at once to the general of the day at the staff headquarters of his imperial majesty." [23] Pushkin hastily made preparations for the road, sent
to Trigorskoe for his pistols, without which he never traveled,
and calmed the weeping Arina Rodionovna. At dawn he set out
for Pskov.

"Not in the position of a prisoner" might stand as a description of Pushkin's status for the rest of his life. The terms of the
tsar's order gave no hint of what his future lot might be. He
knew that he was not under arrest, but neither was he a free
person. Was it to Siberia or to liberty that he was going? Perhaps at the moment of departure he did not care much; at
least he was leaving Mikhailovskoe.

CHAPTER XIV

Moscow Again

So now you are not the former
Pushkin, but my Pushkin!
Nicholas I to Pushkin

On the road to Pskov Pushkin was in a happy, joking frame
of mind. He stopped at an official station to change horses and
to eat. The food was vile, and he scratched a scurrilous quatrain on the window with his ring to the effect that von Aderkas
was as bad a governor as a tavern keeper. In the morning he
reached Pskov and sent a reassuring note to Praskovya Osipova.
It was a thoughtful act, for very early that same morning the
household at Trigorskoe had been thrown into turmoil by the
sudden appearance of Arina Rodionovna. The old nurse, her
gray hair disheveled, and all out of breath, sobbed her startling
story of the messenger who had come the previous night to take
her nursling to Moscow. Much disturbed over this news, they
asked her if any of Pushkin's papers had been confiscated. No,
nothing had been taken or destroyed, but she herself had destroyed something. "What was it?" "That damn cheese,"
answered Arina, "which Alexander Sergeevich loved to eat and
which I can't stand; the smell of German cheese is vile." [1]
Besides smelling badly, thought the good Arina, German cheese
was foreign and hence might be used as evidence against her
master.

On the night of the fourth of September, escorted by the imperial courier, Pushkin set out for Moscow, a distance of some
five hundred miles. No doubt the uncertainty of his immediate
future gave him plenty to think about on the long journey.
There were times at Mikhailovskoe when he had felt that any
change in his situation would be an improvement. The accession of Nicholas had given him hope which not even the Decembrist Revolt had destroyed, for after this event he had writ-

ten Delvig that he would place his trust in the magnanimity of the young tsar. He lost some of this faith when the cruel sentence of the conspirators was announced. With himself in mind he had written to Vyazemski: "I still have hope in the coronation. Those who are hanged are hanged, but penal servitude for one hundred and twenty friends, brothers, and comrades is horrible." [2]

Pushkin had no illusions concerning his personal relations with the conspirators. He had never belonged to a secret society, but his conscience was not altogether clear concerning what might be called the symbolic part he had played in the catastrophe. People in Moscow and Petersburg, aware of his liberal views and actions, were expressing surprise that Pushkin had not been numbered among the guilty. A good deal of speculation has arisen on this point and on his subsequent dealings with the government. Some have loosely condemned him as a reactionary and a traitor to his own convictions.

Whatever change Pushkin's political attitude underwent after the revolt, the part he played in the conspiracy is clear enough. Pushkin was a liberal, and until the day of his death he remained a liberal. The abuses of the Russian government he abhorred, and if he differed with some of his rasher contemporaries on the means of correcting them, it was not because he was less liberal than they but more farsighted. He has been named with Radishchev, Voltaire, and Rousseau as an inspirer of liberal thought in Russia, and this statement requires no justification. As a youth in Petersburg he had boldly written and spoken his resentment of despotic government, with a frankness that frightened the conspirators of that time. There was much youthful bravado in his actions then, but their sincerity is unquestionable. He was also the first of these liberals to suffer punishment for the cause, a fact often forgotten by some of the Decembrists who set him down as a reactionary. Pushkin would have joined the conspiracy if he had been asked. But the conspirators distrusted his frankness and unstable nature; and perhaps a discerning few felt that his great talent ought not to be risked in such a cause. Pushkin himself declared modestly that he was not worth the honor. It is true that he had none of the political idealism and reforming fanaticism of the noblest of the conspirators. But if he had been enrolled among their number, there is no reason to suppose that he would have been unworthy of the honor. His forbidden verses were everywhere recited by the Decembrists, and their stirring lines served as slogans. The evidence presented to the tsar's Committee of Inquiry proved conclusively that Pushkin's inflammatory poetry had been used as highly effective propaganda. Another fact easily forgotten is that for five years Pushkin had been an exile, a marked man continually under the surveillance of the authorities. Such a situation would have made it extremely hazardous for him and his associates had he been allowed to join the conspiracy.

Despite his natural alliance with the liberals, it must be admitted that Pushkin had no special talent for revolutionary activity, nor had he any deeply-rooted inclination to espouse the cause other than through his poetry. Essentially he was, as he said, a peaceful man. His impulsive feelings might easily have drawn him into heroic action, but this would have come from the heart, not from the head. His main business, his whole life, was poetry. Like many a liberal, he wished for reform, but he preferred to see it brought about by intelligent development rather than by bloody revolution.

Once the failure of the revolt had become an accomplished fact, Pushkin accepted the situation. It is nonsense to say that he recanted his liberalism at this point. In the letter to Delvig mentioned above, he sensibly remarked about the failure: "Let us be neither superstitious nor one-sided, like the French tragedians; let us look on the tragedy with the eyes of a Shakespeare." [3] He had no intention of opposing the inevitable. To Zhukovski, in the letter of March 7, in which he asks him to intercede in his behalf, Pushkin frankly and courageously says: "Whatever may have been the form of my thoughts, political and religious, I will preserve it in its integrity, but I have no desire to oppose foolishly the generally accepted order and necessity." [4] For a man of Pushkin's temperament, whose chief interest was his art, political justice had to give way to political necessity in the dark period of reactionary government that immediately followed the accession of Nicholas. He was not exactly making a virtue of necessity in this instance. There were times when he had to compromise with the "generally accepted order" for the safety of his own skin. But his private thoughts he kept to himself.

On his long ride to Moscow Pushkin may have meditated on what he would say if he were allowed an audience with the tsar. He felt that Nicholas had shown more sense than dignity in the manner in which he had quelled the revolt and punished the participators. Although he hoped for a pardon, he was determined not to lose any of his own dignity in appealing to the tsar's reason. The fate of his Decembrist friends was on his conscience.

Pushkin arrived in Moscow on the eighth of September, having covered the distance, by uninterrupted driving, in the extraordinary time of four days. Unshaven, dirty, weary, and a bit ill, he reported to the officer of the day, who at once sent a message to the chief of the general staff, Baron Dibich. The tsar was immediately informed, and Pushkin was ordered to present himself in his majesty's study in the Chudov Palace at four o'clock that very day.

II

> No, I don't flatter when in free
> Praise of the tsar I use my art.
> *Stanzas*

Still in his dirty traveling clothes, Pushkin entered the Kremlin and was closeted with the Tsar of all the Russias, a man only three years older than himself. There have been many accounts of this famous interview, which lasted over an hour, but the true story was never told in detail by either of the principals. In the excitement of the occasion Pushkin forgot much that took place. Some shreds of the conversation have been handed down as reported by the poet and the tsar, and hence have gained a certain authenticity. The room was cold, and Pushkin stood with his back to the stove, warming his feet while he spoke to the emperor, a breach of etiquette which seemed to annoy Nicholas. The tsar is credited with saying:

"You hate me because I have crushed the party to which you belonged. But, believe me, I also love Russia, I am no enemy to the Russian people; I desire its freedom, but first it must be strengthened." [5]

Nicholas asked him if he were not a friend of many of the conspirators who had been sent to Siberia.

"It is true, Sire," Pushkin answered. "I loved and esteemed many of them, and I continue to nourish the same feeling for them." [6]

Then Nicholas inquired: "What would you have done if you had been in Petersburg on the fourteenth of December?"

"I should have been in the ranks of the rebels," [7] Pushkin frankly answered.

This well-known reply, which neither the tsar nor the poet ever denied, ought to set at rest any doubt concerning Pushkin's real sympathy for the cause of the Decembrists. According to Baron Korf, Nicholas also said:

"To my question of whether or not he would change his form of thought and give me his word to think and act otherwise, he replied with many compliments about the 14th of December, but he hesitated for some time to make a direct answer, and only after a long silence did he extend his hand with the promise to behave differently." [8]

Upon being questioned about his writing, Pushkin complained of difficulties with the censor, and the tsar said: "You will send me everything you write; from now on I will be your censor." [9]

Nicholas finally informed Pushkin that he was free, free to go wherever he wished in the empire, with the exception of Petersburg. A special permission was required to visit this city. At the conclusion of the interview the tsar is reported to have led the poet into an adjoining room filled with courtiers. "Gentlemen," he said, "here is the new Pushkin for you; let us forget about the old Pushkin." [10] The poet left the palace with tears in his eyes.

Pushkin's exile was over. He hurried to uncle Vasili's house to break the joyful news. From all accounts he conducted himself well in this audience. As a private citizen he had preserved his dignity before his sovereign and had said nothing of which he was ever ashamed. Apparently Nicholas himself had been much impressed. That evening at a ball given by the French ambassador, he remarked to one of his generals concerning Pushkin: "Do you know, today I talked for a long time with the most intelligent man in Russia." [11]

The happy outcome of the interview had not been anticipated in the least by Pushkin. A curious fact indicates that he had been prepared for the worst. Either on the road to Moscow, or shortly before this, he had composed four incomplete verses which may have been intended as a concluding quatrain to *The Prophet*. One tradition maintains that he lost them on the palace stairs and found them upon leaving the Kremlin. Later he destroyed the manuscript. The story goes that if the tsar had decided to punish him further, Pushkin had planned to hand him the following verses as a last gesture of farewell:

> Arise, arise, O Russian prophet,[12]
> And in thy vestments now dishonored,
> Around thy humbled neck a halter,
> To the tsar . . . appear!*

The news of Pushkin's pardon was on everybody's lips, and people praised the kindness of Nicholas. Pushkin himself was completely taken in and deeply appreciative of the tsar's behavior toward him. But he was an optimist by nature. Had Nicholas really pardoned him? Or were his actions dictated by ulterior motives? For the tsar cast a baneful shadow over the remainder of Pushkin's life. Fairly recent investigations in the secret archives of the government, made possible since the October Revolution, have brought to light documents which provide new and interesting information on this important phase of Pushkin's biography.

---

* These lines and the story connected with them have been rejected by some critics, but on the basis of contemporary evidence there seems no good reason for refusing to accept the verses as Pushkin's, or the story connected with them.

On July 13 the five Decembrists had been hanged in Petersburg. The next day the tsar and his court, purified by a solemn *Te Deum*, left for Moscow, where the coronation was to take place on the twenty-second of August. Nicholas ascended the throne with blood on his hands; and he never forgot the mad mob on Senate Square. A soldierly sense of duty was perhaps the finest virtue of this young monarch. He was not remarkable for his intellectual powers, nor did he have any thirst for culture. If it had not been for the Decembrist Revolt his reign might have been of happier memory, and certain much-needed reforms might have been achieved. As it was, he did dismiss the despised Arakcheev and other hated toadies of Alexander I. But the revolt cankered his mind and turned him forever against the old Russian nobility and the liberalism of the intellectuals. The severe punishment he meted out to the conspirators and his uncompromising attitude toward them clearly indicated that he intended to rule his country with sternness and force.

Nicholas was closely associated with his Commission of Inquiry and examined the conspirators himself. He and the Commission had been much impressed by the widespread influence of Pushkin's revolutionary poems. Of course, they must have known of their existence, but the nature and significance of this verse had escaped them previously. Now, although they could not connect Pushkin directly with the conspiracy, they were convinced that he was a dangerous man. Apart from other evidence, a parody on the national anthem, *God Save the Tsar*, had been attributed to him. The quiet, inoffensive Pletnev was placed under surveillance by the emperor's order for no other reason than his friendship for Pushkin. Apparently the authorities preferred to have Pushkin on their side, for exile, they realized, would not prevent him from writing seditious poetry. The members of the Commission and Nicholas were indifferent to literature; for them Pushkin was merely an obnoxious freethinker and political suspect. Ryleev was a poet, but he had been hanged without compunction.

Though poetry and literature had no real value in the tsar's eyes, one may be sure that such influential men as Zhukovski and Karamzin did their best to impress Nicholas with the fact that the great poet Pushkin would be an adornment to his reign. And the tsar was definitely interested in such adornments. He would pardon Pushkin — but only on two conditions. First, Pushkin must give over his freethinking; second, his literary talent must be made to serve the government. No doubt Nicholas had also calculated the beneficial and moral effect that an apparent pardon of Pushkin would have on his sullen subjects. Here was an ideal dessert to serve at the coronation festivities.

At about this time an incident occurred which might easily have been fatal to Pushkin's chances for freedom. A poem, *André Chénier*,[13] had been published in his thin volume of January 1826. With the exception of one section, the censor had certified it. Chénier's verse had influenced Pushkin, and the execution of this young French revolutionist had powerfully stirred his imagination. The poem is a bold elegy on Chénier in which Pushkin praises him as the "singer of freedom" and excoriates his enemies. Unfortunately, manuscript copies of the uncensored version got into circulation under the title of *The Fourteenth of December*, and in some cases copies of Ryleev's well-known letter to his wife before his death were appended. It was not difficult to construe certain lines of the poem as referring to the events of the fourteenth of December. By the beginning of August 1826 the matter had come to the attention of the police. Of course, the tsar was informed of this before his interview with Pushkin, but the authorities had not yet finished their investigation of the matter. The possibility has been pointed out, and it is not at all unlikely, that the tsar's summons to Pushkin, which was issued on August 28, had some bearing on the Chénier poem.[14] One may be certain that Nicholas asked Pushkin in the interview whether he had written this poem about the fourteenth of December. It was easy for Pushkin to prove that he had written *André Chénier* before the revolt; that it had nothing to do with the fourteenth of December; and that he was not at all responsible for the manuscript copies in the hands of the police. The outcome of the famous interview might have been quite different if Pushkin had not been able to give the tsar a satisfactory explanation. But he had not heard the last of this matter.

There is another interesting fact which indicates that the "pardon" of the tsar was a hollow sham intended to beguile Pushkin and to win public sympathy. In the summer of 1826 Pushkin's parents and sister were vacationing at Reval. The poet had already sent in his request to the tsar for a recall from exile. In the meantime Vyazemski, who was also at Reval, persuaded Nadezhda Osipovna to write the new emperor, asking that her son be pardoned. It even appears that Vyazemski himself composed this letter for Nadezhda Osipovna. The request was received on the thirty-first of August, but owing to the pressing business of the coronation ceremonies, it was not considered by the Board of Pardons until January 4, 1827. The letter has not been found, but its contents are clear from the Board's report. Pushkin's mother pleaded the cause of her son's aneurysm once again, and begged the tsar to pardon him, adding a new note with her statement that Pushkin wished to return to the bosom of his family. The matter was brought to the attention of Nicholas on the thirtieth of January, over four months after Pushkin's interview with him. Quite clearly the tsar mistook this request of the mother for a plea made since he had given Pushkin his "freedom" on the memorable eighth of September. His decision, written in on the report of the Board by the secretary of state, reads simply: "His majesty's assent to the request of Pushkina is withheld." [15] It is obvious that, despite his so-called pardon at the meeting with Pushkin, four months later Nicholas could not find it in his heart to issue an official pardon.

In his relations with people Pushkin was simple and sincere. There was no guile in his nature. He never understood the tsar's real opinion of him, for the tsar was careful never to express it. Pushkin emphatically separated the person of the emperor from the political system he headed, and he accepted his sovereign's pardon in all good faith and honestly tried to live

up to its conditions. He was grateful to Nicholas and professed
something of admiration for him. In a poem of 1828 he frankly
expressed this gratitude:

> In me he honored inspiration;
> He set my thoughts at liberty.
> Shall I not with sincere emotion
> Proclaim his praise in fealty? [16]

For a time he even believed that the tsar's rule reflected the
views of the people. But Nicholas never for a moment lost his
dark suspicions of Pushkin. For him he was always a member
of the old nobility that had ushered in his reign with bloodshed
and revolt. He wished to bind the poet to him with silken
chains; but any serious overt act would have meant iron
shackles. Nicholas was very clever in his dealings with people.
When he wished to exert himself, his personality was charming
and his regal bearing impressive. But he could play the hypo-
crite. The poet Tiutchev justly said of him: "He has the façade
of a great man." [17] Not long after his audience, Pushkin was
made to realize that he was a "free" man only when and as the
tsar wished.

At the very beginning of his reign Nicholas had established a
new department of secret police connected with the Third Section of his private chancery, and at the head of it was his most
faithful adviser, Count Benkendorf. The pardoned Pushkin
at once fell under the surveillance of this secret police. His cage
was simply a little larger. A complicated network of spies
spread over all of Russia. Wherever he went Pushkin came
under the eyes of these agents. Not only his own correspondence but the letters of friends and relatives were opened in order
to discover evidence against him. Pushkin would have thought
twice about his new-found liberty if he could have read the following report of one of the agents, which was sent to Benkendorf just nine days after his interview in the Kremlin: "Upon
leaving Pskov Pushkin wrote a letter to his close friend and
schoolfellow, Delvig, informing him of this news and asking him
to send him money to be used for carousing and champagne.
This gentleman [Pushkin] is known as a philosopher in the full

sense of that word, a man who preaches a consistent egoism, with a scorn for people, a hatred for feelings, as well as for virtue; finally, he has a lively inclination to achieve worldly happiness at the expense of everything that is sacred. This ambitious individual, devoured by a craze for lust, as they say, has such a vile head that it will be necessary to give him a lesson on the first suitable occasion. They say that the emperor has just tendered him a favorable reception and that he does not deserve the kindness which his majesty has shown him." [18]

III

> In hope of glory and of good
> I hail the future unafraid.
> *Stanzas*

For the first time in six years Pushkin was free. At least, so he thought, and for the present thinking made it so. Moscow rejoiced. The city was crowded with celebrities and foreigners who had come for the coronation. The stage was set, and the pardoned poet became the darling of the hour. This occasion marked the high point in Pushkin's popularity. No Russian author had ever received such public acclaim. More than fifty years passed before ancient Moscow hailed a literary figure with equal enthusiasm. This was Dostoevski, and, curiously enough, the occasion was his memorable speech at the unveiling of the Pushkin statue at Moscow which suddenly aroused popular admiration for the novelist's genius.

For several years, exaggerated rumor, spicy anecdotes, and brilliant poetry had built up a reputation for the exiled Pushkin in the public mind. His dramatic arrival in Moscow and the interview with the tsar at this moment made a national hero of him. "Pushkin, Pushkin has come!" [19] cried the children of Vyazemski when he first visited their house, and this greeting of surprise and delight reflects the type of reception accorded him by the whole city. The moment Pushkin entered the theater the audience no longer bothered about the spectacle. All attention, all glances were directed at the great poet. Distinguished families vied with each other for his presence at evening gatherings. At balls women continually chose him for the mazurka or the cotillion. Even a police report to Benkendorf at this time carefully notes the adoration of Pushkin. "The ladies flatter and spoil the young man," writes the secret agent. "For example, in the course of his expressing a desire to enter the service, several ladies exclaimed at the same time: 'Why serve! Enrich our literature with your sublime productions. And besides, do you not already serve the nine muses?'" [20] The journalist V. V. Izmailov wrote Pushkin on the twenty-ninth of September: "How unfortunate that I cannot see and hear you because of my poor health, that I cannot wonder at you in person and share in your triumph in the capital. I envy Moscow. It has crowned an emperor; now it crowns a poet." [21] Nothing would do but that the well-known artist Tropinin should paint his portrait. They pointed him out in restaurants, and crowds followed him on the street. Enthusiasts compared him to Shakespeare, and some, not knowing with whom to compare him, declared that he was incomparable.

This prolonged hymn of praise was sweet music to Pushkin's ears. The news of the pardon quickly spread beyond Moscow. Vyazemski hastened to send the glad tidings to A. I. Turgenev and Zhukovski, who were abroad. His old friend Chaadaev of the Tsarskoe Selo Hussars shared his joy in Moscow. Warm letters of congratulation from friends began to arrive — from Delvig in Petersburg, N. S. Alekseev in Kishinev, Tumanski in Odessa. The unusual favor conferred on Pushkin by the tsar made a powerful impression on his mother and father. The distinction of a private audience with Nicholas, the pardon, and the honor of having a tsar for a censor delighted these fairweather parents. Delvig wrote of the ecstasy of Nadezhda Osipovna and begged Pushkin to send a kind word to his mother and father in Petersburg.

Upon his arrival Pushkin stayed at the Hotel Europa, but he eventually moved to the quarters of S. A. Sobolevski, whom he had met in Petersburg before his exile. Sobolevski and Lev Pushkin had attended the same school and were close friends. In Moscow Sobolevski worked in the Department of Foreign

Affairs, which provided an easygoing career eagerly sought after by noble youths of the city. His life was that of a rich young bachelor with much time on his hands. He was a shining light at balls and routs, and notorious for gastronomical feats and rakish adventures. "Falstaff" and "Caliban" were Pushkin's nicknames for him. Despite his social activities, Sobolevski had a genuine interest in literature and was regarded as one of the best writers of epigrams at a time when epigram-writing was a fine art. Pushkin and other authors valued his critical judgment. This Moscow epicure became very intimate with Pushkin, who confided to him the most personal affairs of his life. Their strong friendship remained unbroken until the poet's death.

Sobolevski belonged to a group of brilliant intellectuals who called themselves "Lovers of Wisdom." Their guiding spirit was Dmitri Venevitinov, a poet of extraordinary promise. The set included such figures as Pogodin, Koshelev, Shevyrev, Rozhalin, Melgunov, Titov, Maltsov, V. Odoevski, and the Kireevski brothers. These men were full of German romanticism. Goethe in literature and Schelling in philosophy were their models, and their vague purpose was to promote an idealistic love for art and to stimulate thought along transcendental lines.

Sobolevski at once introduced Pushkin to this Moscow group. He hardly needed an introduction, for they had all read his works and were prepared to hail him as their leader. Two days after his arrival in the city Pushkin read *Boris Godunov* to the Lovers of Wisdom at Venevitinov's house. Other readings were called for, and the group went into raptures over the drama. Pogodin describes the effect produced: "It was as though we had simply lost our minds. We grew hot and cold. One's hair stood on end. . . . The reading ended. For a long time we looked at one another and then threw ourselves on Pushkin. Embraces began, a turmoil arose, laughter was heard, and tears flowed amid the congratulations!" [22] Such a reaction is partly understandable. These intellectuals had never heard anything in Russian comparable to *Boris Godunov*. Its blank verse, so effectively read by Pushkin, astounded them, and the complete objectivity of the play fulfilled their fond ideal of dispassionate, Goethe-like poetry. In *Boris Godunov* they saw the beginning of a great period of Russian drama.

The Lovers of Wisdom were particularly desirous of obtaining Pushkin's aid in establishing a literary journal. For some time he had been interested in a magazine, either as owner or editor. Besides, such publications were natural outlets for his poetry. He had contributed to the *Polar Star* of Ryleev and Bestuzhev, but the Decembrist Revolt had ended that paper, and although the *Northern Flowers* [23] of Delvig published much of Pushkin's poetry, it had the disadvantage of being a yearly almanac. The popular *Moscow Telegraph*,[24] edited by Polevoi, was in the forefront of the new romantic movement, and eager for contributions from Pushkin. But he was not enthusiastic about it. He respected Polevoi as an editor but not as a man. Consequently, he willingly gave his counsel and practical assistance to the project of the Lovers of Wisdom. In 1827 the new magazine, the *Moscow Messenger*,[25] was launched in brilliant fashion as a monthly. But for various reasons Pushkin eventually grew cold to the publication, which flagged after Venevitinov's early death, when it fell under the complete control of Pogodin. Pushkin learned to distrust Pogodin almost as much as Polevoi.

Pushkin's initial enthusiasm for the Lovers of Wisdom quickly waned. They were too fond of German metaphysics to suit him. He had no love for philosophy, nor did he believe that abstract thought was the parent of poetic inspiration. In this rarefied region he felt ill at ease. He listened to these Moscow philosophers and took part in their discussions, and no doubt they added to his store of knowledge. But he gained impressions rather than new ideas from their meetings. He had a high regard for some of the Lovers of Wisdom, and for Venevitinov a great admiration. One of their tenets, which they obtained from Schelling's philosophy, namely the doctrine of the lofty place of the Poet in the scheme of things, Pushkin cordially accepted. But he had previously arrived at this opinion himself, without the aid of philosophy. For him the Poet was a special being, and in him breathed an inspired spirit. But the Poet does not seek for perfection; he seeks freedom. The crowd fails to understand this; if the crowd feels the power of poetry at all, it feels it almost physiologically. He had expressed this view earlier in *The Conversation of a Bookseller with a Poet*. And he continued to express it in a more emphatic and austere fashion.

IV

> Thou wilt call up remembrances
> Of days that have been lost by
> thee.
> *To Sofya F. Pushkina*

As the lion of the moment, absorbed in his fame, Pushkin plunged into worldly as well as literary society. He had not doffed his traveling clothes before he enlisted Sobolevski's services in issuing a challenge to Count F. I. Tolstoi. A malicious rumor, allegedly spread by Tolstoi, of a whipping he had received from the police had been rankling in Pushkin's mind since his Petersburg days. He never forgot an injury of this sort. Fortunately, the count, an expert and fearless duelist, was not then in Moscow. Later a reconciliation was brought about, and they ultimately became good friends.

Pushkin visited the *salons* of the city with an avidity that seemed to be born of his long deprivation. He appeared very frequently at the notable gatherings of the beautiful Princess Zinaida Volkonskaya, an accomplished singer and poetess. At this house gathered the intellectual and artistic people of Moscow. They often played charades, in which Pushkin distinguished himself. Once he had to represent a rock in the desert during the migration of the Israelites. He jumped up on the table and covered himself entirely with a red shawl. When the man in the role of Moses touched the rock with his iron rod (in this case the fan of the hostess), Pushkin peeped from under his shawl and poured water on the floor from a decanter. At Volkonskaya's he heard the unique improvisations of the great Polish poet, Mickiewicz. With his unfailing literary generosity, he praised Mickiewicz highly. The Pole wrote home to a friend: "I have become acquainted with him, and we see each other often. Pushkin is almost my equal. . . . In conversation he is

very clever and ardent, has read much and knows contemporary
literature well; his conception of poetry is pure and elevat-
ing." [26]   Despite the pointed reservation in this letter, Mickiewicz admired and thoroughly understood Pushkin.

At this house Pushkin, in December, met the sister-in-law of
the hostess, Mariya Volkonskaya, the daughter of General
Raevski and the girl whose little feet had captured his poetic
fancy in the Caucasus six years before. If she was his famous
"lost love," it seems strange that their last meeting and farewell did not find some echo in his poetry at this time.* For she
was on her way to Siberia to join her Decembrist husband,
Prince Sergei Volkonski. The future lot of this brave woman
brought painfully to Pushkin's mind the fate of his exiled comrades. On the eve of her departure for Siberia he wished to
give her a poem for the revolutionists, but she left sooner than
he expected. The wife of another Decembrist, Alexandra
Muraveva, carried the verses instead. In this poem the revolutionary voice of Pushkin is heard once again, bearing a daring
message of comfort and hope to the exiles:

> In thy Siberian mines keep
> That patience proud and slowly wrought,
> Nor will thy mournful work be lost,
> Or the high soaring of thy thought.
> .   .   .   .
>
> Behind thy gloomy dungeon bars,
> Friendship and love will thee rejoice,
> When once within thy convict holes
> Will come my freedom-loving voice.
>
> Thy heavy chains will fall away,
> Thy prisons crumble; liberty
> With joy will greet thee at the entrance;
> Brothers will pass the sword to thee.[27]

From far-off Siberia came the answer of the Decembrist poet,
A. I. Odoevski:

> The sounds of thy prophetic strains
> Have reached our ears!

---

* It has already been pointed out (p. 111) that his dedication to *Poltava* (1828) is
thought by some critics to refer to Mariya Volkonskaya. But the evidence is very thin.

They had taken up the sword and found chains instead. But Odoevski rejects the "patience" and "hope" of the sympathetic Pushkin:

> Poet, be not disturbed: in chains,
> Buried behind these dungeon bars,
> We contemplate our fate with pride,
> And laugh in spirit over tsars.
>
> . . . .
>
> With swords we'll strike our chains away,
> And freedom's flame again will soar,
> With it we'll thunder at our tsars —
> The land will freely breathe once more! [28]

These courageous words from the remote fastness of Siberia were a prophecy indeed, but one which neither Pushkin nor Odoevski lived to see fulfilled. Fortunately, the verses of both poets escaped the eternal vigilance of the secret police.

The tone of Zinaida Volkonskaya's *salon* was cosmopolitan; but the home of Mariya Rimskaya-Korsakova was a favorite gathering place for members of the best Moscow nobility. Pushkin was a regular guest and even fell a bit in love with one of the daughters, Alexandra, who achieved a place in the "Don Juan List." He also frequented the hospitable home of the Urusovs, where he became involved in one of his usual scrapes. He met there a young artillery officer, Solomirski, who affected a Byronic pose and resented the attention paid to Pushkin by the whole Urusov family. On one occasion he took exception to an amusing story that Pushkin told about a woman known to both. The next day he received a challenge. Pushkin's laconic answer of one sentence recalls Onegin's to Lenski: "At once, if you desire; come with a witness." [29] Happily both seconds were aware of the great responsibility they had assumed. The safety of the poet worried them, and they consulted Sobolevski. With his help, peace was made.

Perhaps among none of these well-known families of Moscow did Pushkin feel as much at home as in the household of the Ushakovs. Not only immediately after the termination of his exile, but in later years, on his periodic trips to Moscow, he rarely failed to visit them. To be sure, there was a special at-

traction in the two daughters, both of whom he courted after a
fashion. Elizaveta, the younger, was very beautiful, but Pushkin preferred Ekaterina. This merry family, with its many
visitors and relatives, reminds one of the Rostovs in *War and
Peace*. Here Pushkin's name was a household word; editions of
his poems were everywhere, and his verses, set to music, were
on the piano rack. He paid Ekaterina marked attention, wrote
poems to her, and drew caricatures in her album. It was in the
album of the younger sister that Pushkin wrote out his "Don
Juan List," which contains Ekaterina's name but not Elizaveta's. The rumor soon spread that he had proposed to Ekaterina. They were sincerely attached to each other, but he was
never deeply in love with her. From all accounts she would
have made him an excellent wife. When Ekaterina finally
married, her husband, jealous of her affection for Pushkin,
destroyed a bracelet he had given to her and the album in which
he had written.

This rumored proposal, however, suggests an inclination for
marriage which took possession of Pushkin after his departure
from Mikhailovskoe, an inclination that soon became an urgent
need. He had not entirely put aside the familiar cynicism of
youth towards marriage, but he was beginning to experience the
natural desire of a man of twenty-seven to settle down. Pushkin had been in Moscow only a few days when he became acquainted with Vasili Zubkov. They had a common bond in
their friendship for the exiled Pushchin. At Zubkov's house he
met his sister-in-law, Sofya Pushkina, a distant relative. She
was a tall, well-formed brunette, with black eyes and refined
features.* With his usual swift reaction he fell in love, but this
time he asked the lady to be his wife, proposing to her in October 1826. Sofya declined. She was on the point of becoming
engaged to a Moscow gentleman and successful careerist, V. A.
Panin. Though not averse to a flirtation, she could not take the
poet seriously.

* There is another opinion that Sofya Pushkina was a blonde and small in stature.
But the evidence of her portrait and the descriptions of Pushkin's friends indicate that
this notion, as Veresaev pointed out, has arisen from confusing Sofya with her sister.

PUSHKIN

This rejection depressed Pushkin and contributed to his sudden determination to leave Moscow for Mikhailovskoe before he had been in the city two months. To be sure, the intensive social life had begun to pall on him, and he also felt a strong urge to get back to writing poetry. At the time of departure, November 2, he wrote a note to Zubkov which clearly reveals his frame of mind: "I hoped to see and speak to you before leaving, but my evil fate pursues me in all that I desire. Farewell, dear friend, I am going to inter myself in the country until the first of January — I leave with death in my heart." [30] He fancied this last phrase, and before long he used it again on a similar occasion. On the road he wrote to Princess Vyazemskaya. Since his Odessa days he had formed the habit of confiding his love affairs to the understanding wife of his close friend. In the midst of his description of the trip, Pushkin interpolated: "S. P.* is my good angel; but *the other* is my demon; this most irrelevantly troubles me in my poetic and amorous meditations." [31] The journey, however, had taken him through no vale of tears, if we may judge from the humorous poetic account of the pleasures of the road which he wrote to Sobolevski; or else he was trying bravely to drown his grief. The coachman was obliged to get rid of a load of empty bottles at every station.

The separation did little to destroy the lingering hope that Sofya might still change her mind. He wrote to Vyazemski that he expected to be back by the first of the month as "she had commanded!" [32] And in a letter to Zubkov (December 1) his passion flames up anew. This letter throws some light on Pushkin's changing attitude towards marriage. "I am 27 years old, dear friend," he writes. "It is time to live, that is to say, to learn happiness. You tell me that it can be eternal: splendid news! [Zubkov was very happily married.] But it is not my own happiness that troubles me. Why should I not be the happiest of men with her? I fear only when I think of the fate which perhaps awaits her; I fear my inability to give her the happiness

---

* To these initials of Sofya Pushkina he adds the footnote: "It is self-evident that this is not Sergei Pushkin." The quarrel with his father had not yet been healed. By "*the other*" Pushkin means Anna Vulf, who still languished for him at Trigorskoe.

that I desire. My life up to the present time, so wandering, so stormy; my uneven character, jealous, susceptible, violent, and weak all at the same time — that is what gives me moments of painful reflection. Ought I to join a fate so sad and a character so unhappy to the fate of a creature so sweet, so beautiful? My God, but she is pretty! And my conduct with her has been ridiculous. Dear friend, try to efface the bad impression I have made on her — tell her that I am more sensible than I seem, and as for proof — well, anything that comes into your head. That vile Panin was in love with her for two years and only got around to proposing to her the week after Easter Sunday — but I see her once in a theater box, a second time at a ball, and the third time I propose to her! If she finds that Panin is right, then she must think that I am mad — is it not so? Explain to her then that I am right, that once having seen her, one does not hesitate; that I cannot pretend to charm her, and hence have done quite correctly in coming to the point; that the moment one loves her one cannot possibly love her more, just as it is impossible to find her more beautiful with the passing of time, for it is impossible to be more beautiful. My angel, persuade her, beg her to frighten off her vile Panin and marry me." [33]

This is not the letter of a man who is sincerely and profoundly in love. A year previously he had written such letters to Anna Kern, with the difference that he made no secret of what he wanted. Now he is willing to talk marriage with the first woman for whom he has conceived a passion. Fortunately, Sofya soon married her "vile Panin," and Pushkin quickly dismissed her from his thoughts. She was not the ideal woman he wished to make his wife.

v

Pushkin's momentary weariness with Moscow had been real. He loved fame but was easily surfeited. "Moscow has left a disagreeable impression on me," he wrote to Vyazemski. In the country he thought he would find rest and the leisure to write. "The village brought something into my heart," he says in this

same letter. "There is a certain poetic happiness in returning
free to my forlorn prison." [34] But he was restless, and his pen
stuck. In answer to Vyazemski's inquiry whether he had
plunged into a fit of verses or was still recovering from his Moscow morning-after, he replied: "I have written despised prose,
but inspiration does not soar. In Pskov, instead of writing the
7th chapter of *Onegin*, I lost the fourth at faro. Is it not
amusing?" [35]

The "despised prose" refers to an article on education which
Nicholas I had requested him to write. Pushkin was already
beginning to feel the burden of being the favored poet of an
emperor. He was also beginning to understand a little more
clearly what his "freedom" meant, and what a mixed blessing
it was to have a tsar for censor. He regarded Nicholas through
the prism of the generosity he had displayed at the interview.
But he did not sense at once the tsar's deliberate intention to
place him under a special moral obligation to behave and do
what he was told in return for his majesty's kindness. This
moral obligation, which he was never allowed to forget, weighed
on his conscience and ultimately stung and tortured his sense of
pride. For freedom of movement (which at best was hardly
real) he had sacrificed his moral freedom.

In public Pushkin did not hesitate to express his gratitude to
the tsar, and at this time he wrote his famous *Stanzas* addressed
to Nicholas. The lines are sincere and scrupulously avoid the
sticky flattery with which poets often honor a patron, particularly if he be a sovereign. Pushkin's hero among Russian rulers
was Peter the Great, and he paid Nicholas the compliment of
comparing him to this famous monarch. But he did not spare
the tsar an appeal for moderation or the advice to imitate the
virtues of his great predecessor:

> Be proud, then, of this family likeness,
> Be like your grandsire in every sense:
> Like him, unwearying and firm;
> Like him, unmindful of offense.[36]

The sincerity of the sentiments he expressed, however, did not
save him from the charge of sycophancy.

After his meeting with the tsar Pushkin was soon informed of his official status. On the thirtieth of September Count Benkendorf, head of the Third Section and chief of its secret police, wrote him a polite letter. "His majesty," Benkendorf tells Pushkin, "has complete confidence that you will employ your distinguished talents for the good of our glorious fatherland, transmitting it together with your immortal name." And as an earnest of the tsar's confidence, Benkendorf conveys his majesty's desire that Pushkin write something on the education of youth. He then informs him, "No one will examine your works; they will have no censor; the emperor himself will be the first judge of your productions and your censor." [37]

Pushkin had every reason to feel pleased with this reasonably courteous letter. Benkendorf simply reaffirmed the tsar's flattering promises. But the head of the secret police had as yet no occasion to show his claws. Benkendorf had already made his mark in the service of Alexander I by ferreting out the political conspiracy before the Decembrists ever struck. Conspiracies became a kind of obsession with him, and it seems that he never quite forgave Pushkin for not belonging to one. He was not well educated, lacked a saving sense of humor, and was dry and cold in official circles. For literature he had no regard. Nicholas trusted him implicitly, and he repaid the tsar by great personal devotion, although he was reckoned a lazy and not too efficient executive. Pushkin's sister described his appearance as "hardly attractive, with a sort of bittersweet smile, as though he had just bitten into a lemon." [38] And Sobolevski hit him off in an ironic epigram for Pushkin's amusement:

> Your first friend was Count Benkendorf;
> His only rival — Baron Korf.[39]

A true representative of the iron age of Nicholas I, Benkendorf believed that zeal and unconditional submission were incomparably higher than all virtues and talents. He had a despot's instinctive dislike for any kind of freedom, and especially for freedom of thought and speech. For him Pushkin was a necessary evil, politically unreliable, and a writer. He treated him like a mischievous schoolboy who must be pulled up and punished for every little offense. His sleuthing efforts contributed much to the misery of Pushkin's remaining years.

Pushkin had not been in Moscow more than two weeks before Benkendorf's clever spies were sending in reports of his behavior. One bit of information that came to his attention concerned the readings of *Boris Godunov*. On the twenty-second of November, at Mikhailovskoe, Pushkin received a chilly letter from Benkendorf. He was asked why he had not acknowledged a previous letter from him concerning the fact that he must submit any new poems to the tsar. Benkendorf knew that he got the letter, "for you have spoken about its contents to certain persons." [40] (This was the "freedom" of an emperor.) Benkendorf then goes on to inform him that he had committed an offense in reading a play to a group without first submitting it to the tsar. And he ends with a reminder of the tsar's kindness to him. Pushkin was surprised and rudely enlightened on his obligations to his imperial censor — it had not occurred to him that his unprinted works must not even be read without the tsar's approval. He hastened to reply to Benkendorf, contritely excusing himself on the score of his failure to understand properly the terms of the emperor's offer to be his censor. The manuscript of *Boris Godunov* would be forwarded at once; and now, sensing the endless red tape before him, he begged permission to submit certain short poems to the regular censor, for he was unwilling to bother busy high officials with such trifles.

In less than a month Pushkin received the first judgment of the royal censor. "I had the happiness to present to the emperor your comedy* on Tsar Boris and Grishka Otrepev," wrote Benkendorf. "His majesty has deigned to read the same with great satisfaction, and I present the following report on this subject in his own hand: 'I consider that Mr. Pushkin's purpose would be attained if, with some necessary chastening, he turned his comedy into an historical tale or romance after the manner of Walter Scott.'" [41] And Benkendorf advised him

* In the manuscript Pushkin entitled his play "The Comedy of Boris Godunov," a mannerism which was dropped in the printed edition.

to follow the tsar's advice. This was a cruel blow. Proud of his play, Pushkin placed great hope in it as the inspiration and starting point of a renascence in Russian drama. The real importance of the work, its Shakespearean form, had been completely missed in this ridiculous suggestion that it be turned into an historical romance. Firmly, and a little sarcastically, he answered Benkendorf: "One may agree that it is closer to an historical romance than to a tragedy, as his majesty deigned to observe. I regret that it is not in my power now to transform what has once been written by me." [42] To make matters worse, Benkendorf had also informed him that all his productions, even his short poems, must first be submitted to his majesty.

It is very unlikely that Nicholas read the play at all. The matter was one for his chief of the secret police to handle. But, as one of his own colleagues said, Benkendorf "learned nothing and read nothing." [43] In the case of *Boris Godunov* — and the method applies to many of the works Pushkin submitted to the tsar — Nicholas ordered Benkendorf to have "some trusty person" read the drama and present a report.[44] This report has survived in the archives of the Third Section, and it is perfectly clear that the tsar's criticism, which Benkendorf quoted, was lifted directly from it. The identity of the critic has been pretty definitely established.[45] It was no less a person than F. V. Bulgarin, renegade Pole, privileged journalist, agent of the secret police, and eventually Pushkin's bitterest critic and vilifier. In 1829 Bulgarin published his historical romance, *The False Dmitri*,[46] treating the same subject as Pushkin's play, which did not appear in print until 1831. There is little doubt that Bulgarin got his idea for an historical romance and certain aspects of his plot from his reading of the manuscript of *Boris Godunov* in 1826.

Meanwhile, Pushkin had finished his article, "On Public Education," [47] which the tsar had requested. This first "command" performance had come hard, for he was poorly prepared for such a task. He tried on the one hand to express his own sincere views about education and on the other to propose reforms which would meet the approval of his royal patron. The article was submitted, and again came a snub from Benkendorf. The tsar had read it with pleasure but had deigned to notice that Pushkin had placed too much stress on genius and sheer knowledge, to the neglect of such necessary virtues in Russian education as discipline and morality. Even this definite attempt to please had failed. Pushkin had not effaced himself and his ideas sufficiently to satisfy Nicholas and Benkendorf. Sadly he remarked to Aleksei Vulf about his rejected article: "It would have been easy for me to write what they wished, but one ought not to pass up such an opportunity to do some good." [48] He began to wonder how it would be possible to make a living at literature if his royal censor continued to be so difficult to please.

A little dejected over these two setbacks from the authorities, Pushkin returned to Moscow on the nineteenth of December. He had not been in the city long before the vexatious business of the *André Chénier* poem came up again and entangled him in the red tape of the police. The situation had serious aspects. Since Pushkin's audience with Nicholas in September, the government had been busily engaged in unraveling the mystery of the dissemination of the poem. Officials became convinced that these verses on the French Revolution referred to the events of the fourteenth of December, and they wanted to know who had put the manuscript into circulation. A student of Moscow University, Leopoldov, had been arrested for having the poem in his possession, and he testified that he had obtained it from Ensign Molchanov, who was also taken into custody. Molchanov swore that it had been written by Pushkin, and that his copy of the manuscript had come from Captain Alekseev. The latter officer was then arrested and examined, but he stuck to his story that he could not remember from whom he had obtained the poem. Alekseev at first was condemned to death, probably to frighten him into a confession, for the sentence was later changed. The head of the Moscow police insisted that Pushkin be made to answer for the verses, and he was finally summoned. Thoroughly disgusted with the whole matter, which he considered stupid in the extreme, he testified in writing, in January 1827, that the verses were his but not the title, "The Fourteenth of December," and that they had been written before this event and referred to the French Revolution. He concluded: "Not one of these verses, without obvious absurdity, can be made to refer to the fourteenth of December. I do not know who placed the erroneous title over them." [49] The authorities, however, were not willing to let the matter rest there. The case dragged on, and the secret police pushed their investigation zealously, determined to trace the poem's wandering existence in manuscript form. It was not until June 1828 that the process ended. The three arrested men were punished with some harshness for having the verses in their possession, and Pushkin was placed under stricter surveillance. It is difficult to understand why Pushkin, having admitted his authorship, was not severely punished, since the authorities seemed convinced that the poem referred to the fourteenth of December.

Still another disagreeable reminder of the silken chains that bound him to the throne increased Pushkin's irritation at this time. He had instructed Delvig in Petersburg to send several poems to Benkendorf (fragments from the third chapter of *Eugene Onegin*, *The Gypsies*, *The Nineteenth of October*, and *To A. P. Kern*), for he proposed to publish them in Delvig's almanac, the *Northern Flowers*. Benkendorf wrote Pushkin a stuffy letter in which he expressed surprise that Baron Delvig, "whom I have not even the honor to know," [50] had submitted to him certain poems. And he indicated that it was discourteous to appoint an intermediary in an arrangement that depended upon his majesty's authorization. But Benkendorf and Nicholas had had no scruples in appointing an intermediary of their own to report on the poems. In this instance, however, the unknown censor of the Third Section approved, although a few minor changes were suggested.

In the few months that followed his second return to Moscow in December, Pushkin tended to slip back into the dissipated life which had characterized his existence in Petersburg. The young blades surrounding the epicurean Sobolevski, with whom Pushkin continued to live, no doubt provided much incentive for this gay social whirl. Pushkin took to gambling again and lost large sums. Balls, parties, and drinking-bouts occupied his time. Somehow or other he could not get down to solid work. The ever-watchful secret police dutifully itemized his waywardness in a report of March 5: "He is accepted in every home, and, it seems, does not so much busy himself with poetry now as with gambling." [51] Pushkin's customary restlessness seized him. In February he dashed off to the district of Tver to spend two weeks with the Trigorskoe Lovelace, Aleksei Vulf. Back in Moscow again, he resumed his bachelor amusements. His restlessness was not simply the result of a nervous, active nature. Pushkin was almost twenty-eight; his youth had ended, and the desire for a more settled form of existence persistently dogged his thoughts. Marriage seemed the logical remedy. Then, too, the fine edge of the fame and excitement that Moscow had offered him was wearing off. His dissipated life alienated some of his worshipers. Vaguely he began to perceive that many of these Moscow aristocrats honored him, not as a social equal and a descendant of a noble line, but as a writer and the lion of the moment. Nothing could be more calculated to hurt his pride. Gossip began to spring up. Enemies talked disparagingly of his relations with the tsar, and the activities of police spies increased his discontent. Suddenly, in April, he requested Benkendorf to allow him to go to Petersburg on family business. (It will be remembered that Petersburg was forbidden him without special permission.) The request was granted, with the cool reminder that, since he had given his word, he would be expected to comport himself honorably in the capital. On the evening of his departure (May 19) a number of friends gathered at Sobolevski's summer place on the outskirts of Moscow to see their hero off in proper bachelor fashion. Pushkin arrived for the party very late and remained only a short time. He was moody and uncommunicative. His mystified friends bade him farewell, and after his departure they discussed his strange and unnatural behavior on such an occasion.

CHAPTER XV

"Pompous City, Wretched City"

Just seven years before, Pushkin had left Petersburg, a much-chastened "Cricket," sad and disillusioned. Upon his return in May 1827, his disillusion was of a different sort. He had now grown introspective. His past was not a happy memory, and the future stretched out before him like an infinity of pain. In the beautiful poem, *Remembrance*, composed not long after his arrival in the city, he writes of the memories that run through his mind in the quiet of a sleepless night:

> And with disgust I read the lengthy scroll of years,
> I shudder, and I curse too late;
> I bitterly regret and shed my bitter tears,
> But can't erase the lines of fate.[1]

Only a radical change in his life could cure this spiritual illness.

Pushkin did not live in the home of his parents on the Fontanka; he took rooms at Demuth's, a hotel hardly within his means. He did not flatter his family with frequent visits, either now or later in his stays in Petersburg. Both mother and father had grown proud of their famous son since those stormy days of exile at Mikhailovskoe. Nadezhda Osipovna, in particular, had softened. She tried to entice him to the family hearth with meals of his favorite dish, baked potatoes. But meals at the Pushkins' were not very attractive. Their dwindling income and the growing miserliness of Sergei Lvovich made for plain fare. Jokingly Delvig once invited Pushkin in verse to dine at his father's house on "rank butter and rotten eggs."[2] But Pushkin was not disposed now to resist the well-intentioned overtures of his parents. He was ready to be friendly, provided they did not interfere in his life, a condition not always observed.

Delvig's house, of course, was one of the first visited. The two poets wept and laughed from joy, and kissed each other's hands, a custom they always observed on meeting. Their hallowed friendship comforted Pushkin at this time. Delvig was a most amiable host. "He was the best of friends because he was the best of men," wrote one who knew him well. "I never saw him boring or disagreeable, weak or uneven." [3] For the first time Pushkin met Delvig's wife, Sofya. He had feared that she would break up his friendship for her husband, but they liked each other at once. Cheerful and sympathetic, Sofya had long been an admirer of Pushkin through his verse and from the example of her husband. Shortly after their meeting she wrote a friend: "Here is our dear, kind Pushkin for you. This portrait is a striking resemblance — as if you were looking at the man himself. How you would love him if you could see him as I do every day! He is a man who grows on you the longer you know him." [4] At this hospitable home gathered close literary friends and old Lyceum comrades. Zhukovski and Vyazemski visited, Krylov dozed peacefully in the corner, and Izmailov, the impossibly lazy journalist, waited patiently for the feasting to begin. Mickiewicz offered his improvisations, and Illichevski, Yakovlev, and Danzas recalled their Lyceum days. On one of these evenings Pushkin arrived with a skull which Aleksei Vulf had given to him, said to have been taken from the Riga grave of one of Delvig's ancestors. Pushkin presented it with the well-known verses beginning:

> Delvig, accept this skull from me,
> For it belongs to thee by right.
> Baron, I will relate to thee
> The story of its Gothic might.[5]

And in the fashion of Byron and his reveling companions, the ancestral skull was filled with wine and passed around to the guests, who drank to Delvig's health.

In this same house lived Anna Kern, whom Pushkin encountered very shortly after his arrival. Now definitely separated from her husband, she had settled in the capital. Many of Pushkin's friends, especially the literary ones — she seemed to have a weakness for authors — were already hers. She had become intimate with the Delvigs and the whole Pushkin family, which she visited frequently. She had already turned young Lev's head; Sergei Lvovich liked her, and some years later, after his wife's death, he professed a foolish old man's passion for Anna's daughter. Aleksei Vulf was the favorite of the moment, but Venevitinov had courted her, and Illïchevski wrote her loving verses. By inclination, or because of her unprotected position, Anna showed a partiality for male company which did not help her damaged reputation. Pushkin himself had lost a good deal of the respect which Anna had inspired in their meeting at Trigorskoe. One is inclined to think that vicious scandalmongering, in which her own husband was not the least offender, had dealt rather harshly with Anna Kern. A short time before his exile ended, Pushkin had written a letter to Aleksei Vulf at Dorpat, in which he inquired unfeelingly after "the Babylonian fornicatress," [6] Anna Kern. Pushkin was not simply pandering to the jargon of the Trigorskoe Lovelace; Aleksei Vulf had finally been successful in an affair with his beautiful cousin. Pushkin now followed suit. He saw a good deal of Anna Kern. Less than a year later he wrote to Sobolevski: "You write me nothing about the 2100 rubles I owe you, but you write about Mme. Kern, whom, with the help of God, I will . . . . one of these days." [7] Their intimacy lasted some time, but Pushkin finally grew cold toward her. His "genius of pure loveliness" had become just another woman in his life.

The affection of dear friends and the pleasures of the capital he had not seen for seven years did little to allay Pushkin's growing unrest. Petersburg had changed, and he had changed. At the beginning of July he wrote to Praskovya Osipova in a spirit of discontent: "The insipidity and stupidity of our two capitals are equal, although diverse, and since I have pretensions to impartiality, I would say that if a choice were given me between the two, then I would choose Trigorskoe." [8] Pushkin liked to flatter this good woman, but in his restlessness he was really turning his eyes towards Mikhailovskoe almost before he had got settled in Petersburg.

A passage of arms with Benkendorf toward the end of July

added to his general dissatisfaction. He appealed to the head of
the Third Section for redress from a publisher who had pirated
his *Prisoner of the Caucasus*. Benkendorf politely but flatly refused assistance. Meanwhile, the government sleuths continued
their activities. They bothered him again with the *André
Chénier* affair, demanding further testimony on his part. And
Benkendorf wrote to the chief of the Moscow secret police to
investigate the significance of a suspicious-looking vignette
which had been printed on the cover of the recently published
Gypsies. The arch detective was convinced that Pushkin had
selected this design, which contained a scroll, dagger, and
chains, with some politically subversive motive in mind. After
a thorough investigation the Moscow official was obliged to
report that the vignette was French in origin, was employed by
several printers, and had been used in many productions. Benkendorf was foiled again. A less evil-minded man would have
been satisfied with the favorable accounts of Pushkin's behavior which were sent in by Petersburg agents. "He seems
very much changed," remarked one of the spies, "and occupies
himself only with finances, trying to sell his literary productions
at advantageous terms." [9] On the twelfth of July Benkendorf
himself begrudgingly reported to the tsar: "Pushkin, after
meeting with me, spoke with rapture about your majesty in the
English Club, and obliged those dining with him to drink to
your majesty's health. He is a good enough scapegrace, however, and if we succeed in directing his pen and speech, it will be
profitable." [10]

But the "scapegrace" had no intention of allowing his pen
and speech to be directed. Four days after Benkendorf's hopeful report to the tsar, Pushkin wrote a short poem, *Arion*, which
was never published in his lifetime under his name. It is a transparent allegory based on the old Greek myth of Arion. The
meaning of the poem is clear. He describes a boat loaded with
men who toil at oars and sail. "Full of trust, I am their carefree
singer," he says. A sudden storm sweeps all away, but he alone
is saved. Yet he continues to sing his "former hymns." [11] The
men in the boat, of course, are the Decembrists. Pushkin was

their "singer," an excellent and precise description of the part
he played in the conspiracy. Furthermore, he intended to remain their singer, the singer of freedom. The poem is symbolic
of Pushkin's position after he made his peace with the tsar. The
moral level of society had fallen very low after the revolt. All
development had ceased, for all who favored progress were piti-
lessly persecuted by the government. The survivors were weak
and fearful. But in the midst of them was Pushkin, saved by a
miracle. His ideas on social and political problems during the
new régime changed somewhat, as did the ideas of many of the
exiled Decembrists. Circumstances might force him to exhibit
a certain outward conformity, but a suspicious and repressive
government could not shackle his free thought. In his heart he
remained a liberal. That he should revert to the theme of the
Decembrists at this time is significant. One is inclined to think
that much of his restlessness and his disturbed state of mind
were connected with the fate of his revolutionary comrades and
the fact that he had not shared it.

Pushkin felt lonely in Petersburg. He was already bored, irritable, and nervous, and his dream of an independent existence
seemed as far from fulfillment as ever. He had hoped to get to
work in the capital, but as in Moscow he lacked both the will
and inspiration. Perhaps the country quiet of Mikhailovskoe,
he hopefully thought again, would encourage the muse. At the
end of July, having remained about two months in Petersburg,
he set out for his village.

II

> O youth, O fading youth:
> May I regret thee still?
> *To Yazykov*

Pushkin enjoyed a brief interval of contentment and work at
Mikhailovskoe. Now that the element of compulsion was removed, he could take delight in the country, at least for a short
time. He slipped easily into the daily routine he had followed
during his exile in the village. There were the usual visits to his
good friends at Trigorskoe, and long conversations with his
pupil, Aleksei Vulf, who by now was well on the way to surpass-

ing his teacher in "the science of the tender passions." But work was his chief concern. He needed money; it was rumored that in his two months in Petersburg Pushkin had lost as much as seventeen thousand rubles at cards. Despite his efforts, he was obliged to write Delvig: "There is still no inspiration; meanwhile, I have turned to prose." [12] In reality he was absorbed in an historical romance, *The Negro of Peter the Great*.[13] The hero of the story is his great-grandfather Abram, and the historical background is adequately filled in. Pushkin was enthusiastic about Peter and his period, which he considered the greatest in Russian history. In the course of the next few years he devoted much time to investigating and writing about this epoch. Although he worked hard at the novel, he did not finish it, largely owing to a radical change in the plot which he intended to make. It is interesting to see him turning to prose, and the practice increased as the years went on. The failure of poetic inspiration had something to do with it. But it was a natural course to take in view of his growing interest in realism.

A little more than two months of country quiet and Pushkin had had enough. The unfinished *Negro of Peter the Great* and a few short poems made up his total literary output during this stay at Mikhailovskoe. The itch to be off possessed him. By the middle of October he was on the road to Petersburg. At a way station he played cards with an hussar. Time after time he lost, until finally he had gambled away sixteen hundred rubles. Angry over his bad luck, he borrowed two hundred more and proceeded to the next station. While waiting here he read some Schiller. Suddenly a company of prisoners drove up, headed by a government courier. One of the convicts attracted Pushkin's attention. He was a tall, thin, pale young man in a frieze overcoat. Pushkin recognized his old Lyceum comrade, Kiukhelbeker! They rushed to embrace. Guards tried to separate them. The courier, seizing Pushkin's arm, showered threats and curses. Kiukhelbeker had a fainting spell. Pushkin tried to give the courier money for his friend. The offer was refused, and he roundly abused the courier, swearing that he would report him to the emperor. They placed Kiukhelbeker in the carriage, and

the company drove off. He was being transferred to the Dina-
burg prison for the part he had played in the Decembrist Revolt. Under such circumstances this chance meeting with his
old schoolmate, the lovable, mad, and inoffensive "Kiukhlya,"
must have opened the wound of Pushkin's conscience once
again. Of those Lyceum comrades whom he deeply cared for,
only Delvig remained a free man. Pushkin continued to write
comforting letters to Kiukhelbeker after he had been sent to
Siberia, a hazardous business for one in Pushkin's position.
This meeting on the road, and Pushkin's behavior, were duly
reported to the authorities by the courier.

In Petersburg by the end of October, the wandering poet
sought an anodyne for his disturbed spirit in the winter social
life of the capital. The gay Sobolevski was on a visit from Moscow, and the two friends trod the primrose path together. From
the end of 1827 to the first half of the next year Pushkin led one
of the stormiest and most restless periods of his existence. He
continued to keep his quarters at Demuth's, but he was rarely
there, leaving early in the day and returning late at night. When
he remained in the hotel he spent most of his time in bed, reading or writing. If a caller arrived, he got up and chatted while
sitting at his dressing table, cleaning and paring his long nails.
Moscow literary friends were in despair over his failure to send
in promised contributions to their magazine. One of the Lovers
of Wisdom wrote to Pogodin, the editor: "Without doubt the
greatest service I could perform for you would be to rein Pushkin in, but I am not capable of this. He is at home only at nine
in the morning." [14]

The famous poet became the "notorious poet" in certain
circles. Pushkin sampled all levels of society, but in some he was
more welcome than in others. At the Karamzins he was a familiar figure. The great historian had died (1826), but his wife,
Katerina Andreevna, still maintained a *salon* where the most
cultured people of the city were to be found. This Petersburg
bluestocking prescribed two rules for her guests: no cards, and
Russian, not French, must be spoken. Like her famous husband, Katerina Andreevna watched over Pushkin's career with

solicitous care, deprecating his excesses and always ready to intercede in his behalf.

A similar role, though with a certain difference, was played by Elizaveta Khitrovo. She takes a place among those older women, the kind Samaritans in Pushkin's life, who never doubted his real goodness though they chided him for some instances of misbehavior. Khitrovo was the favorite daughter of the great Field Marshal Kutuzov, the warrior of Borodino and Napoleon's nemesis. In society she wore the ribbon of Kutuzov's decoration of St. George and a watch which, she told the curious, and often those who were not curious, had been carried by her illustrious father at Borodino. Twice married and twice widowed, she settled down in Petersburg after extensive travel abroad and conducted one of the city's most celebrated *salons*. Her daughter, Countess Fikelmon (Ficquelmont), was married to the Austrian ambassador to Russia. Through this connection with the diplomatic world, and by virtue of her own interests, a special political tone pervaded Khitrovo's *salon*. But all the intellectuals and writers attended her gatherings. Here she proudly pointed out Pushkin's chair, Zhukovski's divan, and Gogol's corner. Not brilliant herself, she possessed that capacity for listening and appearing very much interested which makes for the successful hostess. Elizaveta Khitrovo was one of those beautiful souls whose "philosophy of good" and "love for life" exasperated her protégés. Yet her kind deeds were numerous, and she took a deep interest in Pushkin's welfare and literary career. Although she was sixteen years older than the poet, her interest, like that of Praskovya Osipova, soon took on the appearance of a genuine passion which became the talk of Petersburg. She wrote Pushkin many letters in which she tried desperately to move within his intellectual and literary world. He always replied politely, but cautiously kept the correspondence away from the subject of love. Eventually he grew annoyed with her persistent attention, and among his friends he encouraged an attitude of ridicule toward her passion for him. Khitrovo was very vain of her fat white shoulders, which she displayed rather shamelessly in public. The fault was capitalized in a cruel epigram, attributed to Pushkin, in which she was referred to as "the naked Liza." Despite his levity in their relations, Elizaveta Khitrovo never ceased her efforts to aid him, particularly in government circles, where she had important contacts.

Pushkin told one of his friends a curious tale which seems to concern Countess "Dolly" Fikelmon, the daughter of Khitrovo. She was a beautiful young woman, whose *salon* became as popular as her mother's. Pushkin was a favored guest, and where the mother failed the daughter succeeded — Countess Dolly strongly attracted him. The story goes that she consented to a rendezvous. Pushkin hid himself under the divan one evening, and when the coast was clear he declared himself to this beautiful wife of the Austrian ambassador. They locked themselves in her bedroom, and time sped so swiftly in their dalliance that Pushkin was not aware that it was broad daylight until he suddenly pushed the curtains aside. The problem now was to get out of the house, for the exit obliged him to pass the ambassador's room. Only by enlisting the aid of a servant, whom he later rewarded in handsome fashion, did he succeed in escaping. The intimate relations of Pushkin and Dolly appeared to lapse after this incident. He told the story to his friend Nashchokin without mentioning any names. Some biographers have since concluded, on the basis of various bits of evidence, that the woman in the case was really Countess Fikelmon. An incident in his famous short story, *The Queen of Spades*,[15] resembles the account narrated above so closely as to make it seem autobiographical. Of course, one cannot say with certainty that the story as told by Pushkin was true, or that Countess Fikelmon was actually the woman in the case. But the evidence, direct and presumptive, is rather convincing.[16]

Apparently Pushkin had many such affairs in these dissipated Petersburg days when he seemed bent on relieving his distraught state of mind by one last desperate fling at bachelor life. Among the fugitive names of women that have survived, one definite personality stands out — the Countess Agrafena Zakrevskaya, wife of the minister of internal affairs, a man notorious for his uncommon ignorance in the official world.

Tall, handsome, and extremely passionate, she turned the heads of all the young men and was celebrated in society as the "Bronze Venus" and the "Cleopatra of the Neva." Baratynski wrote flaming verses to her, and Vyazemski courted her. The countess took a special pleasure in scorning the conventions of society. A reputation for loose morals never seemed to bother the Bronze Venus, and she shocked the ladies and delighted the men by appearing at parties in transparent gowns that silhouetted her majestic figure against the light. Pushkin had a brief, impetuous liaison with Agrafena, and at its conclusion she curiously compensated him for his continued interest by making him a confidant of her many love affairs. As the "brilliant Nina Vronskaya" [17] he brought her into *Eugene Onegin*, comparing her "marble beauty" to that of the transformed Tatyana; and it is very likely that she was in his mind when he created the modern Cleopatra in the *Egyptian Nights*.[18] He dedicated several fine lyrics to Agrafena Zakrevskaya, the best known of which is *The Portrait*:

> With all her swift rebellious passions,
> She with her soul of flame goes forth;
> At times among you she appears,
> O frozen women of the North.
> With all her powers she contends,
> Unmindful of the world's stern bars;
> She is a lawless comet in
> The calculated round of stars.[19]

In the midst of bachelor parties and love affairs Pushkin could not banish his recently-formed desire for marriage and the settled life. He visited his old friends the Olenins, at whose house he had first met Anna Kern in 1819. At that time the daughter, Anna Olenina, was just emerging from girlhood. Now she had grown into an attractive woman whose tiny feet and golden hair fascinated Pushkin. In the spring of 1828 he frequented this household and began to think very seriously of the daughter. He wrote verses to Anna. In his copybook he sketched her face and inscribed in French the name "Annete Pouschkine," and then carefully drew a line through it. It is said that in a moment of passion he actually proposed to her. The family was highly cultured and wealthy, and the father, who greatly admired Pushkin, would have been pleased to have him as a son-in-law. Instead of a wedding, however, there was a sudden break with the family, and the rumor went around that his offer had been rejected. The whole matter was shrouded in mystery until a recent investigator brought certain facts to light.[20] It now appears that Pushkin was not refused. The father arranged a large dinner, inviting many relatives and friends, with the purpose of announcing the engagement. All the guests arrived, but no bridegroom. After waiting a long time the embarrassed host asked the company to be seated. Pushkin finally came very late, the dinner having long since ended. The father took him into his study for a heart-to-heart talk. The engagement was never announced. Pushkin had changed his mind. After thinking it over, he had decided that Anna Olenina was not his ideal woman. It was an extremely awkward situation, and Pushkin could never think of the Olenins without a feeling of annoyance with himself. The only compensation he could make for his shoddy treatment of Anna was to encourage the rumor that his proposal had been rejected.

III

> And clouds now gather over me
> In secret silence, as before;
> A stern and jealous destiny
> Threatens disaster still once more.
>
> *Foreboding*

The illusion of escape did not last long. Women and drinking began to take their toll of Pushkin's bodily and spiritual health, and excessive gambling reduced his material circumstances to a desperate plight. In a cynical mood he wrote to his devoted guardian, Elizaveta Khitrovo: "More than anything in the world I fear respectable women. Long live the grisettes! — this is the easier way and much more satisfactory. . . . Do you want me to speak frankly? I may be refined and decent in my writings, but at heart I am entirely vulgar, and all my inclinations are completely bourgeois. I am satiated with intrigues, sentiments, and correspondence." [21] This may have been an unsubtle attempt to discourage the attentions of Khitrovo, but the letter also reflects the disillusion into which he had sunk. In February 1828 Pushkin's excesses brought on a severe illness, but upon recovering he resumed his disorderly existence. Close friends grew deeply concerned. Vyazemski wrote to A. I. Turgenev in April: "Pushkin pursues a most dissipated life here, and Petersburg may destroy him." [22] His moody and often quarrelsome behavior in society annoyed many and provoked slanderous reprisals. Certain of the uncultured bureaucrats, who had come into power with the reign of Nicholas, were not disposed to show him any favors. They reflected the government's suspicion. Pushkin was proud of his position as a poet, but his genius, he believed, was something apart from himself, an essence intimately connected with the glory of Russia. Any indication that his fame as a writer was his chief recommendation to high society infuriated him. Yet this was precisely his position among many aristocratic members of the Petersburg social world. They merely tolerated him as an artist, a kind of uninvited guest from a sphere of society alien to theirs and infinitely beneath them. Pushkin, however, felt that his birth entitled him to an equal place in this worldly society, and its snobbism cut deeply and set up an antagonism which did much to corrode his natural quality of friendliness. Russia was not a democratic country then, and the notion of social superiority was something that Pushkin had inherited from his family and accepted as naturally as his poetic talent. To be looked down upon by people whom he knew to be his intellectual and cultural inferiors wounded his pride but also provoked his utter scorn. *The Crowd*, the stinging poem that he wrote at the end of 1828, is not simply a powerful reaffirmation of his oft-repeated theory of the poet's elevated place in society. By the "crowd" he also had in mind those uncultured bureaucrats of the capital's upper crust for whom he was merely "Pushkin, the writer." Fiercely he addressed them:

> Go hold thy peace, thou senseless crowd,
> Hired workers, slaves of need and care!
> For I detest thy murmurs loud.
> Thou art earth's worms, not sons of air! [23]

A change of scene had always been Pushkin's remedy for
emotional unrest and extreme dissatisfaction with his manner
of life. It is interesting to observe how often in his lifetime he
sought to escape from a sphere of activities that had become
loathsome to him. Such an escape appeared to be an absolute
necessity now. A war with Turkey was in progress. Sometime
at the end of February or early in March, obsessed with the
desire to get far away from Petersburg, Pushkin applied to
Benkendorf for permission to join the troops being sent to the
Caucasus. It was of no consequence to him in what capacity he
served. About the same time Vyazemski made a similar request. Pushkin had some reason to expect an acceptance of his
services, for since his arrival in the capital his public conduct
toward the government had been exemplary. The reports of
the secret police had not failed to reveal his dissoluteness, but
they also conveyed to Benkendorf Pushkin's praise of the tsar,
which he uttered in public places — usually when he had had a
drink too much. Furthermore, at the beginning of 1828 he had
written his well-known poem on Nicholas, mentioned elsewhere,
which begins:

> No, I don't flatter when in free
> Praise of the tsar I use my art:
> I boldly give vent to my feelings,
> I speak the language of the heart.
>
> I simply have grown to love him:
> Us firmly, honestly he leads;
> Again he gives new life to Russia
> In battle, in hopes, and in deeds.[24]

Pushkin sincerely felt these sentiments at the time he wrote
them. The poem was sent to the tsar for permission to print.
Nicholas was immensely pleased. He refused to allow the verses
to be published, but indicated, hypocritically, that they might
be freely disseminated. And he vaguely promised Pushkin a
reward in the form of an appointment. Pushkin had waited
upon Benkendorf to discover the nature of this reward, but the
latter continually avoided the issue. Pushkin's desire to get out
of Petersburg grew so strong that eventually he was willing to
substitute an appointment to the army for the tsar's promised
reward.

Pushkin's hopes were soon dashed. On the twentieth of April Benkendorf politely informed him that there was no opening in the army, but that his majesty "will not forget you and on the first occasion will take advantage of the opportunity to employ your distinguished talents in the service of the fatherland." [25] Vyazemski's similar request was turned down at the same time. "One might think," Vyazemski sarcastically remarked, "that I had asked for the command of some detachment, corps, or at least a division in the active army." [26] A correct notion of the imperial reaction to the requests of both friends may be gathered from a letter of the tsar's brother, Constantine Pavlovich, to Benkendorf: "Is it possible for you to think that Pushkin and Prince Vyazemski were really guided by a desire to serve his majesty as loyal subjects when they asked permission to join the imperial headquarters? No, there was nothing of the kind; they have already shown themselves so morally depraved that they could not possibly nourish any honorable feeling. Believe me, in their request they have some other purpose, such as to find a new field for the dissemination of their own immoral principles, which would be quickly taken up by the majority of their adherents among the young officers." [27] The ghosts of the fourteenth of December still haunted the royal household. There is some reason to believe that Benkendorf had the supreme effrontery to offer Pushkin a position in his own Third Section as a kind of compensation for the tsar's unwillingness to send him to the Caucasus!

The refusal literally reduced Pushkin to illness. Benkendorf, upon hearing of this, had the kindness to send a message to the effect that the tsar valued his life too much to risk it in the active army, and that his majesty would soon use him in a way more suitable to his special talents. Despite the obvious flattery, which no doubt was Benkendorf's own concoction, Pushkin quickly applied for permission to go to Paris to get out an edition of his works. But this request was also denied. In a visit to Kronstadt it was said that Pushkin toyed with the idea of stowing away on one of the ships in the harbor in the hope of reaching a foreign port. His enervated spirits sank still lower with the growing conviction that he was as much a prisoner as he had been at Mikhailovskoe during his exile. His detention camp was simply larger.

A sudden danger that carried with it a strong threat of Siberia was added to his burden of misery. The long-drawn-out process concerning the *André Chénier* poem had not yet been concluded when a Captain V. F. Mitkov was arrested for having in his possession a manuscript copy of the *Gavriliada*. His servants had complained to the authorities that their master debauched their religious faith by reading this blasphemous poem to them. The matter was brought to the attention of the tsar, and a special commission appointed to investigate. On the twenty-fifth of July, 1828, Pushkin was summoned before the military governor general of Petersburg to be examined. The situation was extremely serious. An admission of authorship of such a thoroughly irreverent production would most certainly have earned him severe punishment. Nicholas I professed to be a devout ruler, and the powerful church would exact the last pound of flesh for such an offense. The surprising fact, considering the number of copies of the *Gavriliada* that had been in circulation since 1820, is that the poem had not been discovered by the police sooner.

Early in August Pushkin presented written testimony that he had read the poem but had not composed it. The tsar, apparently unwilling to lose this opportunity to push an advantage, refused to accept his simple denial. The authorities summoned Pushkin again, and he answered the questions put to him more fully in writing. "The manuscript," he testified, "had circulated among the officers of the Hussar regiment [at Tsarskoe Selo], but from whom I obtained mine I do not at all remember. My own copy I burned, no doubt in 1820. I make bold to add that in none of my works, even in those which I especially regret, are there any traces of disbelief or blasphemy. It is all the more distressing to have ascribed to me a production so wretched and shameful." [28]

This document was presented to the tsar, but again he refused to be convinced. There is the strong probability that he had some secret information, unknown to the authorities, and hence was not fooled by Pushkin's pious lying. Nicholas returned the testimony to the commission with the cleverly calculated advice that they were to summon Pushkin once more and "to tell him in my name that, knowing Pushkin personally, I believe his word. But I desire that he aid the government in discovering who could have composed such an abomination and who could offend Pushkin by placing it under his name."[29]

Pushkin received this communication in silence, and after much deliberation he asked permission to send a sealed letter to the emperor. The permission was granted. Apparently the statement of Nicholas had appealed to his essential honesty and truthfulness. He wrote a letter which was delivered to the tsar. Its contents were never revealed. But it is a pretty safe assumption that he frankly confessed his authorship of the *Gavriliada*, expressed his sincere regrets, and threw himself upon the mercy of Nicholas. At any rate, the whole case was suddenly and mysteriously dropped by order of the tsar. Pushkin's moral obligation to Nicholas was now more binding. The silken chains were drawn a little tighter.

The accumulated disappointments and adversities of 1828 no doubt encouraged Pushkin's dissolute existence in Petersburg, and the patronage and guardianship of the emperor throttled his natural free impulses. On the twenty-sixth of May he wrote the following well-known poem, which clearly reflects the bitter spiritual misery under which he labored:

> Gift in vain, and gift of chance,
> Life, why wert thou given me?
> Why have I been thus condemned
> To a secret fate by thee?
>
> Who with some strange hostile power
> Summoned me from nothingness,
> And disturbed my mind with doubt,
> Filled my soul with passion's stress?
>
> Goal there's none before me now:
> Empty heart and idle brain,
> Life's monotonous roaring sound
> Burdens me with endless pain.[30]

IV

> We poets in tranquillity
> Find refuge in our endless
> dreaming.
>
> *Tokens*

The poetic inspiration that Pushkin had vainly sought in the country quiet of Mikhailovskoe he found, curiously enough, in the excitement and dissipation of the city. One is reminded of the stormy period after his graduation from the Lyceum, when he persistently hammered away at *Ruslan and Liudmila* in the midst of his youthful orgies in the capital. By the end of February 1828 he had published five of the six chapters of *Eugene Onegin* which he had finished during his exile. In the spring he drafted the seventh chapter. As the autumn of this year approached, he experienced a lively urge for composition. Autumn was his favorite time for writing. This somber season of the year affected Pushkin in the way that spring traditionally affects most poets. When summer's beauty faded, his creative power grew unusually active, and an insistent desire to write took possession of him. It was scarcely force of habit, though this may have had something to do with it. He was thoroughly aware of this seasonal influence, as were many of his friends, and the bulk of his best work was written in autumn.

During October 1828 Pushkin forsook his worldly pleasures, shut himself up in his rooms, and devoted himself to writing a long poem in three cantos, *Poltava*. The design of the work had been in his mind for some time, and the poem advanced with incredible swiftness. He had finished the first canto by the third, the second by the ninth, and the third by the sixteenth of the month. He literally lived poetry during these three weeks, writing all day and most of the night. Verses came to him in his sleep, and he jumped up to set them down on paper. When hunger overtook him, he hurried to a neighboring restaurant. The lines pursued him there, and with a piece of bread in his hand he dashed home to write before he forgot the verses that were running through his head. When thoughts refused to take the form of poetry, he set them down in prose, which he later versified. Thus hundreds of lines were composed.

Poltava, written in such a white heat of inspiration, is a significant work in Pushkin's literary development. It is an unusual combination of two themes, one purely romantic, the other heroic. The former concerns the love of the wily old Hetman Mazepa for his goddaughter, Mariya Kochubei, who runs away from her father's home to live with Mazepa. This story is connected with the heroic theme — the historic struggle between Peter the Great and Charles XII of Sweden — by the treason of Mazepa. The father of Mariya, deeply offended by her actions, reveals Mazepa's treasonous plan to join the forces of Charles. Peter does not believe him and turns the father over to the hetman, who promptly executes him. Mariya hears of her father's fate too late to plead his cause. She goes mad and refuses to return to Mazepa. The heroic theme is taken up at this point, and the third canto contains the superb description of the battle of Poltava in which Peter defeats the combined forces of Charles and Mazepa.

The juxtaposition of these two strikingly dissimilar themes represents, perhaps, an artistic flaw. In a sense, the romantic element is a continuation of Pushkin's early Southern verse tales. But the heroic theme, the best part of the poem, is a striking expression of Pushkin's new literary objectivity and of his creative interest in Russian history, which had been manifested in *Boris Godunov*. In portraying the figure of Peter, who is elevated to godlike proportions, Pushkin expresses a patriotic fervor which was deeply ingrained in his nature. He identifies himself with the nation as the singer of its glories and as a member of an old historic family. The treatment of the historic theme, which is completely objective, and the diction advance along the lines of his latest development. The diction of *Poltava* entirely eschews the easy mellifluous quality of the early tales. It is hard, compact, metallic — heroic in the best sense of the word.

Poltava ended, Pushkin attended a rollicking alumni meeting of his Lyceum class on the nineteenth of October and then left for Malinniki, the estate of Aleksei Vulf and his mother at Tver. Here he found this old Trigorskoe friend and her two daughters,

Anna and Evpraksiya Vulf. At Malinniki he wrote the splendid and mysterious dedication of *Poltava*, and finished the seventh chapter of *Eugene Onegin*. Several short poems were also composed, including *Anchar*, the poisonous Upas tree that stands alone in the desert, another example of Pushkin's rare quality of terse, compact expression, to which no translation can do justice. He thoroughly enjoyed himself on this estate. Neighbors came from all the countryside to see the great poet. There was much diversion to be found in the company of Praskovya Osipova's two daughters and her many relatives and friends. He flirted with Elizaveta Poltoratskaya, sister of Anna Kern and, like her, much in love with Aleksei Vulf. (The Trigorskoe Lovelace was jealous of his teacher's attention to Elizaveta.) He also wrote enthusiastically to Vulf in Petersburg of a young girl whom he met at Malinniki, Mariya Borisova: "She is a flower in the desert, a nightingale in the thicket, a pearl in the sea, and in a few days I intend to fall in love with her." [31] This was the love-language of his friend, and Pushkin was no doubt purposely annoying him, for with his unusual capacity, Aleksei also had designs on Mariya. Teacher and pupil were often rivals, and not always friendly ones, in these transient affairs.

The creative time of autumn was over. Winter had set in. The road called him again. Pushkin left Malinniki on the sixth of December. But he did not return to Petersburg. The winter social season of Moscow was proverbial for its splendor and activity, and he headed there. Once in the city, the round of visits began among the Lovers of Wisdom, the Ushakovs, the Volkonskis, and the Korsakovs. In the home of his friend, Sergei Kiselev, he read *Poltava*. Count F. I. Tolstoi, one-time enemy and now his friend, was present, and also Vyazemski. The performance was somewhat spoiled by one of the guests, who got drunk and sick during the reading. Pushkin also saw something of Pavel Nashchokin. This unusual man occupies an important place in the remaining years of his life. Pushkin valued friendship very highly, and some of his finest lines are devoted to the theme. But of his many friends there were only a few in whom he felt free to confide his most intimate thoughts and feelings. These were Delvig, Pushchin, Sobolevski, and Nashchokin. His devotion to all of them was rare, and they in turn were never found wanting in time of need. Nashchokin was a gentleman whose only fault was his extreme kindness and utter selflessness. He possessed several fortunes in his lifetime but lost them in gambling and in helping his friends. His house was a refuge for all the poor writers and artists of the city, and innumerable paintings and statues, which he had bought to aid his artist-friends, gave it the appearance of a museum. He had an original mind and considerable ability, but he was lacking in training and mental discipline. Completely incapable of protecting his own interests, Nashchokin's material circumstances fluctuated between the two extremes of spending thousands of rubles to build a miniature house and burning invaluable antique furniture to keep himself warm.

Pushkin had perhaps met Nashchokin during his Lyceum days, but it was not until his appearance at Moscow, after his exile, that he came to know him well. From then on, their friendship grew, and on his visits to Moscow Pushkin often stayed with him in the "Pushkin Room," as Nashchokin called the quarters in his own house which he always kept ready for Pushkin's arrival. They shared with one another their cares and joys, and lent each other money. Pushkin asked his advice in important matters, often read his works for Nashchokin's criticism, and even desired that they be buried together. On this second visit to Moscow Nashchokin was living with a gypsy girl, and this contact helped to encourage Pushkin's love for gypsy entertainers and their unique singing. He spent much time with the Moscow gypsies.

Pushkin attended many of the winter social events. At one of these huge balls he saw a young girl in a fluffy gown and with a golden tiara on her head. This was the sixteen-year-old Natalya Nikolaevna Goncharova, who had only recently donned long dresses for her entrance into society. Her budding charms carried with them a prophecy of enthralling womanly beauty. More than a year later Pushkin wrote of "Natasha" Goncharova: "When I saw her for the first time, her beauty was just being noticed in society; I loved her, my head was turned." [32] But his actions in this instance of falling in love were quite contrary to his usual practice. Without any apparent reason, Pushkin left for Petersburg (January 4–5) shortly after seeing Natasha Goncharova at the ball. Natasha, however, was very much in his thoughts.

v

> No, no! Is it possible that I shall soon be thirty years old? I await this fateful time, but I have not yet said farewell to youth.
> *Pushkin to Ks. A. Polevoi*

Since Malinniki was conveniently on the road to Petersburg, Pushkin stopped off for a few days. Aleksei Vulf was there, eager to introduce his preceptor to all the local victims, past, present, and prospective, of his Lovelace technique. They traveled about together to the estates of Vulf's many relatives who had settled in the district. It is interesting to observe how thoroughly Pushkin's reputation had been established in these villages. The simple country people knew of his fame, although many had not read his poetry. They regarded him as a kind of intellectual giant whose freethinking was to be feared. The girls worshiped him, even thought him handsome, and, frightened at his long nails, called him a "devil with claws." Vulf and Pushkin had a jolly time playing cards, dancing, and flirting with provincial damsels and servants. Together they continued the journey to Petersburg, where they arrived on the eighteenth of January.

In the capital Pushkin resumed the form of life he had run away from three months before. Although he had made his peace with his father, he rarely visited the family, which now had been somewhat broken up. Arina Rodionovna had died; Lev had joined the army and was in the Caucasus fighting the Turks. In 1828 Olga eloped and married Nikolai Pavlishchev. Her parents, especially Nadezhda Osipovna, were furious, and though Pushkin tried to reconcile them to the couple, they never quite forgave the husband. Had he been of higher birth, the parents might well have been pleased, for Olga was now in her thirties. In truth, it was not a very advantageous match. Pavlishchev was an unimaginative, sour, and unsuccessful man, who eventually caused Pushkin considerable difficulty in money matters.

Pushkin's distaste for the social whirl grew more pronounced. He had not been back in Petersburg a week when he wrote to Vyazemski: "We go in for routs, because one requires in them no intelligence, gaiety, or general conversation on politics or literature." [33] His one refuge was the company of close literary friends. Here he received the acknowledgment he felt his due. Journals vied with each other for his poetry. Young writers sought him out for advice and assistance. It was about this time (January 1829) that Gogol came up to Petersburg to seek his fortune. Filled with a schoolboy worship of Pushkin, he made bold to call on him rather late one night. Courage deserted him at the door, and he repaired to a bar nearby to fortify himself with spirits. On the next try he bravely summoned the servant, who told him that his master was resting. "Is it true that he works all night?" asked Gogol. "What do you mean, 'works'?" replied the servant. "He plays cards!" [34] Young Gogol was much chagrined upon learning of this mundane occupation of his poetic idol. But he soon came to know Pushkin well, and the latter's encouragement and practical assistance helped to start Gogol on the road to a fame which eclipsed his own.

Delvig's house was the gathering place of Pushkin's particular literary group, and scarcely a day went by that he failed to visit this best of friends. Here the conversation was often brilliant. Although regarded as their leader and oracle, Pushkin did not always distinguish himself in these discussions, for he was as unequal in conversation as he was in his actions. There was little or nothing in him of the literary lion who calculates effects in public and will not follow where he cannot lead. Nor in company did he consciously play the part of the absorbed "genius" who believes that there is a special virtue in silence. Pushkin naturally dramatized himself and exploded in conversation, or he was naturally moody and uncommunicative. There is no end of contemporary testimony concerning both his brilliance and wisdom in discussion. Neither audience nor glittering occasion was necessary to make him scintillate. The subject had merely to strike the steel of his mind and the sparks flew; as his brother said, Pushkin's talk was incomparably greater than his poetry. Alexandra Smirnova, who knew him well, and whose own fine intelligence qualified her as an excellent judge, said of him: "I never knew a more clever man than Pushkin. Neither Zhukovski nor Prince Vyazemski could argue with him — he would entirely overcome them. Vyazemski, who did not wish Pushkin to seem cleverer than he, would sulk and become silent, but Zhukovski would laughingly say: 'You, brother Pushkin, the devil knows what you are — indeed, I feel that you speak nonsense, but I cannot argue you down.'" [35] His general information was extensive, and he was capable of holding forth on a variety of subjects with as much penetration and authority as he displayed in the field of literature. In this respect Mickiewicz, an acute and exacting observer, remarked: "Pushkin captivated and amazed his listeners by the liveliness, acuteness, and clarity of his mind; he was gifted with an unusual memory, showed correct judgment, a refined and excellent taste. When he spoke about European and native politics, one would think that he was listening to a man trained in governmental affairs and saturated with daily readings of parliamentary debates." [36]

Yet he offended as often as he delighted in this circle of intellectuals at Delvig's. Unfeeling remarks, brutal frankness, and sarcasm wounded and made enemies. Often he seemed anything but wise. And during the winter of 1829 he was more prone to irritate than to please. A fancied slight, and he was ready with a challenge. Friends noticed that he had changed. His high-spirited, ebullient nature had become morose and apathetic. His thirtieth birthday was at hand, and he was beginning to feel old — with that false but none the less poignant senility of a man who has reached the end of youth. Only very close friends seemed to sense the struggle going on within him.

Physical action had always served Pushkin as a kind of antidote for moral weariness. His whole being cried out for such physical action now. But the government stood in his way. Suddenly, on March 9, as one of his impulsive and characteristic gestures of despair, he fled from the capital without bothering to ask anybody's permission. His destination was the army in the Caucasus. But he would go by way of Moscow. The image of Natasha Goncharova had grown brighter in his mind during these dark Petersburg days.

Pushkin stayed with Nashchokin in Moscow. Rumor was already explaining that he had come to propose to Ekaterina Ushakova. (Pushkin's friends were as determined to get him married off as he was himself.) He visited the Ushakovs often during this stay, but he had no intention of proposing to Ekaterina. It was said that he visited her house every day simply to pass by the window of Natasha Goncharova twice a day. Count F. I. Tolstoi knew the Goncharovs, and through his efforts Pushkin was soon introduced into the family. He was modest and awkward at this first visit, confused by the importance and conviction of his own intentions. And the young Natasha was painfully self-conscious. But her girlish modesty only made her all the more attractive in his eyes.

Before long Pushkin was calling as often as propriety would permit. He got on well enough with the family, but he soon had sharp differences with the mother, Natalya Ivanovna. She had positive ideas about religious devotion and the glorious character of the late Emperor Alexander I, ideas which Pushkin unwisely objected to. But he eventually felt that his position was strong enough to make a definite proposal, which he did through Count Tolstoi. The mother was evasive, putting him off with the excuse that it was necessary to wait a bit, for her daughter was still too young to be thinking of marriage.

Discouraged, but still nourishing hope, Pushkin set out for the army in the Caucasus on the first of May. That same day he wrote to the mother of his beloved: "I ought to write you on my knees while shedding tears of gratitude over your answer, which Count Tolstoi has just brought me. This answer is not a refusal; you still permit me to hope. However, if I still complain, if sadness and bitterness mingle with my feelings of happiness, do not accuse me of ingratitude; I understand the prudence and tenderness of a mother! But forgive the impatience of a heart sick with happiness. I am departing at once, and I carry in the depths of my soul the image of a celestial being to whom you gave life." [37]

CHAPTER XVI

Marriage

> God has sent thee down to me,
> my Madonna,
> The purest image of the purest
> charm.
>
> *Madonna*

Pushkin did not leave Moscow for the Caucasus because his proposal to Natasha Goncharova had been rejected. He was not foolish enough to suppose that the evasive answer of her mother amounted to anything more than the polite refusal which convention demanded under such circumstances. The mother simply had other plans for her daughter. The Caucasus and war would give him time to think, and perhaps to forget. His mind had been set on this trip two months before. But the failure of the marriage plans unquestionably sealed his determination to be off for the wars. Some contemporaries hinted that the journey was a kind of gambling junket arranged by card sharps. Their idea was to use Pushkin to beguile wealthy and gullible army officers into games for heavy stakes. Nothing that we know of Pushkin's conduct on this trip, however, supports such a preposterous notion. Apart from a desire for action and new scenes to offset his spiritual and emotional weariness, he earnestly wished to see his brother, as well as Nikolai Raevski and other friends who were serving with the Caucasian army.

Pushkin's first indiscretion was to travel a good deal out of his way to visit the famous General Ermolov, who was then living in retirement in Orël. For years Ermolov had fought Russia's battles in the wilds of the Caucasus, and after conquering the country had become its governor general. But he had a reputation for liberalism, and was even considered by the Decembrists as a possible leader of the provisional government

they had intended to set up. Naturally, Nicholas I lost no time
in displacing this man, really a national hero, giving his command to General, later Field Marshal, Ivan Paskevich, who
was now leading the Caucasian army. Pushkin spent a day in
the company of Ermolov, whom he described as having "the
head of a tiger on a herculean torso." [1] The conversation of the
great poet and the great soldier left them deeply impressed
with one another. "On this first occasion I was with him only
for a short time," wrote Ermolov, "but what power of lofty
talent was there!" [2] Later Pushkin intended to write a life of
Ermolov, a task which he never lived to perform. As might
be expected, the police reported this meeting of two such
suspicious persons to the authorities in Petersburg.

From Orël Pushkin went forward by swift stages to Tiflis. He
arrived on the twenty-seventh of May and sent a request to
Paskevich at the front for permission to join the active forces.
Meanwhile, he made the most of his stay in the Georgian capital. Pushkin's fame had preceded him — and also the police
reports. When he left Petersburg in March, Benkendorf had
been informed by a secret agent of his intentions to go to the
Caucasus. A dispatch was quickly sent to Paskevich, who was
told to be on the lookout for Pushkin and to keep him under
surveillance. The general communicated with the authorities
at Tiflis, and Pushkin's every move was watched.

Local admirers arranged a sumptuous feast in honor of the
visit of the great poet. All manner of Eastern food, music, and
dancing was presented for his entertainment. Pushkin was
deeply touched, wept, and made a speech which he concluded:
"I do not remember a day in which I have been as happy as
now; I see how they love, understand, and value me — and
how happy this makes me!" [3] But on the whole, he did not like
Tiflis; the food was bad, and he thought the prices sheer
robbery.

Pushkin was overjoyed when on the eighth of June he finally
received Paskevich's permission to join the army. He made all
haste over a difficult country and in bad weather, displaying
unusual endurance and covering as much as fifty miles a day on

horseback. On the thirteenth he caught up with the troops near the village of Kotanla by the Kars-chaya river shortly before they went into action. The war was simply an extension to the Caucasus of the hostilities that had broken out between Russia and Turkey along the Danube in 1828. Kars, a formidable stronghold, had already fallen, and Paskevich was trying to bring the struggle to an end by capturing the enemy's principal city of Erzerum.

Pushkin's immediate concern was to find his brother, an adjutant in the Nizhni Novgorod Dragoon regiment, which his old friend Nikolai Raevski commanded. The meeting was noisy. Friends surrounded him, for he knew many of these officers. Among them were his Lyceum comrade, Valkhovski, and Mikhail Pushchin, the brother of another schoolmate. But conversation had to wait, for the army was preparing to march against the enemy. Not until nightfall, after camp had been pitched, was Pushkin presented to General Paskevich, who received him pleasantly enough.

The next day Pushkin's eagerness for action was granted. A remnant of his old ambition for an army career still lingered. He wanted to see Turks, to engage in a hand-to-hand struggle with them; for Pushkin the army signified only heroic deeds. In the afternoon a large party of Kurds suddenly attacked the Russian advance line of Cossacks. Shots rang out. In a twinkling Pushkin leaped on a horse and galloped off in the direction of the enemy, gallantly waving a saber. Friends feared his impetuous nature and had strictly warned him to remain in the rear. They started in pursuit. Fortunately, a detachment of cavalry arrived to disperse the invaders, and Pushkin did not get a chance to try his saber on a Turkish head. Perhaps in this instance he was lucky to keep his own head on his shoulders. One may well imagine the surprise of the warlike Cossacks at seeing in their midst this poet turned Mars, charging along with saber, Caucasian cloak, and top hat. They took him for an army chaplain.

For a short time Pushkin enjoyed this life, riding with the troops in his civilian clothes and carrying a Cossack whip. On

the march he lived in Raevski's tent, sharing the officers' board
and pleasures. From all accounts, camp life had its bright spots
in an army that was overwhelmingly superior to the enemy.
There was much merry conversation, and excellent feasts of
Eastern *shashlyk* and champagne chilled in mountain snow.
Pushkin even introduced a literary note by reading his verses,
for many of these officers were interested in poetry.

As the campaign lagged, however, Pushkin began to lose his
initial enthusiasm. The enemy were strange fighters. They
never seemed to come out in the open in this mountainous
country, and he never got an opportunity to slaughter a Turk.
The Russians advanced with some ease, and Pushkin took
great pride in their victories. But the extreme heat and the
task of keeping up with the troops on long marches began to
tell on his strength, unused to such continual exertion. He also
began to observe conditions in the army more closely, and war
lost much of the glamour with which his poetic imagination had
always invested it. The poverty and the hard lot of the common soldier aroused his sympathy. As the campaign neared its
end, he did not throw himself forward so eagerly. In fact, he
grew very weary of it all and soon had had enough of army life.

Erzerum fell on the twenty-seventh of June, scarcely offering
any resistance. Pushkin entered the town with the victors. He
expected to find a little Moslem Bagdad, filled with all the
exotic pleasures of Oriental refinement. Instead, he beheld un-
believable dirt, poverty, and disease. He spent three weeks in
Erzerum. Pushkin mentions the plague, which broke out in the
town, as his reason for leaving it and the army. However,
there were certainly other contributing factors. He had attached himself to the Nizhni Novgorod Dragoons, and after the
taking of Erzerum this connection ended. His close friends were
detailed elsewhere. Left alone, he was obliged to spend much of
his time with Paskevich. Now he missed the clever conversation of his intellectual officer-friends at the commander's staff
dinners which he had to attend. Paskevich was primarily interested in his own military glory. At first Pushkin had been
well received by him, for the commander no doubt hoped that

the great poet would immortalize his victories in verse. But Pushkin was no more disposed to sing the commander's praise than he had been in the case of Count Vorontsov in Odessa. Perhaps Paskevich was piqued by the silence of Pushkin's muse; at any rate, he soon began to regard the poet as an annoying liability in the army. Among Pushkin's officer-friends were many former Decembrists who had been lowered in rank and relegated to line regiments. Spies sent in exaggerated reports to the commander of his conversations with these offenders. Furthermore, Pushkin's independent attitude was irritating, and he appears to have assimilated something of the dislike which many of the officers had for the general. Paskevich quickly grew cold, and he realized that the feeling was mutual. According to one account, they even had an open quarrel, the upshot of which was Paskevich's order that Pushkin leave the army immediately. With the present of a Turkish saber from the commander as a peace token, he left Erzerum about the twenty-first of July.

After a few days at Tiflis, Pushkin made his way back in leisurely fashion through a country which he had come to know well in 1820. He halted at Vladikavkaz, Pyatigorsk, and Kislovodsk. There was much drinking and gambling with friends he picked up on the way. Everybody knew that the famous poet had been with the army, and upon his return they expected thrilling verse on Russia's victories and heroes. Pushkin published nothing, and his silence was severely criticized, especially by Bulgarin. His Caucasian experiences inspired a few short pieces, however, and several years later (1836) he wrote his prose *Journey to Erzerum*,[4] which is, in part, a kind of apology for any offense his silence may have given to the hospitality of Paskevich. Yet the work is anything but a hymn of praise to the illustrious commander. Bulgarin mocked its appearance in print.

If Pushkin had a notion that this period of more than four months of travel and life in a martial atmosphere would kill his passion for Natasha Goncharova, he was much mistaken. He had written once to her mother from the Caucasus but received no answer. Now he was returning to try his luck again with the beautiful daughter.

II

Pushkin arrived in Moscow towards the end of September. It was morning, and he went directly to the Goncharovs. The mother, who was not yet up, received him in her bedroom. She behaved coldly, and Natasha treated him with calculated indifference. Deeply discouraged, he soon departed for Malinniki. He later wrote that he left Moscow "with death in my heart,"[5] the same expression he had used several years before when Sofya Pushkina had rejected his proposal. Now there was a difference in the kind of despair. His feeling for Natasha Goncharova was no transient infatuation. He had grown older, time was flying, and the possibilities of marriage seemed more remote than ever.

Why did the Goncharovs spurn an offer from Russia's greatest poet, an offer that many families would have been flattered to receive? Afanasi Goncharov, the founder of the family in the seventeenth century, was a merchant who had amassed an enormous fortune in paper and linen manufacturing in Kaluga. The Goncharov products had become known throughout Russia and were even marketed abroad. But a grandson squandered the family wealth, and the business declined rapidly. Nikolai Afanasevich, the next in line, married Natalya Ivanovna Zagryazhskaya, the mother of Pushkin's Natasha. She came from an aristocratic family that had fallen on evil times. Only after her marriage did she discover that the reputed Goncharov wealth had already passed into the realm of legend. Her husband made a brave attempt to repair the family fortunes, but his spendthrift and mad father continually hindered his efforts. Six children were born to the couple, three sons and three daughters, of whom Natasha was the youngest. To add to their misfortunes, Nikolai Afanasevich, after a severe accident, showed positive signs of the insanity that ran through the Goncharov strain.

When Pushkin became acquainted with the Goncharovs they

NATALYA NIKOLAEVNA PUSHKINA

1844

had settled in Moscow. While trying to present the appearance of a well-to-do family to the social world, they were really living a hand-to-mouth existence. With the husband now entirely incapacitated, the wife dominated the household. Adversities encouraged a tendency to religious mania in Natalya Ivanovna which eventually clouded the last years of her life. She ran her house like a convent, was continually surrounded by priests, monks, and pilgrims, and spent many hours a day in prayer. Family questions were referred to priests, and she rarely made a decision without appealing to God and the Bible for inspiration. She brought up her children, especially the daughters, in blind obedience to her every wish, and promised them hell and damnation for the slightest infraction of her stern regimen. Apart from religious training, the daughters received even less than the meager education of Moscow girls of good families. They learned French at the expense of Russian, a little music, and fancy embroidery. Of the world and its wicked temptations they were taught a pious fear. Most of their cloistered existence was devoted to cultivating the polite affectations and feminine arts which were thought necessary to catch husbands. For the daughters this was the mother's only aim — a rich husband would repair the family fortunes. Despite all her efforts, however, the two eldest daughters, Ekaterina and Alexandra, had failed to find suitable husbands. They were rather plain girls and had no compensating attractions that would make them especially desirable to the critical Moscow youths. In fact, the mother had virtually lost all hope for her two elder daughters, and now she concentrated her efforts on Natasha.

Natasha was truly beautiful and had some reason to expect a brilliant marriage. But apart from her looks, she had little to recommend her. The Moscow youths paid Natasha many compliments, but for some reason or other they went no further. She was still very young, to be sure, but her lack of immediate success may be attributed to the material conditions of her family. Even with beauty the Moscow cavalier expected a dowry, and it was no secret that the Goncharovs could not afford one. Pushkin had been sized up by the mother, not as a great poet, but as a prospective match for her daughter. She had no interest in literature or literary fame. What she wanted was a fashionable and wealthy husband for Natasha. Furthermore, she had heard, like everybody else, of Pushkin's rakish reputation and the fact that he was under police surveillance. She had no particular relish for such a son-in-law. However, since Natasha had not received any other offers, Natalya Ivanovna was not ready to reject Pushkin unconditionally. Her position was simply one of hopeful waiting. If at any time in the negotiations a proposal from a more desirable party had been made, the mother would gladly have given Pushkin an emphatic "no." And one may be sure that her pretty daughter would have readily concurred.

III

Pushkin left Moscow on the twelfth of October and spent several weeks at Malinniki. For a man with "death in his heart," he seems to have whiled away the time very pleasantly at this jolly Tver estate of Praskovya Osipova and her son. Aleksei Vulf was in the Caucasus, and Pushkin wrote him of his doings at Malinniki. The letter is an itemized account of the local beauties. The Trigorskoe Lovelace was credited with having a harem of twelve girls on the estate, and with exercising the *jus primae noctis* among his serfs. Netty Vulf occupies a prominent place in the letter. "For three days now I have been in love with her," [6] Pushkin wrote. This news prompted Aleksei to remark about his preceptor: "He does not change with the years, and he has returned from Erzerum precisely as he went — a most cynical lady-chaser." [7]

But Aleksei Vulf could never see in Pushkin anything other than the Mephistopheles who had given him his first lessons in the "science of the tender passions." In reality, Pushkin cared nothing for these provincial damsels of Malinniki. Not one of them, in his eyes, could compare with the beautiful Natasha in Moscow. Fretful and restless, he was soon on his way to Petersburg. When he arrived in the first week of November, another misfortune awaited him in the nature of an angry letter from Benkendorf. "His majesty has deigned to command me," wrote the head of the secret police, "to ask you by whose permission you undertook this journey [to the Caucasus]. On my side, I most humbly request you to inform me why, not living up to your word, you did not apply to me, but went to the Caucasus without telling me of your intention of making this trip." [8] The "freedom" granted him by the tsar was obviously an empty promise. Pushkin had long understood this fact, but now he was weary of it all. And wearily he replied to Benkendorf, abjectly begging the tsar's pardon for his "offense." Even the spirit of resistance seemed to fail him.

"Here in Petersburg there is anguish, anguish!" [9] Pushkin soon wrote to a friend in Moscow. It was the anguish in his own soul that he complained against. The city's pleasures now provided no escape. He continued to indulge his passion for gambling — as usual, unsuccessfully; and he was still bored by the benevolent attentions of Elizaveta Khitrovo. Happily, at this time a new literary enterprise occupied his mind. His popularity had begun to wane, largely through the efforts of hostile critics, such as Nadezhdin and Bulgarin. At first the line of attack had been to praise his early works at the expense of his recent productions; Pushkin's powers were failing, said the critics. But when *Poltava* appeared in 1829 and the seventh chapter of *Eugene Onegin* the following year, the scurrilous criticism of the works made it clear to Pushkin that he had a literary war on his hands. In reality two camps had been formed. Pushkin found himself at the head of the older, more conservative writers, a kind of literary aristocracy. The other camp consisted mostly of the journalists, such as Polevoi, Bulgarin, and Nadezhdin, who often essayed belles-lettres. By this time romanticism had pretty much won the day over the old French neo-classical influence. Along with most of the younger writers and critics, Pushkin accepted this fact. He was by no means opposed to innovation. But he wished to prevent literature from becoming completely commercialized and to raise its social standard by keeping criticism out of the realm of per-

sonal spite and arrant favoritism, toward which it was rapidly
tending.

The enemy, however, held a strong position and was un-
scrupulous in its tactics. The editors Bulgarin, Grech, and
Senkovski virtually controlled the journalistic world. Bulgarin's *Northern Bee* was the only daily paper allowed to publish political news, and his favored position with the government
as a secret police agent enabled him to dictate. For, by exerting
his influence, he invariably succeeded in ruining the efforts of
competing journalists who did not belong to his particular
group.

Pushkin and his adherents realized that only by establishing
a journal of their own, which would serve as an outlet for their
personal views and criticism, could they hope to contend successfully with Bulgarin and his followers. The *Moscow Messenger* had been a gesture in this direction, but under Pogodin
the magazine was rapidly being turned into an historical publication. The situation increased Pushkin's desire to edit his
own journal, but as yet the authorities were not disposed to
grant him this favor. The devious type of censorship which
controlled his every production also limited his effectiveness
as a contributor. A way was eventually found to circumvent
these difficulties. After much opposition the government finally
gave Delvig permission to edit a strictly non-political paper,
the *Literary Gazette*.[10] In many respects Pushkin himself was
the editor, since he formulated the policies and worked in complete harmony with Delvig, who shared his literary views. He
was the chief contributor and got around the censorship by
printing his articles anonymously.

The first number of the *Literary Gazette* appeared on January
5, 1830. It at once set a high literary standard. Besides Delvig
and Pushkin, contributions were solicited from such friends as
Vyazemski, Baratynski, and Zhukovski. The magazine's purpose of opposing Bulgarin and his group was no secret, and
Pushkin played a leading part in these polemics. In the case
of his own poetry he had aways been reluctant to reply to
hostile criticism. But he relished the task of raising the cudgels

in defense of the works of others when he felt that they had been treated unfairly. His contributions to the *Literary Gazette* reveal him as a superb journalist and a critic of unusual insight. His views are always stated with perfect clarity in the terse, unadorned style which he cultivated in prose. His little masterpieces of polemics are written with the same economy and neatness as his lyrics. Nor was he lacking in stinging satiric wit in these journalistic battles. Bulgarin, enraged at his success, was soon making every effort to have the *Literary Gazette* suppressed.

These activities helped to absorb Pushkin's energies during the winter of 1829–1830, but they did little to cure his chronic unrest or to make him forget his failure at Moscow. On the seventh of January he once again appealed to Benkendorf for permission to leave Russia. He begins his letter very pointedly: "Since I am not yet married or attached to the service, I should like to make a journey either to France or Italy. However, if this may not be allowed, I should like leave to go to China with the mission which is being sent there." [11] It made no difference, France, Italy, or China — anywhere, so long as he got out of Russia! Benkendorf could hardly miss the despair in this request, but refusing Pushkin had become almost a routine matter with him. His majesty, Benkendorf explained, feared that a trip abroad would be too expensive for Pushkin, and besides it would take him away from his occupations. (Pushkin must have felt this last reason an insult to his intelligence.) As for the diplomatic mission to China, which the government was on the point of sending, Benkendorf informed him that all the positions had been filled. Despite the chagrin with which Pushkin received this rather stupid refusal, it is interesting to observe him humbling his pride in a good cause in the letter of acknowledgment which he wrote the very next day. In this he makes a personal plea to Benkendorf to procure a pension for the forgotten widow of his old friend, General Raevski. It is doubtful whether Pushkin's generous attempt carried any weight with the tsar, but the widow was soon granted a pension.

It would have been easier for Pushkin to stomach the government's hostile attitude if he had felt that he was in any way deserving of it. He believed that he had made his peace with the tsar, that he was a favored person, and that he had outwardly, at least, lived up to his moral obligation to Nicholas. Since he had no certain knowledge that the tsar still regarded him as a troublesome and dangerous subject, he was now convinced that the persistent refusals of his request indicated that he was out of favor with Nicholas. This conviction pained him deeply. Instead of being regarded as a person of consequence, he was treated like a pardoned malefactor who had not been restored to grace. And the authorities lost no chance of rubbing it in. Once he appeared in civilian dress at a ball given by the French ambassador. Promptly he received an indignant communication from Benkendorf, informing him of the tsar's displeasure over the fact that he had not worn the uniform of a noble. The government was determined to keep him in line and to make him feel that his very existence was on sufferance of the tsar. But encroachments on his personal liberties during most of his mature life had not inured Pushkin to this form of enslavement. His temperament was not of the submissive kind, and although he was dealing with an all-powerful autocrat, he was capable of striking back. His natural love of freedom could never die within him.

A fragmentary poem of this time suggests that Pushkin's longing for travel was prompted by the hope of forgetting Natasha Goncharova:

> Let's go wherever you desire, my friend;
> I'm ready now to follow to the end.
> Fleeing the proud one, I'm for anywhere,
> Even to distant China's wall, or there
> In seething Paris town, or where at night
> The oarsman used to sing of Tasso's plight,
> Where 'neath the dust the ancient relics rare
> Still sleep, and cypress groves perfume the air —
> I'm ready, friend, so let us say good-by.
> Tell me, in travel will my passion die?
> Shall I forget this maid and my cruel pain?
> Or to her feet and to her young disdain
> Shall I once more my loving tribute bring? [12]

But the nepenthe of China or seething Paris or Tasso's native land had been denied him. There was no fleeing the proud one, and it is safe to say that had his desire for foreign travel been fulfilled, he would still have brought back his "loving tribute" to Natasha. Like a lovesick youth who had lost all hope, Pushkin's thoughts dwelt on death:

> Whether the noisy streets I wander,
> Or in the crowded temple pray,
> Or sit with foolish youths, I ponder
> And steep myself in thought. I say:
>
> How years speed past, so swiftly ending,
> While to us all there's much unclear;
> Into eternal vaults descending
> Will be our lot; our hour is near.
>
> .   .   .   .
>
> Each day and year of mortal pining
> There lives with me the self-same gloom,
> Among them ceaselessly divining
> The coming holiday of doom.[13]

Yet thoughts of death did not prevent him from keeping an ear cocked for news of Natasha Goncharova from Moscow. The winter social season of the ancient city might quickly put an end to what little hope remained. Reports soon began to dribble into Petersburg. Yes, Natasha was taking a prominent part in balls and entertainments. Pushkin heard that as Dido's sister, in one of the classical tableau representations much in fashion then, Natasha had achieved a signal success. Everybody was talking of her beauty. And then came to Pushkin's ear the expected rumor of a suitor. Hurriedly he wrote to Vyazemski in Moscow: "Is it true that my Goncharova will marry the archivist Meshcherski?" [14] Shortly after this inquiry, Pushkin himself was on his way to Moscow, still not ready to accept defeat.

IV

> My road is sad.
> *Elegy*

The police dutifully reported Pushkin's arrival in Moscow on March 12. He wrote to Vyazemski that he jumped from his carriage into a concert hall and there beheld Natasha Goncharova. She was more beautiful than ever, and she was not engaged to anyone! His hopes soared, and the pursuit was taken up once more. "Mama Kars"—Pushkin's nickname for Natasha's mother, suggested to him by the formidable fortress of Kars — was still unassailable, but the chances of her capitulation had improved since the siege of a few months ago. Rumor persisted that he was seeking the hand of Ekaterina Ushakova in Moscow, for Pushkin had kept his courting of Goncharova a secret, even from his close friends. He now felt his case so promising that he actually hinted of the affair to Vyazemski.

Pushkin carefully refrained from duplicating his disorderly Petersburg life in Moscow. Pious Mama Kars already held this against him, and he had no desire to offend her further. He even became somewhat domesticated during this waiting period, remaining at home with respectable friends and smoking his pipe. To be sure, there were stolen moments of gambling and furtive visits to gypsy singers, but his behavior, in comparison with that of the past two years, was exemplary. Doting Elizaveta Khitrovo wrote him nearly every day from Petersburg and plaintively regretted his failure to reply. She worried excessively over his health and promised to keep him informed of the social world of the capital, of literature and politics. Joyfully she repeated the compliments paid him by the tsar's brother in her presence. "How I love anyone who loves you!" [15] she pathetically concluded. Pushkin appreciated her devotion, but he had no time or patience now for this indirect love-making of a woman almost thirty years older than Natasha Goncharova. With irritation he wrote to Vyazemski: "If you can fall in love with Eliza yourself, then do me this divine favor." [16]

The ubiquitous Benkendorf soon interrupted his comparative calm. A haughty letter of the seventeenth of March demanded to know why he had gone to Moscow without asking permission. And again he was charged with breaking his word. In his reply Pushkin did not conceal his vexation. He bluntly pointed out Benkendorf's inconsistency in requesting a reason for his trip to Moscow on this occasion and failing to do so in previous instances. Meanwhile, open warfare had flared up between Pushkin and the editor Bulgarin. An anonymous article, actually written by Delvig, had appeared in the *Literary Gazette* on March 7, attacking Bulgarin's historical romance, *The False Dmitri*. Bulgarin, attributing the article to Pushkin, had printed an extremely vicious lampoon on the poet in his *Northern Bee*. Like most of his literary friends, Pushkin knew of Bulgarin's connection with the secret police, and he no doubt suspected that Benkendorf countenanced the lampoon. This was actually true. In the continuation of the journalistic war Benkendorf defended Bulgarin when even the tsar felt that he had gone too far in his vilification of Pushkin. Enraged over the attack, and with Benkendorf's letter of the seventeenth of March still rankling, Pushkin finally turned on his official guardian. "Despite four years of blameless conduct," he wrote Benkendorf, "I have not been able to obtain the confidence of the authorities! With pain I see that my every step arouses suspicion and ill will. General, pardon the freedom with which I complain, but in heaven's name deign to enter for a moment into my position and see how embarrassing it is. It is so precarious that every moment I feel myself on the verge of a misfortune which I cannot foresee or escape. If up to this time I have not fallen into some disgrace, I owe it not to a consciousness of my own rights, of my duty, but uniquely to your personal good will. I shall be thrown into prison on the very day after you cease to be minister. Mr. Bulgarin, who, in his own words, makes use of your influence, has become one of my bitterest enemies because of a critical essay which he has attributed to me. After the infamous article which he has published about me, I believe him capable of anything." [17] It is very likely that Pushkin toned down his anger a bit, in view of the fact that he desired permission to visit Nikolai Raevski in Pskov. However, the request was refused, by order of the tsar, who at that time was displeased with the behavior of Raevski. Benkendorf saw something of the mettle of Pushkin in this communication. Yet it did not change his attitude toward the poet. Nor was the spy Bulgarin muzzled in the least. He continued his journalistic diatribes, and because of a protected position he came off best in this war, but not before he had earned an unenviable immortality in the satire of Pushkin.

For the moment Benkendorf's rebuffs and the hostile criticism of the press were forgotten in the imminent fall of Mama Kars. No acceptable offers of marriage had been made by any of the desirable young blades of Moscow. And Pushkin's position was greatly strengthened by the fact that he would ask for no dowry, an important consideration with the Goncharovs. At the beginning of April he thought the time ripe to make a second proposal. The mother apparently asked him to state his position in writing. His letter is interesting. Pushkin rehearses the courtship up to his return from the Caucasus, mentioning the cold reception he had received on that occasion. He does not attempt to justify his wayward past, but maintains that vicious scandal has exaggerated the faults of his character. "I felt," he writes of his early efforts to win Natasha, "that I played a very ridiculous role; I was timid for the first time in my life, and this timidity in a man of my age could hardly please a young person of your daughter's age." But now, filled with a new hope, he is willing to state his intentions frankly: "Habit and long intimacy alone would help me to gain the affection of your daughter; in the course of time I can hope to bind her to me, but I have nothing with which to please her; if she consents to give me her hand, I shall see in this only a proof of the tranquil indifference of her heart. But, surrounded with admiration, homage, seductions, will this tranquillity endure? It will be said that an unfortunate fate has prevented her from forming other connections more equal, more brilliant, more worthy of her — perhaps these remarks will be sincere, but it is certain that she will believe them as such. Will she not have regrets? Will she not regard me as an obstacle, as a fraudulent ravisher? Will she not take an aversion to me? God is my witness that I am ready to die for her, but to have to die only to leave a dazzling widow who the next day is free to choose a new husband — this idea — this is hell.

"Let us speak of my fortune; it is little enough. Until now my possessions have been sufficient for me. Will they be suffi-

cient for a married man? For nothing in the world should I want
my wife to know privation, or that she should not be able to go
wherever she is called to shine, to amuse herself. She has the
right to exact it. In order to satisfy her, I am ready to sacrifice
all my tastes, all the passions of my life, and an existence quite
free and adventurous. However, will she not complain that her
position in the world is not as brilliant as she merits and as I
should desire? Such are my anxieties in part — I tremble at the
thought that you will find them reasonable enough." [18]

The sincerity and frankness of this letter are commendable,
and there is a fatal note of prophecy in the obstacles to future
happiness which he conjures up. Pushkin seems to have had
more than an inkling of the difficulties ahead of him, but one is
puzzled by the expressed conviction that the woman whom he
hopes to make his wife is not at all in love with him. Of course,
such a situation was not uncommon in marriages of this time.
But his tacit acceptance of it argues either that he was passionately in love and determined to get married, or that he had
supreme confidence in his ability to instill in this young girl a
lasting devotion to him. Perhaps both conditions obtained.
Pushkin had not come easily by his desire to marry. Until his
return from exile, no thought of it appears to have entered his
head in his many affairs with women. When Baratynski had
taken a wife a few years before, Pushkin had scornfully remarked: "Marriage castrates the mind." [19] However, a feeling
that he was approaching the autumn of life, and a longing, as he
said, to learn happiness, had convinced him that it was time
to take the step. Sofya Pushkina, Ekaterina Ushakova, and
Anna Olenina had not measured up to his ideal woman. One
may be certain that he had such an ideal, for he portrayed her
in the character of Tatyana in *Eugene Onegin*. And he no doubt
found something of Tatyana in Natasha Goncharova. Beauty,
youth, freshness, and an angelic innocence were part of this
ideal. Natasha Goncharova possessed these attributes, though
her angelic innocence might well be described as "quasi." It
was the madonna type, a word he often used in referring to
Natasha, that dominated his poetic imagination. But she must

be a madonna of the great world. Tatyana had not completed
her development until she had become the peerless ruler of
society, beautiful, perfectly self-possessed, proper in all things,
and faithful to her husband. About other conditions Pushkin
did not seem to care. He felt that he would be able to form a
young wife to his own ideals. Whether Natasha had the intelligence to appreciate him, and the charm and tact necessary to
make a success in society, was a question which Pushkin unfortunately did not pause to ask himself at this time.

At last Mama Kars fell. Pushkin's proposal was accepted,
and his cup of joy flowed over. Always superstitious, he attributed the success of this second proposal to a frock coat which
Nashchokin had loaned him for his momentous visit to the
Goncharovs. Immediately he announced the news to his friends,
who warmly congratulated him. To Vyazemski's wife he wrote:
"My marriage with Natalya (who, parenthetically, is my
hundred-and-thirteenth love) is decided." [20]

New obstacles created by Mama Kars quickly soured his
happiness. A son-in-law of hers, she said, ought to have an
estate of his own. And she continued to nag him on the score
that the tsar held him in disfavor and that he was an object of
police surveillance. At this point Pushkin was willing to go to
any lengths to preserve peace. Humbling his pride, which in
this instance must have cost him much, he wrote to his parents,
telling them the news and asking their blessings. He then
hinted that some sort of allowance would be deeply appreciated.
(On such an occasion, a son had every right to expect a portion
of his parents' estate.) The mother and father were delighted
to tears with the engagement. At last their wayward son was
going to settle down. Vyazemski, who was at their house when
they learned the news, wrote to Pushkin: "I became all the
more convinced of the truth of your engagement after your
father poured us a second bottle of champagne upon receiving
your last letter. With this, I saw clearly that the matter was no
joke. I could not believe your letter or his tears, but I could
not fail to believe his champagne." [21] Even among Pushkin's
friends the niggardliness of his father had become a byword.

But the parents were sincerely, almost deliriously, happy. After much reckoning they wrote their son a joint letter filled with tears, "immeasurable joy," and praise to God. Sergei Lvovich agreed to give him two hundred serfs from the village of Kistenevo near his Boldino estate. This would furnish an income of four thousand rubles a year. Such a sum was a mere pittance compared to what he would need, but considering the financial condition of the parents it was a very graceful gesture.

Pushkin was now a landed proprietor, and Mama Kars was satisfied on this score. His next efforts were with Benkendorf. He wrote him a long explanatory letter, telling of his approaching marriage and requesting some testimony of the tsar's favor and also permission to print *Boris Godunov* to help in his pecuniary difficulties. The reply is a masterpiece of diplomatic chicanery, yet precisely what Pushkin required. Benkendorf assured him of the felicitations of the emperor and the empress, both of whom had heard of Natalya Goncharova. (In fact, Nicholas had seen her at a ball in March and had spoken of her dazzling beauty.) Then Benkendorf gallantly produced the following lie: "His majesty the emperor, filled with a paternal solicitude for you, has deigned to charge me, General Benkendorf, not as chief of the police, but as a man in whom he is pleased to place his confidence, with observing you and guiding you with advice; never have the police been ordered to keep you under surveillance." [22] And he concluded with permission to show this letter to any interested person, and to print *Boris Godunov* on his "own responsibility."

The Goncharovs were delighted with this show of imperial favor. Instead of being a kind of literary outcast, Pushkin now seemed to them an excellent medium for making contacts with important people. The official betrothal was announced on the sixth of May. Everything ought to have been serene. But it was far from that. Mama Kars was a difficult person to deal with, and she continued to vex her prospective son-in-law with various money matters. Dark rumors were whispered that the engagement would be broken, and Pushkin himself began to have doubts. He wrote to Vyazemski, asking him to tell his old friend, Katerina Karamzina, of the engagement, because "at heart I need her words, for now I am not entirely happy." [23]

In a strange fragmentary confession, written at this time (May 12–13), which he curiously represented as translated from the French, Pushkin set down the confused thoughts that troubled his brain. It is worth translating in part, for it will reflect his torturing doubts.

"My fate is decided — I am to be married. She whom I loved for two whole years, whom my eyes at first sought out everywhere, with whom a meeting seemed bliss, my God, she is almost mine! The expectation of a decisive answer was the most painful feeling of my life. The expectation of the last lingering card, remorse of conscience, the dream before a duel — all this in comparison signifies nothing. . . .

"I am to be married; that is, I sacrifice my independence, my carefree, whimsical independence, my luxurious habits, my aimless wanderings, solitude, and inconstancy. . . . I never bothered about happiness; I could get along without it. Now I need it for two, and where am I to get it? . . .

"While I am unmarried, what are my obligations? . . . In the morning I get up when I wish, I receive whom I wish, I decide to go out — they saddle my wise, docile Jenny. I go up the side streets, I look in the windows of the low-built houses . . . I dress carelessly if I go out as a guest — with all possible attention if I dine in a restaurant, where I read either a new romance or the journals. If Walter Scott or Cooper has written nothing, and there is no criminal trial in the papers, then I call for a bottle of champagne on ice. I watch the glass frost from the cold, I drink slowly, rejoicing that the meal costs only seventeen rubles and that I can permit myself this frolic. . . . Such is my bachelor life.

"At that minute they hand me a note; an answer to my letter. My fiancée's father kindly summons me. There is no doubt; my proposal has been accepted. Nadinka, my angel — she is mine! All my sad doubts vanish before this heavenly thought. I throw myself in a carriage and gallop to their home. . . . The father and mother sit in the parlor. The former meets me with an open embrace, pulls a handkerchief from his pocket and wants to weep, but he cannot, and resolves to blow his nose instead. The mother's eyes are red. They present Nadinka to me; she is pale and awkward. . . . They bless us. Nadinka gives me her cold, timid hand. The mother speaks of the trousseau, the father about his Saratov estate — and I am a bridegroom.

"Now it is already not the secret of two hearts. Today it is domestic news, tomorrow the news of the market place. Like a poem, contemplated in the seclusion of a summer night by the light of the moon, and then sold in the bookshops and criticized in the journals by fools.

"All rejoice at my happiness; all congratulate and take a fancy to me. . . . Young people begin to stand on ceremony with me — they already look upon me as an enemy. In my presence the ladies praise my choice, but behind my back they pity my bride. 'Poor thing! She is so young, so innocent, and he is such a loose, immoral fellow!'

"I confess this begins to bore me. I like the customs of certain ancient peoples: the bridegroom secretly ravishes his bride and the next day presents her to the town gossips as his wife."[24]

These were not very pleasant thoughts on the eve of his marriage. But the business attitude of Mama Kars sickened him. Romance was pushed into the background amidst the constant bickering over money matters. The Goncharovs were making heavy demands upon him for the trousseau. In desperation he appealed to friends for aid. Pogodin scraped together a small sum. Pletnev helped out. Elizaveta Khitrovo, who in her generous desire "to be useful to others" had gracefully surrendered him to Natasha, busied herself in his interests. And, incidentally, she gave him good advice — to abandon society after his marriage and settle in the country — advice that would have saved his life had he followed it. A potential godsend loomed on the horizon. The possibility developed that old grandfather Goncharov might offer a dowry. At the end of May Pushkin and the Goncharovs packed off to Linen Factory in

Kaluga, the estate of the half-mad grandfather. But the wily old man had nothing to offer. He simply wished to use Pushkin's connection with the court in his own interests. He made the extraordinary proposal that Pushkin should use his influence to obtain a loan of two or three hundred thousand rubles on the linen business, and that he should ask permission from the tsar to melt up a colossal bronze statue of Catherine the Great which was in the possession of the Goncharov family. The half-mad grandfather claimed that he had been offered forty thousand rubles for the metal. Pushkin promised to do his best on the first request; and he immediately wrote to Benkendorf for leave to melt the statue. Even the secret police, on reading this letter, thought it a joke. Permission was granted, but the statue was not sold for years, and the sum it brought was a mere fraction of the old man's figure.

The grandfather's dowry vanished into thin air. Worried and restless, Pushkin spent the rest of the summer in travel, much of it in an effort to raise money for himself and the Goncharovs. As though anxious to renew the memories of his childhood before marriage, he paid a short visit to his dead grandmother's old estate of Zakharovo. On the sixteenth of July he left for Petersburg. But in the capital his attempts to borrow money for grandfather Goncharov had little success. In the middle of August he was back in Moscow in time to be present at the death of his jolly old uncle Vasili. Poet and connoisseur of literature to the end, he died while murmuring his criticism of a recent article on poetry. "Poor uncle Vasili," Pushkin wrote to Pletnev. "Do you know what his last words were? . . . 'How boring is Katenin's article!' and not a word more. What do you think of that? That is how an honorable warrior dies, in harness and with the war cry on his lips!" [25]

In Moscow again new vexations were encountered. Mama Kars made life most unpleasant for him. Pushkin wished to hasten the marriage, but she would have none of it. Infinite preparations had to be made. Obedient Natasha said nothing. Quarrels resulted, and finally a particularly disagreeable scene with Mama Kars convinced Pushkin that all was over. At the

end of August he gloomily left for Boldino in the Nizhni Novgorod district to look over his newly-acquired estate. On the
eve of departure Pushkin wrote to Natasha: "I have set out
for Nizhni without any assurance of my fate. If your mother is
resolved to disrupt our marriage, and you are willing to obey
her, I will subscribe to any motive which she may be pleased to
offer for her resolution, and in this case even if it be as reasonable as the scene she made yesterday and as the insults which
she was pleased to heap on me. Perhaps she is right and I am
wrong in thinking for a moment that I was created for happiness. In any case, you are entirely free; as for me, I give you
my word of honor to belong only to you or never to marry." [26]
Pushkin was most miserable, and in his misery all the doubt of
the past few months rose to the surface to make him wonder
whether this marriage ought ever to take place. His pessimism
is clearly revealed in a letter to Pletnev, written about the
same time as that to Natasha: "My dear, I shall tell you all
that is in my heart: I am sad — misery, misery! The life of a
bridegroom of thirty is worse than the thirty years of the life of
a gambler. The affairs of my future mother-in-law are all upset. My marriage is put off day after day. Meanwhile, I grow
cold; I think about the cares of the married man and then about
the charms of bachelor life." [27]

V

> I shall tell you (as a secret)
> that at Boldino I wrote as I
> haven't written for a long time.
> *Pushkin in a letter*
> *to Pletnev, 1830*

An encouraging letter from Natasha, soon after his arrival
at Boldino, did much to dissipate Pushkin's deep gloom. Once
again his marriage became something more than a straw to
clutch at. He had intended to remain in the village only a short
time, but suddenly a cholera epidemic broke out. Contagion,
it was thought, spread through the air. Strict quarantines were
established throughout the whole district. Pushkin was iso-

lated. He grew frantic. All the roads to Moscow were heavily guarded, and in order to reach the city it was necessary to pass through five quarantine stations, remaining fourteen days in each. Nevertheless, he set out, endeavoring to avoid the quarantines, but he was held up and obliged to return to Boldino. Instead of a few weeks he had to remain in the village for three months.

He poured out letters to Natasha, explaining the situation in great detail, as though he believed that a different construction would be placed upon his absence from Moscow. The cholera had reached the city, and he feared for her safety. These letters alternate between furtive endearments and extreme exasperation over his enforced delay. Only her love sustains him in his misery, he writes. She is his "angel"; and "I kiss the tips of your wings, as Voltaire said about people who were not worth as much as you." [28] He continually complains of the infrequency of her letters and the fact that they are as short as a visiting card. Indeed, one may question the existence of her love, although the feelings of Natasha in the course of their whole stormy courtship were hardly given a chance to develop. A dominating mother, who demanded and received implicit obedience, had resolutely pushed her daughter into the background during the negotiations. It is unlikely that Pushkin had seen much of Natasha alone, and the formal language of address in his letters speaks eloquently of the proprieties the couple had been forced to observe. It is certain that the mother dictated her daughter's every move. No doubt the reason for Natasha's few and brief letters was the fact that Mama Kars disapproved of her writing to Pushkin, and supervised her letters when she did write. Under such circumstances it is little wonder that Pushkin's father informed him at this time of a Moscow rumor that his engagement had been broken.

Boldino was not very picturesque, nor was the manor house comfortable. But worries, doubts, and the constant irritation of his seclusion did not prevent Pushkin from applying himself to literature with unexampled vigor. It was his favorite time of autumn, and during these three months at Boldino he enjoyed an extraordinary period of composition — in a sense, his last great sustained period.

Pushkin was no longer the universally acclaimed poet of the days after his return from exile to Moscow. His glory had waned, and the opposition party in the journalistic world showed him scant respect. He and his friends had fought back and delivered telling blows, but popular opinion was largely controlled by the enemy's press. Hostile critics were ready to pounce upon everything he printed. *To a Nobleman* (1830),[29] a poem in Alexandrines in honor of the highly-cultured Prince N. B. Iusupov, in which Pushkin extols his Aristotelian virtue of magnificence, was at once stupidly ridiculed by his "democratic" foes. They accused him of flattering the great for gain. In reality, no such idea had entered his head, and he bitterly replied that a Russian gentleman had no social superiors and hence no need of flattering anyone. Criticism had never troubled him much, but this despicable and personal abuse of mercenary journalists, which tended to degrade the very poetic art that he loved, only served to exaggerate his literary aloofness and his contempt for the "crowd." In *To the Poet* he turned on his critics and their followers:

> O poet, never value popular acclaim!
> For thou dost hear fools' judgments and the crowd's reproof;
> The present roar of zealous praise turns into blame;
> But thou remainest steadfast, quiet, and aloof.
>
> For thou art king: live by thyself. In exaltation
> Travel the free road, whither thy free mind will lead,
> Perfecting the fruits of thy darling meditation,
> And never asking reward for a noble deed.[30]

But with the autumn at hand and the fury of composition upon him, Pushkin forgot the critics, the crowd, and even Natasha. Now he wrote, and wrote to please himself. "You cannot imagine," he exclaims in a letter to Pletnev, "how jolly it is to run off from a fiancée, just to sit and write verses! . . . Ach, my dear! how charming the country is at present! Imagine: steppes and steppes, not a soul of a neighbor; I ride to my heart's content, write at home as much as may be meditated upon; no one visits."[31] Under such ideal conditions Pushkin

wrote in the huge butcher's books, which he always carried
about with him, swiftly and freely. The rhymes often came
easily. But the first draft was only a beginning. The preservation of nearly everything Pushkin wrote in these manuscript
books provides a unique opportunity to study the development
and perfecting of poetic ideas in form and expression. Pushkin
never dashed off his verse, like Byron, while shaving in the
morning. He was a slave to perfection. There was no end to
the pains he would take in order to search out the right word,
image, and rhyme. The first draft was often followed by a
second, a third, and even a fourth and fifth. And each was
worked over with endless care. When he finished, his manuscript was almost undecipherable because of the numerous corrections. When the right word evaded him, Pushkin's idling
pen would take to drawing, at which he had considerable talent,
on the page before him. Sometimes these drawings have biographical significance; often he attempts to sketch on his manuscript concrete representations of the image, scene, or persons
of his poems. But when the words came again, his verses flew on,
as he describes in *Eugene Onegin*:

> I write; my heart no longer grieves;
> The pen, forgetting, does not draw
> Beside my incompleted lines
> Either the feet or heads of women.[32]

Only a few lyrics were written during the remarkable Boldino
period. The lyric is the poetry of youth, and Pushkin was leaving youth behind. After 1830 he rarely had occasion to use this
form. But these few lyrics are among his very best. Thoughts
of the dead fill them, as though Pushkin were seeking the comfort of forgotten memories at a time when the uncertainty of
his married future troubled him. Now he wrote the three beautiful elegies which, as has been mentioned,* may have been
dedicated to the shade of Amaliya Riznich, his passionate
love in Odessa. The woman of these poems has left for her native
country:

> Thou didst desert this foreign strand
> For distant shores of thine own land.[33]

* See p. 172.

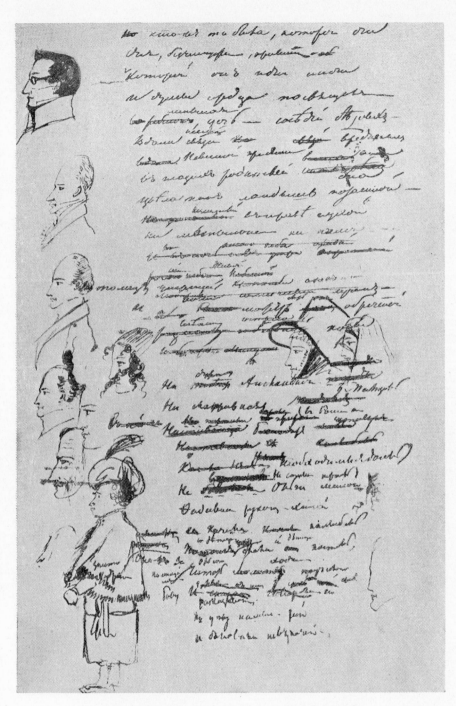

MANUSCRIPT PAGE OF *EUGENE ONEGIN*

But the woman has died, and in a poignant second elegy Pushkin writes:

> Oh, if 'tis true, that in the night
> When all that lives serenely sleeps,
> And from the sky the moon's pale light
> Among the gravestones softly creeps,
>
> If then 'tis true from their cold bed
> The quiet graves send forth their dead —
> Leila, I call, I wait for thee:
> My friend, come hither, come to me! [34]

Long and more substantial poems and prose, however, were
Pushkin's principal occupation at Boldino. The account of the
wanderings of Eugene Onegin, the rejected eighth chapter, was
completed, and the brilliant concluding chapter of his great
masterpiece was written. Almost, as it were, by a feat of artistic legerdemain, he recaptured in this last chapter much of
the lightness and sparkle of the first, written eight years previously. But a gentle melancholy runs through the final stanzas.
His long and arduous task was finished, but he was sorry to part
with his hero and heroine. The end seemed to symbolize an end
of one stage of his life, which in a sense it did, and with misgivings he sadly contemplated a new existence. Later Pushkin
could not resist tinkering with the poem and actually contemplated a continuation, but he wisely abandoned the idea. Yet
he did start a tenth chapter at Boldino. His intention, apparently, was to develop the hero's life after Tatyana finally
rejected him, and it appears that Eugene was to have become involved in the Decembrist conspiracy. But he burned what he
had written of this tenth chapter at Boldino. Only a few fragments remain, which are disguised in a cipher, for he feared
that their political subject might get him into difficulties with
the police.

Another narrative poem, *The Little House in Kolomna*, was
written at this time. It is a light, whimsical piece, recalling
Byron's *Beppo* in form and treatment. There is much irrelevant
playing with the subject in the Byronic manner, one which
Pushkin made thoroughly his own. But the poem actually tells
a story, simple and irritating though it may be. In Kolomna,

a poor section of Petersburg, live a widow and her daughter.
A cook, their only servant, dies, and the daughter brings to the
house a young woman who will work for almost nothing. Although a bad cook, the new servant is quiet and well-behaved.
All goes well until the widow comes home from church early and
finds her servant shaving before the mirror. The mother faints,
the cook vanishes, and the story ends. Symbolist critics have
found material of deep significance in this droll work, and it has
even served as a medium for revealing hidden sexual themes in
Pushkin's poetry. The story perhaps contains a joking satire
on contemporary literature, but if he had any more subtle motives, Pushkin buried them very deeply. There is no moral, he
humorously adds at the end, unless it be that "to shave a beard
is incompatible with the nature of a lady." [35]

One of the outstanding achievements of the Boldino period is
the *Dramatic Scenes*, which contains the four short plays, *The
Stone Guest, Mozart and Salieri, The Feast during the Plague*, and
The Avaricious Knight.[36] Pushkin obtained the idea of composing these little tragedies from the similar *Dramatic Scenes* of
Barry Cornwall.[37] The plays, written in blank verse, vary in
length from about two hundred to five hundred lines. These
little dramas in each case concern a single theme, which is developed in a psychological manner, and it is clear that Pushkin
designed them for reading rather than stage production.

The Stone Guest is a variation of the old Don Juan theme,
treated in this instance with a rare economy of effort. What is
most admirable about the play is the complete success with
which Pushkin reproduces Southern European reality in both
action and characterization, a reality which he had no means of
knowing through personal contact. Even the dialogue of foreigners is caught in a realistic manner, never for a moment
ringing unnaturally. The illusion of locale is complete. In
every respect *The Stone Guest* is a masterpiece in miniature.

The shortest of the little tragedies is *Mozart and Salieri*,
which is based on the tradition of the poisoning of the great
musician by his envious rival. The psychological development
of the talented and hard-working Salieri, who bitterly resents

the easy accomplishment of the God-gifted genius Mozart, is unsurpassed for passionate, convincing reasoning. Pushkin cleverly avoids cheapening the character of Salieri by justifying his envy with motives that seem perfectly logical on Salieri's own premises.

The Feast during the Plague differs from the other plays in that it is a fairly close translation of a scene from John Wilson's (Christopher North) *The City of the Plague*. But the translation gains enormously over the original through the transforming power of genius. Despite the almost word-for-word rendering, Pushkin's perfection in verse and diction is something entirely beyond the power of Wilson. He adds two songs, certainly suggested by the original, which are written in his inimitable lyric manner and give this play a special distinction.

The Avaricious Knight is a brilliant psychological study of greed and consists of three short scenes, developing the miserliness of an old baron towards his brave but thriftless son. The dialogue is a masterpiece of compression, and the characters are revealed rather by suggestive touches, contrasts, and parallels than by direct delineation. The father's avarice is pathological. He hoards gold for the feeling of power that it gives him. Yet he never uses this power, and while conjuring up visions of the luxurious existence he might lead, he continues to live in wretched poverty. Belinski said of the play: "In its well-sustained characters (the miser, his son, the Duke, and the Jew), its skillful arrangement, the fearful force of its pathos, its wonderful poetry — in short, in everything this drama is a very great production, worthy of the genius of Shakespeare himself." [38] With our own hallowed admiration of Shakespeare it is difficult to accept such praise. But *The Avaricious Knight* is by no means unworthy of the great dramatist. Pushkin was not a little influenced by Shakespeare in the *Dramatic Scenes*, and particularly in the blank verse, where he has finally overcome the faults of the verse of *Boris Godunov*. In the famous monologue of the baron in the second scene of *The Avaricious Knight*, a passage which Russian schoolboys learn by heart, the free swing of Pushkin's verse, the clever use of enjambement, and the policy of syllabic equivalence are all in Shakespeare's later verse manner. It will be instructive to translate a few lines of this monologue as an example of Pushkin's style in the *Dramatic Scenes*:

In a Vault

Baron.   Just like a youthful madcap who awaits
His rendezvous with some intriguing wanton,
Or with some fool beguiled by him, so I
Have waited for this moment to descend
Into my secret vault to faithful chests.
O happy hour! that time when I can throw
Into my chest, the sixth (that one not filled)
My handful of accumulated gold.
It seems a trifle; yet by such mites
These treasures prosper. Somewhere I have read
That once a king commanded all his troops
To gather earth by handfuls in a heap,
And a proud hill was raised, and the king
From this high ground could contemplate with joy
The stretch of plain concealed by his white tents,
Likewise the sea where ships were scudding by.
So I, in bringing a poor handful here
Into the vault, my customary tribute,
Shall raise my mound — and from its height can I
View everything that is to me submissive.
And what is not submissive to me? Like
Some demon I can rule the world from here;
I wish — and palaces will raise themselves;
In my entrancing gardens there the nymphs
Will leap about in merrymaking troupes;
The muses, too, will pay to me their tribute;
Free genius will enslave itself to me;
Both sleepless toil and virtue will then wait
Attentively upon my recompense.
I need but whistle, and obedient
To me will bloodstained crime creep timidly,
And it will lick my hand, and in my eyes
Will seek to read my wishes by their glance.
To me all is submissive, I — to nothing;
I am above all wishes; I am calm;
I know my power; and for me this knowledge
Is sufficient.[39]

A very considerable part of Pushkin's literary activity at Boldino was devoted to prose. For several years now he had been concerned with the development of prose for the purposes of fiction. Karamzin had shown the way toward an acceptable style in historical exposition; Vyazemski and Pushkin himself had already set a fine example in critical prose. But as yet writers of Russian novels and short stories had not achieved a distinguished style or, for that matter, any distinguished fiction. The unfinished *Negro of Peter the Great* had been an attempt in this direction. Walter Scott, whose historical romances were all the rage in Russia, influenced Pushkin in this work, and continued to influence him in later prose productions. But neither Scott's loose prose nor his narrative method could satisfy Pushkin. At Boldino he wrote the *Tales of Belkin*.[40] These five short stories (*The Shot*, *The Snowstorm*, *The Stationmaster*, *The Undertaker*, and *The Lady-Rustic*) are admittedly in the nature of an experiment. He published them anonymously, and they were poorly received by the critics. Yet Pushkin attached great importance to these tales, since they were intended to be models of the right way to tell a story. For the most part they are mere anecdotes, and every vestige of psychology, of irrelevant reflection and description, is scrupulously avoided. The prose is studied, almost too much so, and while achieving a definite cadence and balance, it is shorn of all rhetoric, being terse, tight, and simple in the extreme. Only much later were the *Tales of Belkin* recognized for what Pushkin intended them to be — perfect models of narrative structure. In *The History of the Village of Goriukhino*,[41] also written at Boldino but never finished, Pushkin further developed his imaginary storyteller Belkin, who relates the five tales mentioned above, and was on the way to creating one of the most humorous and pathetic figures in Russian fiction.

Once more winter had set in. The wonderful Boldino autumn was behind him. Many works, and the plans and drafts of others, make up his total accomplishment during these three months. Never again did inspiration flow so freely or were his efforts so uniformly successful. The quarantine bars had been let down, and by the fifth of December Pushkin was back in Moscow. A new life stretched before him, but his dream of a happy future was not unmixed with dark foreboding.

VI

> I do not wish, O friends, to die;
> I want to live, to think and suffer.
> *Elegy*

Upon his return Pushkin was given no intimation that his absence of three months at this crucial time had caused any heartburning. As a matter of fact, the Goncharovs received him coldly. Mama Kars had not sweetened in the interval, and Natasha was still under her thumb. He began to wonder if the rumors about a broken engagement did not have some basis in facts unknown to him. Certainly his more cynical friends placed no faith in the projected marriage. When Aleksei Vulf learned of the betrothal, he wrote: "I wish him happiness, but with his morals and form of thought, I do not know if it is possible to hope for this. If mutual responsibility is in the order of things, then how unfortunate it will be for him to wear horns — it is more probable that his first concern will be to debauch his wife. I hope I am mistaken in all this." [42] Another acquaintance even had the bad taste to remark that the poem, *Madonna*, which he dedicated to Natasha at this time, had actually been written for another woman.

The whole affair seemed so hopeless to Pushkin that in a moment of deep despair he contemplated going to Poland to fight in the rebellion that had broken out there. Like most Russians, even like many of the old Decembrists, he had no sympathy for the patriotic Poles. However, Nashchokin, who was his best counselor and most helpful friend during these dark days, persuaded him of the rashness of such a step. To add to his low spirits he learned in January of the death of Delvig. Benkendorf had summoned Delvig for an article in the *Literary Gazette*, which he had aimed at Bulgarin. The chief of the secret police had fiercely rebuked the soft, gentle Delvig, threatened him with Siberia, and sternly forbade him to edit the magazine in the future. Delvig's sensitive feelings were deeply wounded by such harsh treatment. His health had never been good, and after this dressing-down by Benkendorf he became apathetic and uninterested in anything, so that an attack

of illness easily carried him off. It was a terrible blow to Pushkin. Delvig was his closest and dearest friend. Mention of the
death runs through his letters like a grief-filled litany. To
Pletnev he wrote: "I am sad, miserable. This is the first death
that I have wept over. . . . No one in the world was closer
to me than Delvig. Of all the connections of my childhood, he
alone remained — about him our poor little group gathered.
Without him we are completely orphaned. . . . Yesterday I
was with Nashchokin, who was powerfully affected by his
death — they spoke about him, calling him the late Delvig,
and this epithet was so strange, so terrible. Well, there is
nothing to do! We are agreed. The late Delvig. So be it." [43]
More than anything else the death of Delvig seemed to symbolize for Pushkin the disintegration of his own little world.
All was flux and change. He, too, was changing, and he sadly
wondered whether it was for the best.

At last the date of the marriage was definitely set, but this
fact did not put an end to his disputes with Mama Kars.
Firmly he wrote to Pletnev in Petersburg: "My dear, here is
the plan of my life for you: I shall marry in about a month; I
shall live in Moscow for about a half year, and in the summer
I shall come to you. I do not like Moscow life. Here you live,
not as you wish, but as the aunts wish. My mother-in-law is
like an aunt." [44] The quarrels were usually over the perennial
subject of money. Apart from taking care of all the expenses of
the wedding, Pushkin was actually asked to provide Natasha
with a dowry. Even on the very day of the wedding Mama
Kars sent to him for money to pay for the carriage. From
every possible source he sought funds to meet the heavy demands placed upon him. He mortgaged the serfs his father had
given him. *Boris Godunov* finally came out, and for this he received a considerable sum — and, it may be mentioned, a
note from Benkendorf telling him that the tsar had read the
printed play with great satisfaction (no doubt for the first time,
despite the fact that the manuscript had been submitted to him
for censoring).

As the momentous day approached Pushkin's low spirits did

not rise, nor were his dark doubts banished. The uncertainty, the constant wrangling, and the mercenary aspect of all the preparations shrouded the coming event in gloom. His early enthusiasm had been reduced to a kind of cold deliberateness. One almost feels that if any acceptable retreat had presented itself at this juncture, he would have gladly seized it. In a curious letter, written just eight days before the wedding to N. I. Krivtsov, an old friend of his bachelor days, Pushkin frankly declares his thoughts: "I am married — or almost. Everything you could say to me about the benefits of bachelor life and against marriage, all this I have already thought over. In cold blood I have weighed the advantages and disadvantages of the position I have selected. My youth was noisy and unfruitful. Up to now I have lived otherwise than as people usually live. I was not happy. There is no happiness outside the common spheres. I am thirty years old. At thirty people ordinarily marry — I am behaving like such people, and no doubt I shall regret it. In fact, I am marrying without rapture, without any childish illusions. The future does not appear rosy to me, but in all its stern nakedness. Misfortunes will not surprise me: they enter into my domestic calculations. For me every joy will be unexpected." [45] On the eve of the wedding Pushkin gave his last bachelor party to a few select friends. He read some verses in which he bade farewell to his youth, and all the guests noticed that he was unusually sad.

The marriage took place on the eighteenth of February, 1831, in the Great Ascension Church in the west end of Moscow. Vyazemski was best man. Natasha was incomparably beautiful in her bridal gown. In changing hands one of the rings fell, and during the ceremony a cross and a Bible fell from the pulpit. The superstitious Pushkin grew pale and muttered, "These are all bad omens!" [46]

CHAPTER XVII

Honeymoon and Wormwood

> Love in marriage — this is the very
> summit of human dignity in love.
> *Pushkin to A. O. Smirnova*

Wishful thinkers among Moscow pessimists did not overlook the bad omens. They had anticipated the failure of this match during the period of betrothal; after the wedding they were sure of it. "Don't think it will be the last stupidity that I shall commit in my life," [1] Pushkin was reported to have said of the event. They compared the future fate of the young bride to that of Lady Byron. If Natasha's account be true, her husband certainly delivered himself of a Byronic gesture the very day after the wedding. He arose that morning and foregathered with some friends, meanwhile forgetting all about his wife. Left alone in a strange house, Natasha spent the time weeping, for Pushkin did not return to his bride of a day until dinner. And there is an unpleasant Byronic flavor in some doggerel which he is credited with writing on his marriage:

> If you wish to be polite — admire,
> If you wish to rise — stoop;
> If you wish to be in heaven — pray,
> If you wish to be in hell — marry! [2]

Close and discerning friends also regretted the match. A difference of thirteen years in age did not augur well. They were convinced of Pushkin's desire to settle down; but would a captivating young bride, who had already sampled the flattery of society, be willing to adapt herself to a quiet domestic existence? And what of the latent danger in the fact that he had no assured income sufficient to take care of a married couple in the expensive world of high society? Finally, these friends mournfully asked, would Pushkin now have the leisure to write?

Despite these gloomy premonitions, rumors, and reports, Pushkin began his married life most auspiciously. A week after the wedding he wrote to Pletnev: "I am married — and happy. My one desire is that nothing in my present life should change — nothing better can be expected. This situation is so new for me that I seem to have been reborn." [3] Moscow friends quickly detected the settled air of domesticity that came over him. He was ripe and eager for the new life. A palatial house in the Arbat section served the newlyweds as a temporary home. There were many visitors. The girl-bride was charming but moved awkwardly in her new surroundings. Curious guests observed that little taste was evident in the furnishings, and that napkins and table covers were soiled. The couple were invited everywhere — to balls, concerts, and the homes of friends. And every where they were noticed and commented on. The short, swarthy, unhandsome, curly-headed poet cut an odd figure standing beside his tall, beautiful young bride. "Vulcan and Venus" was the description of one wit. But all were agreed that they behaved in public like a pair of doves.

Two worries disturbed the happy honeymoon period — money and Mama Kars; the two were practically synonymous. Although Pushkin had been obliged to give Natasha a dowry of eleven thousand rubles out of the sum received from mortgaging his serfs, his mother-in-law did not feel that this was sufficient. So accustomed had she grown to the blind obedience of her daughter that she continued to snap her whip, failing to realize that Natasha had been released from her exacting control. She volunteered unflattering advice to the wife, and was responsible for exaggerated stories concerning the husband's character. Rumors on this score arose once again to plague Pushkin. He took prompt action. By the end of March he wrote to Pletnev that he could no longer live in Moscow. He wanted quiet, relief from gossip, and as many miles as possible between him and his mother-in-law. Would Pletnev rent a little house for him in Tsarskoe Selo? It must be inexpensive. No garden was necessary. Something very simple, just for him and Natasha. It would be pleasant to live in this village, the scene of his schooldays. But Pushkin carefully forestalled any rumors of a rupture. He regretted nothing, he told Pletnev; his wife was charming and he was ready to make any sacrifices for her. However, he could not get away from Moscow until the middle of May. With a feeling of relief he wrote Nashchokin from Tsarskoe Selo: "Now, it seems, all is smoothed over, and I shall live tranquilly, without a mother-in-law, without equipage — hence without any great expense and without gossip." [4]

II

The little house had been found, and the next five months among the country surroundings of Tsarskoe Selo were the happiest in Pushkin's married life. Financial worries did not cease. In most of his correspondence at this time, and later, the question of money appears with painful regularity. Despite many sad experiences, he had never learned to save, for he was a spendthrift by nature. He squandered large sums easily, always hoping with a gambler's hope that a sudden turn of luck would save the day. Marriage did not alter these habits, except that it worried him excessively when poverty affected his wife as well as himself. He conscientiously endeavored to provide Natasha with everything she desired, and under the circumstances her demands were often inconsiderate. She was as thriftless as he, and a bad manager of the household. Pushkin had piled up large debts in Moscow, and his creditors were now beginning to harass him. Nashchokin took upon himself the disagreeable task of trying to straighten out his friend's financial obligations. Often, however, the situation grew serious. Jewels that the mother-in-law had finally surrendered in lieu of a dowry were pawned. And at times, as Pushkin himself confessed, there was not a groat in the house.

But even financial worries could not spoil the summer happiness at Tsarskoe Selo. Everyone thought Natasha most charming, and all marveled at her beauty. Contemporary accounts testify to her striking appearance. Count V. A. Sologub wrote: "In my time I have seen many beautiful women, and I have met women more fascinating than Pushkina, but I have never beheld one who united in herself such perfection of classically correct features and figure. She was tall, with an incredibly thin waist, well-developed shoulders and bosom, and her small head, like a lily on a stalk, swayed gracefully on her slender neck; such a beautiful and perfect profile I have never seen, and then her complexion, eyes, teeth, mouth! Yes, she was a real beauty, and all other women, even the most attractive, faded when she appeared." [5] Indeed, in the society in which she moved Natasha was generally considered the first beauty of her time. In poetry Pushkin wrote of "the beauty of Goncharova" [6] with the same simple conviction that he would have written of the beauty of Venus. He thought that she closely resembled the Madonna of Perugino. This famous picture was then in Russia, .and Pushkin told his wife that he wished to buy it for her, but the price of forty thousand rubles was safely beyond his reach. Upon being introduced to Natasha, Countess Fikelmon remarked that the melancholy and quiet expression of her face prophesied unhappiness. Natasha was presented to the Empress Alexandra Fedorovna, who was delighted with her and predicted that she would be the most interesting woman of the next social season.

Deeply in love with his wife and serenely happy in his love, Pushkin had at last found a kind of spiritual rest after years of stormy existence, wanderings, and uncertainties. As yet he had scarcely had time to wonder whether his girl-bride possessed anything other than the quality that had first attracted him — her remarkable beauty. He regarded her as a child and treated her as one, not caring in his present happiness about the vast spiritual and mental chasm between them. Arm in arm they promenaded through the gardens of Tsarskoe Selo. He introduced her to his literary friends — Zhukovski, Gogol, Pletnev, Karamzina, and A. O. Rosset (later Smirnova). Natasha was half afraid of these people, often bored with their everlasting literary conversation, and not a little jealous of the hold they had on her husband's affections.

Cholera had reappeared in Petersburg, and the couple were obliged to remain in Tsarskoe Selo. But they continued to enjoy the seclusion of the tsar's summer village. Pushkin visited his old Lyceum, and the students received him with rapt school-boy awe. They dogged his footsteps in the garden, waiting for a favorable opportunity to meet and talk with the great poet. On such occasions he was simple and frank, chatting easily with these boys about their school life and the days when he had attended the Lyceum.

The quiet happiness of their summer retreat and the urgings of his literary friends encouraged Pushkin to resume writing. Besides, the profits of his pen were now absolutely essential. The *Tales of Belkin* were polished for the press; Onegin's letter to Tatyana was written for the last chapter, which was also prepared for printing. Of more significance is the folk tale, *Tsar Saltan*, based on a story told by Arina Rodionovna. Push-kin was to turn more and more to these simple tales of the folk as a medium for poetry. In them he is entirely the creator. The story is borrowed, as Shakespeare might borrow the plot of a play, but the finished product becomes an original work of beauty. Pushkin had learned to move easily and surely in this world of complete fantasy. The artlessness of the folk is never subordinated to the sophisticated rules of art. Meaning or understanding or logic is not allowed to obtrude upon the natural laws of folk-tale narration. The story moves on, as it were, by its own volition. And Pushkin's recognition of this inherent artlessness and his complete acceptance of it serve to make these folk tales his most perfect creations.

In their little house at Tsarskoe Selo the young bride was now treated to the spectacle of a poet at work, and it can hardly be said that the process of literary creation impressed her. As a matter of fact, she was rather annoyed by it all. When the fury of composition seized Pushkin, he shut himself up in his study and worked all day, often, indeed, far into the night. Natasha soon learned that he was not to be disturbed. When writing, Pushkin could be as irritable as a pregnant woman, as his sister observed. Natasha had to sit downstairs and amuse herself as best she might. Her mind was extremely limited. She had no interest in poetry and scarcely knew the titles of her husband's works or of the books he read. Pushkin did not expect an eighteen-year-old girl, with her background and lack of education, to appreciate and understand his compositions. Generally speaking, he did not have a very high opinion of the capacity of women to appreciate poetry. He censured them for their preference for French and their comparative ignorance of Russian. "Nature has bestowed on them," he writes, "a sparse intelligence and a most peevish sensitivity, and has almost denied them any feeling for the beautiful. Poetry evades them, never reaching the soul; they are insensitive to its harmony. Observe how they sing popular songs, how they alter the most natural verses, distort the measure, and destroy the rhyme. Listen to their literary judgments, and you will be surprised at the inappositeness and even at the stupidity of their understanding. Exceptions are rare." [7]

This criticism is a little hard on Russian women, who at that time rarely enjoyed the educational opportunities of men. Certainly Pushkin did not place his wife among the "exceptions." But he did imagine that she would respect his work, although she might be incapable of understanding it. He soon discovered otherwise. Apart from her beauty, Natasha was a very ordinary young wife, entirely self-centered and eager for male attention. Perhaps Pushkin made a mistake in treating her like a child and thereby emphasizing the tremendous intellectual difference between them. At the end of the day he would emerge from his study, weary from work but eager to read his latest composition to some critical friend. He did not ask his wife to listen, for he had already observed how bored she grew when he read poetry to his literary guests. His first impulse was to go to Zhukovski or to that brilliant and attractive young maid of honor, A. O. Rosset, whom he did include among the "exceptions." Natasha demurred. She had not seen him all day. Why could he not read his newest work to her? She was even a bit jealous of the intellectual Rosset, who considered her stupid. Pushkin would dismiss the request as a childish caprice, and with a laugh he would dash off to one of his literary friends. Naturally, Natasha resented such treatment, and it encouraged her inclination to seek refuge in purely social activities where she could shine.

Among Pushkin's literary endeavors at Tsarskoe Selo was a generous attempt to get out an edition of Delvig's old almanac, the *Northern Flowers* (the proceeds to be used to aid the late poet's impoverished wife and two brothers). He contributed several of his own works to this project, and begged articles and poems from his friends. He also resurrected his old dream of founding a political and literary journal. Twice, in May and July, he specifically requested permission from Benkendorf to edit such a journal. "If it will please his imperial majesty to make use of my pen," Pushkin wrote, "then I shall try with accuracy and zeal to fulfill the will of his majesty, for I am ready to serve him to the extent of my ability." [8] His plan was to include, along with belles-lettres, Russian and foreign political news, for, as he explained to Benkendorf, political opinion could thus be directed so as to serve the best interests of the government. At the same time he also asked for permission to reënter the service, for a raise in rank of two degrees, and for leave to use the archives in order to write a history of Peter the Great. The tsar refused the request to edit a literary and political journal. The *Northern Bee* of the subsidized Bulgarin already served this purpose to the government's satisfaction. Nicholas I had no desire to allow Pushkin to attempt to direct political opinion in Russia. But his rank was raised to that of titular counselor, and he was readmitted into the College of Foreign Affairs, for the purpose of using the archives, with a salary of five thousand rubles a year. Pleased with these favors, Pushkin wrote to Pletnev in July: "The tsar has taken me into the service — but not into the chancellery, or into the court or war service — no, he gave me a gratuity, opened up the archives to me in order that I might dig there and do nothing. This is very kind on his part, is it not true? He has said: 'Since he is married and is not rich, he must keep his pot boiling.' Good God, but he is kind to me!" [9]

This offer to employ his pen in the service of the tsar and his currying favor with the government may seem to indicate a marked change in Pushkin's political and social point of view. And his reaction to the Polish revolution, which at this time was being vigorously suppressed, may well be construed as another indication of a reactionary tendency. Aflame with patriotism, he wrote three poems in defense and praise of Russia's imperialistic designs. The best known of these, *To the Slanderers of Russia*,[10] even offended certain warm liberal friends and was unfavorably commented on in the foreign press. Zhukovski, a favorite of the tsar, was eager to further the interests of his newly-married friend at court. Pushkin saw a great deal of him at Tsarskoe Selo, and it is pretty certain that his old teacher in poetry tried to bring him and the monarch closer together. In his walks in the palace gardens Pushkin met Nicholas, and their conversations were most flattering to the poet. It is even noticeable that his letters at this time often mention the tsar in a highly laudatory manner. And there can be little doubt that Pushkin now sought a closer intimacy with the aristocracy that surrounded the throne, a tendency that grew as time went on.

Had Pushkin really turned reactionary, and if so, had his marriage anything to do with the transformation? The question is difficult to answer, since we are dealing with a country and a time when to be anything other than reactionary was extremely dangerous. It has already been said, however, that Pushkin had not changed in his attitude toward political and social questions. He had simply developed, and this development preserves a certain consistency during the remainder of his life. It is idle to think of him as a man who had a definite political platform, and though one may try to read a political philosophy into his works, the results will have no validity. The most that can be gained is a general impression of what Pushkin thought about such matters. As a youth, he had evinced the radicalism of youth. He shared the conviction of the liberals of his day that a political and social change for Russia was desirable. The Decembrist Revolt had put an end to all that; the liberals had lost — at least, for the time being. Pushkin accepted the fact realistically. Most sensible people in Russia did. He became convinced that the time for radical change was not ripe, and he made his peace with the tsar. No one will know how much this submission tortured his conscience or how deeply he grieved over comrades who suffered for the cause; but there is evidence enough to indicate that his mental distress was considerable. He was not a political idealist or a professional revolutionist, and for a man in his public position, and one who knew that he was continually spied upon, it would have been sheer suicide to oppose openly, or even covertly, a reactionary government that was quick to punish such offenders. Yet he actually took chances in this respect, as his poems to comrades in Siberia and his continued contacts with liberal and persecuted friends testify. After his marriage Pushkin was faced with the sobering responsibility of providing for his wife, and he took this responsibility very seriously. The major portion of his income he derived from writing, and this in turn depended upon the good opinion of the tsar. Very naturally, he sought the favor of the government. It was a matter of bread and butter. Furthermore, he was convinced that his birth entitled him to a place in aristocratic circles, for which he certainly had a predilection; and the social ambitions of his wife, her very happiness, made it almost essential for him to move in such circles. As for his espousing the cause of Russia against Poland, here Pushkin simply followed the dictates of his convictions. He had never made any secret of his patriotism. Yet one can be a liberal and a patriot at the same time.

Had Pushkin been a strictly free man, able to speak out fearlessly what he thought, it is not hard to imagine what he would have said about conditions in Russia. He hated oppression, the abuse of the peasantry, and the despotism of autocracy. But he would have advocated reforms by peaceful and wise legislation, not by bloody revolt. Shortly before his death Pushkin wrote to Chaadaev and frankly expressed his discontent with the state of things in Russia. "Although personally attached to the emperor," he says in part, "I am far from admiring all that I see about me. . . . One must admit that our social existence is a sad thing. The absence of public opinion, the indifference to duty, justice, and truth, the cynical contempt for the thought and dignity of man — all these things are truly desolating." [11]

No, Pushkin had not become a reactionary; he simply had to face the stark problem of existence. He remained a liberal, or, as Vyazemski has better described him, a liberal conservative. Even at this time, when the government's additional favors drew the silken chains that bound him to the tsar more closely, Pushkin began to fear the consequences of this bondage. He was happy with his wife, and instinctively he felt that he could preserve this happiness only by striking out on a new path. At this very time he wrote to Praskovya Osipova at Trigorskoe, asking her about the possibilities of buying a small place near her estate. There he would settle with Natasha and lead a peaceful existence away from the capital and the baneful influence of the government. Unfortunately, nothing came of the project. For the remainder of his life Pushkin strove to realize this dream. But as time passed it became increasingly difficult to retreat, for the silken chains grew tighter.

III

> At heart I wish her happiness and peace
>   of mind,
> All the carefree pleasures, all the goods
>   of life,
> Yes, all — and even joy to him who
>   married her,
> To him who honored this dear girl with
>   name of wife.
>   *To N. L. Sollogub*

By the middle of October the cholera epidemic in Petersburg had subsided, and the couple thought it safe to move to the capital. They rented expensive quarters. Natasha proved useless in the business of setting up housekeeping. Her husband had to take care of all the details — furnishings, servants, equipage. Preparations for her debut in Petersburg society were Natasha's chief concern. The winter season was at hand. Gowns had to be bought. Money vanished and new loans had to be obtained. Her kind aunt, E. I. Zagryazhskaya, who frequented the best circles, aided with gifts and influence.

The debut was a glorious success. The empress had been correct; Natasha proved to be the most interesting woman of the season. But one must understand "interesting" in terms of beauty. Natasha had little else to offer. At the balls she conquered all by her beauty. "Psyche" was the pet name adoring admirers conferred on her. "As for my sister-in-law," wrote Pushkin's sister, "she is the woman most in fashion here. She is now in society, and they say that she is most beautiful." [12] Natasha had found her proper milieu. Pushkin gallantly danced attendance. For this frivolous aristocracy the title of poet had no significance, and in the company of courtiers who continually surrounded her he was already beginning to feel like "the husband of Madame."

Money problems once more, and the desire to use the archives for his history, soon took Pushkin away from social activities. He left for Moscow on the third of December, and upon his arrival stayed with Nashchokin. One of the objects of this visit was to pawn the jewels given Natasha by her mother. His research in the archives also got under way. During this first absence from Natasha, Pushkin began the remarkable series of letters to his wife which represents one of his highest achievements in prose. The nature of their relations is clearly revealed in the correspondence. There is occasional banter and much stern advice, in tone more like the advice of a father to his daughter than that of a husband to his wife. On the whole, Pushkin avoids writing about his literary endeavors, realizing that these would have little interest for Natasha. But in all these letters sounds the constant note of his deep, unchanging love.

Patiently and with humor he relates at length the news of her native city and of all the people he has visited. But without her he is sad, and now, particularly, the separation frightens him. Natasha was already pregnant. "You will not sit at home," he scolds. "You will go to the palace, and if you don't watch out you will have a miscarriage on the hundred-and-fifth step of the commandant's stairway. My dear, my wife, my angel! Do me this favor: remain two hours a day in your room,

and take care of yourself." [13] In another letter he warns
Natasha not to lace herself too tightly, not to sit with her legs
crossed, not to go dancing, and to beware of making friends with
certain countesses of shady reputation. Then he sweetens his
advice by telling her that he was mad to leave her alone in
Petersburg, for "I love you so, my angel, that I cannot express
it in words." [14] But Natasha was not worrying about her health.
At the very time Pushkin was cautioning her to avoid dancing,
she was attending the Petersburg balls and flirting with the
officers.

Pushkin hurried his business in Moscow and by the end of the
month returned to the capital. He found his wife in good
health, despite, as he wrote to Nashchokin, "her girlish indiscretion. She dances at balls, exchanges compliments with the
emperor, and runs up and down the stairs. She must be placed
in the hands of a midwife." [15] The eternal hunt for money continued. From a wealthy friend Pushkin attempted to borrow
twenty-five thousand rubles. Even grandfather Goncharov's
colossal bronze statue of Catherine the Great was brought
forth again. It had not yet been sold or melted down, and now
Pushkin conveniently discovered that it was really a beautiful
work of art. He boldly proposed to Benkendorf that the government buy the huge monument for twenty-five thousand
rubles and set it up in Petersburg in honor of the famous empress. His offer was politely refused.

In the spring of 1832 Pushkin moved — the first of many
changes in his living quarters in Petersburg. And on May 19 a
daughter, Mariya, was born. He grew more serious, more concerned about the future of his family. In September he went to
Moscow again to consult with Nashchokin about money matters
and to resume work in the archives.

He visited the University of Moscow to hear a lecture on
Russian literature. At its conclusion the students were told
that the lecture had been on the theory of art, but that in the
auditorium they had Pushkin, art itself. In raptures the students crowded about him, and a warm discussion was held on
literary matters.

Pushkin wrote Natasha frequently, and when he received her answers he went into ecstasies, kissing the letters and reading them again and again. "How dear, how sweet! What a long letter! How clever it is! I am grateful, little wife. Continue as you have begun and I will pray to God for you forever." [16] He thanks her for taking lessons in chess, which is "absolutely necessary in any well-arranged household." [17] The customary advice persists. She must avoid riding horseback and go to bed early. Particularly he cautions her about flirting. He had observed her capacity for this, and he seemed obsessed by the fear that she would go too far, that her actions would discredit her in society. He warns her of coquetting with members of the diplomatic corps. People will talk. She in turn complained about his flirtations and made a great play at being jealous. But one strongly suspects that her jealousy, as one critic put it, was the jealousy of manner, not of fact. At best, she was offended because he neglected a beautiful wife for the lesser charms of other women. Whatever feeling Natasha may have had for her husband, it was not that of passionate love. She had married him without love, and Pushkin knew it. He had hoped to awaken such an emotion in her, yet, despite his own profound love, he never succeeded. She dutifully gave herself to him as a wife, never as a lover. As though seeking an excuse for his failure, he at first attributed her lack of feeling to the knowledge she had of his youthful amours. This note is struck in a verse fragment:

> When I enclose thy slender body
> In my embrace, and willingly
> I play the spendthrift, squandering
> My tender words of love on thee—
> Thy supple form in silence freeing
> From clasping arms, thou, with relief,
> Dost then reply to me, my friend,
> With a cold smile of disbelief:
> Carefully hoarding in thy mind
> The tales of my unfaithfulness,
> Gloomily listening without
> Sympathy or attentiveness.
> I curse the crafty diligence
> Of youthful culpable delights,

The meetings and the expectations
In gardens in the quiet nights;
I hate those whispered loving speeches,
The secret melody of verses,
The kisses of believing girls,
Their tears and their belated curses.[18]

It was not the irregularities of his past, however, that prompted
Natasha's indifference. The bitterness of repulses and the protracted coaxing that chilled his passion had taught him otherwise. Another bit of verse, found among his manuscripts after
his death, seems to refer to his intimate relations with his wife:

Ah no, I place no store in riotous revelry,
In transports, frenzy, or in sensual ecstasy,
Or in the cries and moaning of a youthful Grace,
When like a serpent, writhing soft in my embrace,
She hastens the moment of final convulsion
With wounding kisses and her aching impulsion.

But how more charming art thou, submissive to me!
And how more painfully I take delight in thee!
After surrendering to lengthy supplication,
Thou yieldest tenderly to me, without elation,
Heedless of everything, ashamed and coyly cold;
Thou dost not answer to my ecstasies so bold,
But more and more the flame in thee increases still —
At last my flame thou sharest, much against thy will.[19]

This dutiful but unwilling submission characterized their entire relationship. There was no real spiritual, intellectual, and
physical union. Natasha never tried to understand or appreciate him. She was just a wife, and even this status she sometimes resented.

After his return to the capital in October he soon found it
necessary to move again. The winter social season of 1832–
1833 drew the Pushkins into a whirl of balls and entertainments.
Natasha still rode the wave of popularity. All the fashionable
youths pursued her. Despite her husband's warnings, she persisted in her flirtations, which were often in bad taste and not
entirely free from vulgarity. All continued to praise Natasha's
beauty, but no one said anything of her heart, her mind, her
soul, or her modesty. Indeed, nothing seemed to concern her
except dancing and being the center of attraction in the ballroom. She had no interest in the theater, music, art, or litera-

ture. Natasha lived as children live, without thought or care. Her life was a series of festivities, balls, promenades, and preoccupations with her toilet. The fact that she was pregnant again did not interfere with her strenuous pleasures.

The effect of this constant round of balls and masquerades on Natasha's health worried Pushkin. Nor had his own health been any too good, for he had been suffering from rheumatism. Yet he insisted on accompanying her to all these affairs. "You never see Pushkin anywhere, except at balls," Gogol wrote to a friend. "Thus he will squander his whole life if some occasion or other, or even necessity, does not drive him into the country." [20] Close friends, zealous protectors of his glory, grew angry at what they thought a willful and stupid waste of time. The ever-helpful Pletnev wrote to Zhukovski: "You now are right in disdaining such idlers as Pushkin, who does nothing at all, except in the morning to sift into a box the old letters sent him, and in the evening to take his wife to balls, not so much for her amusement as for his own." [21]

Even friends could hardly be expected to understand the inner compulsion that obliged Pushkin to humor his girl-wife. He was proud of Natasha and her beauty, and proud to be seen with her. If achieving a social success made her happy, he felt it necessary to further her ambition. But he had no real desire for this incessant social activity. Almost at the same time that Pletnev sent his censorious letter to Zhukovski (February 17, 1833), Pushkin wrote to Nashchokin: "My existence in Petersburg is neither here nor there. The cares of life worry me to death. But I have no leisure, none of the free bachelor life necessary for a writer. I whirl about in society, my wife is all the rage — all this requires money; money is obtained through work, and work requires seclusion. . . . I need a journey, morally and physically." [22]

Since that happy summer at Tsarskoe Selo, however, Pushkin had not been idling. In reality, he had been full of literary schemes and was making the most of the precious little leisure at his disposal to carry them out. In December 1832 he had been elected a member of the Russian Academy, a rather obsolete and· lifeless body that occupied itself with dull questions on the Russian language. There was something ironic in his elevation to this ultra-conservative institution, the head of which was Admiral Shishkov, who had been the standing joke of the long-defunct Arzamas Society of Pushkin's youth. But he was pleased. The membership brought him certain privileges and also a recognition of his literary services from ancient enemies.

The authorities had been more coöperative over this period, but their surveillance was not relaxed in the slightest, and every trip he made was still carefully chronicled by the police and a watch kept on his actions. Benkendorf had also taken him to task for printing his perfect little poem, *Anchar*, in the benefit edition of Delvig's *Northern Flowers*. (Pushkin had allowed the poem to go through the ordinary censor without submitting it for the tsar's approval.) On the other hand, Benkendorf had melted to the point of performing real favors. On Pushkin's request he had interceded for brother Lev, obtaining him a transfer from the Caucasus to the Russian forces in Poland. There is a pretty authentic story that the editor Grech offered Pushkin a position on his magazine and on that of Bulgarin, carrying with it a very considerable salary. Despite his desperate need for money, Pushkin refused to ally himself with these literary foes. But again he revived his own fond scheme for a political and literary magazine, and on this occasion Benkendorf at first encouraged him. The possibility of such a publication thrilled Pushkin. He began making plans, and talked with friends about the formation of a staff. Then, at the last minute, Benkendorf prescribed so many conditions that the magazine would have been completely emasculated. Once more Pushkin had to abandon his darling project.

Historical researches occupied most of his time. His original idea of a history of Peter the Great had been temporarily put aside for another scheme, a history of Pugachev's revolt in the time of Catherine II. In reality, he had a twofold plan in mind — the history and an historical romance based on the period. He went about the collecting of material in a thorough manner.

Everything connected with the period interested him. He burrowed in the archives, consulted with historical specialists, and sought out rare manuscripts. The authorities aided him in his investigations, although the tsar was suspicious of this interest in the revolt of the masses under Pugachev. In seeking permission to use material in the archives Pushkin cleverly tried to avoid appealing directly to the tsar. He wrote to subordinates, but the requests were invariably referred to Nicholas. In one instance the wary tsar flatly refused access to certain documents. "What does he want these papers for?" Nicholas wrote to the official who had transmitted the request. "They have been lying untouched in the archives since my grandmother ordered them placed there. Even I have not read them. Let Pushkin get along without them. Does he wish to obtain from them scandalous material paralleling the canto of *Don Juan* in which Byron dishonored the memory of my grandmother? No, indeeed!" [23] Pushkin's only reply was to express surprise that the tsar had ever read *Don Juan*. But it would have been more surprising if Nicholas had failed to read Byron's classic description of his grandmother:

> In Catherine's reign, whom glory still adores,
> As greatest of all sovereigns and w . . . . s. [24]

Before the end of 1833 Pushkin had actually begun drafting his history of the Pugachev revolt. And in January of the same year he sketched the historical romance, *The Captain's Daughter*, [25] which is based on the Pugachev period. Another prose work is connected with his investigation of Catherine's time — the incomplete novel, *Dubrovski*. It is the romantic story of a poor landowner who has been ruined by a wealthy neighbor. *Dubrovski* is complicated in plot, contains plenty of action, and provides a remarkably realistic picture of rural life in the time of Catherine II. The characters are among the most lively and the best creations of Pushkin.

Poetry was not forsaken entirely for "scornful prose," as Pushkin called it. "How sorry are those poets who begin to write prose," he told one of his acquaintances. "I confess that, if I were not obliged by circumstances, I would not dip my pen in ink for prose." [26] In March 1833 the first edition of the entire *Eugene Onegin* was published, just ten years after he had begun this great novel in verse. At about the same time he finished his *Songs of the Western Slavs*,[27] on which he had long been working. To these poems, drawn from Prosper Mérimée's *La Guzla*, an excellent forgery of Serbian folk songs, Pushkin added a few songs from other sources and cast the whole in the meter of the Russian folk epic. It was the first time that a poet had used this measure with any consistency and skill, and the songs represent a triumph in the impersonal narrative style which he had been cultivating. Folk themes, as already indicated, were becoming favorite material for poetry with Pushkin. In the spring of 1832 he had written the incomplete but altogether wonderful folk drama, *Rusalka*. It is the story, not original with Pushkin, of a miller's daughter who has been seduced by a prince. He finally abandons her and marries a princess. The betrayed girl throws herself into the Dnieper and becomes a *rusalka* (a river nymph). Before long the prince becomes bored with his noble wife and wanders along the river bank. Meanwhile, the betrayed girl, who is now queen of the *rusalkas*, has given birth to a daughter. Determined to revenge herself on the seducer, she sends her other-world daughter to entice her mortal father. And here the fragment ends. In this poem, which is written in his best blank verse, Pushkin recreates the whole world of Russian folk romance with amazingly realistic vividness. The tragic element is touching but most artistically restrained, and over the whole breathes the atmosphere of the fairy world, convincingly real yet unforgettably haunting in its eerie effects. *Rusalka* is an inimitable achievement.

In the late summer of 1833 Pushkin hired a house in a suburb of Petersburg, and there, on the sixth of July, his son Alexander was born. For several months now an irrepressible desire to be on the road had been agitating him. As happened so often in his bachelor days, he felt the need of a change. A journey, as he had told Nashchokin, was a moral and physical necessity.

Family cares and the social whirl of the capital were weighing him down. Everything interfered with his work. In May he had written Praskovya Osipova that Petersburg did not agree either with his tastes or his means. Little Mariya had been ill. "I suppose," he writes his Trigorskoe friend, "that she is cutting teeth. Up to this time she has not had one. Even though you convince yourself that everyone has experienced all this, yet these creatures are so frail that it is impossible to watch them suffer without trembling." [28] He yearns to go to Mikhailovskoe, but Natasha does not like the country. Now, however, he discovered a very legitimate excuse for a trip. He had to visit the regions of Orenburg and Kazan, where the Pugachev revolt had raged, in order to consult the local archives for his history. Pushkin asked Benkendorf for a furlough of two or three months for this purpose. He cautiously refrained from telling his official guardian that he also wished to visit this region in order to assimilate local color for his historical romance. The ever-suspicious tsar, however, desired to know more precisely the reasons for such a trip. In irritation Pushkin replied that he required two months of seclusion in order to rest and to finish his history. His expenses in the capital were mounting as his family increased, he explained, and hence he badly needed the money which the sale of this work would bring him. Begrudgingly, permission was granted, and on the eighteenth of August Pushkin left Petersburg.

IV

> Remain young, because you are young — and rule, because you are beautiful.
>
> *Pushkin in a letter to his wife, 1833*

The open road and the jolly company of Sobolevski, who was on his way to Moscow, revived Pushkin's spirits and brought back happy memories of his bachelor days. They stopped off at Malinniki, but since the Vulf estate was practically deserted they soon resumed their journey. Further on the road Pushkin interrupted his trip to pay a short visit to Yaropolets, the village of his mother-in-law. By now she had pretty much accepted Pushkin. Perhaps her married daughter's success in the capital had helped to soften Mama Kars' opinion of him. She received him kindly, and the visit was the pleasantest he had ever had with her.

Pushkin arrived in Moscow on the twenty-fifth of August and remained there for four days. It was an enjoyable stay. He met many of his old comrades of bachelor conviviality, and in their gay company, toasts, frequent and deep, were drunk to the peerless beauty of Natasha. The next stop was Nizhni Novgorod, and from there Pushkin proceeded to the Pugachev country, arriving in Kazan on the fifth of September. Here he got down to the business of collecting material in a serious manner. He consulted local historians, dug in the town archives, visited the ancient camp site of Pugachev, and stayed up until the early hours of the morning to write out his notes. There were some old natives in the district who claimed to have had personal contacts with Pugachev and to have taken part in the stirring events of the rebellion. Pushkin zealously hunted them out and interviewed them. He took extensive notes of their accounts, eager to recover the slightest fragment of contemporary local color. The illiterate natives were suspicious of this ardent curiosity, and in one instance afraid to take the money he offered. Because of his appearance and unusually long nails they decided that he must be "Antichrist."

But Pugachev's field of action had been large, and there was still much more ground to cover in this search for historical data. He went on to Simbirsk, made a side trip to the estate of his friend, the poet, Yazykov, and then continued further into the Cossack country, visiting Orenburg and Uralsk. In those days of travel such a journey through the sparsely populated Ural territory was an heroic feat, and Pushkin encountered many difficulties on the road. He now felt satisfied with his investigations, and started back. It was autumn, and mindful of the brilliant period of composition that he had enjoyed at Boldino before his marriage, he hopefully directed his steps there. He arrived at the village on the first of October, weary from his incessant traveling, but eager to get down to writing.

His expectations were not disappointed. In the next six weeks Pushkin experienced another period of incredibly swift composition, not as prolific as the Boldino autumn of 1830, but in its accomplishment amazing enough. He finished, including even the introduction, *The History of Pugachev*. This was Pushkin's title. When it was published in 1834 the tsar ordered that it be called *The History of the Pugachev Rebellion*.[29] For Nicholas I a rebel could not have a history. The work consisted of two volumes, one of text, the other of notes. Pushkin never lived to finish his history of Peter the Great, although he left many highly interesting and discerning fragments on the subject. His place as an historian therefore depends largely on his handling of the Pugachev rebellion. The final product is history written by a literary artist, yet he was by no means inattentive to the strictly formal aspects of such a task. His historical insight and research deserve the highest respect, even on the basis of modern standards. Certain important sources were denied him, but those at his command were handled with skill. He underestimates the significance of social and economic factors, and is too prone to concentrate on dramatic incidents and individuals. But both as history and literature the work is a first-rate performance.

There were other prose pieces written at Boldino, fragmentary for the most part, and of a critical and biographical nature. But the time Pushkin stole from his history was largely devoted to poetry. He continued to find inspiration in his favorite folk material, and wrote in effortless fashion two tales, *The Dead Princess and the Seven Champions* and *The Tale of the Fisherman and the Fish*.[30] The first is not so successful as his other folk stories, but *The Tale of the Fisherman and the Fish* is a delightful story. The artlessness and complete impersonality of *Tsar Saltan* are attained once more. It is the old story of the poor fisherman who is allowed to wish for anything he desires in return for releasing a fish that he has caught. His shrewish and ambitious wife, of course, carries things too far, and the harassed fisherman is glad to return to his former impoverished but peaceful state. In general, these folk tales were scorned as silly and meaningless poems by contemporary critics, but it was agreed that the story of the fisherman was superior to the others.

As though he were attempting a poetic exercise in the art of condensation, Pushkin reduced Shakespeare's *Measure for Measure* to a short narrative poem under the title of *Angelo*. With a few changes, which tend to make a more tragic figure of Angelo, the story and many of the lines of the original are retained. Against the background of the play the results are curious, yet the work is indelibly stamped with Pushkin's genius. The critics scoffed at it, but Pushkin, either because of an author's love for a maligned brain child, or because he actually believed it, always maintained that he had written nothing better than *Angelo*. At this time he also wrote a few short poems, the most notable of which is *May God Keep Me from Going Mad*.[31] The fear of insanity now haunted his thoughts frequently, and in these lines it finds an expression filled with horror and deep pathos.

The most remarkable achievement of this second Boldino period is a poem of over five hundred lines — *The Bronze Horseman*.[32] It is often rated higher than *Eugene Onegin*, and critics are not lacking who maintain that it is the greatest of all Russian poems. Curiously enough, it grew out of Pushkin's desire to write a sequel to *Eugene Onegin*. He abandoned the idea in favor of a new poem whose hero was to bear the name of Eugene. The pedigree of this hero he wrote at Boldino (*The Genealogy of My Hero*),[33] but finally he eliminated the pedigree and used the plot for *The Bronze Horseman*, which is written in unstanzaed octosyllabics. The central situation of the poem is the disastrous Petersburg flood of 1824. A poor clerk, Eugene, is in love with Parasha. She and her house disappear in the flood, and the grief-stricken Eugene finally goes mad over his loss. Homeless, starved, and wild-eyed, he roams the streets, plagued by urchins and beaten by coachmen. Once, as he is passing Senate Square, he sees the huge bronze equestrian statue of Peter the Great, the work of the famous French sculptor, Falconet. To Eugene's deranged mind the bronze emperor appears to be the cause of all his misery. As he curses the statue it suddenly becomes animated and threatens him with outstretched arm. The terrified Eugene flees and is pursued by the bronze horseman through the city's streets. The resounding clang of the hoofs roars relentlessly in his ears until he is finally forced to the river. At the end of the poem his body is found on a little island hard by the remains of his sweetheart's home.

A vein of transparent symbolism runs through *The Bronze Horseman*. Its tragic theme is the opposition between the rights of the individual and the all-powerful, despotic empire, typified by the statue of Peter the Great. The pitiful citizen Eugene has no more right to question the will of the bronze figure than had the toiling masses who gave their lives that Peter's great city might exist. Yet Pushkin does not minimize the tragedy of the weak, defenseless Eugene, who is driven to destruction by the unjust and inhuman power of the bronze horseman. Worship of the city and its illustrious founder, which Pushkin carefully sustains throughout the whole poem, contrasts fearfully with the misery and persecution of the un-heroic Eugene. *The Bronze Horseman* is the most mature and finished of Pushkin's productions, the most tragic, profound, and brilliant in thought and conception, the most intense, powerful, and compact in language and structure. Despite the fantastic device of plot, which is pure poetry, all romantic adornment is eschewed in favor of strictly realistic imagery and language. Pushkin's royal censor refused permission to print it unless certain changes were made. Perhaps the symbolism suggested too clearly a contradiction in human justice that was not flattering to an autocrat. Pushkin refused to make the changes, but, fully conscious of the poem's worth, he continued to modify and polish it until his death. In some respects *The Bronze Horseman* reads like an allegory of the tragic opposition of Pushkin's own life — the individual in conflict with a despotic tsar.

As on his previous trip, nearly all Pushkin's correspondence was devoted to Natasha during this absence of three months. He wrote often, sometimes twice a day. The letters are gossipy, chatty, filled with the small details of his "Odyssey." In Push-

kin's large correspondence with various people he displays an
unerring faculty for adapting the contents of his letters to the
individual taste and intellect of the recipient. He realizes that
light gossip and little details are what would interest his wife
most. Accordingly, he tells her of the people he met, of their
mutual acquaintances, of the hare and priest that crossed his
path and aroused his superstitions, and of all the trifling adventures of the road. But we find scarcely anything of the
deeper thoughts and the profound feelings that agitate his
mind, or of the vast literary plans that constantly occupy him.
When he writes of his own affairs, he does it half jokingly, as
though afraid to bore her. He knows that she regards his
poetry only as a means of making money, and on the few occasions when he does mention it, he rarely fails to remark about
his hopes of financial returns. Domestic concerns are a constant
topic. He is anxious about her health, fears that she is pregnant again, is afraid that she lacks money; and he continually
asks for the children, warning her not to spoil little Masha by
petting her too much.

His love for Natasha, or rather the fear that she would fail to
believe in this love, is reflected in all these letters. He bows
before her as before a goddess. Perhaps with unconscious design, his compliments often take the form of the extravagant
flattery that Natasha was accustomed to receive from her
many admirers in the social world. The women he meets in his
travels are purposely described as unattractive in order not to
arouse her jealousy. None of them compares with her. "Look
in the mirror," he writes, "and you will be convinced that it is
impossible to compare anything in the world with your face.
But I love your soul even more than your face. Farewell, my
angel, I kiss you affectionately." [34]

Pushkin, however, continually worries over her flirting, and
the theme runs through his whole correspondence with his wife
like a leitmotiv. Natasha's letters to her husband, with very
few and inconsequential exceptions, have not survived. But
from the contents of his own it is easy to see that she made
a special point of telling him of all her conquests. It was a

fatal weakness. He warns her against flirting with Sobolevski or the tsar, who had already begun to show her marked attention. "Do not terrify me, little wife," he writes her in a pathetic vein from Boldino. "Do not say that you have been flirting; I shall return to you without having succeeded in writing anything — and without money we shall run on the rocks. You had better leave me in peace, and I will work and hustle." [35] Pushkin's Tatyana-like ideal of the proud, reserved, and tactful queen of society was rapidly disintegrating. Without thinking for a moment that she would be unfaithful to him, he was nevertheless beginning to distrust her mind, heart, and character. From his own experience he knew that flirting itself might signify nothing, but that vicious gossip soon ruined the reputation of both the innocent and the guilty. "You rejoice in the fact," he angrily writes, "that these dogs run after you, as after a bitch, raising their tails straight as pipes and sniffing at your rear. What is there to rejoice over? . . . So, my angel, please do not flirt. I am not jealous, and I realize that you do not go off at a tangent; but you know that I don't like anything that smacks of the Moscow damsel, that is not *comme il faut*, that is vulgar. If on my return I find that your dear, simple, aristocratic tone has changed — and I shall investigate — then, by Christ, I shall go off with the soldiers in despair." [36]

Despite the half-playful threat, Pushkin was deeply serious. Yet he feared that he had been too severe, and in his next letter he softened his tone. "I repeat to you more gently that flirting leads to no good; although it has its own pleasant side, yet nothing so quickly deprives a young woman of that without which there can be no felicity or peace in a family's relations to society: *esteem*. . . . Think about this, my beauty, and do not worry me to no purpose. I shall soon return, but for some time I shall remain in Moscow on business. Little wife, little wife! I have been traveling the great road, living for three months in the wild steppes; I shall stay in filthy Moscow, which I hate — for what? For you, little wife, in order that you may be tranquil and shine in health, as is proper at your age and with your beauty. Heed me, then. To a man's inevitable concerns with life do not add family worries, jealousy, etc., etc., without mentioning cuckoldry, about which I read a whole dissertation by Brantôme a few days ago." [37]

In all this Pushkin may seem to be laboring a point with husbandly obtuseness. Flirting was much in fashion, especially in the aristocratic society in which he and his wife were now moving. Pushkin had done his share of flirting in the past, and it now seemed puritanical to object to it in his wife. But he did not set any great store by Natasha's brains or tact. He fully realized the dubious position he held in Petersburg high society. And he knew that at the first opportunity this society would take delight in ruining his wife's reputation and in ridiculing him. Whatever such a situation would signify to Natasha, for Pushkin it would be intolerable. He valued his honor — the esteem of society — more than anything in life. This honor must be kept unsullied at any cost. His carping at her flirtations was indeed no small matter. With his passionate temperament it bore all the elements of tragedy.

CHAPTER XVIII

A Prisoner of the Tsar's Court

> In chains they bind thee with
> the fools,
> And come to plague thee
> through the bars,
> As they would plague a beast.
> *May God Keep Me from Going
> Mad*

With manuscript books and a full-grown beard Pushkin left Boldino. After a short halt in Moscow he returned to Petersburg on the evening of November 20, hoping to surprise Natasha by his sudden appearance in a new beard. She was attending a ball at the Karamzins. He went directly there and waited outside while a servant summoned her home on a pretext. Natasha ignored the call, for she was busy dancing a mazurka with Prince Vyazemski. A second and more urgent request succeeded. Upon entering the carriage she found herself in her husband's arms. Filled with the excitement of the dance, Natasha did not receive this unexpected interruption very graciously. And the full beard was soon abbreviated to Pushkin's customary side whiskers.

The quiet and peaceful literary labors of Boldino were exchanged for the noise and fatiguing pleasures of the ballroom. Again the capital's social season was under way. Even if her husband's company was not sought after, Natasha's was everywhere in demand. Her absence from the exclusive court balls at the Anichkov Palace had been noticed by the tsar. Pushkin's rank did not entitle him to take part in these functions. Nicholas found a remedy; at the end of 1833 his majesty made Pushkin a gentleman of the chamber. This court dignity virtually obliged him and his wife to be present at the palace balls.

The honor deeply offended Pushkin. He was thirty-four years of age, a great poet, and a public figure. The appointment of gentleman of the chamber was ordinarily conferred on eighteen-year-old aristocratic youths who were seeking their first contact with the court. Although he wished to avoid the conclusion, there was no doubt in his mind concerning the true reason for this insulting honor. Between 1833 and 1835 Pushkin kept a diary of the daily events of his life, perhaps intending to use it as a basis for writing his memoirs. The entries are coldly impersonal, compressed, at times almost cryptic, as though he feared the possibility that the document might fall into the hands of the authorities. For January 1, 1834, he wrote in his diary: "The day before yesterday I was made a gentleman of the chamber (that is quite improper at my age). But the court wanted N[atalya] N[ikolaevna] to dance at Anichkov." [1]

Pushkin's first impulse was to decline the position most emphatically. But close friends assured him that Nicholas had no motive other than to honor him. They feared the tsar's anger should he refuse. Natasha, in a seventh heaven, added her irresistible pleas to those of friends. Weakening, he complained that he had no money to buy the expensive uniform, but a friend came to his aid and presented him with a complete outfit. With many misgivings, Pushkin finally accepted the appointment. He was afraid of what people would say, and he knew full well that his acceptance placed him under further obligations to the crown. The tsar was drawing the silken chains still tighter.

Pushkin was right. Society laughed over the spectacle of a poet of thirty-four taking his place among the youthful and foppish gentlemen of the chamber. Some whispered that the tsar simply desired the beautiful Natasha at his dances; others said more openly that Pushkin had begged for the honor himself. The tsar's brother, Mikhail Pavlovich, congratulated him, and Pushkin noted his ironic answer in his diary: "Up to now all have felt it necessary to ridicule me; you are the first to congratulate me." [2]

The new duties further complicated his social life, adding tribulation and vexations from which he had hitherto been free. His attendance at court functions became mandatory. The tsar was a stickler for etiquette, and the distracted poet everlastingly fell afoul of the rules. At one ball he appeared in his uniform when a frock coat was ordered. He hastily departed, and the tsar showed his displeasure. A gentleman of the chamber, remarked Nicholas, ought to take the trouble to change his dress and return. Pushkin earned a rebuke for this negligence. Instead of the round hat of his official dress, he appeared in a three-cornered hat; or the buttons of his uniform failed to comply with accepted standards — such details the tsar noticed and charged against him. Gentleman of the Chamber Pushkin did not turn up at the palace church on Palm Sunday — immediately his superior invited him to explain his absence. And like a misbehaved schoolboy he had to think up convincing excuses. On another occasion he fled the capital in order to avoid appearing with the youths of the chamber at a special function. He explained that he was ill, and wondered why the angry tsar did not send a courier or his physician after him.

While Pushkin fretted and fumed, Natasha gaily danced. On the seventeenth of January she was presented at her first court ball. The tsar danced a quadrille with her and at supper gave her the place of honor beside him. He also talked with the husband, and Pushkin coldly notes in his diary that he did not thank Nicholas for his recent appointment. Balls and masquerades followed in quick succession. This season of 1833–1834 was an unusually busy one. It was a positive relief for him to be able to steal a little time for reading or for a visit with an old friend. Natasha, however, was in her element. She would return from the dance at four or five in the morning, sleep all day, have dinner at eight, and be off to another ball. The expected eventually happened. In March Pushkin wrote to Nashchokin: "This winter has been terribly crowded with balls. At Shrovetide we danced even twice a day. It finally came to an end on the last Sunday before Lent. Think I: Thank God! these balls are off my mind! My wife is at the palace. Suddenly I look — something is the matter with her — I escort her out, and after arriving home, she has a miscarriage." [3]

Doctors prescribed a rest. On the fifteenth of April Natasha and the children were sent to Linen Factory, the Kaluga estate of the Goncharovs. Pushkin was grateful for this termination of his social activities, but he gloomily anticipated the next season. He felt that he had cut a sorry, even silly, figure — the "singer of freedom" in the uniform of a gentleman of the chamber accompanying his beautiful wife to the court balls! Were not his liberal friends laughing over the poet who once threatened a tsar in his verse and who now appeared to be a servile member of the court of a more reactionary tsar? Had not a lampoon been published, ridiculing his strange position? Were not scandalmongers already beginning to gossip about the attention Nicholas I was paying his beautiful Natasha? Rebellious thoughts of independence, of release from this vicious society, from the court and its ruler, awoke in him.

II

> Then to spit on Petersburg, retire, scamper off to Boldino, and live like a lord.
> *Pushkin in a letter to his wife,*
> *1834*

After the departure of his wife, Pushkin's existence became relatively calm in comparison with the social hurly-burly of the preceding months, but his mind seethed with discontent. "One advantage of your absence," he wrote Natasha, "is that I am not obliged to doze at balls or to gorge myself on ices." [4] His presence was still required at court functions, but he maintained the fiction of illness, even at the risk of offending the tsar. He spent the days quietly, working at home until four o'clock, and then going to Demuth's to dine with Sobolevski or with some other bachelor friend. Often he whiled away the evenings playing billiards at the English Club.

Pushkin's disturbed state of mind is clearly revealed in his correspondence with Natasha. In these letters he shows himself a harassed man, and now he makes no effort to conceal his heavy thoughts from his wife. Their relations had ceased to be altogether serene. The tenderness of his former correspondence is rarely absent, but a letter begun with kind intentions often ends, as he confesses, with a "slap in the face." As though he distrusts her care for the children, he makes a point of inquiring after their health and of giving her advice on how they should be treated. Pushkin was a stern but good father and deeply interested in his children. He continually fears that Natasha will spoil them and strictly warns her against this. The boy was his favorite, and he whimsically tells his wife that he hopes Sasha will not follow in his father's footsteps and write poetry and quarrel with tsars. There is no lack of affection, but his advice, now more abundant and pointed, seems to spring from his irritation over the fact that Natasha fails to understand their domestic affairs realistically or to perceive how precarious their economic situation has become. Perhaps she regarded his advice as that of a peevish husband who was growing old too soon. At any rate, she paid little attention to it. Vexed, he writes: "Little wife, little wife! if you do not mind me in such small things, what am I to think?" [5] But far from soothing his troubled mind, she filled her letters with stories of dances and flirtations at Kaluga, despite the fact that she had gone away for a rest. With a curious mixture of anger and tenderness he storms at her: "I begged you not to wear yourself out at Kaluga, but obviously that is your nature. I shall say no more about your flirtatious relations with the neighbors. I have allowed you to coquette; but I do not have to read an entire page of detailed description about it. Having scolded you, I take you tenderly by the ear and kiss you: thanks for this, that you pray to God in your room. I pray very little to God, and I hope that your pure prayer is better than mine, both for my sake and for ours." [6]

The exasperation so evident in this correspondence springs not only from the vanishing illusion that in marriage lay his future happiness. New adversities were helping to fray his sorely tried nerves. Like a stalking ghost, money difficulties continued to haunt him at every turn. His parents urgently summoned him. They begged him — the mother in tears and Sergei Lvovich on the verge of collapse — to save the remnant of their estate, which they were in danger of losing because of unpaid debts. In order to remedy the situation Pushkin advised them to settle at Mikhailovskoe, but the ageing and impractical couple refused to sacrifice their expensive city life. Then the poverty-stricken husband of his sister Olga descended upon him, demanding money from the family estate, money which Pushkin could not give him. Brother Lev's gambling debts were dumped at his doorstep, and he had to come to the rescue. Even Nashchokin had fallen on evil times and was asking for badly-needed funds.

These demands, on top of his own financial problems, were a heavy burden indeed. To make matters worse, the thoughtless Natasha wrote from Kaluga that she was going to bring her two sisters to live with them in Petersburg. Neither Ekaterina nor Alexandra Goncharova had succeeded in getting a husband, and life with their exacting mother was extremely difficult. With her new contacts at court and the aid of her influential aunt, Natasha had conceived the brilliant idea of getting her sisters established as maids of honor. This, at least, would be a step in the direction of matrimony. Although he was sorry for the sisters and desirous of helping them, Pushkin vigorously opposed his wife's plan. He knew that for Nicholas, as for most of the tsars before him, maids of honor at the court had always been regarded as "dainty morsels." And he had no desire that his sisters-in-law should get involved in the scandalous doings of the court, nor did he wish to have his wife under any obligations to the tsar. But there were other and more practical reasons for opposing the scheme. "Think," he wrote to Natasha, "what nasty interpretations swinish Petersburg will place on this. You will be well-advised, my angel, to refuse your petitioners. . . . My advice to you and your sisters is to get further away from the court; there is little sense in it. You are not rich. It is impossible for you to pile everything on your aunt." [7] But his wife argued the point, and Pushkin finally turned on her: "Here is my opinion: a family ought to be alone under its own roof: husband, wife, children, are they too few? Parents, yes, when they are old, but there will be no end of trouble, and there will be no family peace." [8] Natasha disregarded his good advice. The sisters were eventually brought on and quartered in the household, with results even more dire than Pushkin had anticipated.

With alternating vexation and affection, Pushkin calls his wife a "fool" in one letter and in the next begs her to see that only their straitened circumstances and her failure to consider them make him angry with her. What would happen if he suddenly died, he asks? There would be no estate for her to fall back on, no subsistence for little Masha and Sasha. He regrets the necessity of mentioning the matter of money so often. "Dependence is disagreeable; especially when for twenty years I have been independent. This is no reproach to you but a complaint against myself." 9 Yet Natasha insisted on understanding his statement as a reproach. Kindly and patiently, he explained: "You are young, but you are the mother of a family, and I am convinced that it will not be difficult for you to perform the duties of a good mother, as you perform the duties of an honorable and good wife. Dependence and disorder in the management of a household are terrible; and none of the pleasures of vanity can compensate for peace of mind and contentment." 10 It was this dependence, he told her, which necessity or ambition thrust upon a man, that eventually destroyed him. "They look upon me now as on a groveler with whom one may behave as he pleases." 11

The despicable spying of the authorities contributed greatly to Pushkin's mental and moral misery. A letter to his wife was opened by the post-office officials at Moscow. In it Pushkin had been telling Natasha of his difficulties with three tsars. And he concludes: "The third, although he made me a page of the chamber in my old age, I do not desire to change for a fourth: let well enough alone." 12 This was thought to be offensive, and a copy of the letter was made and sent to the tsar. It angered Nicholas, and only the kind offices of Zhukovski, who placed a favorable interpretation on the statement, smoothed things over. The story got around, and Pushkin heard it. Bitterly he wrote in his diary: "I can be devoted, even slavishly so, but I will not be a slave or a fool, even for the King of Heaven. However, what profound immorality in the customs of our government! The police open the letters of a husband to his wife and take them to the tsar to read (a well-bred and honorable man), and the tsar is not ashamed to admit this — and he furthers intrigue worthy of Vidocq * and Bulgarin!" [13]

Pushkin was maddened to the point of explosion. The "swinishness" of the postal officials he despised, and the knowledge that his letters were being opened made it difficult for him to write. He finally informed Natasha of the incident, warning her not to show his letters to anyone and to be careful of what she said in hers: "If the post office has opened the letter of a husband to his wife, then this is its affair and a disagreeable one: the secrets of family relations are subjected to nasty and dishonorable treatment; but if you are at fault, this would pain me. No one must know what takes place between us; no one must be allowed to enter our bedroom. Without secrecy there is no family life." [14] In a second letter on the subject he sternly remarks: "It is very possible to live without political freedom, but without the inviolability of the family it is impossible. Penal servitude is better by far." "This is not written for you," [15] he concludes defiantly, hoping that the police would also read this statement. They unquestionably did. And another letter, in which he fiercely arraigns the culpable director of the Moscow post office for not being ashamed to open mail or to peddle his own daughters, never reached Natasha.

The incident affected Pushkin's relations with the tsar; in his eyes Nicholas I had ceased to be an honorable man. It brought to a head an extreme decision which the accumulated adversities of the past months had suggested. Pushkin felt that he must retire from the service, relinquish his hated duties as gentleman of the chamber, and settle down in the country. He yearned to get away from the oppressive, scandalmongering society of Petersburg, to remove Natasha from the vicious influences of the capital which were destroying his married life. In the country he would find the possibility of bettering his

---

* François-Eugene Vidocq (1775–1857), a criminal who used his knowledge of the underworld to good advantage as a police spy and finally won distinction in the French police service.

financial plight, and the peace and contentment that would enable him to write. When he communicated this desire to his wife, she naturally objected. To be buried in the country, far removed from the glitter and pleasures of the capital, was a dreary existence for the beautiful Natasha to contemplate. But to her husband there seemed no other way of avoiding the specter of approaching catastrophe. He must escape before it was too late. Above all, he must regain his independence. On the twenty-fifth of June, 1834, Pushkin sent a brief note to Benkendorf, requesting that he be allowed to retire from the service because of family affairs, and asking the single favor of retaining his privilege of using the archives for historical research.

The tsar was indignant at what he thought a display of ingratitude on Pushkin's part. Benkendorf's cool answer soon arrived. His majesty had no desire to hold anyone in the service against his will. Therefore Pushkin was free to retire. But permission to use the archives was withdrawn, "for this privilege may be given only to persons enjoying the particular confidence of the authorities." [16] In such picayune spitefulness one may discern the personal spleen of Nicholas, for he knew full well that Pushkin had suspected the motives behind his appointment of gentleman of the chamber, and that he scorned the office itself. As a matter of fact, the tsar had sensed the change in Pushkin's regard for him. The monarch Pushkin had celebrated in the eulogistic poems, written after his release from exile, had fallen in his esteem. Then he had compared Nicholas to his hero, Peter the Great. Now he writes in his diary of this tsar who connived at the opening of a husband's letter to his wife: "Someone said of the emperor: 'In him there is much of the ensign and little of Peter the Great.'" [17] And by this "someone" Pushkin means himself.

It was not easy to accept the loss of his privilege of using the archives, for it meant the end of his historical studies. But there is every reason to suspect that Pushkin, if he had been let alone, would have stuck by his guns in this instance and gone into retirement. However, a letter from Zhukovski arrived. He had been talking with the tsar about the resignation. Nicholas had been hurt by the request, said Zhukovski, yet he wanted it understood that the door was still open. Pushkin must not be an ingrate. And Zhukovski advised him to recall his letter.

Pushkin was thrown into confusion. The charge of ungratefulness never failed to wring his conscience. Briefly he wrote to Benkendorf again, trying to explain his position. But Zhukovski was still dissatisfied. The tsar, he reported, had said that all was over between them. He must write a full letter of apology. Pushkin could not understand for what he should apologize. He was not ungrateful. Family circumstances alone had obliged him to retire. Zhukovski insisted. His influence on Pushkin was enormous. Worn down and defeated, he wrote two more letters to Benkendorf in which he humbly withdrew his request for retirement, asking simply for several months in the country in order to finish some work. The permission was granted, and he was restored to the service.

However, Pushkin had hardly been restored to the good graces of Nicholas. In his report to the tsar Benkendorf suggests that the letter of resignation be forgotten: "It is better for him to be in the service than to be left to his own devices." [18] And in reply the tsar scribbled on the report: "I pardon him; but invite him and explain once more that what might be forgiven in a twenty-year-old madcap cannot be pardoned in a man of thirty-five, a husband and the father of a family." [19] Nicholas had gained his point. Pushkin would remain bound to the service and to his ridiculous duties of gentleman of the chamber, and his beautiful wife would continue to adorn the court balls. Pushkin's close and kind friend, Zhukovski, had performed him a fatal service. The weight of disastrous circumstances crushing his life was never to be removed; the silken chains were never to be broken.

III

Throughout these weeks of separation from his wife, and despite the atmosphere of constant worry in which he was living, Pushkin worked steadily at the task of seeing *The History of the Pugachev Rebellion* through the press. The government

had lent him twenty thousand rubles to print it, and he hoped
to make a good profit on the enterprise. He missed Natasha,
and her failure to write was a constant irritation. She seemed
to be leading a very gay existence at Kaluga, flirting and dancing with the provincial cavaliers. And she continued to irritate
him with the history of her successes. Whether this was naïve
candor or feminine cunning it is hard to say. But she did succeed in arousing his jealousy. "I hope," he writes, "that you
will appear before me as pure and truthful when we meet as
when we parted." [20] Finally, exasperated by her frivolous behavior, he angrily remarks: "You work only with your feet at
balls and help your husband squander money." [21]

Growing more and more impatient to see his wife, Pushkin
hurried through the last proof sheets of the history, and on the
twenty-fifth of August he was free to go to Kaluga. He passed
two pleasant weeks at Linen Factory with Natasha. But his
favorite time of autumn was at hand and the urge to get down
to writing seized him. Once again he turned to Boldino, which
had by now become identified with so many of his productions.
Having accompanied Natasha as far as Moscow on her way
back to the capital, he proceeded alone to Boldino, where he
arrived on the thirteenth of September.

The first snow had fallen, and the little village presented the
quiet haven of inspiration that he had anticipated. But somehow or other inspiration did not flow. He wrote *The Golden
Cockerel*,[22] another of those perfect little folk tales. Though
more or less on a par with *Tsar Saltan* as a poetic accomplishment, it contains a new note of irony which increases the intellectual pleasure it affords but detracts somewhat from its pure
folk quality. Apart from this poem he did nothing else. "I am
lonesome," he writes Natasha, "and when I am lonesome my
thoughts go out to you, as you cling to me when you are frightened." [23] Try as he might, the verses would not come. His head
was filled with other things. "I read Walter Scott and the
Bible, but I am always thinking of you," he writes in a second
letter to his wife. "I am disturbed about many things. Clearly
there is no use remaining any longer in Boldino this autumn." [24]

Family cares, social duties, and deep disquietude over his future prospects had contrived to make the period between 1834 and 1835 one of the most meager in Pushkin's literary output. He wrote little and slowly, occupied himself with old designs, and drafted new ones which were never finished. The strain of intimate lyricism had almost ceased. The transition which he had been undergoing from the personal lyric to the heroic lyric and epic subject material had been completed, and the tendency to sacrifice verse for prose was more pronounced. He now favored themes of a folk nature, or he wrote on historical, religious, social, political, and philosophical subjects. Of the short occasional poems there were none written in 1834 and few in 1835. He had published *The History of the Pugachev Rebellion* and did some work on his historical romance, *The Captain's Daughter*. But besides these, the only completed prose work in 1834 was the famous short story, *The Queen of Spades*.[25] It is entirely different from his other tales, suggesting in a sense the horror tales of Poe. The story concerns a young army engineer who learns a lucky gambling secret from the ghost of an old woman whom he has frightened to death. The secret works twice, but on the third try the young engineer loses his entire fortune and goes mad. The plot amounts to nothing more than a clever anecdote, and the genius of the tale consists in the telling. For sheer narrative Pushkin never surpassed *The Queen of Spades*. It is a classic in the short story genre. The cold fury of the tale and its mad effects are built up with an irresistible logic and economic psychological analysis that create an illusion of complete reality. The style is nervous, compact, and hard with the cold hardness of ice. Not a word is wasted; everything is neat and clean; and the effects seem like the results of ordered laws of nature rather than those of the careful designs of art. In addition, the author manages to suffuse the whole with an irony that imparts a universality to the tale.

Pushkin soon grew discouraged with his vain attempts at composition at Boldino. Such literary impoverishment during this season of the year and in a locale that had proved so ideal on previous occasions frightened him. If he could not write, where would he get money? His parents were on the verge of ruin. They were even asking him to pay a debt they had contracted with his old Trigorskoe friend, Praskovya Osipova. A new social season, with all its attendant expenses, faced him in Petersburg. He returned to the capital in the middle of October, having remained scarcely a month at Boldino.

IV

> Again I visited
> That corner of the earth
> where once I spent
> Two unforgettable years in
> sorry exile.
> *Again I Visited*

The pleasures of homecoming were dampened by new responsibilities. Natasha's two sisters had arrived. A larger house had been taken, and the increase in the family meant an increase in Pushkin's expenses. Ekaterina and Alexandra soon began to appear everywhere in society with their younger sister, and Natasha's beauty seemed all the more dazzling in contrast with their plain appearance. Good aunt Zagryazhskaya played the fairy godmother to all three, and without her aid the situation would have been more difficult. Largely through her influence, Ekaterina was appointed a maid of honor to the empress in December.

During the social season of 1834–1835 Natasha was at the height of her success. She was pregnant again, but pregnancy and childbearing never appeared to diminish her beauty and were not allowed to interfere very much with her amusements. A cultured observer of the time wrote of her: "Suddenly — I shall never forget this — a lady entered, straight as a palm tree, in a gown of black satin, reaching to the throat (the court was then in mourning). This was the wife of Pushkin, the first beauty of the day. Such stature and such stateliness I have never seen — *incessu dea patebat!* Her noble, classical features reminded me of the Euterpe in the Louvre Museum." [26]

The three sisters monopolized conversation in the Pushkin household with their chatter about clothes, balls, and specta-

cles. The poet felt himself in alien territory. Like the aristocratic youths and guardsmen who flirted with them, the sisters did
not accept him as a genuine part of their social world. His uniform of a gentleman of the chamber struck them as a laughable
incongruity. Natasha preferred the pleasures of the ballroom
to all the poetry in the world. At times she seemed a little annoyed with her position — she, a social lioness par excellence,
married to a mere man of letters. Yet Natasha was not above
exploiting her husband's literary fame. Pushkin now tried to
avoid his social duties as much as possible. Careless of censure,
he remained home from the balls or left them early. People
noticed his bored, often grim countenance at these entertainments. There were few with whom he could talk at court balls.
His brilliant conversational powers were wasted in this cultural
desert of superficial amusements. And his pride of birth was
wounded by the fact that these aristocrats did not show him any
marked attention. Nor did they defer to his genius. They set
him down as an inferior, unsociable and badly bred, and he
repaid them with stinging sarcasm and obvious contempt.

The most unpleasant results of the social season were new
debts, and the sums he now owed had reached staggering proportions. The profits from *The History of the Pugachev Rebellion*
had been considerable, but they were quickly swallowed up by
old debts. Brother Lev, Pavlishchev, and his parents were all
looking to him for financial aid. Surfeited with the whole business, and sick of the capital and the feminine babble of his
household, Pushkin ran off to Mikhailovskoe in the first week
of May. Never had the country air seemed so fragrant to him
or the quiet of the village so attractive. He visited Trigorskoe,
and Praskovya Osipova noticed how sad and disillusioned her
friend appeared. "God! how well off you are here!" he exclaimed. "But there, there in Petersburg, what misery often
stifles me!" [27] Circumstances did not permit him to enjoy the
charms of the country for long. Natasha was nearing her time.
He arrived home on the fifteenth of May, the day after the
birth of his third child, Grigori.

This visit to Mikhailovskoe, however, had only sharpened

Pushkin's desire to settle down in the country. He knew that
Natasha would strongly oppose such a move, but once more it
seemed to him the only logical way out of his many difficulties.
There were his official duties at the court to reckon with, and
any plan he devised must take them into account. On the first
of June he wrote a determined letter to Benkendorf. Neither
he nor his wife had any fortune, he explained. "To work for a
living is certainly not humiliating for me; but, accustomed as I
am to independence, it is quite impossible for me to write for
money, and the idea alone suffices to reduce me to mere imitation. Life in Petersburg is horribly expensive. . . . Three or
four years of retreat in the country will place me in a position to
return to Petersburg to the occupations which I owe still to the
bounty of his majesty." [28] But remembering the tsar's attitude
towards his previous request, he besought Benkendorf to realize
that his desire for an extended furlough was prompted by no
motive other than absolute necessity.

Again the answer was "no." If he wished to leave the service
and retire to the country, he was free to do so. But the tsar refused to allow him to remain in the service and be away from
Petersburg for three or four years. Once more Pushkin's fears
were aroused and his determination wavered. He was afraid of
losing the small salary he received from the government and his
privilege of using the archives. More than this, he was afraid of
the old charge of ungratefulness, of falling down on his moral
obligations to the tsar. Nicholas simply would not understand
his desperate plight. He hastened to write two other letters to
Benkendorf, explaining the situation in detail, in an effort to
justify his request. "During the last five years of my sojourn in
Petersburg, I have contracted debts of almost sixty thousand
rubles. I have been obliged to take over the affairs of my
family, and this has inconvenienced me so that I have had to
forfeit my own heritage; and the only means at my disposal to
put my affairs in order is to retire to the country or to borrow
once and for all a very large sum of money." [29] Pushkin ends the
letter by affirming his intention to submit entirely to his
majesty's will.

Nicholas was adamant. He wanted Pushkin to remain in the capital. But as a kind of compensation two favors were granted him. The government loaned him thirty thousand rubles, with his own salary as collateral, and he was given a leave of four months to go to Mikhailovskoe. In accepting this compromise, Pushkin perhaps displayed a certain weakness of character. There is no doubt that he could have retired and settled down in the country. Yet there is some extenuation. It is clear that confusion existed in his own mind concerning the course he ought to pursue. His situation had grown so desperate that he was like the proverbial drowning man catching at any straw. His living expenses in the capital had increased to about twenty-five thousand rubles a year; his total debt at this time was certainly more than sixty thousand rubles. There was little help to be had, obviously, from his government salary of five thousand. To economize while he remained an active member of Petersburg society was impossible. On the contrary, his expenses were increasing all the time. A wife, three children, and two sisters-in-law were dependents, and to some extent he was obliged to help his parents and his brother and sister. His own patrimony was impoverished and mortgaged up to the hilt, as was the estate of his mother and father. Literature, then, was his chief source of income, but during the last four years his literary output, for various reasons, had been relatively slight, and the popular demand for it not so great as formerly. He knew that his wish to retire to the country was an economic gamble. Living expenses would be cut down considerably. But the question remained whether he would be able to earn enough by his writing to support his family, for he would lose his government salary and the right to use the archives for unfinished historical work on which he had already spent much time. No doubt Pushkin had developed a kind of dependence on the favor of the tsar, and he did not wish to lose this favor. It represented a certain security, even though an intangible one. And he was deeply conscious of his obligations to the tsar, obligations of which Benkendorf never ceased to remind him. Furthermore, Natasha had convinced him that Petersburg was absolutely essential to her

happiness. To remain in the capital certainly amounted to following the line of least resistance. To abandon it all and live in
the country was an extreme remedy that might prove worse
than the disease. It is true that his reasons for escape were not
only economic; they were also mental and moral. In these
latter respects, however, he had not yet reached the breaking
point. If he possessed even the hope of economic security, he
was willing to remain in Petersburg for the time being rather
than defy the forces that contrived to hold him there. No longer
a bachelor, he feared to burn all the bridges behind him because
of his family responsibilities. It was not an easy compromise for
Pushkin to make. Contentment, leisure to write, and his independence were as far removed as ever. As if it were a mirage
in the desert he continued to pursue this vision of a quiet
country life, but his steps were already faltering and soon his
strength would be entirely spent.

v

> Other and better rights are
> dear to me;
> I need another and still better
> freedom!
> *From Pindemonte*

After a summer with his family at Black River, fashionable
suburb of Petersburg, Pushkin decided to make use of his leave
of absence. He left for Mikhailovskoe on the seventh of September, hoping that an autumn there would inspire him to
vigorous composition. The village had not changed much since
his exile ten years before. He missed his old nurse; "and in my
absence," he wrote Natasha, "around my ancient pine tree
friends has grown up a family of young pines, and I look at them
with vexation, as I sometimes look at young cavalier guards at
the balls where I no longer dance." [30] This sad and suggestive
comparison probably elicited no sympathy from his young wife.
"Everywhere," he remarks, "it is said that I am growing old."
Pushkin carried to Mikhailovskoe all his worries, and letters
to his wife are a poignant record of literary frustration: "I have
not yet begun to write and I do not know when I shall begin"; [31]
"I am completely upset and write nothing, yet time flies"; [32]

"Imagine, up to now I have not written a line, and all because I am not easy in mind." [33] He went out for long walks, rode horseback, pored over books, but poetic inspiration refused to come. In despair he revealed his feelings to Natasha: "You cannot conceive in what a lively way the imagination works when we sit alone within four walls or stroll in the woods, when no one hinders us from thinking, thinking until the head whirls. But about what do I think? This is what: How shall we live? My father leaves me no patrimony; he has already squandered half of it; your estate hangs on a hair. The tsar will not permit me to become a landowner or a journalist. God knows, I cannot write books for money. We have not a groat of sure income and certain expenses of 30,000. . . . What will come of this only God knows. Meanwhile, I am sad. If you could but kiss me, perhaps my grief would vanish." [34] His love for her never wavered, even though he now realized how thoroughly incompatible were their mental and spiritual lives. A good deal of his immediate unrest was caused by failure to receive Natasha's letters. Rather carelessly, she had addressed them to the wrong place.

A short poem and a prose fragment, *The Egyptian Nights*,[35] were all the literature he could drag out of his perplexed brain. The fragment is an unusual study of a high-born poet, Charski, who is ashamed of his very genius because it makes him appear ridiculous in aristocratic society. In many respects Charski is a self-portrait, a convincing psychological study in which Pushkin reveals the snobbish side of his own nature.

Unable to write, driven almost frantic by the failure to hear from Natasha, and suddenly learning of his mother's serious illness, he decided to cut short his stay at Mikhailovskoe. By the middle of October he was back in Petersburg. He found his mother so critically ill that it was obvious she had not long to live. The affairs of his parents were in complete chaos, and old Sergei Lvovich behaved hysterically under the strain. The son was much disturbed by exaggerated gossip. Busybodies were saying that Natasha went about in high society in elegant clothes while his parents were in rags and his mother dying in poverty. What had Natasha to do with the situation? If his mother had wished to live with them, his wife would have received her kindly, said Pushkin. "But a cold home," he wrote to Praskovya Osipova, "filled with brats and encumbered by all sorts of people is hardly convenient for a sick person. . . . As for me, I suffer from bile and am entirely upset. Believe me, dear Madame Osipova, although life is such a sweet existence, there is a bitterness in it which makes it disgusting, and society is a vile lake of filth." [36] Pushkin was extremely sensitive to such gossip, and scandalous rumors about him and his family were becoming a favorite topic in Petersburg high society.

An unexpected ray of hope broke through the dark clouds. Towards the end of 1835 the tsar at last made it possible for Pushkin to realize his long-cherished ambition of publishing a magazine. With regret he had to accept the damaging condition that politics must be entirely omitted. But the very fact that he was finally to be editor of his own publication heartened him. Furthermore, he imagined that he would reap a golden harvest — at least thirty thousand rubles a year — from this enterprise. Pushkin planned a quarterly, to be called the *Contemporary*,[37] on the model of the famous British reviews. He hoped to gather about him the best writers and critics in order to make his magazine a mouthpiece of the real literary intelligentsia — the "aristocrats of thought and feeling." He would show the "democrats," the journalists who were debasing Russian letters, what real literature and criticism should be. In many respects he reckoned without the power of the hostile press and the ultra-conservative mantle it had thrust upon him. The new writers, devotees of French and German romanticism, thought they had left him far behind. And the rising young dictator of criticism, Belinski, was already complaining that Pushkin was dead, or at least had swooned away for the time being. He concerned himself too much with resurrecting the past, said Belinski, and was too indifferent to the problems of the present. Pushkin ignored the handwriting on the wall. He was convinced that the public would accept his magazine and like it. With a vigor that he had not shown for some time, he began laying plans in the early months of 1836, preparing material of his own for the first issue, and urging his literary friends to contribute. His right-hand man in the publication was Prince V. F. Odoevski, highly cultured and well-acquainted in Petersburg literary circles. Pushkin valued him, but as an editor he was a far cry from Delvig, a friend whom he missed tremendously at this juncture.

But Pushkin was not allowed to work in peace. His house was eternally filled with the friends of his wife and of her sisters. Natasha was once again pregnant; yet her social activities never ceased. Children and household affairs were abandoned for balls and spectacles, and Pushkin often had to assume the family responsibilities of his wife. Desperate for money, he had to pawn Natasha's jewels, shawls, and the silverware. Resentment against the society that cluttered his existence and monopolized all his wife's time grew into a positive hate. She flirted more brazenly than ever, and people winked knowingly and pitied her husband. An ugly rumor spread that her miscarriage had been caused by a beating Pushkin had given her. The slightest breath of slander now infuriated him. At a ball a harmless remark made by young Count V. A. Sologub to Natasha resulted in an immediate challenge. "Do you really think that I get any pleasure out of shooting?" he asked Sologub when they met to consider the affair. "But what am I to do?" he continued. "I have the misfortune to be a public man, and you know that is worse than being a public woman." [38] The challenge was withdrawn only when Sologub gave him testimony in writing that he had meant no offense. Pushkin wanted the document in order to show it, if necessary, to doubting members of society. Still another collision took place in February. He demanded satisfaction from the aristocratic Prince N. Repnin for an offensive remark which had been reported to him. "I am obliged to protect my honor and the name which I must leave to my children," [39] Pushkin wrote the prince. Fortunately, Repnin satisfactorily explained the offending remark, and peace was made. These quarrels indicate the extreme touchiness of Pushkin's nerves at this time.

On the twenty-ninth of March Pushkin's mother died, and

he was deeply affected. He had never been close to her, but during her last years of illness he had played the part of a very dutiful son. Nadezhda Osipovna, in her turn, had learned to value his qualities for the first time. He accompanied the body to its final resting place in the graveyard of the Svyatogorski Monastery near Mikhailovskoe.

While Pushkin was in Mikhailovskoe the first number of the *Contemporary* appeared (April 11, 1836). It was unfortunate that this exciting event had to take place during a time so difficult for the editor. Pushkin had worked hard to make the issue a success, and perhaps no magazine in Russia had ever begun its existence with contents of such distinction. The editor had been obliged to write almost the whole issue himself, and it included his well-known works, *The Avaricious Knight* and *The Journey to Erzerum*, along with several short poems and critical articles. Gogol contributed a few pieces, among them his famous story, *The Nose*. The *Contemporary* did not bring in any golden harvest. Pushkin's own literary set praised it highly, but the camp of the enemy buried the publication in a conspiracy of silence. He was deeply disappointed and quickly realized that he had a long uphill fight on his hands if the magazine were ever to become popular.

In May, shortly after his return to the capital, Pushkin found it necessary to go to Moscow to work in the archives on his history of Peter the Great and to collect new material for the second number of the *Contemporary*. He stayed with his old friend, Nashchokin. Again he could not get down to work. Time was flying, and the second number of his magazine would soon be due. He learned of the unfavorable reaction of Moscow critics to his publication. The authorities were also troubling him again. A curt letter from Benkendorf called him to account for a contribution in the first issue of his magazine that had not met with the approval of the tsar. Another communication from a subordinate of the chief of the secret police coolly informed him that they knew he had received a letter from his exiled comrade, Kiukhelbeker. He was commanded to hand over the letter and to tell how it had reached him.

Pushkin began to regret his editorship of the *Contemporary*. He wondered if, in turning journalist, he were not placing himself on the same level with his literary enemies. And he now visioned an infinity of difficulties with the authorities. "To purify Russian literature," he wrote his wife from Moscow, "is like purifying the privies, and then one must be dependent upon the police." [40] In still another letter he wrote to her of his journalistic enterprise in a more bitter strain: "Although I am still an honorable man, I have already received a rebuke from the police in which they told me, 'You have deceived us,' and made other such statements. What will they do with me now? Mordvinov * will regard me as he regards Faddei Bulgarin and Nikolai Polevoi — as a spy. Only the devil thought of having me born in Russia with a mind and talent!" [41]

The several letters from Moscow to Natasha are filled with concern and unflagging love. The imminent birth of another child reminds him painfully of his growing expenses. "What of the children? What misery! I perceive that I shall absolutely need an income of 80,000 rubles. But I will get them." [42] Yet what disturbed him more than his mounting expenses were the rumors he heard in Moscow of Natasha's flirtations. Husbands are always the last to hear of their wives' misbehavior, he declares, but that men should go around talking of the attention she had paid them was intolerable. "It is not right, my angel," he sternly warns her. "Modesty is the best ornament of your sex." [43]

An ominous portent occurred on his departure from Moscow. At Nashchokin's farewell dinner Pushkin spilt some butter on the table. This boded misfortune. To take the curse off the bad omen, he waited until after midnight before he would leave. The very night he arrived in Petersburg (May 23) his fourth child, Natalya, was born.

Pushkin plunged into the business of his magazine. Family cares and the many demands on his pocket, time, and energy made him feel like a hunted man who had no possibility of escape. Where could he go to find independence, leisure, and

---

* A. N. Mordvinov, an official in the chancellery of Benkendorf.

financial security for himself and his family? The country was forbidden to him. A foolish, hopeless longing to flee abroad took possession of him. But this was unthinkable. And now his cup of misery was filled by a scandalous rumor that reached his ears. All Petersburg high society was coupling the name of his wife with that of a handsome officer of the Guards, Baron George d'Anthès. There was no doubt that the young officer was madly in love with her. Pushkin's jealousy flared forth. To have his honor impugned, to be ridiculed and pitied by a heartless so-ciety, to have the whispered word "cuckold" applied to him — this seemed the last straw! No, his Natasha, his beautiful madonna, would never be unfaithful to him. He was sure of this, or he wanted to be sure of it. In *Eugene Onegin* he had scoffed at his hero for making honor the sole criterion for his fatal duel with Lenski:

> But whisper and the guffaw of fools. . . .
> Social opinion — there it is!
> The source of honor and our idol!
> And that which makes the world go round! [44]

Yet Pushkin was as much a slave to his honor as Eugene. The rumors persisted. The longing to run away from it all, to escape to some idyllic haven of happiness before it was too late, is pathetically reflected in a verse fragment of this time which he addressed to his wife:

> 'Tis time, my friend, 'tis time! The heart now yearns for peace.
> Days follow days, some part of life still finds release
> In every passing hour, but I along with thee
> Intend to live, to look, before we cease to be.
> There is no joy, but there is peace and liberty.
> Long have I dreamed of a desirable destiny —
> A weary slave, I long since contemplated flight
> To some remote abode of work and pure delight. [45]

CHAPTER XIX

Coadjutor of the Order of Cuckolds

And now, at last, it is my turn;
Dear Delvig, thou dost call to
me!
The Lyceum Celebrates

Baron George d'Anthès, born in 1812, belonged to a good
Alsatian family. He attended the military school of Saint-Cyr,
but since his sympathies were legitimist, he was obliged to leave
the institution after the outbreak of the July Revolution of
1830. As a follower of Charles X, D'Anthès had little hope of
a career in France at this time, and he turned to Prussia, where
his family possessed important connections. The Prussian Prince
Wilhelm, however, advised him to seek his fortune in Russia and
gave him a letter of recommendation to Major General V. F.
Adlerberg, director of the chancellery of the Ministry of War
and a favorite of the tsar. His hopes full-blown by such powerful influence, D'Anthès set out for Russia in the autumn of 1833,
determined to make an army career for himself.

On the way he met Baron Louis van Heeckeren, the Dutch
minister to Russia, who was returning to Petersburg after a
leave of absence. Heeckeren at once grew interested in the
young Frenchman, aided him in a siege of illness on the road,
and allowed him to join his suite for the remainder of the journey. There is some mystery concerning the precise derivation
of Heeckeren, a man of forty-two when he first met D'Anthès.
Rumor had it that he was the natural son of the Dutch king.
But his family name was a distinguished one in the Netherlands, and his career had been highly successful. Nicholas I
had decorated him, and he was one of the best-known figures
in the diplomatic corps of the Russian capital. Although his
position and his polished demeanor made him a welcome guest

in high society, Heeckeren had the reputation of being jesuitical, malicious, and thoroughly immoral.

Along with his letter from Prince Wilhelm, D'Anthès now gladly accepted the patronage of Heeckeren. Such extraordinary good fortune ought to have made him grateful, but this unknown youth accepted it all as his just due. General Adlerberg, the tsar, and the empress interceded in his behalf. Dispensations were granted in the examinations necessary to qualify him as an officer. By February 1834 D'Anthès was admitted to the Horse Guards, and soon he was given the rank of lieutenant. Better than this, his financial and social position was secured by the fact that Heeckeren in 1836 legally adopted him as his son. The diplomat had watched over him with more than paternal care during the first two years of his career and was as much concerned with his success as the youth himself. He saw to it that D'Anthès lacked for nothing, and he introduced him into the highest social circles. It did not take Petersburg gossips long to whisper that the young Frenchman was Heeckeren's natural son. But this notion has no basis in fact. The next rumor was that they were living together in sin, and since the Dutch envoy had a reputation for this perversion, the rumor became a firmly anchored conviction. Subsequent events, while not destroying the possibility of such an unnatural connection, make it difficult to believe.

Of course, D'Anthès did not rise by influence alone. He had an appearance, personality, and pushing qualities that were hard to deny. Blond, tall, and well-formed, he was considered the handsomest man in the regiment and the officer most in fashion. Although a poor soldier, he had a special faculty for making himself well liked. He treated army discipline with scant ceremony, but his unfailing and clever repartee kept his comrades and superiors in good humor. Even the tsar's brother, Mikhail Pavlovich, a great lover of jokes and puns, enjoyed chatting with the witty young Frenchman. What he lacked in culture he made up for by his pleasing disposition and French gallantry; and besides, culture was not a *sine qua non* in the aristocratic society of the time of Nicholas I. There was a certain arrogance about D'Anthès which amused those who liked him and offended some who found a special virtue in sincerity and simplicity. Nor were there lacking those who thought him a giddy, light-minded fop whose pushing tactics were reprehensible and whose jokes smacked too much of barrack-room smut. D'Anthès, as might be expected, had considerable success with the ladies. Besides his natural charm of appearance and manner, he had the usual attraction of the foreigner for women. And he did not hesitate to exploit his position by taking liberties with the ladies which Russian men did not permit themselves in high society.

II

Baron d'Anthès met Pushkin's wife in the autumn of 1834, if not in the course of the preceding winter. At first he was just another guardsman to her, although an unusually attractive one. Natasha flirted with him as she did with all of her many admirers. But her customary passivity merely served to fire the young Frenchman's passion. Before long he was head over heels in love with her. At the Pushkin household D'Anthès was a constant visitor until the husband, becoming aware of his passion, made it clear that his presence was no longer desired. Nothing daunted, D'Anthès made a point of turning up at all the social functions attended by Natasha. When he was not talking or dancing with her, his eager eyes followed her around the ballroom. Among the three Goncharova sisters the question of the officer's presence at dances, public gatherings, or at the theater provided an amusing guessing-game. But the odds were all on D'Anthès' side — he invariably appeared. Ekaterina Goncharova was herself in love with him, and she gladly arranged meetings between the guardsman and her sister simply to feed her own passion in his presence. D'Anthès even contrived to get acquainted with Pushkin's literary friends in the hope of seeing Natasha at their *salons*. Vyazemski's wife warned him that she would refuse him her home if he continued his flagrant courting there; and Mme. Karamzina grew angry over his indiscreet behavior in her house with the wife of

Pushkin. Flirting was in no sense frowned upon in high society, but this persistent and open wooing of D'Anthès, which attracted the attention of everyone, was considered to be in bad taste.

Natasha did not long remain impervious to such ardent devotion. Her cold nature melted before the flame of the Frenchman. He was handsome, lively, and her own age, and he shared fully with her the social excitement of the giddy set in which they both moved. Like any thoughtless young wife, she enjoyed this youthful attention as an interesting substitute for the habitual affection of a husband whose passion she dutifully satisfied but did not encourage. In Natasha's eyes D'Anthès certainly was a more attractive personality than Pushkin. Had fate been a little kinder to her, she might have married just such a man, for he represented nearly everything that was congenial to her nature. In this duel of flirts there is no doubt that the guardsman played the active role, but it is equally certain that Natasha did not discourage him. That she ignored her husband's fierce anger, which she knew well, the gossip that was fouling her reputation, and even the fact that her sister was in love with the same man, can argue only one thing — that Natasha was much attracted to D'Anthès. However, she did not submit to him, either because of finer instincts and fear, or simply because time and circumstances did not allow of such a consummation. As though to prove her innocence, she practically made a confidant of her husband in the whole affair. Like a proud cat, she brought home her victim and deposited him at the feet of her master for his approbation. The love notes of D'Anthès were read to Pushkin and his whispered compliments repeated. Meanwhile, Petersburg high society hummed with the scandal and gleefully awaited the denouement.

Pushkin watched the courting of D'Anthès with mounting fury. Nor was he unaware of the encouragement Natasha gave her lover. Essentially his conception of marriage and of the duties of a wife was old-fashioned, though one generally shared by his contemporaries. However she might behave before her marriage, after it a woman ought to settle down, devote herself to household affairs, and, above all, be absolutely faithful to her husband. His ideal Tatyana in *Eugene Onegin* embodies these qualities as a wife. Although there is some poetical justification for her stand, Tatyana refuses to submit to Eugene, whom she still loves, because she believes it her duty to be true to her husband, even though she does not love him. From his own experience Pushkin knew that a man could flirt with a woman and not have any respect for her. And the same experience had taught him that a husband becomes the laughing-stock of society when a wife is not chary of her honor. The fate of the husbands of Riznich, Davydova, Vorontsova, Kern, and Zakrevskaya, however much he may have contributed to it in each case, was a fate that he had no intention of suffering himself. He was determined that he would not become a laughing-stock on this score. Yet Pushkin did not allow his ideal of the faithful wife to interfere with his own urge to philander. Here again he was being conventional. To be sure, after his marriage he had little desire to resume the wayward conduct of bachelor days, but he was not entirely faithful to Natasha. There were visits to brothels, and in his own home it is pretty certain that he had intimate relations with his sister-in-law, Alexandra Goncharova. In appearance a kind of caricature of Natasha, Alexandra had little of her temperament or love for society. She soon became the stay-at-home, taking care of the children and assuming the household duties that her younger sister neglected. Deeply devoted to Pushkin, she read his poetry with enthusiasm, comforted him in his family cares, and even gave him her personal effects to pawn. Their relationship, which she guarded with wise secrecy, was a real solace in these last troubled months of his life. Natasha affected jealousy, but, as already indicated, her jealousy was little more than an affectation. She even went to the naïve extreme of suspecting her husband of an affair with the fifty-three-year-old Elizaveta Khitrovo.

The pressing business of the *Contemporary* required all Pushkin's attention. Three more numbers were due for 1836, and he was desperately dependent upon their sale for much-needed funds. By herculean efforts the second and third issues were published in July and August. This feat was accomplished in the teeth of innumerable difficulties. His grasping brother-in-law wrote him long, exasperating letters from Mikhailovskoe, demanding money and assistance in straightening out the affairs of the run-down estate. Meanwhile, Pushkin was pawning tableware and jewelry, and he wrote Pavlishchev that he had no funds and that his head was in a whirl. Again he dreamed his old dream of retiring to his village. In a manuscript note of this time he exclaimed: "Oh, shall I soon transfer my penates into the country — fields, a garden, peasants, books; poetical works, my family, love, etc., — religion, death!" [1] But now he lacked even the necessary money to transport his family to the country. In October he wrote his father: "In the village I could work — here I do nothing, except fret myself to death." [2] On the nineteenth of October Pushkin attended the twenty-fifth anniversary of his Lyceum class. The usual poem was expected from him, and such an occasion would ordinarily have been one of mirth and merriment. The empty chairs of absent comrades saddened him. Pushchin and Kiukhelbeker were in exile; several were dead, including his beloved Delvig. Pushkin wondered if he would be the next to go, as though he had a premonition that this was to be his last Lyceum reunion. He got up to recite his commemorating verses and began:

> There was a time: our youthful holiday
> Glittered, was boisterous and crowned with roses . . . [3]

Then the tears came, and he could not continue. His heart was being eaten out by the dogged courting of D'Anthès, which was daily flaunted in his face, and by the rising tide of scandalous gossip. His mind was distracted, and his ability to work vanished under the strain. Pushkin realized that the time was at hand when he must take decisive measures to put an end to the whole affair. He did not have to wait long.

III

> While the heart in us does yearn
> for peace!
>
> *Fragment*

On the morning of November 4 Pushkin received an anonymous letter. The contents were in French and read:

"The Chevaliers of the First Degree, Commanders, and Chevaliers of the most serene Order of Cuckolds, gathered in full assembly under the presidency of the venerable Grand Master of the Order, S. E. D. L. Naryshkin, have unanimously nominated Mr. Alexander Pushkin coadjutor to the Grand Master of the Order of Cuckolds and historiographer of the Order. Perpetual Secretary, Count I. Borch." [4]

That same morning some seven or eight of his close friends received a similar letter, enclosed in an envelope addressed to Pushkin. This was a mortal blow.

There was no doubt in Pushkin's mind that the anonymous letters were directly inspired by the affair between his wife and young D'Anthès. And at once he suspected Heeckeren as the author. Natasha herself told Pushkin that the diplomat played the pander for his adopted son. Heeckeren besought her to submit to D'Anthès, to elope with him abroad, to have mercy on a youth suffering from love of her. From what we know of the diplomat's reputation, the role of go-between in a clandestine love affair would not have taxed his moral scruples. Yet it is difficult to understand the motive behind such a part, particularly if his relations with D'Anthès were of a perverted sort. But distorted natures do not always subscribe to logical motives. If his affection for the young Frenchman were deep enough, and it seems to have been so, anything that contributed to D'Anthès' happiness might easily have been attempted by Heeckeren, even in the face of jealousy and sacrifice. Perhaps he hoped that Natasha's submission would eventually bring the affair to an end. However, it is much more difficult to find a reason, psychologically or on the basis of known facts, for Heeckeren's authorship of the anonymous letter. Here he had everything to lose and nothing to gain. Only a most perverted

Les Grands-Croix, Commandeurs et
Chevaliers du Sérénissime Ordre des
Cocus réunis en grand Chapitre sous la
présidence du vénérable grand-Maître
de l'Ordre, S. E. O. L. Narychkine, ont
nommé à l'unanimité Mr. Alexandre
Pouchkine coadjuteur du grand Maître
de l'Ordre des Cocus et historiographe de
l'Ordre.

Le sécrétaire pérpétuel : Cte J. Borch

THE ANONYMOUS LETTER

and mad sense of intrigue could have prompted such an act on his part. Although he was an intriguer and the instigator of much scandalous gossip about Pushkin, he was not mad or unaware of his own best interests. To him and his adopted son, both foreigners, Pushkin's poetic fame meant little or nothing. Yet he must have realized that such an insulting letter, if attributed to him, might create a scandal that would endanger his career, as well as the life of his adopted son. Heeckeren may well have desired to see the end of D'Anthès' passion for Natasha, but he was altogether too clever to employ such a dangerous device as the anonymous letter. Pushkin's guess was unquestionably wrong.

Then who did write the letter? The problem has never been solved in an entirely satisfactory manner. Pushkin had many enemies, male and female, in Petersburg society. At one time he appears to have entertained the idea that the author was a woman. Countess Nesselrode, wife of the minister of foreign affairs, hated him with a venomous hatred, perhaps initiated by an offensive remark about her father in an epigram ascribed to Pushkin. He professed to wonder whether her enmity was more bitter than that of his mortal foe, the editor Bulgarin. And he was as violently hated, for reasons which are not clearly known, by Idaliya Poletika, the natural daughter of the well-known Count G. Stroganov whom Byron honored in *Don Juan*. Idaliya was Natasha's friend and lent her best efforts to aiding the cause of D'Anthès by way of hurting Pushkin. Suspicion has been cast on each of these women as the author of the anonymous letter, but there is absolutely no proof of their guilt.

At that time rumor also singled out two young men who lived together, Princes I. S. Gagarin and P. V. Dolgorukov. They both belonged to the circle of youths of dubious morals dominated by the malicious Heeckeren. Some six years later Gagarin became a Jesuit, and his entrance into a religious order was popularly attributed to penitence for his crime against Pushkin. Recent investigators have pretty definitely absolved Gagarin from any active part in the affair, although he may well have been implicated. But evidence has been accumulated

which indicates that Dolgorukov was the author. A clever
fellow but quite unprincipled, and a little mad on the subject
of the Romanovs (he maintained that as a direct descendant of
Rurik he had a better claim to the throne than Nicholas I),
Dolgorukov, on the basis of what is known of his character, was
certainly capable of writing the anonymous letter. He had no
close relations with Pushkin. But the dissemination of such
lampoons was not an unfamiliar device of misguided practical
jokesters at this time. Listening to the gossip of Heeckeren,
young Dolgorukov may well have been inspired to write the
letter as the kind of joke that would vastly amuse his own immoral set. Despite the attempt to disguise the writing in the
several letters, a modern expert in calligraphy has made out a
pretty good case against Dolgorukov. And until convincing
evidence to the contrary is produced, his authorship of the fatal
letters is likely to stand. It is unlikely, however, that Dolgorukov acted alone in the venture. Whether he had one or more
confederates, and who they were, are questions to which there
are no positive answers.

Pushkin did not miss the broad and vicious hint in the anonymous letter: "coadjutor to the Grand Master of the Order of
Cuckolds," Naryshkin. For years the beautiful wife of D. L.
Naryshkin had been the well-known mistress of Alexander I.
It was only natural that cuckoldry should continue as it had
begun — with the royal line. The coadjutor must share the
same fate as the Master; and as the newly-elected historiographer of the Order, Pushkin's initial task was to chronicle
his own cuckolding by Nicholas I. Such was the hint. D'Anthès
had simply followed the tsar. Indeed, so far as gossip could
make anything out of mere appearances, Natasha was no less
guilty with the tsar than with D'Anthès.

This hint could not shake Pushkin's faith in Natasha, but it
did place the stamp of approval on a popular rumor which had
been worrying him for months. Time and again he had warned
his wife not to flirt with the tsar. Nicholas I had a reputation
for philandering which was so well established and included so
many victims that a critic of his character found plenty of ma-

terial for a whole article on the subject. Young ladies were selected as maids of honor with an eye to their acceptability to the royal master. And few remained maids before their marriages. The tsar or some member of his immediate family had his way with them; and then the empress saw to it that they got husbands of imperial choice. Pushkin was aware of the love-intrigue and scandalous behavior of the court, and he had no illusions about the faithfulness of the "family-loving" tsar to his own consort. His appointment as gentleman of the chamber had seemed like an obvious excuse for providing Nicholas with frequent opportunities to flirt with Natasha at the exclusive Anichkov balls. From all accounts Nicholas made the most of these occasions. Pushkin told Nashchokin that "the tsar, like any officer, runs after my wife: several times in the mornings he has deliberately ridden past her window, and at evening during the balls he asks why she always has her blinds lowered." [5] The parents of maids of honor and the husbands of wives who caught the eye of the tsar were not inclined to object to the fact. Indeed, many of them felt honored — and favors were often the rewards of a tsar's seductions. But Pushkin had nothing of this meretricious fiber in his makeup. In the gay court of Louis XIV, Molière had laughed much over cuckolds and had himself been cuckolded. Pushkin, the gentleman of the chamber of Nicholas I, had no intention of sharing the fate of the famous French author. The tsar may have begun his pursuit of Natasha; her husband was determined that it should go no further. Horrified now at the thought that some people might put a malicious interpretation on the money he had borrowed from the tsar's government, Pushkin immediately wrote a letter to the minister of finance, declaring his desire to repay at once his huge loan, though it is difficult to imagine how he could have raised the funds. Nor did he hesitate to let the tsar know that he suspected his designs on Natasha. Nicholas himself is authority for the following incident which happened after Pushkin received the anonymous letter. The tsar, because he "sincerely loved" Natasha, warned her to be more careful of her reputation for her own sake and that of her hus-

band. She told Pushkin of this good advice. Upon meeting the
tsar a little later, he thanked him. "Well, can you expect anything else from me?" asked Nicholas. "Sire, I not only can,"
replied Pushkin, "but I frankly confess that I have suspected
you most of all of making love to my wife!" [6]

A subject has no redress against an emperor. D'Anthès,
however, was vulnerable. After the receipt of the anonymous
letter Pushkin had a talk with his wife. Natasha freely admitted the wooing of D'Anthès and the pandering of Heeckeren.
Although she confessed to some responsibility in the matter,
she swore that she had been faithful to her husband. This was
undoubtedly true, and Pushkin believed her. But his own honor
and that of his wife had been sullied. Gladly, even fiercely, he
picked up the challenge of the "cuckold letter." The day after
he received it he sent a challenge to D'Anthès.

The young guardsman was on duty with his regiment, and
Heeckeren received the challenge. Whatever part he may have
had in the dark events leading up to the anonymous letter,
Heeckeren became thoroughly frightened over the possibility
of a bloody termination of the affair. He at once called on Pushkin and asked for twenty-four hours before answering, hoping
that the offended husband would alter his resolve. He returned at the end of this respite and found Pushkin adamant.
With tears in his eyes Heeckeren pleaded his cause and that of
his adopted son. He had dedicated his life to D'Anthès, started
him on a career, and now all would be ruined by a scandalous
duel. Pushkin was touched by Heeckeren's tears, but he stuck
by his purpose to fight. However, when the father finally asked
for a week in which to prepare himself for all eventualities,
Pushkin generously granted him two weeks, with the proviso
that he should keep the whole affair secret until the appointed
day.

The real purpose of Heeckeren's request for a delay was to
give him an opportunity to persuade close friends of Pushkin's
to intercede. And he made the most of this interlude. Zhukovski and kind aunt Zagryazhskaya were appealed to.
Alarmed at the possibility of a duel, they offered every assist-

ance. These two friends and Heeckeren put their heads together. Pushkin had sent the challenge and D'Anthès was ready to fight, but he was also willing to listen to the advice of Heeckeren. The only way out was to persuade Pushkin to withdraw his challenge.

The cunning Heeckeren finally hit upon a solution and one which is most difficult to understand or to explain in the face of the tangled web of details, plots, and counterplots that make up the story of Pushkin's last duel. It was suddenly discovered that D'Anthès had been pursuing not Natasha but her sister Ekaterina, who, as everybody knew, was passionately in love with him. All these meetings between D'Anthès and Natasha, which had usually involved the presence of both sisters, had as their innocent purpose the courting of Ekaterina. Furthermore, Heeckeren explained, his son was now ready to offer her a proposal of marriage. Pushkin would surely understand this and recall his challenge. And Heeckeren had little difficulty in convincing Zhukovski that this was the truth of the whole matter.

When Zhukovski told Pushkin of the "discovery," he flew into a rage. He knew only too well that his wife had been the object of D'Anthès' attention, and the new explanation he took as proof of the guardsman's cowardice. However, he was willing to withdraw his challenge on the condition that D'Anthès marry Ekaterina. Such a condition would amount to a degradation of the Frenchman and would partially satisfy Pushkin's injured honor. Yet Heeckeren had stipulated that Pushkin must call off the duel without motivating his action by the proposed marriage, which he insisted should be kept a secret for the time being. He had no desire to lay his son open to the charge of cowardice. Such tactics confirmed Pushkin's suspicion that the marriage to Ekaterina was a mere dodge, and he held to his resolve to fight unless his own conditions were accepted.

In despair, Zhukovski admitted failure. Aunt Zagryazhskaya next took up the part of mediator. On her plea Pushkin agreed to a meeting with Heeckeren in which the diplomat officially declared that he had given his consent to the marriage. With this confirmation Pushkin softened a bit and was prepared to withdraw his challenge, for he felt that he had gained something of a victory. But D'Anthès, who had allowed Heeckeren to handle the matter up to this point, now entered the negotiations. Pushkin was mistaken in thinking him a coward. D'Anthès did not want to fight a duel, but he was also determined not to compromise his own honor. The real reasons for his agreement to marry Ekaterina Goncharova are extremely difficult to ascertain. Certainly the desire to avoid a duel was not the sole reason. As a matter of fact, the notion of his marrying Ekaterina had existed even before Pushkin received the anonymous letter. It is most unlikely, however, that D'Anthès himself fathered the rumor; it was probably the result of some wishful thinking on the part of Ekaterina. She was deeply in love with him, and although fully aware of D'Anthès' fierce devotion to her sister, she was still willing, even eager, to marry him. But D'Anthès did not love her, and she knew it. Ekaterina, in the opinion of the society of the time, was virtually an old maid. She was not attractive, had no dowry, was four years older than D'Anthès, and on almost every count would have been considered a poor match for the dashing officer. Ambitious and desirous of a brilliant career, he would have preferred a beautiful young heiress with important social connections.

Then why did D'Anthès agree to this unpromising marriage? The fact that he wished, if possible, to avoid a duel is no doubt only one of the several reasons that created the bizarre situation. The reason that he and Heeckeren swore by was a desire to save the reputation of Natasha. If a duel were fought, rumor would surely ascribe it to the infidelity of Pushkin's wife. From what is known of D'Anthès' character it is hard to accept as genuine this knightly gesture of sacrificing himself for a woman's reputation. Perhaps he thought that the marriage would allay the jealousy of Pushkin and that as his brother-in-law he would have freer access to Natasha. If this was his intention, his reasoning was certainly very faulty. It has been suggested that D'Anthès had already been intimate with Ekaterina and had decided to marry her in a hurry in order to avert a scandal.

But the date of the birth of her first child invalidates this theory. Vyazemski, who must have known a great deal about the affair, is responsible for the statement that D'Anthès was completely enmeshed in the dark intrigues of Heeckeren, implying that the wily diplomat had reasons of his own for bringing about the marriage. And our knowledge of Heeckeren's Machiavellian nature would support such an idea. In short, D'Anthès' willingness to marry Ekaterina was no doubt inspired by a variety of motives. Yet it seems clear that they were all more or less subordinate to his consuming passion for Natasha. Perhaps he hoped that she would understand this as a noble gesture which he made in an effort to avert her husband's jealous wrath from her head and to spare her reputation in society, although he had never been a conscientious guardian of Natasha's reputation. A duel would end everything; married to her sister he would, as it were, be in the family and hence close to her. All the subsequent behavior of D'Anthès appears to bear out this line of reasoning.

Afraid that Pushkin, now that he was willing to withdraw his challenge, would think him a coward, D'Anthès sent a letter stipulating the conditions on which he would agree to call off the duel. Naïvely pretending not to have heard anything about the proffered marriage, he wrote: "I desire to know why you have altered your intentions, while not authorizing anyone to present to you the explanations which I proposed to give to you personally. You should first agree, before you take back your word, that each of us must offer explanations in order that afterwards we may be able to refer to each other with esteem." [7] Obviously, his intention was to prevent Pushkin from offering the marriage as a reason for withdrawing. And as another knightly gesture D'Anthès sent his second, Vicomte d'Archiac, secretary to the French embassy, to inform Pushkin that the respite of two weeks had ended and that he was at his service.

The letter convulsed Pushkin with anger. This last insult was too much. The duel was on again, and he took prompt measures to bring about a meeting. On the fourteenth of No-

vember he met young Count V. A. Sologub at a dinner at the
Karamzins. This was the same Sologub with whom he had
almost fought a duel a short time before. Since then they had
become firm friends, for Sologub was a worshiper of Pushkin
and had already offered his services in the business with
D'Anthès. In the course of the conversation around the table
Pushkin whispered to Sologub: "Tomorrow look up D'Archiac.
Arrange conditions with him concerning only the material side
of the duel. The bloodier the better. On no account agree to
any explanations." [8] Then Pushkin continued to talk and joke
as though nothing had happened. But the remarks to Sologub
are filled with the fury of a vengeful passion.

That same evening Pushkin arrived late, and without Natasha, at a large party given by Count Fikelmon. D'Anthès was
there and paid much attention to Ekaterina Goncharova. Pushkin had some hard words with him and forbade Ekaterina to
talk to him. Although the engagement had not been officially
announced, the news was already beginning to leak out.
D'Anthès conversed with Sologub, who was also present, and
declared that he was willing to fight but that he had no
notion of what it was all about, and that he wished to avoid
a scandal.

The next day the two seconds met and went over all the facts
in the case. Both were deeply conscious of their responsibility
for the life of the great poet and heartily wished to avoid a
duel. They also knew that D'Anthès had no desire to fight.
Their only hope was to placate Pushkin. They decided to sacrifice the interests of D'Anthès, convinced that he would peek
through his fingers at any reasonable settlement. Accordingly,
Sologub sent a note to Pushkin in which were specified the time
and conditions of the duel. Then he slyly added that D'Archiac
had told him confidentially that D'Anthès intended to marry
Ekaterina Goncharova but wished to wait until the duel was
ended before making the announcement, for he feared that
otherwise his motive would be misinterpreted. However,
Sologub continued, if Pushkin would admit verbally, before
him or D'Archiac, that he did not ascribe the marriage to any

dishonorable intention, all would end peacefully. This note was accompanied by Sologub's personal plea to remember his family in making his decision.

Pushkin's answer arrived: "I do not hesitate to write that which I can declare verbally. I challenged Mr. G. Heeckeren [D'Anthès] to a duel, and he accepted without entering into any explanations. I ask the gentlemen-witnesses of this affair to be pleased to regard this challenge as not existing, having been informed by rumor that Mr. George Heeckeren has decided to announce his resolve to marry Mlle. Goncharova after the duel. I have no reason to ascribe his decision to any considerations unworthy of an honorable man." [9] In this Pushkin gave little ground. His stand was not much different from the previous one — the implication that the marriage was motivated by the duel is clear in his letter. Such a communication could hardly satisfy the self-esteem of D'Anthès. But the seconds had no intention of showing him the letter. D'Archiac at once declared himself satisfied, and congratulated D'Anthès on his approaching marriage. In turn D'Anthès asked the seconds to thank Pushkin for ending the quarrel, expressing the final hope that they would now become brothers. Sologub and D'Archiac called on Pushkin soon after receiving his letter. He was pale and quiet as he listened to the thanks of D'Archiac.

"On my side," added Sologub, "I have allowed myself to promise that you will behave toward your brother-in-law as toward a friend."

"In vain!" Pushkin shouted vehemently. "That shall never be. Never shall there be anything in common between the house of Pushkin and the house of D'Anthès!"

D'Archiac looked with dismay at Sologub. But Pushkin quickly regained control of himself and continued: "However, I have admitted and am ready to admit that Mr. d'Anthès has acted as an honorable man." [10]

Heaving a sigh of relief after this last remark, D'Archiac hastened to depart before another compromising outbreak. The duel had been avoided. But in all Pushkin's actions and words, before and after the withdrawal, one senses a seething volcano of hate and vengeance toward the young guardsman who had made such an impression on the heart of his wife.

IV

> Beware, I shall bring you un-
> happiness!
> *Pushkin to Ekaterina d'Anthès*
> *Heeckeren*

Even after the formal announcement of the engagement Pushkin found it difficult to believe that D'Anthès would go through with the marriage. His hatred for the young French-man did not lessen, nor for a moment did he lose his conviction that Heeckeren had written the "cuckold letter." Although the business of the duel had ended, he by no means felt that he had settled his score with the Dutch diplomat. Pushkin's nature was not unusually revengeful. He was easily offended, but he just as easily forgave his enemies and forgot their offenses. This sustained hatred for Heeckeren indicates how deeply he had felt the insult of the anonymous letter and how thoroughly his emotional system had become unhinged by the whole nasty mess of rumor and scandal touching Natasha. It is clear that he planned to repay Heeckeren for his part in the affair after the duel had been settled. On the twenty-first of November he wrote a letter to Benkendorf — apparently never sent — which seems designed to protect his interests in view of some reprisal he intended against Heeckeren. In this communication Push-kin recites all the details leading up to the abortive duel and the marriage proposal of D'Anthès. Then he directly accuses Heeckeren of the authorship of the anonymous letter, and con-cludes: "Being sole judge and guardian of my honor and that of my wife, and in consequence demanding neither justice nor vengeance, I cannot and do not wish to deliver to anyone the proofs of that which I advance." [11] The hint is that he will take the matter into his own hands; and the letter, of course, was intended to compromise the Dutch minister in the eyes of the Russian government.

The reprisal, it seems, was to take the form of a vicious letter to Heeckeren. On the day of his communication to Benkendorf,

Count Sologub was in Pushkin's study, and he read him the insulting letter which he intended to send to Heeckeren. "His lips trembled," writes Sologub. "His eyes were bloodshot. At that moment he was terrifying, and only then did I really understand his African derivation." [12] Zhukovski was quickly informed and apparently persuaded Pushkin not to send the letter. He put it aside, but not his hate.

Meanwhile, preparations for the wedding went forward. His home, Pushkin complained, was turned into a fashionable store for ladies' apparel. The sisters, Natasha and Alexandra, threw themselves into the preparations with enthusiasm. D'Anthès was still forbidden to visit the house and had to meet his bride-to-be at her aunt's. Ekaterina, although she must have been fully aware of her secondhand position in this whole affair, never hesitated to accept D'Anthès' proposal. In her passionate devotion to him she at once became his partisan, blaming Pushkin for everything. And in the pre-nuptial stage, at least, D'Anthès treated her with some consideration and affection.

In this babble of excited females and in a state of chronic exasperation, Pushkin was able to do little other than feed his own anger. He tried halfheartedly to work on his history of Peter the Great, and at the end of November he finally got out the fourth and last number of the *Contemporary*. It included a splendid monument to his fame, the short historical novel, *The Captain's Daughter*, which he had begun several years previously. Here Pushkin utilizes the material of the Pugachev rebellion to tell a story in the manner of Scott. But it is a model of narrative neatness compared with Scott's historical romances, pruned almost too thoroughly of those adornments which lend glamour to the tales of the Wizard of the North. Historical fact is closely adhered to, except in the characterization of Pugachev, who is turned into a romantic and popular hero. But the noble Moronovs and the humble yet arrogant servant, Savelich, are treated in severely realistic fashion. On the whole, realism predominates in the work, and *The Captain's Daughter* points in the direction of the great Russian realistic novel and clearly suggests the kind of work that might have come from Pushkin's pen had he lived.

The wedding of Ekaterina and D'Anthès took place on the tenth of January, 1837. The unrelenting Pushkin did not attend it and asked his wife to leave immediately after the ceremony. When the couple paid a bridal visit, he would not receive them. The marriage astonished the Petersburg social world, and the reasons for it became a favorite topic of discussion at many fashionable gatherings. Everybody had expected the handsome, dashing young guardsman to make a brilliant match. Even the empress expressed surprise. In a letter to a society leader she wrote: "I should like to have through you the details of this inconceivable marriage of D'Anthès. Is it possible that the reason for it is the anonymous letter? Indeed, what is it — magnanimity or sacrifice? It seems to me useless — it is too late." [13] Society quickly divided itself into two camps on the question. The more aristocratic members, including, of course, Pushkin's enemies, were convinced that D'Anthès had married the unlovely Ekaterina in order to save the reputation of Natasha. Many interested people, however, believed that the Frenchman had married to escape the duel. All might have ended here, for Pushkin could have been contented with this dubious balm to his injured honor. But the reparation contained the seeds of defeat and tragedy.

Pushkin had made it brutally clear that he desired no contact with D'Anthès, and even after the marriage he continued to refuse him his house. Despite this uncompromising attitude, both the son and father attempted to use the new relationship as a means of reconciliation. D'Anthès not only persisted in attempting to visit Pushkin, but he wrote him at least two friendly letters, no doubt at the suggestion of Heeckeren. To the first Pushkin answered that he had no desire to renew relations with D'Anthès. The second he brought unopened to aunt Zagryazhskaya's to ask her to return it. There he met Heeckeren and gave him the letter, declaring that he wanted no correspondence with D'Anthès, nor did he wish even to hear his name. With a malevolent spirit of provocation Heeckeren refused to take the letter, remarking that it was written to Push-kin and not to him, and hence he could not accept it. Enraged, Pushkin threw the letter in his face, and is reported to have shouted: "Take it, you scoundrel!" [14]

Under such circumstances it would seem that the instincts of gentlemen, had they possessed them, would have prevented Heeckeren and his adopted son from interfering any further in Pushkin's life. On the contrary, the interference continued and in a more aggravating manner. D'Anthès at once took ad-vantage of his new relationship to place himself on a more familiar footing with Natasha. Although forbidden to see Push-kin's wife in her own house, he availed himself of every occasion, both during the period of his betrothal and after his marriage, to meet her at the homes of relatives, to which he now had free access. Then there were the frequent balls of the winter season, at which both he and Natasha rarely failed to be present. As though feeling secure in his position as a relative, D'Anthès now threw all caution to the wind. His courting was of a more open and offensive nature. There were long dances, bold and familiar conversations, and stolen walks. The marked contrast between his behavior towards his wife and Natasha in public was noticed by everybody. Once again people began to talk, and now the opinion was freely advanced that D'Anthès had married one sister in order to make love to the other. By his flagrant, indiscreet attention to Natasha it seemed as though he were trying deliberately to convince Pushkin that this was actually the case. However, such a complete disregard of con-sequences was not simply a desperate effort to prove to Pushkin that he was really a brave man. In his consuming passion for Natasha, D'Anthès was obviously ready to venture anything.

It is difficult to understand the attitude of Natasha toward this renewed and ardent pursuit of D'Anthès. She must have realized, in the light of the previous scandal, that she was run-ning the risk of flirting away her husband's life. His jealous rage and meticulous regard for his and her honor had been force-fully impressed upon Natasha. And she knew the extremes to which he would go to protect his honor. Furthermore, besides the gossip about her own reputation which she was provoking anew, the happiness of her sister was now involved. Ekaterina's situation had been delicate enough before the marriage; now her sister's behavior made it pitiful. In view of these facts Natasha's conduct after the marriage of D'Anthès seems most reprehensible. She encouraged him, but, sure of her own ultimate fidelity to her husband, she still regarded the affair as a flirtation, though an unusual and intensive one for her. Natasha was jolly and happy with D'Anthès; her husband, although his love and faith in her never altered, had grown moody and irritable in the extreme. Had Natasha been passionately in love with D'Anthès and submitted to him, it would be easier to understand and, possibly, to forgive her conduct. But this light, thoughtless attitude of a woman who was concerned merely with indulging her own selfish caprice seems more immoral, under the circumstances, than any forthright act of infidelity to her husband.

The seething volcano was on the point of eruption. A succession of incidents drove Pushkin into a furious hunger for retribution. Heeckeren and his son became fiends incarnate, sticking red-hot pokers into his brain. At a ball at the Vorontsovs' D'Anthès devoted himself to Natasha during the whole evening. She and his wife were served by the same foot doctor, a fact which prompted D'Anthès to pun maliciously: "*Je sais maintenant que votre cor est plus beau, que celui de ma femme!*" [15] Natasha dutifully reported the offensive remark to her husband.* At another ball D'Anthès, taking the arm of his wife, said in a voice that Pushkin could not fail to hear: "Come, my legitimate one!" [16] D'Anthès' ostentatious toasts to Natasha, his ardent conversations, the long dances, and the spiteful innuendoes of Heeckeren all seemed to Pushkin part of a conspiracy against his honor. Now he had little blame for Natasha, who continued to torture him with her tales of D'Anthès' wooing, for he felt that she was being victimized by a pair of scoundrels.

In order to understand the extraordinary behavior of Pushkin

---

* The pun, of course, is on *cor*, "corn," and *corps*, "body."

during January 1837, one must be fully aware of the complete collapse of the material and emotional factors governing his life. He had reached a point where it was difficult to go on living. His total debt had reached one hundred and twenty thousand rubles, a stupendous sum for a man in his position. Nearly everything he owned was mortgaged, and most of the personal effects on which he could borrow had already been pawned. Yet the social life his wife loved increased his living expenses every month. He knew that he was still being spied upon and that he was regarded as a suspicious person by the authorities. His position at the court as gentleman of the chamber made him ridiculous in everybody's eyes and more so in his own. His suspicions concerning the real reason for this appointment had been confirmed by the slanderous hint of the "cuckold letter" about the relations of the tsar to his wife. He still dreamed and talked about retiring to the country, but the favor of Nicholas depended upon his remaining in Petersburg. Peace and leisure for work were denied him, and he felt that his creative powers were failing. People on the street gathered about him and shouted: "Bravo, Pushkin!" When he attended lectures at the university Pletnev hailed him as an immortal, and the students sat worshipfully at his feet. Such tributes were consoling to his enervated spirits. And in a moment of belief in this immortality he wrote his ringing *Exegi Monumentum*:

> I've raised my monument, unwrought by human skill;
> The people's path to it will not be overgrown,
> And its rebellious head will tower higher still
>   Than Alexander's shaft of stone.

> I shall not die — my spirit in the sacred lyre
> My ashes will survive and still escape the flame —
> I shall be great in this sublunar world entire,
>   As long as poets live by fame.

> Throughout the whole of Russia word of me will pierce;
> They will pronounce my name in every living tongue,
> Proud grandson of the Slav, the Finn, the Tungus fierce,
>   The Kalmuck, friend of steppes unsung.

> Among the people I shall long be held a sage,
> Since I awakened with my lyre some tender feeling,
> Because I honored freedom in my cruel age,
>   And summoned favor for the kneeling.

So to the will of God, O Muse, show reverence,
Not fearing an offense or asking for the crown,
Accepting praise or blame with full indifference,
And do not argue with the clown.[17]

But the scornful last line was the real sentiment in his heart
during these bitter days. He knew that he was no longer the
uncontested literary leader. Critics held him up as reactionary,
and journalists ridiculed his works.

Pushkin's drifting away — more apparent than real — from
his liberal comrades now saddened him and made him feel that
he had forsaken his intellectual heritage for the false glitter of
aristocratic tinsel. He understood all the faults, the narrowness,
and emptiness of Petersburg high society. Yet he wished to be
accepted, not because he valued this aristocratic set, but because
it was considered the best in Russia. And he felt that his own
noble birth gave him a prescriptive right to enter this society,
and that his literary attainments should have made him even
more desirable. The poor man who rises never feels himself so
unhappy among aristocrats as the man whose birth places him
on the fringe of that society but who is never quite accepted;
and his unhappiness is all the more acute when he feels that his
talents and intellect are greater than theirs. Petersburg high
society deeply offended Pushkin's pride of birth. And the offense went still deeper when he realized that in many cases he
was tolerated simply because of his beautiful wife. Now this
society was vastly amused because it thought that his beautiful
wife was betraying him with a clever young guardsman. They
laughed when they saw Prince Dolgorukov make the traditional
sign of the horns behind Pushkin's back.

Such was Pushkin's hopeless position in January 1837. His
appearance and whole personality seemed to change. He looked
old, yellow, and harassed. Gone was the characteristic carefree
manner, the spontaneous childlike laughter. For whole days he
walked about the city or locked himself up in his study and
paced the room from corner to corner. When the house bell
rang, he rushed out and shouted to the servants not to receive
any letters postmarked from the city. (He continued to re-

ceive anonymous letters, informing him that D'Anthès' marriage was merely a blind to conceal his relations with Natasha.) Yet if a letter came, he seized it, shut himself in his study, and was heard by the servants talking aloud to himself in French. With his wife he was sepulchral; in company, without her, he displayed a forced gaiety that seemed to be inspired by hysteria. A friend saw him rush past Natasha, D'Anthès, and the latter's wife on the street with a look of concentrated hate on his face. He stood and glowered while D'Anthès danced with Natasha. At one ball he entered the study of his host, which was lined with the horned heads of hunting trophies, and found there a young friend of the Guards. "Why are you here?" he asked. "For a Horse Guard, especially for an unmarried one, this is no place. You see," he pointed to the horns, "this room is for married men, for a husband, for our brethren." [18] The guardsman left the room and caught sight of D'Anthès dancing with Pushkin's wife.

Like Othello, Pushkin was driven to madness by jealousy. And like the Venetian blackamoor, he had lost all tranquillity and was prepared to say farewell to the pride, pomp, and circumstance of life. Unlike Othello, however, Pushkin still believed in the purity of his beautiful Desdemona. Dear friends advised him, since he trusted his Natasha, to forget the whole affair and let time restore his peace of mind. But Pushkin was not merely jealous of his wife; he was jealous of his honor. Pride would not permit him to become the laughingstock of Petersburg society. And when a friend from Trigorskoe visited at this time and told him that even the people in the country were talking about the scandal, this was the last straw. His good name, Pushkin felt, belonged to Russia and to posterity. To have it dragged in the mire of filthy scandal was an insult to all of Russia, and more than he could bear. Later he remarked to D'Anthès' second: "There are two kinds of cuckolds: those who are really such, and they know well how to comport themselves; but the case of those who are cuckolds by the favor of the public is a more embarrassing one, and this is mine." [19] At least the public would learn that he could defend his honor.

Finally an incident occurred that could have but one consequence. Natasha received a letter from D'Anthès begging for
a meeting in private. He had highly important matters to talk
over with her, and he swore that he would respect her honor as
that of his wife's sister. His letter concluded with dark hints of
dire results if she refused to see him. Genuinely frightened,
Natasha agreed. The rendezvous took place in the home of
Pushkin's bitter enemy, Idaliya Poletika. The details of what
happened at the meeting are obscure. It appears that it was
just a subterfuge contrived to give D'Anthès an opportunity to
throw himself at the feet of Natasha and beg her submission.
As soon as she learned his real purpose, she fled the house. The
next day Pushkin received an anonymous note which informed
him of the rendezvous. He questioned his wife, and Natasha
told him of the meeting and her conviction that it had been a
trick to compromise her. Pushkin wanted nothing more. On
the twenty-sixth of January he wrote Heeckeren the following
letter, filled with venom and calculated provocation:

"Baron! Permit me to review what has occurred. The conduct of your son has been known to me for a long time, and I
could not remain indifferent to it. I was content with the role
of observer, free to intervene when I should judge it fitting. An
incident which at any other moment would have been very disagreeable happened most opportunely and obliged me to put an
end to this affair: I received anonymous letters. I saw that
the moment had come, and I profited by it. You know the rest:
I have made your son play a role so pitiful that my wife, astonished by such cowardice and dullness, cannot keep from
laughing, and the emotion which might have appealed to her,
perhaps, as a great and sublime passion has been extinguished
in the calmest scorn and the most merited disgust.

"I am obliged to declare, Baron, that your part has not been
quite suitable to you. You, the representative of a crowned
head, you have been as a father the pimp of your son. It would
appear that all his conduct (clumsy enough, moreover) has been
directed by you. It is you who probably dictated to him the
wretched things that he has uttered and the silliness that he

included in his writing. Like an obscene old man, you have lain in wait for my wife in every corner in order to tell her of the love of your bastard, or so he is called; and when, ill with syphilis, he was obliged to remain at home, you said that he was dying from love of her; you muttered to her: Give me back my son.

"You understand, Baron, that after all this I cannot permit my family to have the slightest relations with yours. It was on this condition that I agreed not to take action in this dirty business, and not to dishonor you in the eyes of your court and ours, as I had the power and intention to do. I cannot allow my wife to continue to listen to your paternal exhortations. After his abject conduct, I cannot permit your son to dare to address a word to my wife, much less to recite to her the jokes of the barrack room, or to show a devotion and unhappy passion, since he is a coward and a scamp. I have been obliged to address myself to you, and to pray you to end all this matter if you desire to avoid a new scandal before which I shall certainly not retreat." [20]

Pushkin had written this fatal letter to Heeckeren purposely, for he believed him to be the guiding spirit behind much of the conduct of his son. He realized that the father, because of his diplomatic position, would hardly be able to fight a duel, and that the obligation would rest on D'Anthès. At any rate, such a letter could be answered only by a duel. This was precisely what Pushkin desired. And "the bloodier the better!"

CHAPTER XX

The Last Duel

> He is no more. The youthful bard
> Has found his end before his time!
> The storm winds blew; the lovely
> flower
> Died in the morning of its life;
> The altar flame has now gone out!
> *Eugene Onegin*

After sending this letter to Heeckeren Pushkin felt as though he had been relieved of some unbearable pain. The accumulated black bile of weeks of suffering had suddenly been discharged. He was quiet, happy, and at times even jolly. That same day (January 26) A. I. Turgenev saw him twice, and on each occasion he conversed in lively fashion, joked, and laughed. This bright exterior may have been designed to deceive his old friend concerning the true state of affairs. But the peace of a man who has made an important and irrevocable resolution had entered Pushkin's heart. Fate would take care of the rest.

Heeckeren received the insulting letter the day on which it was sent. He was just about to go to Count Stroganov's to dine. According to his own story, he hesitated over the proper measures to take in answering such a vile offense. His official position made it difficult for him to challenge Pushkin, and if he did, in view of the previous challenge to his son, D'Anthès might be regarded as a coward. If he accepted and were killed, then D'Anthès would feel it necessary to avenge him; and if the duel proved fatal to his son, his wife might be left entirely without support. He proceeded to Stroganov for counsel, and the count advised that D'Anthès should make the challenge. This suited Heeckeren. He at once wrote to Pushkin:

"Not recognizing either your handwriting or your signature [an insulting falsification], I have had recourse to Vicomte d'Archiac, who brings this letter to you with the request to make known to him whether or not the letter I am answering actually comes from you. Its contents have gone so completely

beyond all possible limits that I refuse to answer to all the details of this epistle. You appear to have forgotten that it was
you who retracted the challenge which you addressed to Baron
George Heeckeren and which was accepted by him. The proof
of what I say exists here, written by your hand, and has reposed
in the hands of seconds. There remains only to say that Vicomte d'Archiac visits you in order to agree upon a place of
meeting with Baron George Heeckeren, and I add that this encounter permits of no delay. Later I will teach you to respect
the dignity with which I am clothed and which no conduct on
your side must offend." [1] The letter was approved and also
signed by D'Anthès.

When D'Archiac arrived, Pushkin accepted the challenge
without even bothering to read Heeckeren's pompous communication. Later in the day D'Archiac wrote Pushkin a note
to the effect that he would remain at home until eleven that
evening to receive his second; after that hour he would be at a
ball given by Countess Razumovskaya.

On this occasion the matter of a second was a troublesome
one for Pushkin. He wanted no repetition of the situation connected with his previous challenge. Everything must be kept a
secret. If close friends discovered his intentions, they would
surely try to prevent the duel. Pushkin was determined that
this duel should take place. Certain of his friends as seconds
could not be trusted to keep the affair from the knowledge of
Zhukovski, Vyazemski, or even from the tsar. And Pushkin
was very successful in keeping his secret. Apart from the active
figures in the challenge, perhaps only two other people learned
of it from him. Alexandra Goncharova knew of the letter to
Heeckeren. In his immediate family this loving, sympathetic
Cinderella of the household was probably the only one to share
his secret, and in her strange relations with Pushkin she had
long since learned the virtue of silence. On the evening of the
twenty-sixth he visited Princess Vyazemskaya, and perhaps out
of sheer habit — she held his confidence in many intimate
matters — he entrusted the news to her. However, as though
to forestall any chance of intervention, Pushkin had already

determined that the duel should be fought as quickly as possible.

On the night of the twenty-sixth, having as yet failed to obtain a second, Pushkin attended the ball at Razumovskaya's. There he met D'Archiac and conversed with him about the difficulty. The attention of Vyazemski was drawn to the pair, and, no doubt thinking some mischief was up, he approached. They quickly broke off their conversation, and Vyazemski was none the wiser. Destiny showed the way, and Pushkin blindly followed. He caught sight of Arthur C. Magenis, an official of the English embassy, whom he valued as an honorable and discreet Englishman. Pushkin now asked him to act as a second. Without definitely accepting, Magenis agreed to talk the matter over with D'Archiac. But D'Archiac refused to discuss the subject with him, since he had not been formally constituted a second. When Magenis sought out Pushkin to report, he had already left for home. Unwilling to visit him at such a late hour, for fear of arousing the suspicions of his wife, Magenis sent him a note at two o'clock in the morning. He refused to be a second, since the possibility of a peaceful settlement had already been precluded. (By rule, the first duty of a second was to try to effect a reconciliation.) Thus the day of the challenge had passed, and Pushkin had failed to obtain a second.

On the morning of the twenty-seventh Pushkin arose at eight o'clock. He drank tea, wrote a bit, and walked about his study in high spirits, singing to himself. This was to be his day of reckoning. At about ten o'clock a letter arrived from D'Archiac. He demanded that Pushkin send him at once a properly accredited second. A sudden fear seized Pushkin that the negotiations would be prolonged and that the news of the intended duel would leak out over the city. All the burning impatience for vengeance behind his calm exterior bursts forth in his answer:

"I have no desire to take the loafers of Petersburg into my confidence concerning my family affairs; consequently, I did not agree to any conversation between seconds. I will appear only at the place of meeting. Since it is Mr. Heeckeren who has challenged me and is offended, he can choose one [a second] if he

BARON GEORGE D'ANTHÈS

feels this necessary; I accept him in advance, even if he be one of his own cavalrymen. As for the hour and the place, I am entirely at his service. According to Russian custom, this is sufficient. Vicomte, I beg you to believe that this is my final word and that there is nothing more for me to answer concerning this affair, and that I shall move only in order to present myself at the place of meeting." [2]

Pushkin, of course, knew perfectly well that his demand was contrary to the rules of the duel. A second of his own choosing was absolutely necessary for legal reasons and those of honor. The letter was simply an impulsive outburst provoked by the exasperating delay and by his own inability to obtain a second. But get one he must.

Whether he met Konstantin Danzas on the street by sheer chance in his search, as is generally asserted, or deliberately selected him, is not positively known. But for various reasons the latter possibility is the more likely. Pushkin probably sent for him. This is the Danzas of the Lyceum days, the fun-loving schoolmate, the "typographer" of the *Lyceum Sage*. He was now a lieutenant colonel in the army, something of an epicure, careless of life and ambition, but brave, honest, and loyal. Pushkin had seen little of him since their graduation, yet they had never ceased to be warm friends. He turned to him now in this last emergency.

Danzas arrived about noon, and Pushkin received him cheerfully. Closeted in his study, he explained the business. Danzas agreed to be his friend's second and left to obtain the pistols, promising to meet him at an appointed place. Meanwhile, an answer to his letter came from D'Archiac, in which he insisted that Pushkin must find his own second and that no further negotiations would be undertaken until he had done so.

A strange calm descended upon Pushkin as he prepared himself. Some small business had to be concluded. An authoress, A. O. Ishimova, whom he wished to persuade to do some translations of Barry Cornwall for the *Contemporary*, had invited him to call that day. He wrote her a letter with his regrets and sent his copy of Cornwall, indicating the passages to be rendered. Then he washed himself, put on clean linen, donned his great bearskin coat, and departed at one o'clock. No one in the house knew his destination.

Having taken a sleigh, he met Danzas, and together they drove to the French embassy, where D'Archiac lived. On the way Pushkin chatted about simple, everyday matters. At the embassy he presented Danzas to D'Archiac. Then he clearly recited before both witnesses everything that had taken place between him, D'Anthès, and Heeckeren. The reason for sending the insulting letter, Pushkin explained, was that the diplomat and his son had violated their promise to leave his wife in peace; and he read the fatal letter aloud. "Now the only thing I have to tell you," he concluded, "is that if the affair is not settled this very day, the first time I meet Heeckeren, father or son, I will spit in his face." [3] Then, turning to Danzas, he officially declared him his second and left both witnesses to decide upon the conditions of the duel.

The conditions were quickly drawn up. The duel was to take place at five o'clock that day at a lonely spot near Black River on the outskirts of the city. Pistols were the weapons. The adversaries were to stand five paces from the barriers, which in turn were to be ten paces apart. At a given signal they were to advance, but under no circumstances might they pass the barriers in order to shoot. If there were misses on both sides, the adversaries would fire again under the same conditions.

There was no retreat now. The duel was a sure thing. With the conditions all carefully written out, Danzas hastened to Volf's well-known confectionery shop on the Nevski Prospekt, where he had promised to rejoin Pushkin.

II

And Lenski, closing his left eye,
Also began to aim — just then
Onegin fired his fatal shot . . . .
The poet's destined hour had
    struck:
Silent, he let his pistol fall.
            Eugene Onegin

Pushkin cared nothing about the conditions which his second showed him. The duel was the thing. After drinking a glass of water or lemonade, he left the confectioner's shop with Danzas at about four o'clock. The meeting was at five. They hired a sleigh and set out towards the Troitski Bridge. The January weather was cold, and a stiff wind blew. Outwardly Pushkin seemed calm; his mind was clear and his conversation cheerful. Dueling was no new experience for him. His courage had been tried on several fields and not found wanting. But this was no ordinary contest arising out of some fancied slight or harsh words in a drunken spree. Fierce resentment, his own honor and that of his wife, and the good opinion of Petersburg society were mingled in the complexity of reasons that drove him to seek a desperate conclusion. The gravity of the cause seemed to portend grave consequences. Yet any deep thoughts that coursed through his brain or any anxiety for his wife and children never came to the surface on this fateful ride.

As they turned into the Palace Quay, Natasha's carriage suddenly approached from the opposite direction. Perhaps she will see him, thought Danzas hopefully. He might tell her of the duel; she would beg him to return home, and all would be saved! The terrible feeling that the great poet might be going to his death had been preying on the second's mind. But Natasha was nearsighted, and Pushkin deliberately turned his face the other way. The two vehicles passed without any sign of recognition from husband or wife. And the little sleigh continued on its destined way.

Groups of Petersburg high society were returning from an afternoon of tobogganing on the hills outside the city. Many of them knew Pushkin and Danzas, and bows were frequently exchanged. Noticing Count I. M. Borkh and his wife in one carriage, Pushkin remarked: "There is a model pair for you." Since Danzas seemed to miss his point, he continued: "Why, the wife lives with the coachman and the husband with the postillion." [4]

Prince V. D. Golitsyn yelled as he passed: "Why are you going so late [to the hills]? Everybody is coming home." [5]

Many of these revelers were well acquainted with the bitter

relations between Pushkin and D'Anthès, but none guessed why he was driving outside the city limits at this late hour in the afternoon. By the frozen Neva loomed the forbidding Peter-Paul fortress which was used as a prison.

Pushkin jokingly asked his comrade: "You are not taking me to the fortress, are you?"

"The road to Black River by way of the fortress is the shortest," [6] Danzas solemnly answered.

Both parties arrived at the same time. The two seconds conversed briefly and finally settled upon a spot for the duel. It was a short distance from the road and concealed by thick bushes, which would prevent the coachmen from witnessing the fight. The snow was knee-deep, and the seconds, with the help of D'Anthès, trampled down a long narrow lane. Pushkin, shrouded in his bearskin coat, sat on a mound of snow and watched the preparations with apparent indifference. When they had cleared a sufficient space, Danzas asked him if it was satisfactory.

"It is all the same to me; only hurry it," he impatiently replied.

Twenty paces were measured off, and the seconds used their capotes to indicate the barriers. They began to load the pistols.

"Well, have you finished?" asked Pushkin, growing more and more impatient to begin.

All was ready. The adversaries took up their positions, weapons in hand. Danzas gave the signal to begin by waving his hat. With firm steps the two enemies advanced towards their respective barriers. Pushkin reached his first and raised his pistol. D'Anthès, who had walked only four paces, fired. Pushkin dropped, exclaiming: "I'm wounded!"

He had fallen on Danzas' capote, his head in the snow and the barrel of the pistol stuck in the snow. Both seconds ran to him, and D'Anthès approached. After several moments of silence Pushkin raised himself on his left elbow and said:

"Wait; I have enough strength to take my shot." [7]

D'Anthès returned to his post, stood sideways, and covered his breast with his right arm. Danzas gave Pushkin another pistol for the one which had dropped in the snow. Supporting himself on his left elbow, Pushkin took steady aim with a firm right hand. He was a dead shot. He fired, and D'Anthès fell.

"Bravo!" [8] shouted Pushkin, throwing his pistol aside. The duel was ended.

But Pushkin had been seriously wounded. The bullet hit the upper part of the thigh bone where it joins the pelvis, and was deflected deep into the lower abdomen. After firing he collapsed in a half-faint. He quickly recovered, however, and asked D'Archiac:

"Is he killed?"

"No, but he has been wounded in the arm and the breast," was the reply.

D'Anthès' arm had received Pushkin's shot. The ball had gone through, striking a button and merely bruising the ribs. His protective gesture had no doubt saved his life.

"It is strange," said Pushkin. "I thought it would give me pleasure to kill him, but I do not feel that now." [9]

D'Archiac tried to mutter words of reconciliation, but Pushkin interrupted him:

"In the end it is all the same; if we both recover, we shall try again." For him there could never be any peace between them.

Pushkin was losing much blood. The coachmen were called, and with their aid a litter of fence poles was constructed. He was carried to the road and placed in the sleigh. They set out, Danzas and D'Archiac on foot and D'Anthès bringing up the rear in his own sleigh. Pushkin suffered much pain but never breathed a word of complaint. After traveling a short distance they met a carriage which had been sent by Heeckeren for just such an occasion. Without saying who sent it, D'Anthès and his second offered it to Pushkin. Danzas accepted, and at the same time refused their proposal to keep his part in the duel a secret.

Pushkin was placed in the carriage and, with Danzas beside him, began the slow, tortuous route back to Petersburg. Pushkin, however, did not appear to suffer much. He chatted with Danzas, joked a bit, and related several anecdotes. The talk concerned duels in general, and he recalled his fight with Zubov in Kishinev. Then he remembered the duel of his friend, Shcherbachev, who had been fatally wounded in the abdomen. As though suddenly sensing the seriousness of his own hurt, Pushkin remarked: "I'm afraid my wound is the same as Shcherbachev's." [10]

Before they reached his house Pushkin gave Danzas detailed instructions about what to say to his wife, for he was afraid of alarming her. When they arrived, at six o'clock, Danzas went into Natasha's room and found her with her sister Alexandra. His sudden appearance surprised Natasha, and she looked at him in fright, as though she expected some bad news. Danzas told her that Pushkin had been wounded in a duel with D'Anthès but not seriously. She rushed to the entrance. Pushkin attempted to quiet her, saying that he was not dangerously hurt and would call for her as soon as he got into bed. Natasha fell in a faint.

Pushkin's old valet carried him in his arms into the house.

"Does it grieve you to have to carry me?" [11] Pushkin asked him.

He was brought into his study, the room he loved best. Clean linen was ordered, and after being undressed he was placed on the divan. Meanwhile, Danzas had run for a doctor.

III

> Friends, are you sorry for the poet?
> In the flower of joyous hopes . . .
> He perished!
>
> *Eugene Onegin*

Doctors were hard to find at that hour. Danzas tried several without success, including Arendt, the tsar's physician. He finally discovered Sholts, an obstetrician, who promised to come at once with another doctor. Danzas returned to Pushkin's house, and by seven o'clock Sholts and Dr. Zadler arrived. Pushkin asked his wife, Danzas, and Pletnev, who had just come on a visit, to leave the study.

"I feel badly," he said, giving his hand to Sholts.

The doctors examined the wound, and Zadler left to get some necessary instruments.

"What do you think of the wound?" Pushkin asked Sholts in a clear voice. "When I was shot I felt a hard blow in the side and a burning pain in the loins; much blood was lost on the road — tell me frankly, how do you find the wound?"

"I cannot hide from you the fact that your wound is dangerous."

"Tell me — is it fatal?"

"I imagine that this will not be concealed from you long," replied Sholts. "But let us hear the opinions of Arendt and Salomon, who have been sent for."

"I thank you. You have behaved like an honorable man with me." Pushkin raised his hand to his forehead. "I must put my house in order." Then, after several minutes of silence, he said: "It seems that I am losing a great deal of blood."

Sholts looked at the wound again and applied a new compress.

"Do you not wish to see some of your close friends?" asked the doctor.

"Farewell, friends!" said Pushkin, glancing around at the books in his study. "Really, do you think that I have not an hour to live?"

"Oh, no, not that; but I thought it would be pleasant for you to see some of them. Mr. Pletnev is here. . . ."

"Yes — but I should like Zhukovski. Give me some water; I am nauseated." [12]

Sholts felt his pulse and found it very weak. Zhukovski was sent for, and Danzas returned. Finally Arendt and Salomon arrived with Zadler at about eight o'clock. Pushkin asked the tsar's physician to tell him exactly what his chances were. He was not afraid of the truth, he said, and then there were certain matters that had to be taken care of if he must expect the worst.

"If that is the case," replied Arendt after examining him, "then I must tell you that your wound is very dangerous, and as for your recovery, I have almost no hope."

Pushkin thanked him. Ice packs were placed on his abdomen, and he was given a cold drink. Arendt said that he had to

return and report to the tsar. Pushkin requested him to ask the
sovereign not to prosecute his second. Arendt promised and
departed. On the way out he said to Danzas: "It is a vile joke:
he will die." [13]

In the meantime, Spasski, Pushkin's family doctor, came.
Pushkin had little faith in him, but now, thoroughly aware of
the seriousness of his condition, he asked Spasski not to give his
wife any false hopes.

"She is not a dissembler," he said. "You know her well. She
must learn all. However, do with me what you wish; I agree to
everything and am ready for anything."

Spasski left the room to attend to Natasha, and on his return
he told Pushkin that she was quieter.

"Poor thing, she suffers in innocence, and she may suffer still
more in the opinion of people," [14] said her husband.

Then, with extraordinary clarity of mind, which rarely deserted him in the midst of his suffering, he suddenly remembered that he had received an invitation that day to attend the
funeral services of Grech's son, who had died from consumption.
He asked Spasski to send his regrets. At this point they prevailed upon him to call a priest. The holy father soon arrived,
and the last rites of the Church were administered.

The news of the duel and of Pushkin's critical condition had
spread throughout the city like wildfire. Friends began to appear — Zhukovski, the Vyazemskis, M. Vielgorski, P. I. Meshcherski, P. A. Valuev, A. I. Turgenev, and aunt Zagryazhskaya.
Every time his wife came into the room or even stood at the
door, he seemed to sense her presence and asked if she were
there. He did not want her to see him suffer.

At midnight Dr. Arendt returned from the tsar. He had nothing to say about Pushkin's request concerning Danzas, but
there is a tradition that he brought a personal note from Nicholas to the wounded man which read: "If God does not permit us
to see thee any more in this world, I send thee my farewell and
this last advice: die a Christian. About thy wife and children
do not worry: I will take care of them." [15]

Touched by the communication, Pushkin is supposed to have

strongly desired to keep this letter, but Arendt had been ordered to return it to the tsar. It is very improbable, however,
that Nicholas ever sent such a personal letter. There is no doubt
that he did entrust a written statement to Arendt himself, and
that this was repeated to Pushkin, but the precise nature of its
contents will never be known.

Pushkin called for Danzas and dictated to him from memory
a list of all his debts for which he had no written record. Then
he took a ring from his finger and gave it to his second as a
keepsake, and he told Danzas that he wanted no one to avenge
him.

In the long hours of the night Pushkin's suffering grew intense. Gangrene had set in, and the pain became unbearable.
He ordered a servant to bring him a box from the writing table.
Danzas entered the room just in time to see him concealing a
pistol under the bedclothes. Pushkin surrendered the weapon,
confessing that his pain was so great that he wished to shoot
himself. This extreme suffering continued unabated until seven
o'clock on the morning of the twenty-eighth. Pain convulsed
him, and he tried to stifle his cries for fear of arousing his wife,
who remained in the living room in a prostrate condition. An
attempt was made to drain the wound in order to relieve his
agony.

After seven o'clock the pain lessened somewhat. He asked
for his wife, for Alexandra Goncharova, and for his children,
since he wished to bid them farewell. The children entered,
half-asleep, and were led up to him. He raised his eyes to each
in turn, placed his hand on their heads, and blessed them. With
a cry Natasha threw herself on her husband. All in the room
wept. Throughout his suffering Pushkin had been most solicitous for her welfare. He did not wish her to remain in the room,
but he summoned her on several occasions. Aware of the moral
torture she was undergoing, he tried to lighten her burden.

"Be quiet; you are not to blame for this," [16] he told her.
And again: "Do not reproach yourself for my death; this is a
matter which concerned me alone." [17]

After his family left the room Pushkin's close friends were

summoned. Zhukovski kissed his cold, outstretched hand and could say nothing. He pressed Vyazemski's hand and murmured: "Farewell; be happy." [18] He embraced A. I. Turgenev and whispered that he loved him. Then he called for his old friend Mme. Karamzina. She came soon, and he asked her to bless him, which she did. He kissed her hand, and she left the room in tears. The ever-faithful Elizaveta Khitrovo stormed the house in a frenzy of grief. They tried to keep her out, but she would not be denied a last visit with the poet whose genius she worshiped.

Crowds of admirers stood outside, on the stairs, and in the anteroom. "Is he better?" "Is there any hope?" were questions asked on every side. One old man, who kept a shop next to the house, exclaimed in wonderment: "The Lord my God! Why I remember once how a field marshal died, but it was not like this!" [19] Many of these onlookers — friends, strangers, and even foreigners — wept. What was it that touched them? Zhukovski gave the answer: In general, genius is good. In the worship of genius all people are akin, and when it leaves this earth forever, all lament with the same brotherly grief. Pushkin, in his genius, was not only the property of Russia but of all Europe.

At midday occurred one of those sudden turns for the better which are so illusory in fatal illnesses. Pushkin's condition seemed to improve, and his spirits rose. Hope gripped those at the bedside. After all, doctors were often wrong. But Pushkin himself was not deceived. About two o'clock his friend V. I. Dal arrived, a physician and writer. Pushkin greeted him with a smile and joked faintly. Dal scarcely left his side thereafter and offered him hope which he refused to accept.

"There is no living for me here; I shall die. That is clear, and it must be so!" he declared.

Toward nightfall the pains began again. His fortitude was extraordinary, his complaints few. Dr. Arendt had seen death on many battlefields and admitted that he had never encountered such endurance. Leeches were applied to relieve the fever, and ice packs were placed on his head. His thoughts went back to his old Lyceum comrades and his schooldays. If only Pushchin and Malinovski were present, he said, it would be easier for him to die. Several times that night he asked what hour it was. And when Dal told him, he replied:

"How long must I suffer so! Please hurry!" [20]

On the morning of the twenty-ninth the press of people outside became so great that Danzas, fearing a demonstration, requested the authorities to send guards. Pushkin was rapidly growing weaker. He lay motionless with his eyes closed. At about two o'clock he suddenly demanded raspberries. When they were brought he asked that his wife be sent in to serve them. On her knees she fed him with a spoon. Pushkin stroked the head of his beautiful Natasha, murmuring:

"There, there, it is nothing. Thank God, all will be well!"

A peaceful expression came over his face, and his words deceived Natasha. As she went out she said to Spasski: "You see, he will live; he will not die!" [21]

Zhukovski and Vielgorski stood at the head of his bed and Turgenev by the side. Dal whispered to Zhukovski:

"He is going."

Once he gave his hand to Dal, and pressing it, said:

"Raise me; come, higher, higher . . . well, come on!" Then, recovering, he continued: "I dreamt that I was climbing up on top of those bookcases with you, up high . . . and I got dizzy."

After a little while he again opened his eyes, and grasping Dal's hand, said:

"Well, let us go now, please, and together."

On his request Dal raised him a bit higher. Suddenly, as if awakening from a sleep, he opened his eyes wide, and his face brightened.

"Life is ended!" he whispered.

"What is ended?" asked Dal, not hearing him clearly.

"Life is ended!" Pushkin repeated audibly and emphatically. "It is difficult to breathe; I am choking!" [22] These were his last words.

At the moment of death Natasha entered the room. She threw herself on her knees before the body. All her thick chestnut hair fell in disorder about her shoulders. Sobbing, she stretched out her hands to her husband and cried:

"Pushkin, Pushkin, are you living?" [23]

Thus in death, as in life, he was for her "Pushkin" — only Pushkin, the poet.

When they had all left the room Zhukovski remained, and in the strange silence that ensued he sat for a long time looking at the face of the dead man. His feelings were memorably recorded:

"I never beheld anything in his face like that which I saw during the first few minutes after death. His head was a little bent; the hands, which a few minutes before had moved so convulsively, were now quietly extended, as though resting after hard work. But what his face expressed I am not able to tell in words. For me it was so new and at the same time so familiar! It was neither sleep nor rest! It was not an intellectual expression, always so natural to this face; nor was it even a poetic expression! No! Some profound, wonderful thought played over it, something like a vision, like some complete, deep, gratifying knowledge. While gazing at his face I wished to ask him: 'What do you see, friend?' And what would have been his answer if at that moment he could have risen again? These are the moments in our lives which perfectly deserve being called great. At that precise moment it may be said that I saw death itself, divinely mysterious, death without its veil. What a stamp it placed on his face, and how wonderfully death expressed its own and his secret! I swear to you I have never seen on his face an expression of such profound, sublime, and triumphal thought. Of course, such a look had flashed across it before. But it was revealed in its purity only when, in the meeting with death, everything earthly had vanished from his face. Such was the end of our Pushkin." [24]

IV

> Now all is quiet, all is dark,
> As in a house that's quite deserted.
> *Eugene Onegin*

Shortly after the end Pushkin's body was removed from the library. Zhukovski was ordered, in the tsar's name, to lock the room and seal it. The authorities wanted to be the first to in-spect the papers of the dead poet. A feeling of indignation over the duel and Pushkin's death quickly spread among the middle class and the intelligentsia of the city. Threats were uttered against the foreigners responsible, D'Anthès and Heeckeren; and not a little popular sentiment was directed against Push-kin's wife, who had fallen into a state of complete collapse. Even the foreign doctors who attended Pushkin came in for some vilification. The government began to have its fears.

On the request of Natasha the body was dressed in civilian clothes. She knew that her husband would have preferred this to the more proper but hated uniform of gentleman of the cham-ber. During the three days in which the body was on view in the house hundreds of people filed past the bier. Poor men and women, children, and students came in crowds to pay their last tribute to a beloved national poet. Thousands of copies of his works, especially of *Eugene Onegin*, which was republished on the day of his death, were sold. Death restored his waning popularity and brought home to the people at large a realization of his greatness. But very few of the admirers at his bier be-longed to the aristocratic society of Petersburg. In the *salons* and boudoirs of this set there was blame for Pushkin and sympathy for the dashing young D'Anthès.

In death Pushkin's face was unusually serious, but its peace-ful expression showed no trace of the excruciating pain he had endured for forty-five hours after he had received his wound. The white expansive brow stood in sharp relief against the mass of dark curly hair, and thick side whiskers fringed the hollow cheeks to the chin. His bloodless lips lost nothing of their char-acteristic expressiveness in death. Despite the throngs of people that visited the body, the silence of awe in the presence of the great dead was preserved.

The second day after Pushkin's end the government began to translate its fears into action. Soldiers were ordered out to picket the house and the neighborhood to prevent any demon-stration by the crowds. Magazines and papers were strictly forbidden to publish anything but the most formal notices of

Pushkin's death. The authorities promptly seized several unfortunate editors for overstepping the limits of what was
thought to be adequate notification. "Why the black border
about the news of the death of a man who was not an official
and who occupied no position in the government service?" one
of the offenders was sternly asked. "And why the expression —
'the sun of poetry!' Then, for goodness' sake, why such an
honor — 'Pushkin died in the middle of his great career!'
What was this career of his?" [25] For official Russia, a poet could
not have a career, to say nothing of a great one.

Some fanatical worshiper of Pushkin sent anonymous letters
to Zhukovski and Count A. F. Orlov, an official in the Third
Section. The foreign slayer of the poet was denounced and the
government warned to take action. Immediately the con-
spiracy-minded Benkendorf scented a political plot. At a late
hour on January 31 the public was refused further permission to
see the body, and the house was filled with police. That same
night some ten of Pushkin's dearest friends gathered about the
body to pay the poet their last respects. But they were not
allowed to perform this hallowed rite in peace. Later Vyazemski
bitterly complained: "It may be said without exaggeration that
more police than friends collected about the bier. I do not speak
of the soldiers picketing the streets. But against whom was
arrayed this military force which filled the home of the deceased
during those minutes when a dozen of his friends and closest
comrades gathered there in order to render him their last homage? What were these disguised men intended for, known to all
as spies? They were there to keep us in sight, to eavesdrop on
our grief, our words, to be witnesses of our tears, our silence." [26]
Vyazemski was right; they were Benkendorf's spies sent to
gather information about the friends of the dead political suspect, Pushkin.

Invitations to the church services were sent out. The place
and time were specifically indicated — St. Isaac's Cathedral, at
eleven o'clock on February 1. Again the government stepped in.
The public services might be a signal for some premeditated
popular outburst. At midnight on January 31 the police or-

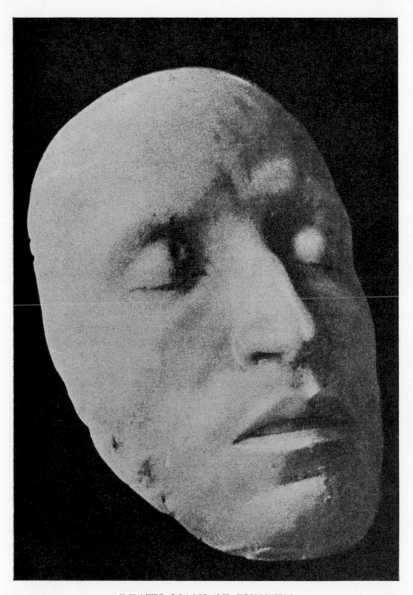

DEATH MASK OF PUSHKIN

dered the body transferred to the Royal Stables Church. The operation was carried on with the greatest secrecy; only Pushkin's closest friends were present.

Although many were deceived by this unannounced change, the news spread, and crowds soon filled the square in front of the church. Professors in the university had been warned to forbid students to cut lectures that day. Nevertheless, many students absented themselves from classes, refusing to obey an order that would prevent them from honoring their great poet. Admission to the church was restricted to those who held tickets or who wore official uniforms. Many of the diplomatic corps were present; and many of the aristocracy refused to come. Yet it was in every sense a national funeral. The church was packed, and sincere grief was expressed on every face. Slowly friends and admirers passed by the bier to give the final kiss. In silence Zhukovski embraced the lifeless form for the last time, bidding a tearful farewell to the pupil who had become his master.

They placed the body in the church crypt, where it remained until the night of February 3. Pushkin had expressed a desire to be buried in Mikhailovskoe. His wife, too ill to accompany the body, had requested the tsar to allow Danzas to act as her representative. Nicholas I refused. Despite Pushkin's plea, the arrest of Danzas for his part in the duel had been ordered. The tsar suggested A. I. Turgenev, who agreed to take charge of the burial. Meanwhile, the authorities in Pskov were instructed to permit only a simple funeral without any public demonstration.

The body was placed in a plain wooden box. Sad at heart, Vyazemski and Zhukovski threw in their gloves, a gesture of devotion which the police regarded as highly suspicious. They loaded the box on a sleigh, and the procession, guarded by police, set out for Mikhailovskoe at midnight on February 3. Turgenev, who had entered Pushkin in the Lyceum twenty-six years before, went along; and the old valet, Nikita Kozlov, who had rocked his master's cradle, now followed him to the grave. In the light of the moon Zhukovski watched the procession until it disappeared around a corner.

At a station not far from Petersburg some people stood about as a sleigh drove up. On it was a simple wooden box covered with straw and a bast mat. Three accompanying policemen argued with the stationmaster, demanding fresh horses.

"What is this?" a woman asked one of the peasants who was idly staring at the box.

"God knows what!" he answered. "You see, someone killed Pushkin — they are whisking him away in a bast mat and straw, may God forgive them, like a dog!" [27]

On the fifth Turgenev arrived at Trigorskoe, near the village where Pushkin had long hoped to retire and lead the life of a country gentleman. The body was sent ahead to the Svyatogorski Monastery, and peasants were ordered to dig a grave. Until a late hour that night Turgenev sat drinking tea with Pushkin's old Trigorskoe friend, Praskovya Osipova. They talked about the dead poet and read the verses he had written in the album of one of the Trigorskoe misses.

Early on the morning of the sixth of February Turgenev, accompanied by the police guards, went to the monastery. Pushkin did not escape the surveillance of the tsar's police until he was entombed forever in the dark prison of the earth. The peasants had not yet finished digging. Turgenev quietly watched until all was ready. A brief and simple service was said in the church. Finally, Pushkin's own peasants and old Nikita bore the coffin and lowered it into the grave. Turgenev threw in a clump of earth. He and the peasants wept a little. The hole was filled, and Turgenev returned to Trigorskoe. Pushkin's grave is beside his mother's. They lay together, much closer in death than they had ever been in life.

Epilogue

Pushkin's real significance had entirely escaped both Heeckeren and D'Anthès. As foreigners who knew no Russian they could not value his literary worth or recognize his importance as a national figure. And the rather sorry position which Pushkin occupied in the aristocratic society of Petersburg did nothing to raise their opinion of him. Had they realized his true greatness, their contemptuous behavior might have been quite different. The public indignation that arose after Pushkin's death, however, quickly convinced Heeckeren and his adopted son that they had made a major mistake which would inevitably result in serious consequences to both of them. The opprobrium that greeted them on every side signified only one thing — the end of their careers in Russia.

D'Anthès was immediately arrested and brought before a court martial. Heeckeren came to his aid, and assistance was expected from friends high in the government. Ordinarily, participants in duels, provided all the proper conditions of private combat were observed, received at the worst only nominal punishment. But this was no ordinary duel. The government could not afford to defy popular opinion, which expected that severe measures would be taken. In a sense Russian national glory had been impugned. D'Anthès was deprived of his rank, discharged from the army, and ordered to be deported under police escort. For his part in the duel Danzas received the lighter sentence of two months in the guardhouse, but he retained his rank and position in the army at the expiration of this period.

The appeals of Heeckeren to influential Russian friends availed him nothing, and the justification that he offered for his behavior in the whole affair was received with little credence. He fell into disfavor with his own government, which ordered his recall. Even the tsar, who was rather sorry for D'Anthès, finally turned against Heeckeren. Nicholas wrote of the tragedy to his brother: "Although no one could accuse Pushkin's wife, not a few have blamed the behavior of D'Anthès and especially that of his odious father." [1] When Heeckeren requested the customary courtesy of a diplomat's final audience, the tsar coldly refused.

On the nineteenth of March D'Anthès, accompanied by his wife, left Russia forever. Ekaterina expressed delight at leaving the country of her birth, and she even had the bad taste to declare that she "pardoned Pushkin" for the misfortune he had brought upon her husband. Perhaps the thought that her vastly more attractive sister would no longer be a temptation to D'Anthès contributed something to Ekaterina's pleasure over this enforced departure. After a few unsettled years D'Anthès once more began a career, this time in politics. Under Louis Napoleon he rose high in the government service and finally became a senator. He lived to old age, his wife having died many years before him. In his travels through Europe he often met Russians, some of them old acquaintances, and more than once he was made to feel the ignominious part he had played in the tragedy of Pushkin. On such occasions he always protested his innocence, and to his credit it must be said that he never failed to defend the good name of the woman he had loved.

Less than a month later Heeckeren followed his protégé out of Russia. He remained in the Netherlands for a time and was soon restored to favor, winning the important post of envoy to Vienna. Heeckeren liked to associate with members of the Russian diplomatic corps at the Austrian capital. But here, as in Petersburg, he soon gained the reputation of being a sharp-tongued, malicious, intriguing old man. He died at a very advanced age, admired by few and loved by none.

Shortly before his end Pushkin is reported to have advised his wife to go to the country after his death, wear mourning for a couple of years, and then marry a respectable man. The loss of her husband had been a terrible shock to Natasha. Illness had prevented her from attending the church services or the burial, and for a time she no doubt suffered as much mentally as physically. Few of her associates in Petersburg high society blamed Natasha for her part in the tragedy; but the majority of Pushkin's intellectual friends, while sorry for the beautiful young widow, were more or less convinced that her unintelligent and indiscreet conduct had been largely responsible for the duel. And popular opinion was unanimous in condemning Natasha. With little variation this unfavorable judgment on her character has persisted to the present day.

There are extenuating factors, however, which mitigate her fault if they do not entirely exculpate her. Intellectually and spiritually she was a very ordinary woman, and it was her great misfortune to be married to a genius. She had married without love, and during the seven years of their life together she had never learned to love or to understand her husband. No doubt it was beyond her limited intellect to understand Pushkin. But if she had been able to return his own great love for her, she might have been inspired to make those sacrifices which would have done much to smooth away the innumerable difficulties that dogged the last years of Pushkin's life. She was reasonably dutiful, faithful, and even jealous, but exasperatingly obtuse in human relations. Unable to take part in Pushkin's intellectual life, she sought an outlet in the giddy pleasures of an exclusive society where she could dazzle all by her beauty. Once she had discovered her proper sphere, it became the passion of her existence, which she indulged to the exclusion of all else. She preferred the whirling of the ballroom and the flirting of her many admirers to the company of her husband and the conversation of his literary friends. No illuminating statements of Natasha's, no expression of fine feeling, no indications of refined taste have survived. She was simply a beautiful doll.

On the basis of the social conventions of the time, Natasha's behavior with D'Anthès before November 1836 deserves little censure. She was aware of the young officer's love for her, but, being confident of her own self-control, she could not see in this anything more than the harmless sort of flirtation which was an accepted practice in her social set. But the "cuckold

letter" and the gossip after Pushkin's November challenge ought
to have been an unequivocal warning to Natasha that the affair
must end. Yet her behavior did not change, and the attention
she paid to D'Anthès after his engagement and marriage has
no justification other than that she was in love with him. Love
has its own justification. But since she did nothing about this
love, and at the same time ignored the terrible moral suffering
that was driving her husband to destruction, Natasha placed
herself in the unenviable position of being the passive motiva-
tion of a tragedy. She never seemed to think, and for posterity she will continue to be, as one writer put it, the important
witness who must always remain under suspicion in the death
of her husband. In this drama Natasha played the part of a
silent character whose extraordinary beauty was the tragic
theme of the play. Perhaps she said nothing because she had
nothing to say.

Shortly after Pushkin's death Natasha retired to the Kaluga
estate of the Goncharovs and remained there for two years.
There was something ironical in this voluntary desertion of
Petersburg society. Two years before, she had opposed her
husband's earnest wish to forsake the capital for the village
because this same society had seemed so necessary to her happiness. Now she lived quietly in the country, regaining her
strength and forgetting her grief. But she missed Petersburg
and readily acceded to the desire of her doting aunt Zagryazhskaya, who was no doubt prompted by people high in court
circles, that she return to the capital. The tsar frequently
inquired about the young widow and made it clear that he
wished her to take a part once more in court festivities. At a
costume ball at the Anichkov Palace, Natasha reëntered society. She had lost little of her striking beauty, which was now
more mature and even somewhat enhanced by the sad expression of her face. The tsar was delighted with her appearance,
paid her a great deal of attention, and had her portrait painted
in the attractive costume which she wore on this occasion.

Her demeanor, however, was much subdued, and she did not
resume social life on the same scale as before. Now her few

activities came more directly under the patronage of the tsar. In 1844 she met P. P. Lanskoi, a major general in the Life Guards Cavalry. Nicholas was very much in favor of a match, and in the course of the same year Natasha married this man.

Lanskoi became a prime favorite with the tsar, and his career advanced very swiftly after his marriage. He was promoted to the rank of adjutant general and served on important commissions. The tsar had given the bride away, sent the pair presents, and attended the christening of their first child. He appears to have become quite intimate with this favored couple, visiting their house in person. Many years after the marriage a story was told which, however, lacks any real authenticity. A man entered the Moscow Historical Museum and offered for sale a watch which bore the monogram of Nicholas I. Since such watches were not rarities, the attendant was surprised at the high price demanded. The man opened the back cover of the watch and revealed on the inner side a miniature portrait of Natasha. Then he explained that his grandfather had served as a valet to the tsar and knew the secret of this picture. When the tsar died the valet took the watch "in order that there should be no awkwardness in the family." [2] The museum did not buy the watch, and the man disappeared without leaving his name.

This second marriage appears to have been a happy one and gave Natasha that spiritual calm, satisfaction, and social contentment which were markedly absent in her unequal union with Pushkin. She died on November 26, 1863.

The conduct of the tsar and his government in all matters relating to the duel is extremely puzzling. Nicholas, of course, knew about the dangerous situation involving Pushkin and D'Anthès. Gossip and Benkendorf's spies would certainly have brought to his attention what he did not observe himself. By virtue of his far-flung espionage system it is very likely that he knew much more about the anonymous letter and the intriguing of Heeckeren than Pushkin. And likewise the November challenge had unquestionably come to his ears. The tsar was perhaps the only man in Russia who could have interrupted the sequence of events leading up to the fatal duel. Had he been solicitous for the welfare of Pushkin, for the protection of the country's greatest poetic genius, he might easily have taken steps to prevent the duel. Yet he did nothing, and one can infer from his own actions and statements that he knowingly let Pushkin march to his death.

By tradition Nicholas is supposed to have disliked family scandals, yet there were occasions when he interfered in such matters in a very decisive way. The situation, no doubt, would have been saved if the tsar had simply agreed to move D'Anthès from Petersburg to a distant army post. It is even on record that General Adlerberg, who became alarmed over the consequences of D'Anthès' behavior, advised that the young officer be shipped away for a time. But the tsar did not approve of such a step. D'Anthès was an adornment at court balls, and the tsar's brother enjoyed his company because of his ready wit. Furthermore, Nicholas may have had reasons of his own for allowing the quarrel to take its destined course.

After Pushkin's death a deliberate attempt was made by close friends to protect the interests of the poet's family and to sanctify his memory for posterity. The well-known letter of Vyazemski to the tsar's brother and that of Zhukovski to Pushkin's father were efforts in this direction. These two friends tried to draw a picture of Pushkin during his last hours which would endear him to the country and the tsar. They portrayed his wife as a blameless woman and Pushkin himself as a worshiper of Nicholas and his system, a good Christian, a man at peace with the world. For his own purposes the tsar was willing to accept this picture, but he was not at all fooled by it. He wished to appear before the people as a protector of the poet and his family, yet he had no intention of making a martyr of him or of contributing anything to his popular glorification. The tsar's message to Pushkin on his deathbed, transmitted by Dr. Arendt, was intended as a gesture of deep sympathy and anxious concern for his family. And the generous provisions he made for the family testify to his good faith. All Pushkin's debts were to be paid; his father's estate was to be released from

PUSHKIN

debt; a pension was to be granted to the widow and her daughters until they married; the sons were to be made pages with fifteen hundred rubles a year until they entered the service; Pushkin's works were to be published at state expense and the profits were to accrue to the widow; and a lump sum of ten thousand rubles was to be allocated for funeral and immediate expenses. This is regal munificence and a spirit of generosity on the part of the tsar which unfortunately manifested itself only after Pushkin's death.

Nicholas has been praised for this show of kindness to the poet's family. But the strange conduct of the government before and after the funeral, and the actions and statements of the tsar himself throw some doubt upon the sincerity of his motives. If Nicholas aided the family, he did not do it in the name of Pushkin or from any conviction of the national significance of the poet's literary accomplishment. There were other considerations. The influence of Zhukovski counted for much, and no doubt his liking for the beautiful Natasha, whom he loved to see at his court balls, was a factor. The tsar was also too clever a monarch to neglect such a splendid opportunity to glorify his own magnanimity in the eyes of the public.

In reality, the opinions of both the tsar and Benkendorf about Pushkin had not essentially altered since that time in 1825 when they became firmly convinced of his connection with the Decembrists. Neither Nicholas nor his chief of police could forget the fearful events of the fourteenth of December. No one who was in any way involved in the revolt was ever entirely removed from suspicion. The fear that Nicholas had experienced on that unfortunate day remained to haunt him throughout his reign. In the last years of his life the poet could never understand why they continued to spy on him and why the tsar persistently conditioned his favor by placing one obstacle after another in his path. The answer is that, for Nicholas, Pushkin was always one of the "friends of the fourteenth." The tsar played an ambiguous role in all his relations with the poet, and it did not cease with Pushkin's death.

Zhukovski was ordered by Nicholas to inspect and catalogue

the posthumous papers of Pushkin. Benkendorf at once interfered. He guessed that among these manuscripts would be material inimical to the government, and he had no difficulty in convincing his sovereign of this. Consequently, an assistant of the Third Section was assigned to supervise the inspection of Zhukovski. The good friend of the poet protested vehemently, but Benkendorf had his way. In one case, at least, the tsar was prepared to prosecute a friend of Pushkin's on evidence discovered among these papers. Poor Zhukovski found himself placed in the ignominious position of a police spy.

When the great historian Karamzin had died, Zhukovski had been allowed to draw up a manifesto of the nation's bereavement. He now requested permission to do the same for Pushkin. Nicholas refused, coldly replying to Zhukovski: "I am ready to do everything for Pushkin, but I cannot compare him in esteem to Karamzin, who died like an angel." [3] The tsar wrote to Paskevich, the general who had sent Pushkin home from the Caucasus, telling him of the death of the poet. Paskevich replied, regretting the tragedy in conventional phrases and adding, "However, he was a vicious man." "I fully share your opinion of Pushkin," [4] wrote Nicholas, an answer which hardly supports the favorable opinion of the poet which the tsar put forth for public consumption.

Nicholas simply did not trust Pushkin, and the extraordinary precautions taken by the government during his last hours and at the funeral are a measure of that distrust. For various reasons Benkendorf had become convinced that Pushkin was a member, and possibly the leader, of a new political conspiracy. He actually feared a popular uprising in Pushkin's name, and every provision was made to guard against a disturbance. Perhaps the agitated state of the populace warranted such fears. Pushkin's personal friends were horrified by the tragedy. These frenzied lines of one of his old Lyceum comrades to another member of the first class are typical of numerous outbursts of indignation: "Pushkin is killed! Yakovlev! Why did you permit it? What villain dared raise his hand against him! Yakovlev! Yakovlev! How could you permit it?" [5] Mickiewicz sent an open challenge to D'Anthès, eager to avenge his friend. And Pushkin's heartbroken brother was barely restrained from calling out the Frenchman to a duel.

What the government feared, however, was the vindictive attitude of huge numbers of the middle class and the intelligentsia. Their resentment was directed against foreigners and members of aristocratic society who, in the minds of these people, were largely to blame for Pushkin's fate. It is an interesting fact that the public at this time regarded Pushkin as a leader of liberal thought and action. Thus the natural and sincerely liberal trend of his mind, which had been under a cloud ever since his "pardon" by the tsar, was discovered by the people only after his death. Very few of the foreign envoys in Petersburg failed to report the tragedy to their respective governments. They considered the fact politically significant because of the popular indignation, which they described as a liberal manifestation against an autocratic power. In some instances they even wrote of Pushkin as the leader of a reform movement. One envoy refused to attend the funeral because he felt that his presence would be interpreted by the government as an indication of liberal leanings.

A few days after Pushkin's death a manuscript poem went the rounds of Petersburg. The author lamented the poet's tragic fate, cursed his foreign murderer, and concluded with a vehement denunciation of those "haughty descendants"

Of celebrated sires whose baseness is their fame,
Who lightly trampled in the dust with servile heel
The hopes of an embittered people and its name!
You, greedy crowd, behind the sovereign's throne you draw,
The hangmen of our freedom, genius, and renown!
You hide yourselves beneath the shelter of the law.
Before you, truth and justice — yet on these you frown!
But God's high court remains, you confidants of crime.
His judgment threatens: He will wait,
Nor is He moved by golden bait;
Your thoughts and actions all He knows before their time.
Before this Judge you whisper slander quite in vain:
It will avail you nothing more,
And never will your shameful blood wipe out again
The murdered poet's gore! [6]

This bitter poem was obviously aimed at Benkendorf and those
aristocratic enemies of Pushkin who had slandered his honor
and still whispered praise of D'Anthès in their exclusive gatherings. The verses were on everybody's lips, and it is little wonder
that the tsar and his chief of police feared the influence of the
dead Pushkin. The author of the poem was a young lieutenant
of the Hussars by the name of Lermontov. He was promptly
arrested, convicted of the offense of honoring Pushkin in this
manner, and sent to the Caucasus. The public immediately
recognized, however, that the mantle of the dead Pushkin had
fallen on the shoulders of this young poet who had mourned his
death in such rhetorical but eloquent verse.

The widespread public indignation over his death and the
popular estimate of him as a liberal force would have surprised
Pushkin. But Lermontov's scathing condemnation of Petersburg aristocratic society in his poem would have delighted him.
For the tragedy of his life was the tragedy of a man crushed by
the society in which he lived and by the rulers whom he was
obliged to obey. Pushkin possessed a brilliant mind and was
endowed with a poetic talent the equal of which Russian literature has never known since. Although proud, passionate, and
conscious of his own worth, at heart he was essentially good,
kind, fair, devoted in friendship, and profoundly sincere in his
convictions. He was wise in the knowledge of the human heart,
but in the daily affairs of his own life he could be childishly
naïve. To people strange to his spirit and interests, Pushkin
seemed inaccessible and even dull. They saw nothing of the
beauty of his spiritual nature, of its complexities and depth. All
those who knew him well, however, valued his genius and loved
him for the rare quality of his rebellious, restless spirit. In the
draft of his fatal letter to Heeckeren he wrote of himself: "I am
good and simple . . . but my heart is sensitive." [7] And this
estimate is entirely just.

Pushkin's life was an endless discord between his inner spiritual being and the external facts of existence. Circumstances
over which he had little control placed him in a difficult and
sometimes unendurable position. His genius demanded freedom

to live and to create as it desired. Instead of this, Pushkin's spiritual and material existence throughout all his mortal days was shackled with chains which he could never break. Instead of enjoying the inner freedom which would have given his genius the possibility of expanding over a broader and deeper sphere of activities, he was condemned to struggle under the maddening conditions of exile, police surveillance, governmental interference, and social obstacles. Instead of enjoying material security he was constantly in debt, harassed by creditors, and forced to shoulder the obligations of his own family and those of his parents. All the facts of existence contrived to wear him down physically and emotionally, and to break the wings of his genius. Although he was an optimist by nature, the prevailing note in Pushkin's poetry is not that of joy. We hear rather a pervasive tone of melancholy, grief, and suffering. The frequent passages of joy and hope only serve to emphasize this consciousness of the inevitable sadness of life.

As the years passed and his difficulties increased, Pushkin desperately sought to escape the bonds that were crushing out his spiritual life and making even the problems of material existence insuperable. But there was no escape. His last desperate effort to free himself succeeded — but his escape was the escape of death.

NOTES

Notes

CHAPTER I

1. *Perepiska Pushkina*, ed. V. I. Saitov (St. Petersburg, 1906–1911), No. 171, I, 232.
2. *Ibid.*, No. 172, I, 233.
3. "Rodoslovnaya Pushkinykh i Gannibalov," *Polnoe Sobranie Sochineni* (4th ed., Moscow, 1934), VI, 382.*
4. *Ibid.*
5. "Nabroski predisloviya k Borisu Godunovu" (VI, 296).
6. "Rodoslovnaya Pushkinykh i Gannibalov" (VI, 383).
7. Cf. *Syn otechestva* (1840), No. 7, II, pp. 464–465; *Sovremennik* (1840), XIX, 102–106.
8. "Rodoslovnaya Pushkinykh i Gannibalov" (VI, 386).

CHAPTER II

1. P. I. Bartenev, "Materialy dlya biografii Pushkina," *Moskovskie Vedomosti* (1854), No. 71.
2. Cf. "Son" (I, 236–237).
3. "Zimni vecher" (I, 418).
4. "Nyane" (II, 202).
5. "Programma zapisok" (VI, 380–381).
6. "Russki Pelam" (IV, 702–703).
7. "O narodnom vospitanii" (VI, 433).
8. "K sestre" (I, 112).
9. "Gorodok" (I, 115).
10. "Molodost A. S. Pushkina po razskazam ego mladshago brata," in L. N. Maikov, *Pushkin: biograficheskie materialy istoriko-literaturnye ocherki* (St. Petersburg, 1899), p. 4.
11. "Bova" (I, 139).

CHAPTER III

1. Cf. *Zapiski I. I. Pushchina o Pushkine* (St. Petersburg, 1907), p. 8.
2. *Ibid.*, pp. 10–11.
3. I. Ya. Seleznev, *Istoricheski ocherk Imperatorskago nyne Aleksandrovskago Litseya za pervoe ego pyatidesyatiletie* (Petersburg, 1861), p. 18.
4. *Ibid.*, pp. 18–23.
5. *Zapiski I. I. Pushchina o Pushkine*, p. 15.
6. *Ibid.*, p. 23.
7. "Byla pora: nash prazdnik molodoi" (II, 255).
8. "K Galichu" (I, 155).
9. "19 Oktyabrya," variant (I, 552).

* Unless otherwise noted, all references to Pushkin's works are to *Polnoe Sobranie Sochineni* (2nd ed., Moscow, 1934), vols. I–VI.

10. "Zapiski M. A. Korfa," in Ya. K. Grot, *Pushkin, ego litseiskie tovarishchi i nastavniki* (St. Petersburg, 1899), p. 219.
11. K. Ya. Grot, *Pushkinski litsei* (St. Petersburg, 1911), p. 361.
12. I. A. Shlyapkin, *Iz neizdannykh bumag Pushkina* (St. Petersburg, 1903), p. 325.
13. *Ibid.*
14. V. P. Gaevski, "Delvig," *Sovremennik* (1853), No. 2, III, 67.
15. *Ibid.*
16. "Mon Portrait" (I, 135).
17. A. S. Griboedov, *Gore ot duma*, Act III, scene 12.
18. Shlyapkin, *Iz neizdannykh bumag Pushkina*, p. 326.
19. S. P. Shevyrev, "Vospominaniya o Pushkine," in L. N. Maikov, *Pushkin*, p. 326.
20. "Zapiski M. A. Korfa," in Ya. K. Grot, *Pushkin, ego litseiskie tovarishchi*, p. 249.
21. *Zapiski I. I. Pushchina o Pushkine*, p. 24.
22. P. V. Annenkov, *Pushkin v Aleksandrovskuiu epokhu* (St. Petersburg, 1874), p. 53.

CHAPTER IV

1. "K molodoi vdove" (I, 244).
2. *Zapiski I. I. Pushchina o Pushkine*, p. 37.
3. "Kn. V. M. Volkonskoi" (I, 528).
4. *Russkaya Starina* (1879), XXV, 378–379 (told by K. A. Shtorkh).
5. K. Ya. Grot, *Pushkinski litsei*, p. 254.
6. *Ibid.*
7. *Ibid.*, p. 35.
8. *Ibid.*, p. 60.
9. *Zapiski I. I. Pushchina o Pushkine*, pp. 25–26.
10. "Zapiski S. D. Komovski," in Ya. K. Grot, *Pushkin, ego litseiskie tovarishchi*, p. 221.
11. *Zapiski I. I. Pushchina o Pushkine*, p. 32.
12. *Perepiska*, No. 1, I, 1.
13. P. V. Annenkov, *Materialy dlya biografii A. S. Pushkina* (St. Petersburg, 1873), p. 34.
14. *Perepiska*, No. 4, I, 5.
15. Ya. K. Grot, *Pushkin, ego litseiskie tovarishchi*, p. 47.
16. *Perepiska*, No. 3, I, 4.
17. "Vospominaniya v Tsarskom Sele" (I, 90).
18. "O Derzhavine" (VI, 337).
19. V. P. Gaevski, in *Sovremennik* (1863), No. 8, p. 370.
20. F. N. Glinka, *Vospominanie o piiticheskoi zhizni Pushkina* (Moscow, 1873), p. 13.
21. K. Ya. Grot, *Pushkinski litsei*, p. 224 ("Iz litseiskikh 'Natsionalnykh Pesni'").
22. "Iz litseiskogo dnevnika, 1815" (VI, 366).
23. *Vestnik Evropy.*
24. "K drugu stikhotvortsu" (I, 79).
25. *Ibid.* (I, 81).
26. "Pushkinu."
27. "Evgeni Onegin," I, viii (IV, 14).
28. "Programma zapisok" (VI, 380).
29. "Zapiski S. D. Komovski," in Ya. K. Grot, *Pushkin, ego litseiskie tovarishchi*, p. 220.
30. "Poslanie k Natali" (I, 96).
31. "Iz litseiskogo dnevnika, 1815" (VI, 365–366).

32. "K Zhivopistsu" (I, 181).
33. "Poslanie k Kn. A. M. Gorchakovu" (I, 256).
34. "Elegiya" (I, 222).
35. "Mesyats" (I, 224).
36. "Elegiya" (I, 226).
37. "Evgeni Onegin," II, x (IV, 39).
38. *Ibid.* (IV, 226).
39. "Piruiushchie studenti" (I, 109).
40. "Poslanie Lide" (I, 211).
41. "Chaadaevu" (I, 311).
42. *Perepiska*, No. 2, I, 3.
43. "Evgeni Onegin," I, vi (IV, 13).
44. *Perepiska*, No. 101, I, 140.
45. Gaevski, "Pushkin v litsee," *Sovremennik* (1863), XCVII, 376.
46. "Zapiski M. A. Korfa" in Ya. K. Grot, *Pushkin, ego litseiskie tovarishchi*, p. 249.
47. "19 Oktyabrya" (I, 414).
48. "Bezverie" (I, 245).

CHAPTER V

1. "Iz avtobiograficheskikh zapisok" (VI, 374).
2. "V. V. Engelhardtu" (I, 280).
3. V. Ertel, "Vypiska iz bumag dyadi Aleksandra," *Russki Almanakh na 1832 i 1833 gody* (St. Petersburg, 1833), pp. 285–300.
4. A. M. Karatygina-Kolosova, "Vospominaniya," *Russkaya Starina* (1880), XXVIII, 568.
5. Cf. "Evgeni Onegin," I, xxxv (IV, 25).
6. *Perepiska*, No. 11, I, II.
7. "Moi zamechaniya o russkom teatre" (VI, 7).
8. Karatygina-Kolosova, "Vospominaniya," p. 568.
9. "Moi zamechaniya o russkom teatre" (VI, 7–13).
10. *Perepiska*, No. 219, I, 308.
11. Kn. P. P. Vyazemski, *Sobranie sochineni* (St. Petersburg, 1893), p. 476.
12. P. I. Bartenev, *Pushkin v iuzhnoi Rossii* (2nd ed., Moscow, 1914), p. 101.
13. O. M. Bodyanski, "Dnevnik," *Russkaya Starina* (1889), LX, 414.
14. I. I. Lazhechnikov, "Znakomstvo moe s Pushkinym," *Sochineniya*, ed. M. O. Volf (St. Petersburg, 1884), IV, 233–238.
15. "Vse prizrak, sueta" (I, 453).
16. P. P. Kaverin, *Tetrad, 1824–1830* (Moscow, 1913), p. 16.
17. "Iurevu" (I, 276).
18. "Iz zapisnoi knizhki, 1820–1822 gg." (VI, 374).
19. *Ostafevski Arkhiv Knyazei Vyazemskikh*, ed. Count S. D. Sheremetev (St. Petersburg, 1899 ff.), I, 174.
20. *Ibid.*, I, 119.
21. *Ibid.*, I, 253.
22. *Ibid.*, I, 200.
23. "Za starye grekhi nakazanny sudboi" (I, 453).
24. L. N. Pavlishchev, *Vospominaniya ob A. S. Pushkine* (Moscow, 1890), p. 17.
25. "Zapiski M. A. Korfa," in Ya. K. Grot, *Pushkin, ego litseiskie tovarishchi*, p. 250.
26. F. N. Glinka, in *Russkaya Starina* (1871), III, 245.
27. *Starina i Novizna*, I, 43.
28. *Osël i Muzhik*.

29. A. P. Kern, "Vospominaniya," in L. N. Maikov, *Pushkin*, p. 236.
30. "K. A. P. Kern" (I, 402).
31. P. V. Annenkov, *Materialy*, p. 50.
32. "Iz avtobiograficheskikh zapisok" (VI, 377).
33. *Ibid.* (VI, 379).
34. *Russki Arkhiv* (1896), III, 208.
35. *Ostafevski Arkhiv*, I, 119.
36. K. N. Batiushkov, *Sochineniya*, ed. P. N. Batiushkov (St. Petersburg, 1886):
    K. N. Batiushkov to A. I. Turgenev, Sept. 10, 1818.
37. Annenkov, *Materialy*, p. 50.
38. *Ostafevski Arkhiv*, I, 174.
39. "Ruslan i Liudmila" (III, 9–93).

CHAPTER VI

1. *Perepiska*, No. 11, I, 11.
2. S. A. Sobolevski, "Tainstvennye primety v zhizni Pushkina," *Russki Arkhiv* (1870), pp. 1328–1386.
3. "Litsiniiu" (I, 427).
4. "K Chaadaevu" (I, 535).
5. *Zapiski I. I. Pushchina o Pushkine*, p. 45.
6. *Ibid.*, pp. 50–51.
7. *Ibid.*, p. 51.
8. Annenkov, *Pushkin v Aleksandrovskuiu epokhu*, p. 85.
9. "Na Fotiya" (I, 538).
10. "Na Gr. A. A. Arakcheeva" (I, 538).
11. "Vospitanny pod barabanom" (I, 542).
12. "Derevnya" (I, 282).
13. "Noël" (I, 533).
14. "Volnost" (I, 269).
15. *Ibid.* (I, 271).
16. *Ibid.* (I, 269).
17. *Zapiski I. I. Pushchina o Pushkine*, p. 46.
18. I. D. Yakushkin, *Zapiski* (Moscow, 1905), p. 67.
19. *Zapiski I. I. Pushchina o Pushkine*, p. 46.
20. *Ibid.*
21. A. I. Mikhailovski-Davilevski, "Zapiski," *Russkaya Starina* (1890), No. 11, p. 505.
22. *Ostafevski Arkhiv*, II, 26.
23. *Pisma Karamzina k Dmitrievu* (St. Petersburg, 1866), pp. 286–287.
24. F. N. Glinka, "Udalenie Pushkina iz Peterburga," *Russki Arkhiv* (1866), p. 918.
25. *Ibid.*
26. *Zapiski I. I. Pushchina o Pushkine*, pp. 53–54.
27. *Ostafevski Arkhiv*, II, 37.
28. *Perepiska*, No. 167, I, 224.
29. "Evgeni Onegin," I, xxxvi (IV, 25).
30. *Perepiska*, No. 13, I, 15.
31. "Pismo Min. In. Del., Gr. K. V. Nesselrode Gen-Leitenantu Inzovu ot 4 maya, 1820 g.," *Russkaya Starina* (1887), LIII, 241.
32. P. I. Bartenev, *Pushkin v iuzhnoi Rossii*, p. 15.
33. A. N. Veselovski, *V. A. Zhukovski* (St. Petersburg, 1904); see frontispiece.

CHAPTER VII

1. M. F. De Pule, *Russki Arkhiv* (1879), III, 136.
2. *Perepiska*, No. 16, I, 19.
3. M. Gershenzon, *Mudrost Pushkina* (Moscow, 1919), p. 156.
4. *Russki Arkhiv* (1863), p. 900.
5. *Perepiska*, No. 16, I, 20.
6. *Ibid.*
7. *Ibid.*, No. 116, I, 159.
8. J. Galt, *Life of Lord Byron* (London, 1830), pp. 65–74.
9. "Pogaslo dnevnoe svetilo" (I, 299).
10. *Perepiska*, No. 16, I, 21.
11. *Ibid.*, No. 116, I, 160.
12. "Evgeni Onegin" I, xxxiii (IV, 24).
13. Kn. M. N. Volkonskaya, *Zapiski*, 2nd ed. (Moscow, 1921), p. 62.
14. Cf. A. de Ribas, "Pismo Pushkina k neizvestnoi, 1822," *Pushkin Vremennik* (Akademiya Nauk, Moscow, 1936), pp. 227–231.
15. "Bakhchisaraiski Fontan" (III, 144).
16. *Perepiska*, No. 53, I, 75.
17. *Ibid.*, No. 84, I, 121.
18. "Epilog. Ruslan i Liudmila" (III, 92).
19. *Perepiska*, No. 16, I, 19.
20. "Demon" (I, 353–354).
21. "Kavkazski plennik" (III, 94).
22. "Kavkazski plennik," "Bratya-razboiniki," "Bakhchisaraiski Fontan," "Tsygani."
23. *Perepiska*, No. 116, I, 160.
24. *Ibid.*
25. *Ibid.*, No. 116, I, 160–161.
26. *Ibid.*, 161.
27. "Posvyashchenie: Kavkazski plennik" (III, 94).

CHAPTER VIII

1. I. P. Liprandi, *Russki Arkhiv* (1866), pp. 1412–1416.
2. "Chernaya shal" (I, 301).
3. V. P. Gorchakov, "Iz dnevnika ob A. S. Pushkine," *Moskvityanin* (1850), No. 2, pp. 152–153.
4. *Perepiska*, No. 17, I, 22.
5. "A. L. Davydovu" (I, 359).
6. "Evgeni Onegin," I, xii (IV, 16).
7. "Koketke" (I, 331).
8. "Inoi imel moiu Aglaiu" (I, 333).
9. Yakushkin, *Zapiski*, p. 49.
10. "Adeli" (I, 340).
11. P. I. Bartenev, "K biografii Pushkina," *Russki Arkhiv* (1866), p. 1131.
12. Yakushkin, *Zapiski*, pp. 51–52.
13. Cf. "Zametki po russkoi istorii XVIII v." (VI, 178–184).
14. See "Neizvestny plan stati Pushkina o feodalizme," *Literaturnoe Nasledstvo* (1934), pp. 880–882; see also Pushkin, "Zametki po istorii frantsuzskoi revoliutsii" (VI, 189–191).

15. "Kinzhal" (I, 317).
16. I. A. Smirnov, *Dela o Pushkine* (Odessa, 1899), p. 9.
17. P. I. Bartenev, *Pushkin v iuzhnoi Rossii*, p. 111.
18. *Ibid.*
19. "Voobrazhaemy razgovor s Aleksandrom I" (VI, 375).
20. "Bessarabskiya vospominaniya A. F. Beltmana," in L. N. Maikov, *Pushkin*, pp. 126–127.
21. Bartenev, *Pushkin v iuzhnoi Rossii*, p. 103.
22. N. Gerbanovski, "Neskolko slov o prebyvanii Pushkina v g. Kishineve," *Novorossiskie Vedomosti* (1869), No. 49.
23. Pushkin, *Pisma*, ed. B. L. Modzalevski (Moscow, 1926), No. 32, I, 26.
24. Bartenev, *Pushkin v iuzhnoi Rossii*, p. 108.
25. *Perepiska*, No. 24, I, 34.
26. "Iz Kishinevskogo dnevnika" (VI, 371).
27. "Voina" (I, 323).
28. "Vosstan, O Gretsiya, vosstan" (II, 225).
29. Pushkin, *Pisma*, No. 22, I, 19.
30. *Perepiska*, No. 82, I, 118–119.
31. V. P. Gorchakov, "Vyderzhki iz dnevnika," *Moskvityanin* (1850), No. 2, p. 156.
32. "Moi drug, uzhe tri dnya" (I, 471).
33. "So slov Kishinevskikh starozhilov," *Russki Arkhiv* (1899), II, 343.
34. "Tsygany" (III, 174).
35. *Perepiska*, No. 49, I, 69.
36. "Grechanke" (I, 341).
37. Cf. *Perepiska*, No. 278, I, 378; see also E. J. Simmons, "Byron and a Greek Maid," *Modern Language Review*, XXVII (1932), No. 3, pp. 318–323.

CHAPTER IX

1. Cf. V. F. Raevski, "Vecher v Kishineve," *Literaturnoe Nasledstvo* (1934), pp. 660–662.
2. "Iz Kishinevskogo dnevnika" (VI, 372).
3. N. V. Basargin, *Zapiski* (ed. "Ogni," 1917), p. 24.
4. *Perepiska*, No. 19, I, 28.
5. "Eugene Onegin," I, xlvii (IV, 28).
6. *Perepiska*, No. 54, I, 78.
7. *Ibid.*, No. 50, I, 71.
8. "Napoleon na Elbe" (I, 150).
9. "Napoleon" (I, 320).
10. "Svod neba mrakom oblozhilsya" (I, 346).
11. "Pesn o veshchem Olege" (I, 334).
12. *Severnoe Obozrenie* (1849), I, 867.
13. "K Ovidiiu" (I, 327).
14. "Boratynskomu iz Bessarabii" (I, 342).
15. *Perepiska*, No. 47, I, 65.
16. "Tsygany" (III, 172).
17. "Tsar Nikita" (I, 474).
18. "Gavriliada" (III, 120).
19. *Russkaya Starina*, Jan. 1887, p. 244.
20. *Ibid.* (1883), XL, 657.
21. *Perepiska*, No. 25, I, 35.

22. *Ibid.*, No. 20, I, 30.
23. *Ibid.*, No. 38, I, 53.
24. *Ibid.*, No. 34, I, 46.
25. *Ibid.*, No. 44, I, 61.
26. *Ibid.*, No. 42, I, 58.
27. *Ostafevski Arkhiv*, II, 187.
28. *Perepiska*, No. 40, I, 55–56.
29. *Ostafevski Arkhiv*, II, 322.
30. *Ibid.*, II, 327.
31. *Perepiska*, No. 289, I, 388.

CHAPTER X

1. *Perepiska*, No. 53, I, 75.
2. "Puteshestvie Onegina" (IV, 191, 192).
3. *Ibid.* (IV, 196).
4. *Perepiska*, No. 53, I, 76.
5. *Russki Arkhiv*, 1873, p. 1795.
6. *Perepiska*, No. 32, I, 44.
7. *Ibid.*, No. 48, I, 67.
8. *Ibid.*, No. 25, I, 35.
9. *Ibid.*, No. 65, I, 94.
10. *Ibid.*, No. 69, I, 102.
11. "Razgovor Knigoprodavtsa s poetom" (I, 369).
12. "Vzglyad na staruiu i novuiu slovesnost v Rossii," *Polyarnaya Zvezda* (1823), pp. 1–44.
13. *Perepiska*, No. 57, I, 83–84.
14. *Ibid.*, No. 65, I, 95.
15. "Tsygany" (III, 178).
16. *Ibid.* (III, 185).
17. *Perepiska*, No. 166, I, 223.
18. "Tsygany" (III, 178).
19. *Ibid.* (III, 186).
20. *Perepiska*, No. 150, I, 202.
21. "K moriu" (I, 369).
22. *Perepiska*, No. 82, I, 118.
23. *Ibid.*, No. 66, I, 97.
24. "Puteshestvie Onegina" (IV, 192).
25. I. P. Liprandi, *Russki Arkhiv* (1866), p. 1472.
26. F. F. Vigel, *Zapiski* (ed. S. Ya. Shtraikh, Moscow, 1928), II, 204–205.
27. *Perepiska*, No. 56, I, 81, 82.
28. V. A. Yakovlev, *Otzyvy o Pushkine s iuga Rossii* (Odessa, 1887), p. 145.
29. *Ibid.*, p. 8.
30. *Perepiska*, No. 61, I, 88.
31. "V posledni raz tvoi obraz miloi," "Zaklinanie," "Dlya beregov otchizny dalnoi" (II, 88, 93, 97).
32. "Prostish li mne revnivye mechti" (I, 352).
33. "Pod nebom golubym . . ." (II, 7).
34. Vigel, *Zapiski*, II, 201.
35. "Talisman" (II, 26).
36. P. I. Bartenev, *Russki Arkhiv* (1884), III, 188.

37. Vigel, *Zapiski*, II, 245.
38. "Kovarnost" (I, 371).
39. *Perepiska*, No. 65, I, 94.
40. A. A. Sivers, "Pismo Gr. M. S. Vorontsova k. P. D. Kiselevu s otzyvom o Pushkine, Odessa, 6 mars, 1824," *Pushkin i ego sovremenniki* (1928), XXXVII, 137; in French.
41. "Na Gr. M. S. Vorontsova" (I, 360).
42. *Russkaya Starina* (1879), XXVI, 292 (Count M. S. Vorontsov to Count K. V. Nesselrode, March 28, 1824; in French).
43. N. O. Lerner, "Zametka o Pushkine," *Pushkin i ego sovremenniki* (1913), XVI, 68.
44. *Perepiska*, No. 70, I, 103.
45. *Russkaya Starina* (1871), IV, 669–673.
46. *Perepiska*, No. 71, I, 103–104.
47. Vigel, *Zapiski*, II, 246.
48. *Perepiska*, No. 75, I, 108–109.
49. "Sarancha" (I, 541).
50. *Perepiska*, No. 79, I, 114–115.
51. *Ibid.*, No. 81, I, 117.
52. *Ibid.*, No. 80, I, 116.
53. *Ostafevski Arkhiv*, V, 103, 109, 121.
54. *Perepiska*, No. 86, I, 124.
55. *Russkaya Starina* (1879), XXVI, 293 (Count K. V. Nesselrode to Count M. S. Vorontsov, July 11, 1824, from St. Petersburg; in French).
56. *Perepiska*, No. 112, I, 154.

CHAPTER XI

1. "Vesely pir" (I, 289).
2. A. Raspovov, "Vstrecha s A. S. Pushkinym," *Russkaya Starina* (1876), XV, 464.
3. *Perepiska*, No. 99, I, 137.
4. *Ibid.*, No. 103, I, 141–142.
5. *Ibid.*, No. 108, I, 147–148.
6. *Ibid.*, No. 111, I, 152.
7. B. L. Modzalevski, *Pushkin pod tainym nadzorom* (St. Petersburg, 1922), p. 32.
8. Chernovik k "Vnov ya posetil" (Lenin Library, tetrad No. 2384, p. 40).
9. "Evgeni Onegin," IV, xxxviii (IV, 88).
10. *Perepiska*, No. 99, I, 137.
11. *Ibid.*, No. 113, I, 156.
12. "Molodost Pushkina po razskazam ego mladshago brata," in L. N. Maikov, *Pushkin*, p. 9.
13. *Perepiska*, No. 101, I, 139.
14. *Zapiski I. I. Pushchina o Pushkine*, p. 56.
15. *Ibid.*, p. 61.
16. *Ibid.*, p. 65.
17. "I. I. Pushchinu" (II, 16).
18. *Zapiski I. I. Pushchina o Pushkine*, p. 66.
19. "Vospominaniya A. P. Markovoi-Vinogradskoi," in L. N. Maikov, *Pushkin*, p. 233.
20. *Ibid.*, p. 238.
21. *Perepiska*, No. 114, I, 157.
22. *Ibid.*, No. 160, I, 215.
23. "Vospominaniya A. P. Markovoi-Vinogradskoi," pp. 240–242.

24. *Ibid.*, p. 242.
25. "K. A. P. Kern" (I, 402).
26. *Perepiska*, No. 177, I, 239–240.
27. *Ibid.*, No. 179, I, 242–243.
28. *Ibid.*, No. 185, I, 249.
29. *Ibid.*, No. 196, I, 262–263.
30. *Ibid.*, No. 199, I, 269.
31. *Ibid.*, No. 200, I, 269–271.
32. *Ibid.*, No. 209, I, 291.
33. *Ibid.*, No. 216, I, 304.
34. "Vospominaniya A. P. Markovoi-Vinogradskoi," p. 246.
35. *Perepiska*, No. 223, I, 313.

CHAPTER XII

1. "19 Oktyabrya" (I, 413).
2. *Perepiska*, No. 237, I, 327.
3. "19 Oktyabrya" (I, 413).
4. *Perepiska*, No. 206, I, 285.
5. N. M. Yazykov, "Baronesse E. N. Vrevskoi (Vulf)."
6. *Perepiska*, No. 251, I, 345.
7. See P. E. Shchegolev, *Pushkin i muzhiki* (Moscow, 1928), pp. 9–57.
8. *Perepiska*, No. 308, II, 10–11.
9. See N. M. Yazykov, "K nyane A. S. Pushkine" and "Na smert nyani A. S. Push-kina."
10. *Perepiska*, No. 101, I, 140.
11. *Ibid.*, No. 112, I, 154.
12. "Zimni vecher" (I, 418).
13. *Perepiska*, No. 184, I, 249.
14. "O predislovii g-na Lemonte k perevodu Basen I. A. Krylova" (V, 18).
15. " 'Puteshestvie v Arzrum': Proekt predisloviya" (IV, 809).
16. "Zametki po povodu stati Kiukhelbekera, *O napravleni nashe poezii*" (VI, 20–21).
17. *Perepiska*, No. 117, I, 164.
18. "Prorok" (II, 15).
19. *Stikhotvoreniya Aleksandra Pushkina.*
20. "Evgeni Onegin," IV, xvi (IV, 79).
21. *Ibid.*, VI, viii (IV, 117).
22. *Ibid.*, VIII, xlii (IV, 177).
23. *Ibid.*, VIII, xlvii (IV, 179).
24. *Ibid.*, VIII, xlviii (IV, 180).
25. *Ibid.*, VIII, li (IV, 181).
26. *Perepiska*, No. 161, I, 216.
27. *Ibid.*, No. 184, I, 248.
28. "Zametka k Grafu Nulinu" (VI, 317).
29. "Graf Nulin" (III, 187).
30. *Perepiska*, No. 379, II, 89.
31. *Ibid.*, No. 379, II, 87.
32. *Ibid.*, No. 214, I, 301.

CHAPTER XIII

1. *Perepiska*, No. 111, I, 153.
2. *Ibid.*, No. 170, I, 231.

3. *Ibid.*, No. 162, I, 216.
4. *Ibid.*, No. 166, I, 222.
5. *Ibid.*, No. 167, I, 225.
6. *Ibid.*, No. 173, I, 233–234.
7. Pushkin, *Pisma*, No. 180a, II, 125.
8. *Perepiska*, No. 117, I, 165.
9. *Ibid.*, No. 154, I, 207.
10. *Ibid.*, No. 182, I, 245.
11. *Ibid.*, No. 215, I, 302.
12. *Ibid.*, No. 208, I, 288.
13. *Ibid.*, No. 224, I, 314.
14. Cf. M. V. Nechkina, *Katorga i ssylka* (Moscow, 1930), p. 21.
15. *Perepiska*, No. 228, I, 317–319.
16. *Ibid.*, No. 229, I, 319.
17. *Ibid.*, No. 243, I, 335.
18. *Ibid.*, No. 248, I, 340.
19. *Ibid.*, No. 257, I, 352.
20. Pushkin, *Pisma*, No. 206, II, 10.
21. Tetrad, 2368, list 38; cf. also A. Efros, *Risunki Poeta* (Academia, Moscow, 1933), pp. 221, 356.
22. B. L. Modzalevski, *Pushkin pod tainym nadzorom*, pp. 13–16.
23. P. V. Annenkov, *Pushkin v Aleksandrovskuiu epokhu*, p. 321.

CHAPTER XIV

1. M. I. Semevski, "Progulka v Trigorskoe," *S. Peterburgskie Vedomosti* (1866), No. 163.
2. *Perepiska*, No. 264, I, 364.
3. *Ibid.*, No. 235, I, 326.
4. *Ibid.*, No. 243, I, 335.
5. Gertsen, *Kolokol*, 1 marta, 1860 g., list 64, p. 534.
6. N. I. Lorer, "Zapiski moego vremyani," *Rukopis v biblioteke Kommunisticheskoi Akademii*, part I, 426–427. Cf. V. V. Veresaev, *Pushkin v zhizni* (5th ed., Academia, Moscow, 1932), I, 203.
7. M. A. Korf, "Zapiski," *Russkaya Starina* (1900), CI, 574.
8. *Ibid.*
9. A. S. Khomutova, "Pushkin," *Russki Arkhiv* (1867), p. 1066.
10. Lorer, "Zapiski moego vremyani."
11. P. I. Bartenev, *Russki Arkhiv* (1865), pp. 96, 389.
12. "Vosstan, vosstan, prorok Rossii" (cf. N. O. Lerner, *Pushkin i ego sovremenniki*, 1910, XIII, 18–29).
13. "Andrei Shene" (I, 393).
14. See P. E. Shchegolev, "Imperator Nikolai I i Pushkin v 1826 godu," *Pushkin, ocherki* (St. Petersburg, 1912) pp. 226–265.
15. B. L. Modzalevski, "Epizod iz zhizni Pushkina," *Krasnaya Gazeta* (1927), No. 34.
16. "Stansy" (II, 35).
17. F. I. Tiutchev, *Stikhotvoreniya*, ed. G. Chulkov (Moscow, 1935), p. 364.
18. B. L. Modzalevski, *Pushkin pod tainym nadzorom*, p. 30.
19. Kn. P. P. Vyazemski, *Sobranie sochineni* (St. Petersburg, 1893), p. 508.
20. Modzalevski, *Pushkin pod tainym nadzorom*, p. 33.
21. *Perepiska*, No. 273, I, 374.

22. M. P. Pogodin, "Iz vospominani o Pushkine," *Russki Arkhiv* (1865), p. 97.
23. *Severnye Tsvety.*
24. *Moskovski Telegraf.*
25. *Moskovski Vestnik.*
26. *Korrespondencya Adama Mickiewicza* (Paris, 1885), IV, 91.
27. "V Sibir" (II, 19).
28. I. A. Kubasov, *Dekabrist A. I. Odoevski* (St. Petersburg, 1922), p. 73.
29. *Perepiska*, No. 314, II, 23.
30. Pushkin, *Pisma*, No. 217, II, 17.
31. *Perepiska*, No. 279, I, 379.
32. *Ibid.*, No. 282, I, 382.
33. *Ibid.*, No. 291, I, 390–391.
34. *Ibid.*, No. 282, I, 382.
35. *Ibid.*, No. 290, I, 390.
36. "Stansy" (II, 17).
37. *Perepiska*, No. 274, I, 375.
38. L. Pavlishchev, *Vospominaniya ob A. S. Pushkine* (Moscow, 1890), p. 256.
39. *Ibid.*, p. 357.
40. *Perepiska*, No. 286, I, 386.
41. *Ibid.*, No. 294, I, 393.
42. *Ibid.*, No. 497, II, 2.
43. M. A. Korf, *Russkaya Starina* (1899), C, 87.
44. *Starina i Novizna*, VI, 4.
45. See G. O. Vinokur, "Kto byl tsenzorom *Borisa Godunova*," *Pushkin Vremennik* (Moscow, 1936), pp. 203–214.
46. *Dmitri Samozvanets.*
47. "O narodnom vospitanii" (VI, 431).
48. "A. N. Vulf i ego dnevnik," in L. N. Maikov, *Pushkin*, p. 177.
49. P. E. Shchegolev, "Pushkin v politicheskom protsesse 1826–1828 gg.," *Pushkin i ego sovremenniki* (1909), XI, 32–33.
50. *Perepiska*, No. 307, II, 10.
51. Modzalevski, *Pushkin pod tainym nadzorom*, p. 64.

CHAPTER XV

1. "Vospominanie" (II, 40).
2. Delvig, *Neizdannye stikhotvoreniya*, ed. M. L. Gofman (St. Petersburg, 1922), p. 111.
3. "Delvig i Pushkin; pismo A. P. Markovoi-Vinogradskoi (Kern) k A. P. Annenkov," *Pushkin i ego sovremenniki* (1907), V, 142.
4. "S. M. Delvig-A. N. Karelinoi, v fevr., 1830," in B. L. Modzalevski, *Pushkin* (Priboi, Moscow, 1929), p. 216.
5. "Cherep" (II, 28).
6. *Perepiska*, No. 252, I, 346.
7. *Ibid.*, No. 354, II, 60.
8. *Ibid.*, No. 322, II, 29.
9. B. L. Modzalevski, *Pushkin pod tainym nadzorom*, p. 37.
10. *Starina i Novizna*, VI, 6.
11. "Arion" (II, 23).
12. *Perepiska*, No. 330, II, 35.
13. "Arap Petra Velikogo" (IV, 249).

14. "V. P. Titov-M. P. Pogodinu, 18 iiulya, 1827 g., iz Peterburga," in N. Barsukov, *Zhizn i trudy Pogodina* (2nd ed., St. Petersburg, 1888), II, 71.

15. "Pikovaya dama" (IV, 805).

16. Cf. M. A. Tsyavlovski, "Pushkin i gr. D. F. Fikelmon," *Golos Minuvshego* (1922), No. 2, pp. 108–123, and *Rasskazy o Pushkine, zapisannye so slov ego druzei P. I. Bartenevym* (Moscow, 1925), pp. 36–37, 98–102; N. V. Izmailov, *Pisma Pushkina k E. M. Khitrovo* (Leningrad, 1927), pp. 72–74.

17. Cf. "Evgeni Onegin," VIII, xvi (IV, 163).

18. "Egipetskie nochi" (IV, 522).

19. "Portret" (II, 41–42).

20. See N. Kozmin, "Pushkin i Olenina," *Sbornik Pushkinskogo Doma na 1923 god* (Petrograd, 1922), pp. 31–34.

21. Pushkin, *Pisma*, No. 285, II, 59.

22. *Arkhiv br. Turgenevykh* (Petrograd, 1921), VI, 65.

23. "Chern" (II, 50).

24. "Stansy" (II, 35).

25. *Perepiska*, No. 357, II, 63.

26. Kn. P. A. Vyazemski, *Polnoe sobranie sochineni*, IX, 98.

27. "Vel. Kn. Konstantin Pavlovich — gen. A. Kh. Benkendorfu, 27 aprelya, 1828 g., iz Varshava," *Russki Arkhiv* (1884), II, 319.

28. *Dela III Otdeleniya ob A. S. Pushkine* (St. Petersburg, 1906), p. 332.

29. *Ibid.*, p. 343.

30. "Dar naprasny . . ." (II, 40–41).

31. *Perepiska*, No. 370, II, 79.

32. *Ibid.*, No. 425, II, 130.

33. *Ibid.*, No. 377, II, 84.

34. P. V. Annenkov, *Materialy*, p. 369.

35. *Golos Minuvshego* (1917), No. 11–12, p. 154.

36. A. Mickiewicz, *Le Globe*, May 25, 1837 (reprinted in Kn. P. A. Vyazemski, *Polnoe sobranie sochineni*, VII, 315).

37. *Perepiska*, No. 384, II, 92–93.

CHAPTER XVI

1. "Puteshestvie v Arzrum vo vremya pokhoda 1829 goda" (IV, 739).

2. *Starina i Novizna*, XXII, 38–39.

3. K. I. Savostyanov, "Rasskaz o vstrechakh s Pushkinym," *Pushkin i ego sovremenniki* (1928), XXXVII, 148.

4. "Puteshestvie v Arzrum vo vremya pokhoda 1829 goda" (IV, 737).

5. *Perepiska*, No. 425, II, 130.

6. *Ibid.*, No. 390, II, 97.

7. A. N. Vulf, "Dnevnik," *Pushkin i ego sovremenniki* (1915), XXI–XXII, 115.

8. *Perepiska*, No. 389, II, 96.

9. *Ibid.*, No. 392, II, 100.

10. *Literaturnaya Gazeta*.

11. *Perepiska*, No. 400, II, 106.

12. "Poedem, ya gotov . . ." (II, 72).

13. "Brozhu li vdol ulits shumnykh" (II, 73).

14. *Perepiska*, No. 409, II, 114.

15. *Ibid.*, No. 417, II, 123.

16. *Ibid.*, No. 420, II, 126.

17. *Ibid.*, No. 421, II, 127.

18. *Ibid.*, No. 425, II, 130–131.

19. *Ibid.*, No. 255, I, 349.

20. *Ibid.*, No. 433, II, 143.

21. *Ibid.*, No. 429, II, 139.

22. *Ibid.*, No. 430, II, 140.

23. *Ibid.*, No. 436, II, 145.

24. "Uchast moya reshena. Ya zhenius" (IV, 686–690).

25. *Perepiska*, No. 475, II, 175.

26. *Ibid.*, No. 470, II, 171.

27. *Ibid.*, No. 472, II, 172.

28. *Ibid.*, No. 478, II, 179.

29. "K velmozhe" (II, 80).

30. "Poetu" (II, 83).

31. *Perepiska*, No. 475, II, 175.

32. "Evgeni Onegin," I, lix (IV, 34).

33. "Dlya beregov . . ." (II, 97).

34. "Zaklinanie" (II, 93).

35. "Domik v Kolomne" (III, 259).

36. "Kamenny gost," "Motsart i Saleri," "Pir vo vremya chumi," "Skupoi rytsar" (III, 395–467).

37. Pushkin no doubt found Cornwall's plays in *The Poetical Works of Milman, Bowles, Wilson, and Cornwall* (Paris, 1829). See E. J. Simmons, "Pushkin and Shenstone," *Modern Language Notes*, Nov., 1930, pp. 454–457; "A. S. Pushkin, *The Avaricious Knight*," *Harvard Studies and Notes in Philology and Literature* (1933), XV, 329–344; *Polnoe sobranie Pushkina* (Akademiya Nauk, Moscow, 1935), VII, 506–609.

38. *Sochineniya V. Belinskago* (Moscow, 1861), VIII, 682.

39. "Skupoi rytsar" (III, 404–408).

40. "Povesti Belkina" (IV, 287).

41. "Istoriya sela Goriukhino" (IV, 365).

42. A. N. Vulf, "Dnevnik," p. 124.

43. *Perepiska*, No. 520, II, 220.

44. *Ibid.*, No. 511, II, 212.

45. *Ibid.*, No. 522, II, 222–223.

46. M. S. Tsyavlovski, *Rasskazy o Pushkine, zapisannye so slov ego druzei P. I. Bartenevym*, p. 64.

CHAPTER XVII

1. *Russki Arkhiv* (1901), III, 482.

2. *Ibid.* (1902), I, 54.

3. *Perepiska*, No. 526, II, 228.

4. *Ibid.*, No. 541, II, 243.

5. V. A. Sologub, *Vospominaniya*, ed. A. S. Suvorin (St. Petersburg, 1887), pp. 117–118.

6. "K velmozhe" (II, 82).

7. "Otryvki iz pisem, mysli i zamechaniya" (V, 21–22).

8. *Perepiska*, No. 571, II, 278.

9. *Ibid.*, No. 577, II, 287.

10. "Klevetnikam Rossii" (II, 105); the other two poems are "Pered grobnitseiu suyatoi" (II, 104), "Borodinskaya godovishchina" (II, 106).

11. *Perepiska*, No. 1083, III, 388–389.
12. "Pisma O. S. Pavlishchevoi k muzhu, N. I. Pavlishchevu," *Pushkin i ego sovremenniki* (1911), XV, 106.
13. *Perepiska*, No. 641, II, 350.
14. *Ibid.*, No. 647, II, 355.
15. *Ibid.*, No. 651, II, 359.
16. *Ibid.*, No. 690, II, 391.
17. *Ibid.*, No. 692, II, 395.
18. "Kogda v obyatiya moi" (II, 233).
19. "Net, ya nè dorozhu . . ." (II, 102).
20. *Pisma Gogolya*, ed. V. I. Shenrok (St. Petersburg, 1902), I, 241.
21. *Sochineniya i perepiska P. A. Pletneva* (St. Petersburg, 1885), III, 524.
22. *Perepiska*, No. 706, III, 8–9.
23. P. E. Shchegelov, "Pushkin i Tardif," *Zvezda* (1930), No. 7, p. 239.
24. Byron, *Don Juan*, VI, xcii.
25. "Kapitanskaya dochka" (IV, 537).
26. A. S. Arkhangelski, *A. S. Pushkin v Kazani* (Kazan, 1899), p. 35.
27. "Pesni Zapadnykh Slavyan" (II, 113).
28. *Perepiska*, No. 721, III, 22.
29. "Istoriya Pugachevskogo bunta" (V, 281).
30. "Skazka o mertvoi tsarevne i o semi bogatyryakh" (II, 318); "Skazka o rybake i rybke" (II, 311).
31. "Ne dai mne bog soiti suma" (II, 170).
32. "Medny vsadnik" (III, 282).
33. "Rodoslovnaya moego geroya" (II, 164).
34. *Perepiska*, No. 737, III, 35.
35. *Ibid.*, No. 739, III, 50.
36. *Ibid.*, No. 752, III, 54–55.
37. *Ibid.*, No. 755, III, 58.

CHAPTER XVIII

1. Pushkin, *Dnevnik*, ed. B. L. Modzalevski (Moscow, 1923), p. 5.
2. *Ibid.*, p. 6.
3. *Perepiska*, No. 783, III, 83.
4. *Ibid.*, No. 817, III, 115.
5. *Ibid.*, No. 809, III, 108.
6. *Ibid.*, No. 861, III, 160.
7. *Ibid.*, No. 829, III, 127.
8. *Ibid.*, No. 856, III, 154.
9. *Ibid.*, No. 820, III, 118.
10. *Ibid.*, No. 824, III, 120.
11. *Ibid.*, No. 828, III, 125.
12. *Ibid.*, No. 805, III, 101.
13. Pushkin, *Dnevnik*, p. 17.
14. *Perepiska*, No. 819, III, 117.
15. *Ibid.*, No. 826, III, 122.
16. *Ibid.*, No. 840, III, 140.
17. Pushkin, *Dnevnik*, p. 18.
18. *Starina i Novizna*, VI, 10.
19. *Ibid.*, VII, 10.
20. *Perepiska*, No. 856, III, 154.

21. *Ibid.*, No. 858, III, 156.
22. "Skazka o zolotom petushke" (II, 334).
23. *Perepiska*, No. 866, III, 165.
24. *Ibid.*, No. 867, III, 165.
25. "Pikovaya dama" (IV, 484).
26. *Russki Arkhiv* (1878), I, 442.
27. M. I. Semevski, "Progulka v Trigorskoe," *S. Peterburgskie Vedomosti* (1866), No. 139.
28. *Perepiska*, No. 909, III, 203–204.
29. *Ibid.*, No. 918, III, 215.
30. *Ibid.*, No. 933, III, 232.
31. *Ibid.*, No. 929, III, 228.
32. *Ibid.*, No. 931, III, 229.
33. *Ibid.*, No. 933, III, 231.
34. *Ibid.*, No. 931, III, 230.
35. "Egipetskie nochi" (IV, 522).
36. *Perepiska*, No. 943, III, 242.
37. *Sovremennik.*
38. "Gr. V. A. Sologub, *Zapiska*," in B. L. Modzalevski, *Pushkin* (Leningrad, 1929), p. 375.
39. *Perepiska*, No. 970, III, 276.
40. *Ibid.*, No. 1011, III, 310.
41. *Ibid.*, No. 1017, III, 316.
42. *Ibid.*, No. 1011, III, 310.
43. *Ibid.*, No. 1011, III, 309.
44. "Evgeni Onegin," VI, xi (IV, 118).
45. "Pora, moi drug, pora . . ." (II, 257).

CHAPTER XIX

1. *Neizdanny Pushkin*, coll. A. F. Onegin (Moscow, 1923), p. 137.
2. B. L. Modzalevski, "Novoe pismo Pushkina," *Pushkin i ego sovremenniki* (1928), XXXVII, 2.
3. "Byla pora . . ." (II, 254).
4. *Perepiska*, No. 1091, III, 398–399.
5. M. A. Tsyavlovski, *Rasskazy o Pushkine*, p. 45.
6. M. A. Korf, *Russkaya Starina* (1900), No. 3, 574.
7. P. E. Shchegolev, *Duel i smert Pushkina* (Moscow, 1928), p. 98.
8. V. A. Sologub, *Vospominaniya*, pp. 180–181.
9. *Perepiska*, No. 1101, III, 409.
10. Sologub, *Vospominaniya*, p. 185.
11. *Perepiska*, No. 1106, III, 417.
12. Sologub, *Vospominaniya*, p. 186.
13. N. V. Izmailov, *Pisma Pushkina k. E. M. Khitrovo* (Leningrad, 1927), p. 200.
14. A. N. Ammosov, *Poslednie dni zhizni i konchina A. S. Pushkina* (St. Petersburg, 1863), p. 15.
15. Shchegolev, *Duel i smert Pushkina*, p. 123.
16. P. I. Bartenev, *Russki Arkhiv* (1888), II, 310.
17. "Exegi monumentum" (II, 190).
18. Shchegolev, *Duel i smert Pushkina*, p. 418.
19. *Ibid.*, p. 123.
20. *Perepiska*, No. 1138, III, 444–445.

CHAPTER XX

1. *Perepiska*, No. 1139, III, 445–446.
2. *Ibid.*, No. 1146, III, 449–450.
3. A. N. Ammosov, *Poslednie dni*, p. 19.
4. P. E. Shchegolev, *Duel i smert Pushkina*, p. 448.
5. Ammosov, *Poslednie dni*, p. 23.
6. *Ibid.*, p. 22.
7. *Ibid.*, p. 24.
8. *Ibid.*, p. 25.
9. Shchegolev, *Duel i smert Pushkina*, pp. 153–154.
10. Ammosov, *Poslednie dni*, p. 26.
11. Shchegolev, *Duel i smert Pushkina*, p. 155.
12. *Ibid.*, p. 200.
13. Ammosov, *Poslednie dni*, pp. 29–30.
14. Shchegolev, *Duel i smert Pushkina*, p. 202.
15. *Ibid.*, p. 183.
16. A. A. Fomin, "Novye materialy dlya biografii Pushkina," *Pushkin i ego sovremenniki* (1908), VI, 50.
17. V. F. Savodnik, "Moskovskie otgoloski dueli i smerti Pushkina," *Moskovski Pushkinist* (1927), I, 50.
18. *Russkaya Starina* (1875), XIV, 94.
19. Ammosov, *Poslednie dni*, p. 33.
20. Shchegolev, *Duel i smert Pushkina*, p. 205.
21. *Ibid.*, p. 193.
22. *Ibid.*, p. 194.
23. Ammosov, *Poslednie dni*, p. 38.
24. Shchegolev, *Duel i smert Pushkina*, pp. 194–195.
25. P. A. Efremov, *Russkaya Starina* (1850), XXVIII, 536.
26. Shchegolev, *Duel i smert Pushkina*, pp. 266–267.
27. A. V. Nikitenko, *Zapiski i dnevnik* (St. Petersburg, 1905), I, 286.

EPILOGUE

1. *Russkaya Starina* (1902), CX, 227.
2. E. E. Yakushkin, "Chasy Nikolaya I," *Moskovski Pushkinist* (1930), II, 267–268.
3. A. A. Fomin, "Novye materialy dlya biografii Pushkina," VI, 61.
4. *Russki Arkhiv* (1897), I, 19.
5. Ya. K. Grot, *Pushkin, ego litseiskie tovarishchi i nastavniki*, p. 74.
6. M. Lermontov, *Na smert Pushkina*.
7. *Perepiska*, No. 1105, III, 414.

BIBLIOGRAPHY

Bibliography

The present bibliographical survey of Pushkin is not intended to be definitive. Scarcely any Russian author has been so exhaustively studied, and a complete descriptive bibliography of editions and investigations would require several volumes. The following survey is designed for students who desire an introduction to the vast amount of material that has been published during the course of the last hundred years. The works cited are the principal ones and will provide the necessary information for those who are seeking "leads" in the more detailed phases of Pushkin's life and works. The All-Union Pushkin Committee, which has been formed in Russia to direct all activities connected with the centennial of the poet's death in February 1937, has projected the publication of many works of the utmost significance. Some of these have already appeared in print; others are still unfinished. The latter, when it seems advisable, will be mentioned.

I. Manuscripts

From his Lyceum days Pushkin carefully preserved his manuscripts, and his custom of writing in large copybooks made it possible to keep together nearly all the original drafts of his works. Fourteen of these copybooks exist, along with many separate manuscript-sheets. No more interesting laboratory material for a study of the creative process is available. In many cases we have not only the finished poem, but a simple statement of the idea, or a rough plan, or merely a list of rhymes, and then the successive corrected drafts. Hence it is possible to investigate the complicated development of a poem from its original conception to its final form. The neat, careful handwriting of the schoolboy, with a minimum of corrections, gradually changes before one's eyes into the strong, careless handwriting of the man. These copybooks also contain many of Pushkin's drawings, frequently of considerable artistic merit, and often his sketches constitute creative illustrations to a poem or provide important biographical information. (For reproductions and interpretations of these drawings, see A. Efros, *Risunki Poeta*, Academia, Moscow, 1933.) Some of Pushkin's notable works (*The Stone Guest*, *The Feast during the Plague*, *The Bronze Horseman*, *Dubrovski*, *The Egyptian Nights*) were not published during his lifetime. Hence the manuscripts, as the chief source of these productions, have the utmost significance for editors.

At the death of Pushkin the copybooks, by the command of the tsar, were turned over to Zhukovski and a police official, General Dubelt, for inspection. All the pages were carefully numbered in red ink and detached papers catalogued. This manuscript material remained in the possession of the poet's family until 1880, when it was deposited in the Rumyantsev Museum of Moscow (now incorporated in the Lenin Public Library of that city), where it is available today. A descriptive catalogue of these manuscripts was published by V. E. Yakushkin (*Russkaya Starina*, 1884).

A second collection of manuscripts (including parts of *Eugene Onegin*, folk tales, letters, etc.) exists in the Leningrad Public Library. L. B. Modzalevski published a description of this material in 1929 (*Rukopisi Pushkina v sobranii Gosudarstvennoi Publichnoi biblioteki v Leningrade*).

A third important collection, containing miscellaneous manuscripts and many letters, is located in the Pushkin House in Leningrad. Under the general direction of the Pushkin Commission, L. B. Modzalevski, B. V. Tomashevski, N. K. Kozmin, and D. P. Yakubovich are compiling a descriptive catalogue of this collection.

Connected with the collection of the Pushkin House is a small body of manuscript material situated in the Onegin Museum of Paris. These manuscripts have been edited and published under the direction of the Pushkin House of the Russian Academy of Science (*Neizdanny Pushkin*, collection of A. F. Onegin, Moscow, 1923).

A fourth and smaller collection — the so-called "Maikovskoe Collection" — exists in the Library of the Russian Academy of Science in Leningrad.

The Government Literary Museum of Moscow contains the well-known "Copybook of Vsevolozhski," the manuscript of Pushkin's first edition of shorter poems, along with a number of miscellaneous papers.

Many hitherto uncollected and unpublished manuscripts have recently been printed by the Pushkin Commission, edited by M. A. Tsyavlovski, L. B. Modzalevski, and T. G. Zenger (*Rukoiu Pushkina*, Academia, Moscow, 1935).

II. Texts

Many works of Pushkin appeared in book form before his death (*Poems*, vols. I and II, 1829; *Boris Godunov*, 1831; *Poems*, vol. III, 1832; *Eugene Onegin*, 1833; *Prose Tales*, 1834; *The History of the Pugachev Rebellion*, 2 vols., 1834; *Narrative Poems and Tales in Verse*, 1835). If we add to these many separate poems and prose works that were printed in various magazines and almanacs, it is clear that the major portion of Pushkin's production was published under his own supervision. (A bibliography of these separate works in magazines and almanacs printed during his lifetime was compiled by N. Sinyavski and M. Tsyavlovski — *Pushkin v pechati, 1814–1837*, Moscow, 1914.)

The works printed without his authorization, or not appearing in collected editions during his lifetime, and the posthumous works present many editorial problems. As a matter of fact, no complete edition has appeared which seems to satisfy the exacting standards of modern editorial practice.

The first posthumous edition of eight volumes was published in 1838, and represents simply a reprint of those works which were printed under Pushkin's own supervision.

In 1841 a three-volume edition appeared under the direction of Zhukovski, who fulfilled his editorial duties in a very independent manner. He introduced changes which were often an expression of his own personal taste.

Between 1855 and 1857 the first great Pushkinist, Annenkov, published an edition which has much historical importance for the specialist. Annenkov had access to the manuscripts and printed a number of poems which had not appeared previously. However, he handled his new texts in an arbitrary manner, sometimes freely reconstructing them from rough drafts. During the next three decades his example was followed by students of Pushkin, who exhausted most of the unfinished poems, publishing them separately in various magazines. During this period there were still a number of poems which could not be printed in Russia under the censorship regulations, and some of these works appeared in the free Russian press abroad. Thus the *Gavriliada* was first published in London by Ogarev in 1861. And many "uncensored" poems, often apocryphal, were printed in Germany and Switzerland.

The expiration of the copyright in 1887 started a new era in editorial policy which was unfortunate in some of its practices. Every line that Pushkin had committed to paper was regarded as precious, and the ideal of the "Complete Works" led some editors into the usual fault of not distinguishing between the text approved by Pushkin himself and their own notions of the text as it should be. Additions to the set canon, restorations, and inchoate fragments have often interfered with the general utility and trustworthy character of such editions.

The most elaborately planned, after the expiration of the copyright, was the edition of the Academy of Science. From 1899 to 1917, however, only five volumes were published, containing those works written before 1828, plus *The History of the Pugachev Rebellion*. Many vicissitudes finally resulted in the abandonment of the project. Its ponderous apparatus of variants, while helpful for the specialist, has limited the usefulness of the edition for the general reader.

A more useful edition is that of P. O. Morozov, in eight volumes (1903–1906). Its compact form and the introductory articles to the principal productions, substituted for more detailed commentaries, give this edition a special value.

P. A. Efremov edited an eight-volume collection which appeared between 1903 and 1905. The commentaries were a distinct addition, but modern scholarship has made their insufficiencies only too apparent.

The imposing Brockhaus-Efron collection, edited by S. A. Vengerov in six huge quarto volumes (1907–1915), has come in for much unfair criticism. It aims at completeness, but there is a lack of any historical study of the texts, and of notes to all the prose; and the general plan of the edition is befuddled by a mass of superfluous material. Yet this edition has assets which are invaluable to the student of Pushkin. The commentaries on the poems were the fullest up to that time, and all of the longer works are prefaced by critical articles, of unequal value, from the pens of specialists. There are also articles of considerable biographical worth on the various phases of the poet's life.

Since the Revolution of 1917 a marked change has been effected in editorial policy, and a tremendous impetus has been given to the popularity of Pushkin among Russian readers. Under the editorship of the well-known poet, Briusov, a complete edition was planned which aimed at scientific accuracy and broad popularity. However, only one volume appeared (Moscow, 1919), containing all the lyrical productions. Unfortunately, the text of this volume is not always correct, and the complicated arrangement of variants and the plan of the work as a whole make this unfinished edition very unwieldy. The commentaries are also too brief and sometimes entirely too subjective.

In 1921 M. L. Gofman published a little book (*Pervaya glava nauki o Pushkine*, Petrograd) which had a salutary influence on succeeding editions of Pushkin. He laid down the principle that a sharp distinction should be made between the strictly canonical works and those which obviously did not have Pushkin's final supervision. Furthermore, he maintained that as far as possible the poet's own arrangement of his productions should be rigidly observed.

These principles were followed by B. Tomashevski and K. Khalabaev in separate editions of the principal works and in a single large volume (Gosizdat, Leningrad, 1924), which includes all the canonical imaginative productions. These books are easy to handle, and the text is most accurate. Unfortunately, their size prevented the use of notes and introductions.

In 1930 the Soviet State Press (Gosizdat) published the complete works in six volumes (*Polnoe sobranie sochineni*). So far as the text and arrangement are concerned, this edition leaves little to be desired, and the full index is most helpful. The absence of prefatory material and notes limits the all-round value of the edition, and the large number of typographical errors (most of which were corrected in later editions) is discouraging in a work of such importance.

Since this time separate works and complete editions have been pouring from the press, and plans for many others have been laid down by the All-Union Pushkin Committee. Since most of these are still in the press or merely planned, it is hardly necessary to mention them here. However, a word ought to be said of the great edition of the Academy of Science which is in the process of publication. This will consist of eighteen volumes, and the foremost Pushkinists are contributing their services as editors. The text will be established on the most scientific basis, and an exhaustive complement of notes, critical articles, and bibliography will leave nothing to be desired in these respects. So far, one volume, the seventh, containing all the dramatic works, has appeared (*Polnoe sobranie sochineni*, ed. D. P. Yakubovich, Akademiya Nauk, vol. VII, Moscow, 1935). If this volume of the dramatic works is any criterion for the remainder of the undertaking, the edition is likely to be the definitive one for many years.

III. Correspondence

Pushkin's letters and a great many written to him were well edited by V. I. Saitov (*Perepiska*, Akademiya Nauk, vols. I–III, St. Petersburg, 1906–1911). No attempt was made at commentaries. Since the appearance of this work, however, a number of additional letters have turned up. A new edition of Pushkin's letters alone was undertaken by B. L. Modzalevski (*Pisma*, Akademiya Nauk, Moscow, 1926). A second volume was published in 1928, including his correspondence up to 1830. Unfortunately, the editor died, but the work has been carried on by his son, L. B. Modzalevski, and in 1935 a third volume was published, carrying the correspondence to 1833. The fourth and last volume is to appear shortly. The notes to this splendid edition far transcend the ordinary editorial comment. They amount virtually to a small encyclopedia of Russian literature and culture over the period of the correspondence, and the work is of first importance to any student of Pushkin. It may be mentioned that the projected eighteen-volume edition of Pushkin's works will also devote four volumes to the correspondence, and no doubt this edition will be absolutely definitive.

IV. Diary

During his life Pushkin started several diaries; one he burned, and fragments of others are included in his collected works. But his *Diary* for 1833–1835, especially valuable for many reasons, has been available only in recent years. It was twice edited (*Dnevnik A. S. Pushkina, 1833–1835*, ed. V. F. Savodnik and M. N. Speranski, Moscow, 1923; *Dnevnik Pushkina, 1833–1835*, ed. B. L. Modzalevski, Moscow, 1923). Both editions contain exhaustive commentaries.

V. Bibliographies

There is no complete bibliographical treatment of the enormous mass of material written on Pushkin's life and works. The period from 1814 to 1886 has been covered, with a number of omissions, by V. I. Mezhov (*Pushkiniana za 1814–1886 gody*, St. Petersburg, 1886).

The many publications of the Jubilee year of 1899 were listed by V. V. Sipovski (*Pushkinskaya iubileinaya literatura, 1899–1900 gg.*, St. Petersburg, 1900). There were later editions (St. Petersburg, 1901, 1902).

The period between 1900 and 1910 was catalogued in the bibliographical study of A. G. Fomin (*Pushkiniana, 1900–1910*, Leningrad, 1929).

A list, by no means complete, of the works about Pushkin from 1910 to 1918 was published by I. V. Vladislavev (*Russkie pisateli XIX st.*, 3rd ed., Moscow, 1918).

Many bibliographies of the productions of separate years may be found in the various numbers of the well-known journal devoted to the study of Pushkin, published by the Academy of Science and edited by B. L. Modzalevski (*Pushkin i ego sovremenniki*, vols. I–XXXIX, St. Petersburg, 1900–1930).

A rather full survey of biographical studies from 1917 to 1935 was made by

V. Kazanski ("Razrabotka biografii Pushkina," *Literaturnoe Nasledstvo*, 1934, pp. 1137-1158).

A complete bibliography for the year 1935 was compiled by S. Gessen ("Pushkiniana, 1935 g.," *Pushkin Vremennik*, Akademiya Nauk, Moscow, 1936, pp. 393-405).

The All-Union Pushkin Committee plans to remedy the gaps in these bibliographical studies. Publications are under way which will complete the bibliographies of the two Jubilee years of 1887 and 1899; and Fomin will extend his bibliography from 1910 to 1918. Eventually the study of Mezhov, covering the period from 1814 to 1886, will be reworked and completed. Finally, a full and descriptive bibliography from 1918 to 1935 will be issued.

VI. Biographical Sources

Up to date there has been no biography of Pushkin in Russian, or in any other language, which could be called definitive. For that matter, none exists which can be accepted as wholly satisfactory. A weakness for special pleading has vitiated most attempts. But the real obstacle has been the inaccessibility of highly important material in the secret archives of the tsar's government. Since the Soviet Revolution, all these documents have been available, and the way is now clear for an exhaustive study of Pushkin's life. Despite the lack of an authoritative full-length biography, there have been a huge number of studies, in book form and in articles, of nearly every phase of Pushkin's life. And most contributing factors, and all the people who entered his life in an important way, have been thoroughly investigated. Many of the articles and original sources are scattered through a variety of magazines, principally the *Russkaya Starina*, *Russki Vestnik*, *Russki Arkhiv*, *Vestnik Evropy*, and *Pushkin i ego sovremenniki*. It would be impossible, and hardly desirable, to give a complete list of these sources here, since they are all listed in the bibliographical studies mentioned above. Furthermore, a great many of them have been cited in the notes to the present biography. However, a highly selective list of such works would be helpful for the student. The fact should not be forgotten that the poet himself has provided us with the chief sources — biographical fragments, diaries, certain poems, official documents, and, most valuable of all, his letters. Next in importance are the extensive memoirs, diaries, and correspondence of many contemporaries, and the accounts of people who knew him personally. The most valuable biographies, chronologically arranged, are:

Annenkov, P. V., *A. S. Pushkin: materialy dlya ego biografii* (St. Petersburg, 1855; 2nd ed., 1873).

Bartenev, P. I., *A. S. Pushkin: materialy dlya ego biografii* (Moscow, 1855).

Chernyshevski, N. G., *A. S. Pushkin: ego zhizn i sochineniya* (St. Petersburg, 1856; 2nd ed., 1864).

Annenkov, P. V., *Pushkin v Aleksandrovskuiu epokhu* (St. Petersburg, 1874).

Stoiunin, V. Ya., *Pushkin* (St. Petersburg, 1880; 2nd ed., 1906).

Venkstern, A. A., *A. S. Pushkin: biograficheski ocherk* (Moscow, 1899; 2nd ed., 1909).

Sipovski, V. V., *Pushkin: zhizn i tvorchestvo* (St. Petersburg, 1907).

Modzalevski, B. L., and others, *Pushkin* (Trudy Pushkinskogo Doma, Petrograd, 1924).

Hofmann, M., *Pouchkine* (Paris, 1931).

The following works contain the most important biographical sources not already mentioned and the most valuable studies of various phases of Pushkin's life. For convenience, the works are arranged alphabetically.

Ammosov, A. N., *Poslednie dni zhizni i konchina Al. S. Pushkina*, ed. Isakov (St. Petersburg, 1863).

Barsukov, N., *Zhizn i trudy M. P. Pogodina* (St. Petersburg, 1888–1910, parts I–22).

Bartenev, P. I., "Rod i detstvo Pushkina," *Otechestvennye Zapiski*, No. 11, 1853.

——, *Pushkin v iuzhnoi Rossii* (2nd ed., Moscow, 1914).

Batiushkov, K. N., *Sochineniya*, ed. P. N. Batiushkov (St. Petersburg, 1886).

Bylashev, G. O., *A. S. Pushkin na iuge Rossii* (Kiev, 1899).

Dela III Otdeleniya ob A. S. Pushkine, ed. Balashov (St. Petersburg, 1906).

Duel Pushkina s Dantesom-Gekkerenom: Podlinnoe voennosudnoe delo 1837 (St. Petersburg, 1900).

Gaevski, V. P., "Pushkin v litsee i litseiskie ego stikhotvoreniya," *Sovremennik* (1863), VII–VIII.

Gastfreind, N. A., *Dokumenty gosud. i s-peterburgskogo glavn. arkhiv. min. inostr. del, otnosyashchiesya k sluzhbe Pushkina* (St. Petersburg, 1900).

Grot, K. Ya., *Pushkinski litsei (1811–1817) bumagi i-go kursa* (St. Petersburg, 1911).

Grot, Ya. K., *Pushkin, ego litseiskie tovarishchi i nastavniki* (2nd ed., St. Petersburg, 1901).

Guber, P. K., *Don-Zhuanski Spisok Pushkina* (Petrograd, 1923).

Lerner, N. O., *Trudy i dni Pushkina* (2nd ed., Akademiya Nauk, St. Petersburg, 1910).

Liprandi, I. P., *Russki Arkhiv* (1866).

Literaturnoe Nasledstvo, XVI–XVIII (Moscow, 1934).

Maikov, L. N., *Pushkin: biograficheskie materialy i istoriko-literaturnye ocherki* (St. Petersburg, 1899).

Modzalevski, B. L., *Pushkin* (Leningrad, 1929).

——, *Pushkin pod tainym nadzorom* (St. Petersburg, 1922).

——, and others, *Novye materialy o dueli i smerti Pushkina* (Leningrad, 1924).

Moskovski Pushkinist (vols. I–II, Moscow, 1927, 1930).

Nedzelski, V., *Pushkin v Krymu* (Simferopol, 1929).

Nikitenko, A. V., *Zapiski i dnevnik* (2nd ed., St. Petersburg, 1905).

Ostafevski Arkhiv knyazei Vyazemskikh, ed. Count S. D. Sheremetev (St. Petersburg, 1899 ff.).

Pavlishchev, L. N., *Vospominaniya ob A. S. Pushkine* (Moscow, 1890).

Polevoi, K. A., *Zapiski* (St. Petersburg, 1888).

Polyakov, A., *O smerti Pushkina: po novym dannym* (Petrograd, 1922).

Pushchin, I. I., *Zapiski o Pushkine i pismo*, ed. S. Ya. Shtraikh (Moscow, 1927).

Pushkin i ego sovremenniki (Akademiya Nauk, vols. I–XXXIX, St. Petersburg, 1900–1930).

Pushkin Vremennik (Akademiya Nauk, Moscow, 1936).

Razgovory Pushkina, collected by S. Gessen and L. Modzalevski (Moscow, 1929).

Shchegolev, P. E., *Novoe o Pushkine* (St. Petersburg, 1902).

——, *Pushkin. Ocherki* (St. Petersburg, 1912).

——, *Duel i smert Pushkina* (3rd ed., Leningrad, 1928).

——, *Pushkin i muzhiki* (Moscow, 1928).

Shlyapkin, I. A., *Iz neizdannykh bumag Pushkina* (St. Petersburg, 1903).

Sologub, V. A., *Vospominaniya*, ed. Suvorin (St. Petersburg, 1887).

Tsyavlovski, M. A., *Rasskazy o Pushkine* (Leningrad, 1925).

Vengerov, S. A., *Pushkin* (6 vols., St. Petersburg, 1907–1915).

Veresaev, V., *Pushkin v zhizni* (5th ed., Academia, Moscow, 1932).

——, *V dvukh planakh: stati o Pushkine* (Moscow, 1929).

Vigel, F. F., *Zapiski*, ed. S. Ya. Shtraikh (2 vols., Moscow, 1928).

Vyazemski, P. A., *Polnoe sobranie sochineni*, ed. Count S. D. Sheremetev (St. Petersburg, 1878–1887).

Vyazemski, P. P., *Sobranie sochineni* (St. Petersburg, 1893).

Yakovlev, V. A., *Otzyvy o Pushkine s iuga Rossii* (Odessa, 1887).

Under the aegis of the All-Union Pushkin Committee an authoritative biography of Pushkin is being prepared by D. D. Blagoi. This work, in two volumes, is scheduled to appear in 1937.

VII. CRITICAL APPRECIATION

During his own lifetime and ever since his death Pushkin's poetry and prose have provided material for Russia's foremost literary critics. Some sense of balance was maintained until the second half of the nineteenth century, when a cult of Pushkin-worship grew up which resulted in a mass of injudicious and peculiarly biased criticism. Pushkin's younger contemporaries, I. Kireevski and S. Shevyrev, were among the first and best of the earlier critics. But another younger contemporary, the famous critic Belinski, was the first to realize the truly great significance of Pushkin in Russian litera-ture. His favorable views on the poet dominated critical opinion for many years and were echoed by distinguished followers, such as Chernyshevski and Dobroliubov. The only dissenting voice was that of the brilliant and truculent critic, D. I. Pisarev (1840–1868), who severely criticized Pushkin for everything that he was not. A sharp change in critical appreciation was inaugurated by Dostoevski in his famous address of 1880 on the occasion of the Pushkin celebration in Moscow (*Dnevnik pisatelya*, 1880). Read-ing his own philosophy into Pushkin, Dostoevski singled out "humility" as his chief Russian virtue, and saw in many of his works an expression of the Slavophile spirit. Able disciples, such as Grigorev and Strakhov, supported Dostoevski's position, which continued to dominate Pushkin criticism until recent times. With some variation the Slavophile view was supported by the Symbolists, especially by Merezhkovski.

There is no complete and authoritative bibliography of criticism on Pushkin. The poet himself wrote some of the most penetrating observations on his own works. All his criticism has recently been gathered together in a single volume, which is splendidly edited (*Pushkin-Kritik*, ed. N. V. Bogoslovski, Academia, Moscow, 1934).

A useful collection of critical works, which includes everything that Belinski wrote on Pushkin, was issued by V. O. Zelinski (*Russkaya kriticheskaya literatura o Pushkine*, 7 parts, Moscow, 1903–1905). Supplementing this is a collection of miscellaneous articles, edited by V. I. Pokrovski (*A. S. Pushkin: sbornik istoriko-literaturnykh statei*, 4th ed., Moscow, 1916).

A good many critical articles, including some of great value, may be found in the volumes of the Vengerov edition of the complete works (*Pushkin*, 6 vols., St. Petersburg, 1907–1915); and there are also many articles of worth scattered through the numbers of *Pushkin i ego sovremenniki* (Akademiya Nauk, vols. I–XXXIX, St. Petersburg, 1900–1930).

Apart from these sources, the more important critical treatments of Pushkin's works and thought are:

Annenkov, P. V., "Obshchestvennye idealy Pushkina," *Vestnik Evropy*, June 1880.

Blagoi, D. D., *Sotsiologiya tvorchestva Pushkina* (2nd ed., Moscow, 1931).

Engelhardt, B., "Istorizm Pushkina i ego obshchestvennye idealy," *Pushkinist*, ed. S. A. Vengerov, vol. II (Petrograd, 1916).

Gershenzon, M. O., *Mudrost Pushkina* (Moscow, 1919).

———, *Stati o Pushkine* (Moscow, 1926).

Gofman, M. L., *Pushkin: ego obshchestvenno-politicheskie vzglyady i nastroeniya* (Chernigov, 1918).

———, *Pushkin: pervaya glava nauki o Pushkine* (Petrograd, 1922).

Grossman, A. P., *Etiudy o Pushkine* (Leningrad, 1929).
Koni, A. F., *Obshchestvennye vzglyady Pushkina* (Petrograd, 1921).
Kotlyarevski, V., *Pushkin i Rossiya* (Petrograd, 1922).
Lerner, N. O., *Proza Pushkina* (4th ed., Petrograd, 1923).
Nikolski, V. V., *Idealy Pushkina* (4th ed., St. Petersburg, 1899).
Zhirmunski, V. M., *Bairon i Pushkin* (Leningrad, 1924).

The best critical studies of Pushkin's poetics and style are:

Bely, Andrei, *Simbolizm* (Moscow, 1910).
Bobrov, S. P., *Novoe o stikhoslozhenii Pushkina* (Moscow, 1915).
Briusov, V. Ya., "Zvukopis Pushkina," *Pechat i revoliutsiya*, part 2 (Moscow, 1923).
Eikhenbaum, B. M., *Problemy poetiki Pushkina* (Petrograd, 1921).
———, *Melodika russkogo liricheskogo stikha* (Petrograd, 1922).
Korsh, F. E., "Razbor voprosa o podlinnosti okonchaniya *Rusalki*," *Izvestiya II Otd. Akad. Nauk* (1898), No. 3; (1899), Nos. 1, 2.
Tomashevski, B. V., *Russkoe stikhoslozhenie* (Petrograd, 1923).
Vinogradov, V. V., *Yazyk Pushkina* (Academia, Moscow, 1935).
Yarkho, B. I., and others, *Metricheski spravochnik k stikhotvoreniyam A. S. Pushkina* (Academia, Moscow, 1934).

Since the October Revolution a materialistic interpretation of Pushkin's works has prevailed among Soviet critics. Many articles in this vein have appeared in various magazines. Bibliographies of this material, and some of the best critical appreciations, may be found in *Literaturnoe Nasledstvo*, XVI–XVIII (Moscow, 1934), and *Pushkin Vremennik* (Akademiya Nauk, Moscow, 1936).

VIII. Pushkin in English

During his lifetime the English magazines took some slight notice of Pushkin, and there were a few scattered translations. Since his death the interest has increased in England and America, but the attention devoted to him has hardly been commensurate with his position as Russia's greatest poet. The first important study of him was made by T. B. Shaw ("Alexander Pushkin," *Blackwood's Edinburgh Magazine*, 1845, LVII, 656–678; LVIII, 28–43, 140–157). This study includes a few rather fine translations of the lyrics. Another fairly good study, with several translations, was made by W. R. Morfill ("Alexander Poushkin," *Westminster Review*, 1883, CXIX, 420–451). Of course, once histories of Russian literature began to appear in English, Pushkin's name and works became better known to the English-speaking public. C. E. Turner devoted considerable space to him in his *Studies in Russian Literature* (London, 1882). And Maurice Baring in two books, *Outline of Russian Literature* (London, 1914) and *Lost Lectures, or the Fruits of Experience* (London, 1932), showed himself a penetrating and appreciative critic and translator of Pushkin. The poet's position in Russian literature is also fully studied by D. S. Mirsky in his *History of Russian Literature from the Origins to the Death of Dostoyevsky* (2nd ed., New York, 1934). And the following works contain critical appreciations: C. H. Herford, *A Russian Shakespearean* (Oxford, 1925); E. J. Simmons, *English Literature and Culture in Russia, 1553–1840* (Cambridge, 1935); Boris Brasol, *The Mighty Three* (New York, 1934). However, the only substantial treatment of Pushkin in English is the excellent handbook of D. S. Mirsky, *Pushkin* (London, 1926). A memorial volume, edited by S. H. Cross and E. J. Simmons, containing a series of critical studies of Pushkin's works by various Slavic scholars in America, is in preparation.

There have been frequent translations of Pushkin's verse and prose in English, many of them scattered through various magazines. Bibliographies of these translations, and of studies in English about Pushkin, may be found in the following works:

Wiener, Leo, *An Anthology of Russian Literature* (New York, 1903), II, 123–125.

Mirsky, D. S., *Pushkin* (London, 1926), pp. 240–242.

Osborne, E. A., "Early Translations from the Russian," *Bookman* (London), LXXXII (1932), 264, 268.

Cross, S. H., "Pouchkine en Angleterre" (in preparation for the Pushkin memorial volume of the *Revue de la littérature comparée*, January 1937).

A chronological list of the better and more accessible translations of Pushkin into English follows:

Shaw, T. B., "Alexander Pushkin," *Blackwood's Edinburgh Magazine*, LVIII (1845), 28–43, 140–157. Twenty-two short poems.

Spalding, H., *Eugene Oneguine* (London, 1881).

Wilson, C. T., *Russian Lyrics* (London, 1887). Ten short poems.

Panin, Ivan, *Poems of Pushkin* (Boston, 1888).

Pollen, J. C., *Rhymes from the Russian* (London, 1891). Five short poems.

Turner, C. E., *Translations from Pushkin* (London, 1899).

Wiener, Leo, *Anthology of Russian Literature* (New York, 1903), II, 125–149. Eleven short poems and fragments by various translators.

Bianchi, Martha, *Russian Lyrics* (New York, 1910). Sixteen lyrics and fragments from longer poems.

Keane, T., *The Prose Tales of A. Poushkin* (London, 1915).

Pollen, J. C., *Russian Songs and Lyrics* (London, 1917).

Beckhofer, C. E., ed., *A Russian Anthology in English* (London, 1917). Translations, by several hands, of selections from *Eugene Onegin*, *The Queen of Spades*, *The Tale of Tsar Saltan*, and *Mozart and Salieri*.

Jarintzov, N., *Russian Poets and Poems* (London, 1917).

Hayes, Alfred, *Boris Godunov* (London, 1918).

Katkoff, N., *The Golden Cockerel* (London, 1918).

Matheson, P. E., *Holy Russia and Other Poems* (London, 1918).

Slavonic Review (London, 1922–1936). The various issues of this magazine contain a number of lyrics, selections from longer poems, and complete renderings of a few long poems.

Yarmolinsky, Avrahm, and Deutsch, Babette, *Modern Russian Poetry* (London, John Lane, 1923).

Eastman, Max, "The Gabriliad," *Transition* (Paris, 1927), No. 4, pp. 116–131. Also issued separately in a limited edition with illustrations by Rockwell Kent, *Gabriel* (New York, 1929).

Duddington, Natalie, *The Captain's Daughter and Other Tales* (Everyman, 1933).

Elton, Oliver, *Verse from Pushkin and Others* (London, 1935). Contains some of the best translations of Pushkin — a few short poems, selections from *Ruslan and Liudmila*, *Poltava*, and *Eugene Onegin*, and complete versions of *Tsar Saltan*, *The Dead Princess and the Seven Champions*, *The Golden Cock*, *The Fisherman and the Little Fish*, *The Pope and His Workman Balda*, and *The Bronze Horseman*.

Yarmolinsky, Avrahm, ed., *The Poems, Prose and Plays of Pushkin* (New York, Random House, 1936). A standard anthology of Pushkin, containing all of *Eugene Onegin*, *Boris Godunov* and other dramatic pieces, the folk tales, many lyrics and ballads, *The Captain's Daughter*, and shorter prose pieces. The translations are done by various hands.

Krup, Jacob, *Six Poems from the Russian* (New York, The Galleon Press, 1936). Includes complete versions of *Ruslan and Liudmila*, *Poltava*, and *The Prisoner of the Caucasus*.

Brasol, Boris, *The Russian Wonderland* (New York, Paisley Press, 1936). Contains versions of *The Golden Cockerel*, *The Tale of the Fisherman and the Little Fish*, and *The Tale of Tsar Saltan*.

Radin, Dorothea P., *Eugene Onegin* (to be published by the University of California Press, 1937).

INDEX

Index